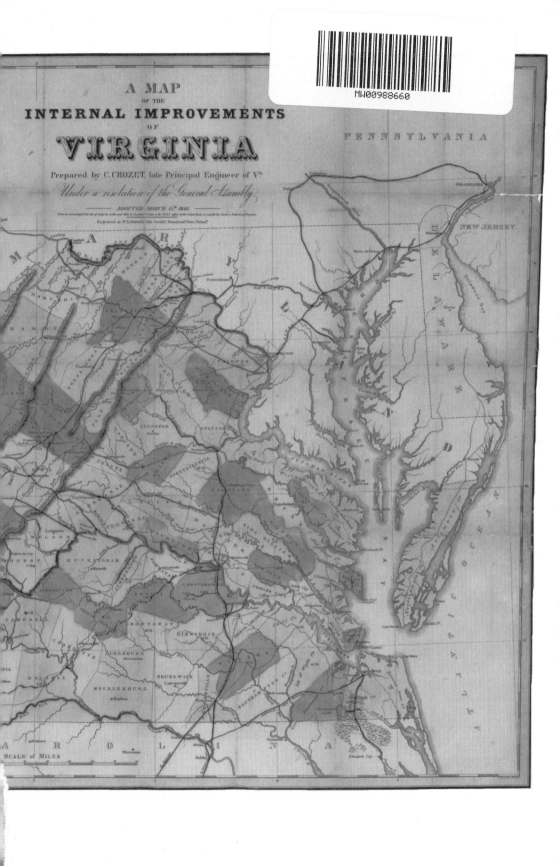

A MAP
OF THE
INTERNAL IMPROVEMENTS
OF
VIRGINIA

Prepared by C. CROZET, late Principal Engineer of V.ᵃ

Under a resolution of the General Assembly

ADOPTED MARCH 15ᵗʰ 1848.

Engraved at P.S. Duval's Lith. Estab.ᵗ Hansland Place, Philad.ᵃ

PENNSYLVANIA

NEW JERSEY

DELAWARE

MARYLAND

ATLANTIC OCEAN

SCALE of MILES

Cradle of America

Cradle of America

FOUR CENTURIES
OF VIRGINIA HISTORY

Peter Wallenstein

University Press of Kansas

Photographs on pages xviii, 62, and front endsheet
map, Virginia Historical Society; on page 124, Library
of Congress. Map on back endsheets by Katie Pritchard.

Published by the University Press of Kansas (Lawrence,
Kansas 66045), which was organized by the Kansas
Board of Regents and is operated and funded by
Emporia State University, Fort Hays State University,
Kansas State University, Pittsburg State University, the
University of Kansas, and Wichita State University

Library of Congress Cataloging-in-Publication Data
Wallenstein, Peter.
Cradle of America : four centuries of Virginia history /
Peter Wallenstein.
p. cm.
Includes bibliographical references and index.
ISBN 978-0-7006-1507-0 (cloth : alk. paper)
1. Virginia—History. I. Title.
F226.W26 2007
975.5—dc22   2006038749

British Library Cataloguing-in-Publication Data is
available.

Printed in the United States of America

10 9 8 7 6 5 4 3 2 1

The paper used in this publication meets the minimum
requirements of the American National Standard for
Permanence of Paper for Printed Library Materials
Z39.48–1992.

Dedicated to

An eclectic group of exemplary historians and human beings I have been privileged to know, and to count as friends, over the years: David Osher, Orest Ranum, Harold Livesay, David Lux, Anne Scott, Jim and Lois Horton, Chaz Joyner, and Paul Finkelman

Charles "Jack" Dudley and the University Honors Program he has built up at Virginia Tech, a monument to what undergraduates can accomplish in research and scholarship

And Sookhan, always, for so much

Contents

....

Illustrations and Sidebars

....

Illustrations

Sidebars

Prologue

Jamestown, Blacksburg, and the Return of Pangaea

....

This book was written in Blacksburg, Virginia, west of the Blue Ridge. Early settlers had reason to view the area as a very Garden of Eden. True, the fruit might not just fall from the trees without human effort, and winters brought at least one week of bitter cold. But the growing season was generous, the water good, the wood supply ample, and land along the creeks plentiful. Bears and deer provided hides for humans to wear and meat for them to eat. More than had the country nearer the Chesapeake Bay, the land seemed uninhabited, plentiful, beckoning people to come, and they came.

More than a place, Blacksburg—and Virginia—can stand as a symbol of the Pangaea of eons ago, when the continents of Europe, Africa, and the Americas all nestled together for a time before they drifted apart again. When they came together, Africa shoved a shoulder into the Chesapeake, and the resulting crunch pushed up a range of mountains we call the Appalachians. The continents drifted apart, but the mountains remained, a monument to the encounter. Over the many thousands of years between then and now, the mountains grew old and, as people often do, grew gentler, bowed, their rough edges smoothed, until settlers in the 1750s found rolling hills—as well as some that seemed less tamed—and waterways meandering among them.

Christopher Columbus led expeditions that took him from Spain to the Caribbean in the 1490s—300 years before the founding of Blacksburg in 1798—and initiated a process by which, through human activity, Pangaea came together again. The continents remained apart, but their peoples merged. People from Africa and Europe migrated in huge numbers across the Atlantic Ocean to what was for them, though hardly for the Native Americans they found living there, a New World. Mixed in various proportions, the three great groups forged new communities. The region around Blacksburg came to be inhabited largely by people whose origins lay in Europe and the British Isles, but members of the other two groups also called the region home and shaped developments there.

Jamestown—far better known than Blacksburg, and marking its 400th anniversary in the year 2007—dates its origins to 1607, nearly 200 years before Blacksburg acquired its name, but also more than 100 years after Columbus sailed into the Western Hemisphere. For generations before the founding of Jamestown, Europeans—especially the Spanish and the French—had been exploring and seeking to settle the New World, and England launched its first efforts to establish a colony a generation before the settling of Jamestown. The effort in the 1580s to found a community at Roanoke Island failed, and multiple times it later appeared as though the Jamestown adventure might fail as well, but it did not. From those various early efforts emerged a vast New World empire claimed by the British, contested by the French and the Spanish, and always controlled or shaped in part as well by the descendants of far-earlier inhabitants and claimants. Jamestown persisted, and English settlements spread.

I have sought to outline what I see as major themes of Virginia's history across four centuries—from the 1580s to the present. As a historical entity, the place that carried the name "Virginia" must be defined in terms of space and time. Virginia simultaneously grew and shrank between the settling of Jamestown in 1607 and the establishment of Blacksburg in 1798. It grew in terms of colonized areas. In the east, settlement pushed westward up the rivers. In the west, it pushed south by southwest out of Pennsylvania, up the Shenandoah Valley, and on south, until it reached the Blacksburg area and beyond, into today's far southwestern Virginia and, often, into Kentucky or Tennessee.

At the same time, Virginia shrank in terms of formal boundaries. During the early years after Jamestown's settlement, "Virginia" lay along the Atlantic Ocean between New France to the north and Spanish Florida to the south, and it included an unimaginably vast area that stretched west to the Pacific Ocean. The end of the French and Indian War in 1763 left Spain in control of the western half of the Mississippi River valley. Later, Virginia relinquished the Northwest Territory, as well as Kentucky, so by the 1790s, Ohio and Kentucky both lay outside its territory, and Virginia's borders encompassed only today's Virginia and West Virginia. The modern boundaries date from the 1860s.

Jamestown, and the lower James River, which flows into the Chesapeake Bay, can stand as a symbol of eastern Virginia and of the first permanent arrival of people from across the Atlantic into a new colony in America. By contrast, the New River flows west into the Ohio River, so Blacksburg can represent not only

Virginia's western extension but also the movement of people both into Virginia west of the Blue Ridge and farther west into the Ohio River valley and beyond.

Long before the 1790s, the dominant language along most of the eastern seaboard of North America was English and the key social, economic, and political institutions were English ones. But the English colonies on the mainland—Virginia, to be sure, and others to both the north and the south of Virginia—grew in human population, in geographical expanse, and in economic power and developed in ways that increasingly distinguished them from England. Distinct or not, their inhabitants found themselves in the late 1770s struggling—successfully—for political independence from the mother country. Within two centuries of the founding of Jamestown, Virginians by the names of George Washington and Thomas Jefferson had taken office as the first and third presidents of a new nation, the United States of America.

Even then, the adventure of Virginia—and of America, and their connections with each other and with a much larger world—could be said to be just beginning. This book traces the stories of the people and events and developments that make up the history of Virginia, both at home and, often, in those larger contexts. It would not be reckless to say that much of modern human history—the era after the return of Pangaea—can be seen in microcosm in the history of Virginia. Yet Virginia has followed its own path through the centuries. This book tells that story.

Whereas many Virginians, like many historical accounts of the state, emphasize harmony among Virginians and relative changelessness across the years, I have tended to emphasize conflict among various groups of Virginians and have often stressed discontinuity. At one point or another, Virginians have differed over a wide range of issues, taking those differences seriously and expressing them with great feeling. I hope to show why, and how, and to what effect Virginians differed among each other. Moreover, Virginia has experienced great change, and I seek to help my readers understand the ways it changed from one era to another. In recounting Virginia's history, I have emphasized black Virginians as well as white Virginians, and the west as well as the east.

In outlining the major developments and highlighting the leading issues of a given time, I have tended to stress three major themes. One is power and policy: who had political power, what they tried to do with it, and how it sometimes shifted from one group to another. Another is education, higher and elementary alike, not only as far as institutions go, but also in a larger sense: what people learned, what they valued, and what culture they sought to transmit from one generation to another. The third is race: how racial identity has operated at different times and over a collection of issues. At various points, these three themes—political power, racial identity, and public education—have powerfully come together, as in Massive Resistance, when the General Assembly directed the governor to close public schools rather than permit them to be desegregated.

I have also addressed what I call "multiple pasts": The past we see can vary, or change, depending on our perspective, the questions we ask, and the sources we use. From time to time, I supply material for readers to consider how we come to understand the past, and how that can differ among us and change over time.

The title of this book is itself an argument—or rather, it is an argument on the one hand and a question on the other. Especially in the nineteenth century, proponents of a very different view than that of Virginia as the "cradle of America" argued for the primacy of Massachusetts Bay over Chesapeake Bay in the founding of what became the United States of America. If it has to be one or the other, this book holds that Jamestown trumps Plymouth. But in fact both areas contributed in vital ways to the founding of the English colonies and a new nation. In the pages that follow, I present Virginia as the "mother of presidents" in the early republic—the birthplace of the Virginia dynasty. In addition, I present Virginia as what I call the "mother of states"—the key to much of the West, the area to the west of the states along the coast from Maine to Florida—in terms of the acquisition of that vast territory by the United States during the years of the Revolution and the early republic, and also in terms of the peopling of much of that territory during the next generation. The great Civil War detour, however, offers ample evidence—the greatest, though hardly the only evidence—that many major characteristics of the evolving nation took their shape in opposition to the vision of leading Virginians.

The subtitle—"Four Centuries of Virginia History"—also warrants comment. In the interests of keeping my book from growing much larger than I wanted, I have had to keep my accounts short about a wide range of people, events, topics, themes, times, and places. Others I have neglected entirely. I have surveyed the colonial era, but I have paid less attention to it than to the time since 1776; so this is much more a history of the state of Virginia than of the colony, more an exploration of the nineteenth and twentieth centuries than of the seventeenth or eighteenth. Not only do the four centuries get unequal space and attention here, but I also emphasize that though Jamestown was founded in 1607, Virginia began in the 1580s.

Two main features of the book are the illustrations and the sidebars. The latter mostly provide primary sources, the raw materials of historical reconstruction, so that readers can see for themselves what was said on various important matters along the way. As for the photographs, some of them illustrate one facet or another of the text, while others expand the narrative, broaden the conversation, by introducing new dimensions. Many of the captions contain brief essays that can help readers pursue the past or see how it might be understood in different ways. Finally, in the bibliography, under "Books for Further Reading," I offer a list of books as possible additional reading for each chapter.

The United States began, long before there was a United States, in a land called Virginia. There, first people from Europe and then people from Africa—and, later, people from other parts of our planet—met people already living there. Together, they created a new world. Virginia has had an enormous impact on the rest of North America and on the rest of the world, just as events outside Virginia have had great force in shaping it. It was not exactly—anywhere, at anytime—what any Virginians wished. But it reflected the conflict and the cooperation among them all. Let's see how it came about.

Part I

1580s–1760s

BETWEEN TWO WORLDS

Two worlds collided when Europeans came to Virginia, and people on each side had to figure out how best to proceed. The puzzle began by the 1570s and persisted into the seventeenth century and beyond. A warrior named Opechancanough and a young woman named Pocahontas suggest the early options from a Native American perspective.

Opechancanough and War

Opechancanough died in 1646, his age thought to be somewhere around 100. He died a captive of the English, after having tried in 1644 to drive the colonists out of the region. Two decades earlier, in 1622, he had made a similar attempt, one that had come even closer to success. Opechancanough saw no good future in the Chesapeake region for Native Americans if the English were to stay. Thus, this warrior and political leader took his stand.

Opechancanough, according to one surmise, in 1606 killed the last survivors of the "Lost Colony." No guesswork is required about who or when, let alone whether, to know that it was Opechancanough who led the Powhatan Uprising in 1622 and another in 1644. If it were possible to prevent colonists—whether from Spain or England or anywhere else across the Atlantic Ocean—from making permanent settlements in the Chesapeake area, he would prevent it. No compromise, no middle way, was possible. It must be war, war to extermination. In this collision of two worlds, one would eliminate the other. Opechancanough hoped it would be his people who came out victors. He died, and his hopes died with him.

Pocahontas and Marriage

Pocahontas, born much later than Opechancanough, died much sooner. Her short life proved as consequential as his. Her way was different. Maybe it was better, maybe not.

Most Virginia schoolchildren know something about Pocahontas, and some of what they know is true. She was a "favorite daughter" of Wahunsenacawh, also known as Powhatan, the chief of his people and the brother of Opechancanough. As a teenager, she married John Rolfe, one of the early settlers in the new English colony on the James River. Their marriage, in 1614, brought a truce in the early wars between the two races. On her trip to England, accompanying her husband and their young son Thomas, she was treated like royalty and was known as Lady Rebecca. English people saw her, daughter of an emperor, as a princess. Alas, the princess fell ill and died in 1617, and her husband returned to Virginia without her. The truce came to an end, and a few years later, after Powhatan, too, had died, Opechancanough led his great uprising of 1622 to kill off the newcomers.

By 1646, both Opechancanough and Pocahontas were dead. The Virginia colony continued to grow. In the collision of two worlds, the English world came to dominate, and the Powhatan people fell into near eclipse. Pocahontas had many descendants through her son Thomas Rolfe, and they took pride in their Powhatan ancestry. But they identified themselves as English, not Indian, and they generally recoiled from people whom they identified as Indians. They hoped that their children would not marry Indians—would not marry Opechancanough's descendants. Some of Opechancanough's kin, too, no doubt live today in Tidewater Virginia, but the world around them is by no means the one that Opechancanough hoped for.

In marrying a leading white settler and thus for a time bringing peace to Virginia, Pocahontas proved the great exception. We can, if we wish, say that Pocahontas was right in the path that she chose for herself—or that destiny brought her. But we cannot say that Opechancanough was wrong in his assessment of the future. Perhaps the truce that Pocahontas and John Rolfe achieved through their marriage gave the English time enough to build to a strength that Opechancanough could not overcome.

Chapter 1

Elizabethan Virginia

....

Sailing for Spain, Christopher Columbus made four voyages to the West Indies, which he mistook for the East Indies, on the other side of the world. After his first voyage, in 1492, he made three more before he died in 1506. A full century lay ahead before the Virginia Company dispatched an expedition that turned up at Jamestown. To put that long period into perspective, the time between Columbus's death and the founding of Jamestown was about as long as the time between Presidents Andrew Johnson in the 1860s and Lyndon Johnson in the 1960s. The century after Columbus supplies essential background to the English adventure on the James River.

One important backdrop to developments during the sixteenth century was the 1494 Treaty of Tordesillas between Spain and Portugal. Two Catholic nations, these seafaring societies sharing the Iberian peninsula obtained papal approval of their plans, and the Treaty of Tordesillas provided a line that chopped the globe in two. Africa—both coasts—as well as west to Brazil and east to the East Indies was open to Portuguese adventuring. The rest of the Americas and much of the Pacific (west, it turned out, to the Philippines) was apportioned to Spain. No European explorer yet knew about the Chesapeake Bay region, but it would not fall in Portugal's half of the planet. It would belong to Spain. No other nation need apply.

The Long Century after Columbus

During the first fifty years after 1492, the Spanish explored and warred through much of the New World. Moreover, Ferdinand Magellan sailed for Spain in 1519 on a round-the-world voyage that, though he did not live to complete it, returned to Spain in 1522. For more and more Europeans, the planet was growing smaller and more familiar. Also in those first fifty years, the Spaniards Álvar

Núñez Cabeza de Vaca, Hernando de Soto, and Francisco Coronado trudged through huge swatches of territory between Florida and California.

England and France sent out feelers during this period as well. England got into the act as early as 1497, when John Cabot—in his native Italian, his name was Giovanni Caboto—reached Nova Scotia, far to the north. Sailing in 1524 for the French, another Italian, Giovanni da Verrazano, cruised north along the Atlantic coast from the Carolinas to Canada, and a Frenchman, Jacques Cartier, explored much of eastern Canada, reaching Montreal. As early as 1534, Cartier identified the St. Lawrence River as a major point of entry into the continent, and in 1541 he attempted, though without success, to establish a colony in the area.

In the Southeast during the second half of the sixteenth century, Spain established a fortress at St. Augustine in Florida in 1565. In the southwest, after heading north from their base in Mexico, Spanish explorers by 1600 had moved into what they named New Mexico, and by 1610 had founded Santa Fe. The Spanish grew ever less impressed with the prospects in eastern North America anywhere north of Florida—moreover, they considered "Florida" to extend well up the coast, and regardless of the prospects there, they did not want interlopers from other lands. The French found this out after they built a settlement near today's Jacksonville in 1564. Upon discovering the intrusion, the Spanish utterly destroyed it.

By 1580, Francis Drake had done Magellan one better, surviving a voyage that took him around the world, during which he sailed north along the California coast. By then, the Spanish, French, and English had explored much of the Gulf coast, the Atlantic coast, and the Pacific coast of what would much later become the contiguous forty-eight states of the United States of America. The Spanish had made far more progress than any other European power in establishing colonies or settlements in the New World. But the French and the English had indicated a considerable interest as well, though neither had yet put down a permanent settlement.

The English, the Spanish, and the People of the Chesapeake Who Discovered Them

In 1492, the year Columbus first sailed off to what he thought was going to be Asia, Spain expelled its non-Catholics—both its Jewish residents and its Muslim residents. People of the three faiths had gotten along quite well for many years, but the time had come, the rulers decided, to push for a religiously more homogeneous society as they built a nation-state.

A half century later, England embarked on a variation of that experience when Henry VIII broke away from the Catholic Church, denying the pope authority over England, in particular any say over Henry's marriages. A struggle between supporters of the Church of England and adherents of the Catholic faith racked the kingdom through much of the reign of Elizabeth I, daughter of Henry VIII by Anne Boleyn, the second of his six wives.

The fact that Spain was Catholic and England not spurred a rivalry between the two that took shape in the eastern Atlantic in a naval struggle and in the western Atlantic in a competition to colonize. The most notable naval encounter took place in 1588 off the coast of England when the great Spanish Armada failed in a mighty effort to humble the apostate English.

All the while the Spanish and the English were embarking on their divergent paths through religious conflict and nation building, not to mention empire building, in the Chesapeake region a different group of people went about their lives. The Virginia Algonquians—the Powhatans—of the Tidewater area west of the Chesapeake Bay also grew in power. Their chief, or commander, in the late sixteenth century was Powhatan, who was probably in his sixties when the English came to Jamestown. His region, the Tsenacommacah, or Tsenacomoco, had a population of perhaps 15,000 in 1607, across a territory that had grown to approximately 60 miles by 100 miles. The last group to fall to Powhatan dominance before Jamestown were the Chesapeakes, early in 1607, in the Norfolk area. At no time had the Powhatans been more powerful—their political control more consolidated, their territory larger.

These were the Americans who discovered Europe when Europeans came to them. But some actually traveled to Europe or to Britain themselves.

Spanish Virginia

At various times during the sixteenth century, the Spanish showed up along the coast of what later became Virginia or North Carolina. When they left after one such occasion, about 1560, they took with them a young man whose Spanish name became Don Luis. For about ten years he lived in Madrid, Havana, or Mexico City. During that time he not only converted to Catholicism but also, no doubt, learned a great deal about Spanish behavior toward Native Americans in the Caribbean, and about Spanish war making as well, as his mentor in Havana was the military governor there. A group of nine Jesuits took him from their base in Havana to the Chesapeake in September 1570, hoping he would act as guide and interpreter and help them establish themselves and evangelize his countrymen. The nine Jesuits spent several months between the James and York rivers, but Don Luis chose to rejoin his people, and in February 1571, he ended the Jesuits' mission by having them killed. Spared among the Spanish was a boy, Alonso, whom a Spanish military expedition from Havana picked up the next year, and from his testimony we know the story of the fate of the Spanish mission on the James.

Spanish and English ships alike visited the Chesapeake area in the 1580s and later. In 1603 a small group described as "Virginia natives" exhibited canoes and how to make use of them—in London. A year or two later, a ship went up the Rappahannock River; it was well received at first, but then things went awry, and a chief of the Indians was shot and killed. None of these visits resulted in a settlement that lasted any longer than had the Spanish mission in 1570–1571, but each gave residents of the region some experience of encounters with strangers, aliens with strange appearances and behavior, who kidnapped, killed, or otherwise mistreated people they ran across. Spain continued to view the region as within its jurisdiction, but the area had never been a focus of their efforts, mission or military, and the one serious venture that took them to eastern Virginia ended in a way that showed why Virginia never became Spanish.

Between Two Worlds, Spanish and Native American: Don Luis and the Scholars

Centuries after a teenaged Indian boy was taken in 1560 by the Spanish to places far away from his Chesapeake homeland, he has remained an important figure in people's imagination and in the historical reconstruction both of how it was that the Spanish did not colonize the Chesapeake region first, and of how the English adventure fared when it finally got under way. A Richmond writer, James Branch Cabell, dubbed Don Luis the "first Virginian." In Cabell's view, Don Luis's treachery prevented Spanish settlement on the Chesapeake and thus preserved Virginia for subsequent English occupation.

One historian, Carl Bridenbaugh, suggested that the Indian leader Opechancanough was in fact Don Luis, so he had direct knowledge of the European world from a lengthy visit to Spain and then to Spanish settlements in the Caribbean islands and in Mexico. In view of Opechancanough's putative age of 100 in 1646, the time line fits. Certainly some teenaged son of a chief had accompanied Spanish explorers in the early 1560s away to Spain and the Caribbean, had spent several years with them, had probably seen the way the Spanish treated their Indian laborers, had accompanied the Spanish group of priests in 1570 to the James River, and, after killing his companions, had taken up the life in the Chesapeake that he had put aside ten years before. That young man postponed European settlement on the James from 1571 to 1607—and may also, according to Bridenbaugh, have been the man who then tried in 1622 and again in 1644 to eliminate that settlement as well.

But most scholars have rejected the Bridenbaugh hypothesis, intriguing though it is. Anthropologist Helen Rountree, for one, notes that if Opechancanough had had as much experience among the Spanish as did Don Luis, he would not have pulled back in 1622 after his devastating initial attacks at Jamestown and elsewhere as though he expected the English, having been so thoroughly pummeled, to pull up stakes and leave.

Spanish Conquistadors in Western Virginia: New Views

The past keeps changing, and recently discovered archaeological and archival materials have revised the known history of sixteenth-century Virginia. Spanish soldiers were in Saltville, in western Virginia, a few years before Spanish missionaries landed on the James River in eastern Virginia.

From 1539 to 1543, Hernando de Soto led a band of marauding Spaniards on the first great expedition by Europeans through the Southeast, an expedition that lasted longer and covered more distance than did the much later westward trip, farther north, of Meriwether Lewis and William Clark. Charles Hudson, an expert on early Indian and Spanish history, came to realize in the 1980s that the expedition led by Juan Pardo, some twenty-five years after Soto's expedition, had covered much of the same route, so Hudson began a study of the Pardo route and sought historian Paul Hoffman's help with the Spanish documents.

Deciphering and translating the spidery writing and archaic language of old documents in the Spanish archives is a highly specialized enterprise, and Hoffman is one of a very few experts at it. The Hudson and Hoffman team prepared a book of new translations in which they speculated about the route the Spanish had taken. Before publishing it in 1990, they had it reviewed by Warren Wilson College archaeologist David Moore, based in western North Carolina, near Asheville, who was attuned to the possibility of an early Spanish presence in his region.

Meanwhile, in 1986, fourteen-year-old Robin Beck picked up some artifacts on a farm owned by his aunt and uncle, Pat and James Berry, in Burke County, a few miles north of Morganton. He took the artifacts to Moore, who identified them as Spanish in origin and urged Beck to be on the lookout for more. Beck then found fragments of a glazed olive jar, a wrought-iron nail, and shards of pottery of a type called grayware that matched specimens known from the Spanish port of Santa Elena on the South Carolina coast. Moore and Hudson were ecstatic. Soto had probably passed through the Morganton area about 1541, but the artifacts at the Berry site came from the 1567 Pardo expedition, which had planted short-lived missions across North Carolina.

Pardo and his *alferez,* or sergeant, Hernando Moyano, were based for a time near Morganton. The Spanish records relate that a mountain chief sent a threat to Sergeant Moyano, who was not averse to a fight, particularly when it would be in the mountains, as, ever since discovering how rich in gold were the Aztecs of Mexico and the Incas of Peru, conquistadors believed cities in the mountains to be a means to great wealth. So he marched north to a place that other Spanish records tell had salt springs from which the Indians made salt—today's Saltville, the only such place in the area. There, the records say, fifteen Spanish soldiers killed more than 1,000 Indians and burned fifty huts, the first recorded battle by Europeans on Virginian soil. Saltville had salt but no gold, however, and Moyano returned to base disappointed.

Stimulated by the discovery of archaeological evidence and a new interest in Pardo, John Worth, doing archival work in Seville, Spain, discovered and translated a previously unknown document that shed further light on Pardo and Moyano. The document, a letter written in 1584 to the king of Spain by an old soldier seeking a pension, confirmed the battle. In that letter, Domingo de León told the king of his service in Moyano's attack on Saltville, and he also said an Indian woman from Saltville (a *casica*) had married a Spaniard and in 1584 was living in the fort of St. Augustine, Florida.

That woman, Luisa Menendez (the records do not tell her Indian name), herself gave testimony at St. Augustine in 1600. She said she was a native of the place where the salt springs flowed and where Moyano had attacked. She had become the young bride of a Spanish soldier named Juan de Ribas, a member of the Pardo expedition, and had moved with her husband first to Santa Elena and then to St. Augustine. As for Ribas, he testified at the same hearing in 1600 that his wife had been a "chieftainess." In 1567, English settlement at Jamestown lay forty years in the future. Preceding Pocahontas—Lady Rebecca, wife of an English soldier—by nearly half a century in what became Virginia was another Indian princess, Luisa Menendez, wife of a Spanish soldier.

Roanoke Island

English America had its beginnings at Roanoke Island, located today on the Outer Banks of North Carolina. In 1584, Elizabeth I gave Sir Walter Ralegh (often spelled Raleigh) authority to explore and colonize an area of North America north of Spanish Florida.

Ralegh's first expedition set out that year, two vessels captained by Philip

Queen Elizabeth I (1533–1603). During Elizabeth's forty-five-year reign the English began venturing in the New World for colonies. Never married, she was known as the Virgin Queen. Virginia Historical Society, Richmond, Virginia.

Sir Walter Ralegh (also spelled Raleigh; c.1552–1618). In the 1580s he named the English settlement in the Roanoke Island area after Elizabeth I, the Virgin Queen. The Jamestown colony was not established until after her death, but the name "Virginia" persisted. Engraving by Simon van de Passe. Library of Congress, Prints and Photographs Division, LC-USZ62-2951.

Amadas and Arthur Barlowe. They reached Roanoke Island, selected it as a possible place for an English settlement, and named the entire Atlantic-coast region "Virginia." A second expedition, under Sir Richard Grenville, followed the next year with seven vessels and 600 men. When Grenville, too, returned to England, he left behind 107 men under Ralph Lane to build houses and a fort on the island. They did so, but they also antagonized local Indians, who responded by making life difficult for them.

The next year, 1586, three expeditions reached Roanoke Island. A relief vessel came, followed by three ships under Grenville, but not before Sir Francis Drake appeared, and Lane and his men chose to leave with Drake for England. Grenville left a new group of fifteen men to hold the fort through the following winter, but they were attacked and killed by Indians. Thus, after not only many visits during three summers but also two groups of men directed to winter on the island, nothing permanent had emerged.

In 1587, an effort was again made to settle the island. Three vessels carried 112 people, among them women and children as well as soldiers. John White, who had accompanied one of the earlier voyages and had produced many drawings of the area and its Indian inhabitants, commanded the 1587 expedition and settlement effort. The community rebuilt the fort, repaired the houses, and settled in at the "Citty of Ralegh." White's daughter, Eleanor Dare, had a daughter, Virginia Dare—named, of course, after the colony of Virginia, to signify her birth as the first English child born in English America. England's effort to colonize the New World was under way.

White left Roanoke Island to return to England for supplies and more settlers. Instead of returning the next year, he had to wait three years. England had gone to war with Spain, Spaniards captured White when he tried to return, and then he had to wait for ships to become available at the end of the war. When he returned in 1590, he found the fort and houses deserted and the colonists nowhere to be seen, and the only clue was the word ".Croatoan" carved in a tree. Roanoke Island became known as the Lost Colony rather than the First Colony. The Spanish Armada was vanquished, but so was England's first stab at founding a colony in North America.

Elizabethan Virginia

As knowledge of the western Atlantic emerged across the second half of the sixteenth century—during the reign of Queen Elizabeth—a few men in England played particularly significant roles in promoting an English attempt to acquire riches, establish trade, thwart the Spanish, explore new areas, or develop

How They Catch Fish. In the 1580s, John White produced various watercolor illustrations (they are housed at the British Museum) of Native American life in the Roanoke Island area, subsequently published as engravings by Theodor de Bry in *Grands Voyages* (1590). This composite shows fishing by spear, weir, and basket, or dip net, with fishing done either wading in the water or moving about in a dugout log canoe. These Carolina Algonquians' lives resembled those of the Virginia Algonquians, the people whom the English met a generation later in the Jamestown area. The Colonial Williamsburg Foundation.

John White's map of Elizabethan Virginia.
Based on a watercolor by John White, this
map, the first to identify "Virginia," was en-
graved by Theodor de Bry and published in
Grands Voyages (1590). Spanish "Florida" ap-
pears to the south (on the left), with Roanoke
Island (toward the right) seen to the left of
the upper of the two ships. Virginia Historical
Society, Richmond, Virginia, gift of the heirs of
John Stewart Bryan.

colonies. Sir Francis Drake, Sir Humphrey Gilbert, and Sir Walter Ralegh were
among the leading figures to have sailed out to the wider world. At home in
England were promoters who never traveled anywhere but nonetheless proved
central to English colonization. Two men—relatives, both named Richard Hakluyt—synthesized and published the information coming in from overseas, and
between them they generated a coherent theory of colonization. The English
would seek to maintain friendly relations with such people as they encountered,
and they would proselytize them, bringing them into the Christian fold. But
regardless, the English would plant permanent settlements. The colonies would
absorb excess English population and supply the home country with raw materials as well as a market for processed goods. The major writings of Richard
Hakluyt the younger appeared at just about the time of the Roanoke adventure.

The last of them, *The Principal Navigations* (1589), recounts the exploits of such English adventurers as Gilbert and Ralegh.

The queen died in 1603, and Elizabethan Virginia faded into lore, before another effort to launch the colony could be made. In 1607, twenty years after the 1587 expedition, England tried again to establish a permanent New World colony in Virginia. This time the attempt was made at Jamestown, and it persisted. One of its purposes, never much accomplished, was to solve the mystery of the Lost Colony. John White's artwork remains to depict the lives of area Indians, the original American people, from the time of his failed effort at colonization during the first launching of Virginia. Roanoke Island eventually fell outside Virginia's boundary and became part of North Carolina—had the place been called Carolina in the 1580s, the baby girl born there in August 1587 might have been named Caroline Dare.

By the early 1600s, the European nations that had been exploring North America began putting down roots farther north than Florida. A French effort succeeded at Quebec in 1608. The French nation would not forever control the vast area around that settlement, but 400 years later most of the people there spoke French and identified themselves as Catholics. The Dutch explored the Hudson River in 1609, and at the mouth of that river they soon established a colony, New Netherlands, from which the great city of New York would emerge. The Dutch, too, were dislodged as a colonial power in North America, but the settlement they began continued under new management, and 400 years later one can still find Dutch architecture there, not to mention places with names like Van Cortlandt Park.

Among settlements by Europeans in North America, St. Augustine came first, with its soldiers and slaves and missions. Four decades later, at pretty much the same time as the French established Quebec to the north and the Spanish founded Santa Fe in the Southwest, the English planted Jamestown. Not only did Jamestown precede Plymouth in New England, it preceded Quebec and Santa Fe, although not by as much.

Chapter 2

Jamestown

....

The beginnings of seventeenth-century Virginia can be sketched through the lives of just a few people among the English and a few Native Americans during the first fifteen years. Among the Powhatan people, these were the Powhatan himself, ruler of his people, as well as his daughter Pocahontas and his brother Opechancanough. Among the newcomers who made their way up the James River were John Smith and John Rolfe, together with George Somers and Sir Thomas Gates, with a supporting cast that included a surfeit of martinets among the leaders and of unfortunates among the followers. Other key players included such ships as *Discovery* and *Patience.*

King James I approved a charter for the Virginia Company in April 1606, and the company had two divisions, the Plymouth Company and the London Company. Both sent expeditions to the New World, to "Virginia," later in 1606. In late December, three ships—the *Susan Constant*, the *Godspeed*, and the smallest, the *Discovery*, with 144 men on board in all, 105 colonists and 39 crewmen—pushed off from London bound for Virginia. To finance the venture, the Virginia Company had sold shares to investors who hoped not only to preserve their capital but also to turn a huge profit. Captaining the *Susan Constant* was Christopher Newport, with years of experience as a privateer raiding Spanish ships making their way, freighted with New World treasures, from the Caribbean to Spain. On board Newport's ship was John Smith, the sole commoner among the seven leaders of the adventure, still in his twenties, with experience warring in strange lands in eastern Europe.

It cannot have been a good omen that the little flotilla spent weeks in sight of England before the weather changed and the trade winds cooperated. Finally under way in early February, the three ships sailed, as planned, south to the Canary Islands and then on west to the Caribbean. There, for a couple of weeks beginning in late March, the men made their way from Dominica to Nevis and then the Virgin Islands, stopping for rest, recreation, and fresh water and food supplies, before pushing north toward the mainland. They sailed into the Chesapeake Bay in late April 1607, twenty years after John White had last seen his daughter, his granddaughter, and the rest of the little colony at Roanoke Island. They sailed up the James River, named to honor their king. On May 14, they landed at a small peninsula, Jamestown, a place they selected as secure against local inhabitants and evidently uninhabited, and where Spanish ships would not likely happen upon them. There they constructed a triangular fort, and English America—Virginia—made a new beginning.

John Smith and the Settlement at Jamestown

Things soon went awry. Relatively secure the Jamestown site may have been, but its drinking water proved deadly. Nearly every day that summer, another of the settlers died, most of them from disease, some from Indian attacks. Just as there had been murmurs before the flotilla ever reached Virginia that they should turn back, by fall there were calls to clamber aboard the *Discovery* and sail away. Powhatan veered from viewing the English as potential allies against his own enemies, and thus being willing to trade for food to keep them going, to seeing them as the great threat to his empire that his advisers had prophesied would arise in the east.

John Smith made possible the settlement's early survival, but he was not yet in charge when Christopher Newport left on the *Susan Constant* to return to England in June 1607. Moreover, only the intervention of the young Pocahontas kept him alive long enough to become the colony's leader. More than once, Pocahontas—ever drawn to Smith, curious about the newcomers, eleven years old when they met—intervened to protect him from her father. After the first of these moments—the most dramatic encounter, in which legend has it that Pocahontas threw herself between her father's warriors and the Englishman they were about to bludgeon to death—Smith returned to Jamestown in January 1608 to find a dozen colonists, out of perhaps forty in all still alive, preparing to push off in the *Discovery* for England. Not only had Smith made constant use of the little ship in exploring the area and trading for corn, but the colony could hardly stand losing such a large fraction of its remaining personnel. Several leaders, anxious to leave and desperate to rid themselves of Smith, arranged to have him executed the next day, but that same evening Newport reappeared, with ample supplies and some sixty new colonists, and Smith had survived again.

John Smith became president, or governor, of the colony in September 1608. Later that month, Newport returned yet again. This time he brought another

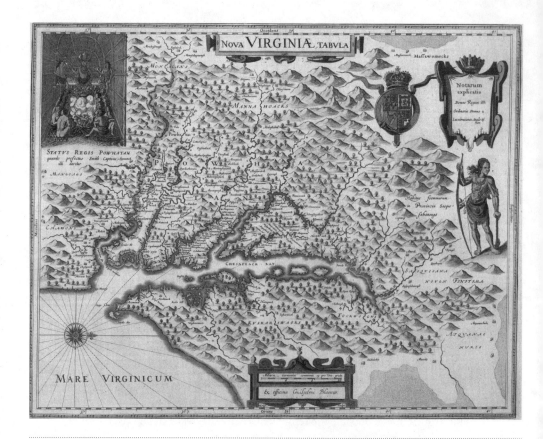

John Smith's map of Jamestown and its surroundings, a composite of English Virginia and the dominion of Powhatan. During his short stay in Virginia, Smith traveled over much of Powhatan's domain, as he reveals in this map, published first in 1612 and later in his *Generall Historie of Virginia* (1624). Like subsequent early maps of Virginia, Smith's, facing west, shows Virginia from the perspective of an approach from the Atlantic. Virginia Historical Society, Richmond, Virginia.

seventy colonists, including the first two women, the wife of a colonist and her maid, who soon found a husband of her own. He also brought orders to find a gold mine, a route to the Pacific, or survivors of the Lost Colony. He failed to bring ample supplies, his sailors consumed much of the food in stock, and when he sailed away in December the colony once again had too little food to carry it through the winter. Smith assembled the colonists and put it to them: "You must obey this now for a law, that he that will not worke shall not eate."

In September 1609, shortly after a "third supply" brought more settlers—including women and children—the company replaced Smith as president, and moreover he suffered a serious accident, so he returned to England. When he left, the colonists numbered some 500. That fall, three dozen of that number abandoned the colony and sailed to England. Smith was no longer available to provide leadership in the colony or engage in trade and diplomacy with Powhatan, who had voiced to Smith the previous winter his suspicion that "your coming hither is not for trade, but to invade my people, and possesse my country." During the winter of 1609–1610, the "starving time," some 400 died, so by March the colonists numbered a mere 60.

A supply ship had been delayed many months from its intended arrival during summer 1609. Coming not by the traditional route via the Caribbean but directly west to the Chesapeake, the *Sea Venture* foundered on a reef just off Bermuda, in a scene that reappeared in William Shakespeare's play *The Tempest*. Sir Thomas Gates, slated to be the next governor, and Sir George Somers, the commander, set about constructing two replacement ships, the *Deliverance* and the *Patience*. In May 1610, they pushed off for Virginia, and this time their trip was quick and uneventful. Yet they were in no way prepared for what they found—a scattering of live human skeletons, a fort in disrepair. Gates and Somers saw no alternative, in view of the scant supplies they had brought, to abandoning the colony, so the colonists all prepared to leave aboard the two ships newly arrived plus the old *Discovery*. Gates resisted the calls of the colonists—wanting to put the nightmare behind them—to burn Jamestown to the ground. Off they went down the river, set to make their way north to Newfoundland.

The next day they discovered to their astonishment that a new supply convoy—three ships, with a year's provisions and 150 additional settlers, under the command of Thomas West, Lord De La Warr—had made the voyage from England, and had in fact made it in less than ten weeks. West carried a commission making him governor "for life," and he ordered Gates to return to Jamestown. The evacuation was reversed. They all returned to Jamestown, which was still standing, and picked up the pieces, establishing a permanent colony in Virginia. Somers, discerning that the Indians had slaughtered the hogs and driven off the deer, headed up an expedition to Bermuda, with the *Patience* and the *Discovery*, hoping to bring back some of the hogs known to be thriving there, so the settlers would have fresh meat once again.

So the colony began anew in 1610. Governing its residents was a draconian new set of "Lawes Divine, Morall and Martiall" outlining behavior that would be required and penalties for infractions. Designed to establish and maintain order under extremely challenging circumstances, the new laws established the death penalty for a wide range of crimes and whipping for some other acts, and they also mandated attendance at divine services in the morning and again in the evening every day. As for the governor for life, West left within the year. By then, the colony was stronger, but violence raged during what historian J. Frederick Fausz calls the "First Anglo-Powhatan War." And though the mortality rate was never again so high as in the winter of 1609–1610, it remained dreadfully high into the 1620s, and indeed, well beyond.

What about the instructions to find not only lots of gold and a northwest passage to the Pacific but also the lost colonists from Roanoke? Some people in England, including King James I, thought their nation might have a stronger claim on the colony against the Spanish if it could be demonstrated that English colonists had been continuously on the scene for two decades by 1607. The Virginia Company instructed Christopher Newport to search for the lost colonists, because any who were found might have helpful information about local native people, not to mention knowing places to obtain gold or copper, and finding survivors might help the company unite under its control both "ould" and "new" Virginia. John Smith and others took a stab at finding any remnants of the lost colonists. According to one line of thought, when the Roanoke colonists left their original place of settlement in the 1580s, at least some went north, and soon after the settlement at Jamestown a ten-year-old boy was seen, quite possibly part Indian and part English, with "a head of haire of perfect yellow." If members of a northern group of lost colonists survived for as long as twenty years, they may have fallen victim, as the Virginia Company phrased it in instructions to Sir Thomas Gates, to "the slaughter of Powhaton . . . upon the first arrivall of our Colonie." Fragmentary evidence of varying sorts—as historian James Horn has sifted it—suggests that most of the lost colonists headed inland, to the west, rather than north along the coast. Several members of the southern group, together with their Indian wives and their children, may well have continued to live in "ould" Virginia beyond 1607.

Contingency enough there was in the original settlement of the Virginia colony at Roanoke Island and its aftermath. Focusing solely on events after 1607, a pamphlet published in 1610 captured the chronic role of contingency in Virginia's persistence—without which there could be no talk four centuries later about England's first permanent settlement dating from 1607. And this passage relates only to developments during summer 1610:

> For if God had not sent Sir Thomas Gates from the Bermudas within four days, they had been all famished. If God had not directed the heart of that worthy knight to save the fort from fire at their shipping, they had been destitute of a present harbor and succor. If they had abandoned the fort any longer time and had not so returned, questionless the Indians would have destroyed the fort. . . . If they had set sail sooner and had launched into the vast ocean, who would have promised that they should have encountered the fleet of Lord La-ware?—especially when they made for Newfoundland, a course contrary to our navy's approaching. If the Lord La-ware had not brought with him a year's provision, what comfort could those souls have received to have been relanded to a second destruction?

John Rolfe

Together with his wife, John Rolfe sailed west with Gates and Somers in 1609 on the *Sea Venture*. While they were shipwrecked at Bermuda, his wife gave birth to a daughter, named Bermuda. But the child died there on the island, and Rolfe's wife died after they reached Virginia. In 1614, the twenty-eight-year-old Rolfe was the principal actor in two dramatic developments at Jamestown that proved absolutely central to Virginia's persistence and growth. Regarding agriculture and the quest for a commodity that could ensure the colony's economic future, he experimented with tobacco and began cultivating a sweet variant from the West Indies, far more enticing to English consumers than the local Chesapeake variety.

And he married Pocahontas—Powhatan's vivacious and fetching teenaged daughter, who had been kidnapped by the English—and thereby secured a peace that endured for several years. He and Pocahontas had a son, Thomas, before all three visited England, where she died in 1617 and left him once more a widower. He returned to Virginia and his tobacco planting, while Thomas—ill himself, so left behind—grew up in England.

What tobacco cultivation in Virginia revealed was an Old World labor force operating on New World land, growing a New World commodity for an Old World market. The fact that Rolfe selected a Caribbean variant of the Chesapeake tobacco expands the story through a larger portion of the North Atlantic world—the ecology and economy of the ocean and the lands on both sides of

Pocahontas, also known as Matoaka and Rebecca (c. 1595–1617). This image was engraved by Simon van de Passe in 1616, while she was visiting England with her husband, John Rolfe, and son, Thomas. First published in John Smith's book *Generall Historie of Virginia* (1624). Virginia Historical Society, Richmond, Virginia.

it. The fact that he and Pocahontas formed a marriage reveals that racial phobias had not yet developed very fully, and the two peoples had some basis for the dream that, under the best of circumstances, they might live peacefully together.

House of Burgesses, Headright System, and Established Church

Virginia kept changing. A key author of one edition of early Virginia must be Sir Edwin Sandys, treasurer of the Virginia Company. According to Sandys, Virginia would have to operate in ways that promoted settlement. The place could not become prosperous unless it attracted more settlers with agricultural skills, and to become more attractive to men, Sandys saw, there would have to be more women. Settlers had detested the governing "Lawes Divine, Morall and Martiall," with their extreme regimentation and extreme penalties, so new regulations must look more like the laws in England.

Among Sandys's proposals, adopted by the company in 1618, the Great Charter replaced landownership by the Virginia Company with a new scheme of landownership, a headright system. First providing for the earliest arrivals, the new scheme provided "ancient" planters 100 acres of land for themselves and an additional 100 acres per share if they were investors in the company. In addition, the new scheme offered 50 acres to each settler after April 1616 who paid his own way to the colony, plus 50 acres to people for every additional person whose passage they paid. A related document called for a "generall Assemblie" of representatives from the scattered settlements to meet and decide on additional local laws. Settlers would have more control over their lives and would therefore be more content, and at the same time they would help with the burden of administering Virginia.

These changes were designed to help the colony succeed and thus help the company survive. A new governor chosen in late 1618, Sir George Yeardley, had responsibility for implementing them. Yeardley arrived in Virginia in April 1619 and soon ordered an election of two men, "burgesses," from each plantation. In addition to what became known as the House of Burgesses was the Virginia Council, whose members were at first chosen by the Virginia Company in London to represent its interests and advise the governor. Together, the Council and the House of Burgesses comprised the "generall Assemblie." The General Assembly met for its first session in 1619 from July 30 to August 4 in the church at Jamestown.

Among the many founding acts of the General Assembly in its early sessions was formal establishment of the Church of England as the official church of the colony. There could be no question but that the colony, representing as it did English authority, would reflect both the Crown of England and the Church of England. It was not so much a matter of church and state, to use the later language, finding some way to relate to each other as it was a matter of church and state being twins that, together, embodied authority and ran the institutional affairs of the colony. People did not choose which church they would attend or belong to. There was only one, though in early Virginia there was often considerable latitude in what people believed or how they practiced their faith. In colonial Virginia, the established church carried out many of the functions that would later be associated with a secular government, including caring for the poor.

White Women and African Virginians

Few women accompanied the English men who sailed in the early years to Jamestown. Those years in Virginia were more like the 1584 and 1585 landings at Roanoke Island than like the 1587 settlement that produced Virginia Dare, but by the early 1620s the colony's population looked more like Roanoke's had in 1587. In 1620, some ninety young women shipped out on the *Jonathan* and the *Merchant of London*. Another thirty-six women sailed on the *Warwick* in 1621. There were others as well, and they went some distance toward narrowing the colony's sex ratio, though it remained unbalanced for many years.

Virtually all of these women, as historian David Ransome has found, were within a few years of twenty years of age, though some were as young as sixteen and a few were over twenty-five. Some of the older ones were widows, but most had never married, and most were missing at least one parent. Like the young men who shipped out as servants, the young women who sailed with the prospect of becoming brides looked to Virginia to provide them a better chance at life. It was a tremendous gamble, but they saw it as worth taking. Sometimes it was.

One other new beginning of enormous consequence dates from this brief period. In late August 1619, a few weeks after the General Assembly's first meeting, the first black Virginians, women as well as men, arrived in the colony. In a letter to the Virginia Company, John Rolfe reported the arrival of "20 and odd Negroes." The *White Lion*, a Dutch warship, had seized the Africans from a Portuguese slave ship, the *San Juan Bautista*, or *São João Bautista*, in the western Gulf of Mexico on its way from Luanda, Angola, to Vera Cruz, Mexico. These first black Virginians had not volunteered to come to Virginia, but they arrived in time to help complete that year's tobacco crop. Trailing the *White Lion* into port by a few days was the *Treasurer*, an English ship out of Jamestown that had teamed up with the Dutch ship in its piracy and slave stealing, and among its cargo was a woman, Angelo or Angela, who soon went to work in the household of William Pierce and his wife, June.

The New Beginnings of 1619

The new governor in 1619, Sir George Yeardley, echoed an observation from a decade earlier, when looking for gold was all the rage. He expressed concern about the focus on tobacco, and the company agreed, noting "the excessive applying of tobacco, and the neglect to plant corne." King James I vented his detestation of tobacco, and John Smith had his doubts too, but it became the basis of agricultural prosperity, too late to save the Virginia Company but not too late to save the colony. Tobacco remained the economic mainstay of much of Virginia through the seventeenth, eighteenth, and nineteenth centuries and indeed nearly all the way to Virginia's 400th anniversary celebration.

The year 1619 has tremendous iconic importance in the history of Virginia and the history of America. The initial meeting of the House of Burgesses in

1619 is often termed the first indication of representative democracy in the New World, the seedbed of American democracy. It was not intended to be so, and democracy did not appear all at once, but that first meeting did in fact prove the seedbed from which an independent legislative body grew. In addition, the new system of land distribution pointed toward the possibility of widespread economic independence. Political democracy and economic democracy, we could say in retrospect, had put in an appearance, or rather, a harbinger of each had emerged in Virginia.

Yet the shift to a headright system, in granting fifty acres for each passenger to Virginia a person paid for, also brought a new age of unfreedom, as some men would systematically acquire other men—would simultaneously obtain both the land and the labor to work it. Indentured servitude characterized the labor force of seventeenth-century Virginia. It provided a method of recruiting a labor force for the new plantations. It also provided people of limited means and few prospects a way to get themselves to the New World, and it raised enormous problems of how to satisfy them once they had paid their debt and could seek the land they yearned to fulfill their dreams of working for themselves. Before the 1640s, many former servants became landowners; but as time went on, that became more difficult.

Unfreedom reached across a new racial boundary that came into view in Virginia in 1619. The arrival of those twenty or so Africans in 1619 is often characterized as the beginning of American slavery. It is also treated as the arrival of the first African Americans. Of course, Africans had accompanied the Spanish in their sixteenth-century forays to Florida and west from there; they had an important presence in Spanish Florida for decades before there was a Jamestown. We are not sure of the status of the first African Virginians, though they no doubt experienced unfreedom, just as did most white newcomers to the colony in the seventeenth century. Regardless of whether they were typically slaves or servants, we can say that before 1620 there were black Virginians as well as white ones, and that without black Virginians, and lots of them, there could have been no plantation slavery as developed before the seventeenth century was out.

The Great Powhatan Assault of 1622

The arrival of many dozens of white women—part of Sir Edwin Sandys's campaign to transform, or at least strengthen, Virginia—made a genuine settler society possible. Then again, their arrival also made it even more imperative that Indians and English find a means to accommodate each other's presence—or there would be war, begun by one side or the other, to gain or regain sole possession of the area. Increasingly, the Powhatan people found themselves denied their traditional land along the banks of the rivers, denied much of their land regardless of its location.

When Powhatan died in 1618, his brothers in turn succeeded him, and soon Opechancanough headed Tsenacommacah. Meanwhile, as Virginia's settler population grew, it spread out to bring under cultivation more and more land for growing tobacco. The combination of more people, living in a sprawled-out fashion, meant that Opechancanough not only could feel alarmed to the point of taking military action against the colony but could also see a prospect of success. In spring 1622 he attacked.

The monstrous event that spring—widespread, well-organized, and deadly—has traditionally been termed a "massacre"; the traditional accounts use the term only when Indians attacked whites, not vice versa. In recent years, the term "uprising" has been frequently used instead. Anthropologist Helen Rountree prefers "the great attack" or "the great assault" of 1622. Whatever it may be called, roughly a third of the colony's settlers, some 300, died, and among the dead were many of the women who had arrived since 1619. The English responded in kind. The settlement's first fifteen years were a treacherous time for English Virginians. The seventeenth century was particularly unkind to Native Virginians.

Opechancanough inflicted enormous damage. It proved not enough to kill off the Virginia colony, but it was enough to kill off the Virginia Company. A new king, Charles I, soon made Virginia a royal colony. The Crown failed to mention any "generall Assemblie," but the group kept meeting anyway, as one governor after another found it useful and called it into session, and in 1639 the king recognized it as a legitimate organ of colonial administration. More and more, the General Assembly—a name it has kept from 1619 to the present, though it has changed in various ways—became a legislature, a colonial counterpart of the British Parliament.

Whatever historical possibilities those first fifteen years either disclosed or curtailed, what happened after 1622 was a rapid growth in the colony's territory, population, and wealth, such that when Opechancanough made another sustained effort to obliterate English Virginia in 1644, the attack produced even more casualties but had even less long-term impact. The attack in 1644 was a last desperate effort to end the experiment to settle an English Virginia, a last desperate attempt to permit Indian Virginia to return to its former condition. Opechancanough died at colonists' hands. The Spanish having receded as a threat, in the Tidewater the Indians did as well. Tsenacommacah vanished. The starving times were over. English men and English women attended Church of England services and raised families of English-speaking white children. Tidewater

Virginia became more and more—year by year, from 1625 to 1650 to 1675—an English world, transplanted to a New World setting. But it was not England, it was America.

Colonial Beginnings Compared: Massachusetts Bay and Chesapeake Bay

The London Company sent out an expedition in December 1606, and in May 1607 it arrived in the Chesapeake Bay. At about the same time, the Plymouth Company sent two expeditions to points farther north, in "North Virginia." One of them left England in August 1606 but was captured in the Caribbean by the Spanish in November, the month before the Jamestown expedition set off. In late May 1607, shortly after the Jamestown expedition reached its destination, a second expedition departed England for North Virginia. It reached the Sagadahoc River (today's Kennebec River) in August, and the new arrivals constructed a fort at what is today Maine's Fort Popham State Historical Site, south of Brunswick, in Sagadahoc County. Half the Englishmen left the colony that December, and the other half—those who had survived the harsh winter—left the following fall, on a boat they had recently constructed, the *Virginia*. So the Sagadahoc colony began shortly after, rather than shortly before, the one at Jamestown, and it lasted barely a year. But the experience facilitated a successful colonization by the Pilgrims at Plymouth in 1620, not to mention the Puritans' settlement at Massachusetts Bay a decade later.

The Virginia Company's John Smith played roles in the English settlements both at Massachusetts Bay and in the Chesapeake Bay area. At Jamestown he was a towering early leader. On a voyage north in 1614, he reconnoitered the coast—mapping the region, and naming it New England—and his reports shaped the settlement that took place at Plymouth in 1620. As for the *Virginia*, after its passengers arrived safely back in England, it made a voyage to Jamestown by way of Bermuda in 1609—and was one of the ships that the colonists climbed aboard when they floated down the James River the next year intending to abandon the colony. Had the colonists not met a supply expedition, and turned back upstream toward the fort to try again, the *Virginia* would have been party to the abandonment of both the English settlements dating from 1607.

The beginnings of the English settlement of the two areas have long been understood as contrasts in colonization. It has long been thought that Jamestown began as a male bastion, whether as a military outpost, a mining town, or a trading post, whereas the Pilgrims came in family groups, as did the Puritans who followed them to New England in the 1630s. From early on, in fact, the northern

These are the Lines that shew thy Face; but those
That shew thy Grace and Glory, brighter bee:
Thy Faire Discoueries and Fowle-Overthrowes
Of Salvages, much Civilliz'd by thee
Best shew thy Spirit; and to it Glory Wyn.
So, thou art Brasse without, but Golde within.
Published by W. Richardson Castle Street Leicester Fields.

John Smith (1580–1631), "Admiral of New England." Virginia Historical Society, Richmond, Virginia.

colonies had considerable numbers of unattached males, too, and there were soon more women in Virginia than is often thought, so the perceived differences on that account ought to be narrowed. It is often thought, too, and rightfully so, that large numbers of early Virginia settlers came as indentured servants, but that turns out to be true for New England as well. The greater differences between New England and Virginia came later. In the first generation, the two areas of settlement were perhaps more similar than not.

As for where English North America began, it has to be Virginia—whether the colony is understood as having originated at Roanoke Island in the 1580s or at Jamestown a generation later. But the Virginia colony remained a very iffy enterprise in its earliest years, something not so true of Plymouth or the larger colony, Massachusetts, that emerged later up the bay from Plymouth at Boston. Virginia got there first, whether we accept the date May 1607 as the time from which continuous settlement can be traced or we say that permanence cannot

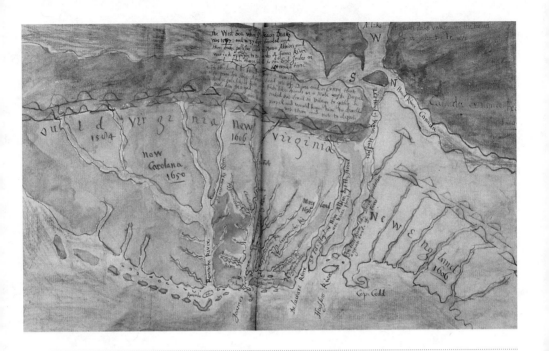

Map of Virginia, 1650, by John Farrer. This map divides the east coast among "Ould Virginia 1584, now Carolana 1650," "New Virginia 1606," and "New England 1606." The James and York rivers appear at the center of the foreground, just as they were at the center of early English colonization, though the Rappahannock and Potomac rivers were also known by this time. Farrer had a pretty good idea of what Virginia looked like as far inland as the fall line, or possibly the Blue Ridge. Beyond that, he conflated the Appalachian Mountains and the Rockies, placing the Pacific Ocean—"the Sea of China and the Indies"— just a few days' hike from Jamestown. A voyage by Sir Francis Drake (c. 1540–1596) up North America's west coast in 1579 provided the basis for subsequent English claims to land "from sea to sea," so what is now coastal California is seen here as the Virginia colony's farthest western reach. Rare Books Division, The New York Public Library, Astor, Lenox and Tilden Foundations.

really be declared before the evacuating settlers met the supply ships and returned to the abandoned colony in June 1610.

In the rivalry between the two regions for historical primacy, the spin artists speaking for Plymouth have often triumphed. The iconic moment from fall 1621, when the Pilgrims hosted the "first Thanksgiving," stands out in this regard. Yet the Pilgrims did not repeat the performance each year, making it an annual affair; rather, that particular event was, many years later, pointed to as the beginning—or simply the first iteration—of the modern U.S. holiday. Virginia's rebuttal has merit: that an early Thanksgiving, a decade before the

Pilgrims set sail, took place at Jamestown during the spring after the starving time of winter 1609–1610, to celebrate the arrival of resupply ships bearing food. Even earlier events—not English, but European—have since been marked as the "first Thanksgiving" in what is now the United States, whether by the Spanish in Texas in 1541 or the French in Florida in 1564.

Not only did Jamestown precede Plymouth, not only did all manner of colonial phenomena occur in Virginia "before the Mayflower" (as writer Lerone Bennett said of African immigrants to the English colonies), but Virginia also proved more of a model than did the Plymouth colony for the America that followed, as so many people—the servants, the maidens—volunteered to go there to reinvent themselves in a new social and economic environment. Plymouth particularly attracted people who had already become who they wanted to be but sought a more favorable cultural and political environment for their identities. Virginia proved a place, in what became the quintessentially American way, to start over. We can say, regardless, of the two areas of English settlement that they both grew, and both changed, and the English took over the European colonies that had begun to sprout in the region between, whether at New Netherlands on the Hudson River or at New Sweden on the Delaware River.

Colonizing Critters

Some years ago, the scholar Alfred Crosby began insisting that humans did not work alone in colonizing the new worlds they came upon. Rather, they brought, whether intentionally or unwittingly, all manner of life forms—animals, plants, and microbes—that went far to shape the colonial encounter. Early Virginia illustrates the phenomenon.

The English in Virginia had in mind, some of them at least for a time, extracting gold and taking it back to the Old World. They had in mind trading for furs and shipping them back. And they had in mind establishing a settler society that would be just like the one they had left behind, only better. In their cultural toolkit, they brought with them attitudes, beliefs, and behavior about their relationship with the natural world. And their natural world included domesticated animals, quadrupeds they owned and depended on—sheep, goats, horses, hogs, cattle. These animals represented property, wealth; they supplied motive power for things and people; and they generated milk, meat, and hides or wool. One other quadruped, the dog, supplied companionship and protection and served as a fellow hunter. How did Indians, colonists, and the four-legged newcomers interact to change the Chesapeake world?

Animal husbandry—the care and handling of domestic animals—as practiced in the Old World and the New World differed in one material way: The Chesapeake region was without animal husbandry, by definition among the Indians and to a considerable extent by neglect among the colonists. The only counterparts to Europeans' livestock previously known to the Native Americans were animals that ran wild (especially deer), which were not domestic animals at all, or dogs, which were hardly domesticated either. As for the English Virginians, company treasurer Sir Edwin Sandys mourned in 1620 about the costs of the tobacco boom: "Corne and Cattell we passe over, being only for sustenance of the People." Assembling shelters for livestock would not have taken a long time, but caring for confined animals would. So plantation owners and farmers left most of their property wooded and unfenced and allowed the animals to forage for themselves.

Beef cattle, horses, and swine proved tough enough to survive wild conditions. Sheep and milk cows did not. Goats were another story—they proved hearty enough to weather the climate and more than capable of providing for themselves, but they stripped the bark off apple trees to supplement their diets, and the colonists depended on hard cider to replace beer, since they had no time to grow barley between tobacco crops. Sheep—a major food source in England—fell too easily to the thriving wolf population in Virginia, and even if they weren't killed in the wild, their wool was so mangled by underbrush that it ceased to be usable. Milk cows fell victim to the Chesapeake's stifling humidity in the summer and to starvation brought on by neglect in the winter. These factors cut milk production, and what milk the cows did give was low in fat, useless for making butter or cheese. Furthermore, milking was a woman's job, so with few women in the colony the cows were largely left alone.

Left to wander the common woods, animals caused confusion for their owners. Where, when you needed it, was a pig for meat or a horse to ride into Jamestown? Wandering groups of swine, horses, and cattle often traveled too far ever to be found again, and they bred and died without interference from their owners. Animals that escaped poachers, wolves, and accidental injury in the forest turned feral, and these stronger animals sprouted thick coats, were shorter owing to malnutrition, and sometimes bred with finer domestic livestock. In hopes of reining in the chaos, the House of Burgesses encouraged each settlement to appoint a cow keeper, but the man usually spent more time watching for Indians than keeping track of the animals. When enough free-roaming pigs and cattle had uprooted and trampled tobacco crops, the House of Burgesses asked farmers to fence them in. Farmers ignored the decree, so instead the planters fenced in their fields. Exemplifying one solution to the wandering, field-destroying pig problem was the so-called Ile of Hogges on the James River near Jamestown—

like similar places later, a small island flushed of its wolf population and refilled with pigs. Planters preserved their crops, owners kept their pigs, and the animals tended themselves.

Indians and colonists differed in multiple ways over livestock, as historian Virginia DeJohn Anderson details. Colonists were aggrieved when Indians swiped livestock, yet the Indians' corn proved a favorite meal of swine and cattle, and the animals were a particular nuisance to Indian women, who were responsible for producing their villages' vegetables. In addition, the newcomer quadrupeds were in direct competition for food with the large game species; they trampled the riverbanks, causing erosion that jeopardized the fish supply; and the livestock that roamed the forests carried foreign diseases that hurt the deer population. Indian and colonial cultures held vastly different perspectives regarding animal life. To colonists, domesticated animals were kept for the sole purpose of satisfying human needs, and humans were the only living beings with any sort of spirituality. The Indians were far less anthropocentric.

Masters of Nature

John Smith wrote that framing Chief Powhatan's treasure temple were four statues: a dragon, a leopard, a bear, and a human. Rather than the lords and masters of nature, the Indians considered themselves to be their prey's equals. The Algonquians believed in a power called "manitou," furnished by a creature's guardian spirit. An animal particularly difficult to catch or whose carcass had immense utility was seen as endowed with immense manitou. When a deer was killed, it was butchered with respect, according to Indians' ancient laws. Thus its protecting spirits would not be angered, and they would allow Indians success in future hunts. When John Smith's Indian guides encountered their first pigs, they stood transfixed. What Smith at first interpreted as a fear of the new animal he soon saw as more a fear of angering the pigs' guardian spirits, with whose demands the Indians were unacquainted.

The equality and spirituality that Indians associated with their animal counterparts made the concept of animal ownership difficult to grasp. After they grew more accustomed to the livestock wandering the forests, they began to hunt them as they would any other creature—showing respect to their guardian spirits, although not to their colonial owners. In time, the Indians of the Chesapeake adopted some husbandry techniques, but they never fully assimilated either English livestock into their culture or the colonists' perspective of human-animal relations. The colonists also changed their ways, though not their belief in humankind's centrality among life forms. As the seventeenth century turned into the eighteenth, horses became ever more important to the gentry. From an early dependence on hunted deer, the settler society moved more and more to a dependence on hog meat. They adopted a hybrid diet that combined, as mainstays, the corn they had learned of from Indians and the hogs they had brought to the New World.

Furthermore, the settlers and their livestock pressed ever more heavily on Indians' crops and hunting grounds. The human newcomers were, in their own minds, at the center of the natural world. As they—especially those who managed the greatest power—understood it, and intended it, they were at the center of the human world as well. The world would be theirs, created in their image, even if that image evolved from one decade, one generation, to another. How they sought to re-create the Chesapeake world in their image, and how that image changed from one generation to another, one century to another, is the subject of chapter 3.

Chapter 3

Land and Labor

....

By 1620, the colony of Virginia was beginning to look like a permanent enterprise, though events in the next couple of years demonstrated that its persistence was something less than a sure thing. The enormously destructive attack by Indians in 1622 left much in doubt, but the colony persisted and soon resumed its growth. The combination of tobacco and servants supplied the menu for a settler society that could work, even if at enormous cost and under continued uncertainty. Would the servants survive, would they work, would they rebel, would they run away? Would there be enough of them? What about tobacco prices? Would the market persist, would it grow, would it provide sufficient rewards to maintain the enterprise? These questions were all based on one fundamental premise: The newcomers from across the ocean—aside from those primarily interested in trading with Indians—wanted the Indians' land, without the Indians on it.

The twin components of servants and tobacco proved to be the colony's social and economic foundation across much of the seventeenth century and, at the same time, its greatest challenge. For one thing, servants, if they survived, became former servants, and former servants were free to seek what they had come to the colony for in the first place: to own their own land. For another, the more successful the colony, the more servants would be required, so maintaining a steady supply of newcomers—itself in doubt—could hardly satisfy the colony's needs.

Indentured Servants

Approximately 80,000 newcomers from across the Atlantic ventured to Virginia in the seventeenth century. The bulk of them came as servants with indentures. Some willing, some kidnapped, they had their transportation costs covered and were provided meals and lodging in return for a number of years of labor, often seven. Because they had, as a rule, some say in whether they went to Virginia, they could negotiate the terms, and men with particular skills might be able to reach terms of no more than four or five years' labor. Regardless of their volition, and regardless of the terms, they had little control over whom they worked with, what work they did, or how they lived. Many died before their time was up and their liberty their own. Many, trying to fast-forward the process, ran away (see sidebar, page 34). From their employer's perspective, a new supply of workers would eventually be needed, since no matter how long the term of indenture, it was finite.

At the conclusion of their terms, servants received freedom dues—typically some food and clothing, but little else. Technically free, they could aspire to landownership, but there had to be land available, and they had to be able to afford it. Many, even most, found themselves hiring on as laborers or staying on as tenants, sometimes with their former employer. Either way, former servants were still working someone else's land, not their own (see sidebar, page 36).

Virginia was volatile. Indians and English contested each other over security and subsistence, and especially they contested each other's claims to control the land. The English threatened each other, too, as servants ran off, tried to maintain their stolen freedom, and were often captured and returned to servitude, punished by the infliction of pain and the extension of their servitude. The English threatened both each other and Indians, when former servants expressed their determination not only to own themselves but also to possess land, to obtain not only liberty but also property—as Bacon's Rebellion demonstrated.

Bacon's Rebellion—and a Shift from Servants to Slaves

A drawn-out incident along the Potomac River between Indians and a white man that began in July 1675 occasioned a series of indiscriminate attacks by settlers against Indians. News coming to Virginia about King Philip's War in New England heightened local fears of what might be coming from Indians in Virginia. Nathaniel Bacon, a young planter who had been in the colony only a short time but had been given a seat on the Virginia Council, led a vigilante group against various groups of Indians. Though he was socially and politically prominent, Bacon's followers included not only numbers of servants and slaves but also a good many restive former servants, for whom land, if it was going to become available, must be coming from the Indians.

Going directly against instructions from Governor William Berkeley, Bacon found himself declared in May 1676 to be in rebellion. In turn, he attacked

THREE RUNAWAYS FROM VIRGINIA SERVITUDE IN 1640

On July 9, 1640, the Virginia Council and General Court disposed of a case of three runaways who had been captured and brought back to resume their service and incur whatever punishments were deemed appropriate. As was reported:

Whereas Hugh Gwyn hath by order of this Board Brought back from Maryland three servants formerly run away from the said Gwyn, the court doth therefore order that the said three servants shall receive the punishment of whipping and to have thirty stripes apiece one called Victor, a dutchman, the other a Scotchman called James Gregory, shall first serve out their times with their master according to their Indentures, and one whole year apiece after the time of their service is Expired. By their said Indentures in recompense of his Loss sustained by their absence and after that service to their said master is Expired to serve the colony for three whole years apiece, and the third being a negro named John Punch shall serve his said master or his assigns for the time of his natural Life here or elsewhere.

One might consider these questions: How is the ethnicity of each of these three men characterized? Did John Punch get a greater punishment or a lesser one than James Gregory and Victor, and if so, why? Was he a slave after 1640?

Berkeley. The colony descended into civil war, and in September, Bacon's men burned the capital at Jamestown. Bacon died the next month, and Berkeley retrieved control, but then he was removed as governor for having lost control in the first place, and he soon died as well. The incident revealed that Indians were still sometimes a force, at least along the moving frontier, and that settlers and their government might go on the warpath against either Indians—friendly or not—or each other.

Servants continued to be important to Virginia's society and economy through the end of the colonial era—but ever less so in the century after Bacon's Rebellion. For one thing, the demand for labor continued to grow, so even a constant supply of new servants could never suffice. For another, changes in England's society and economy diminished the supply. And for Virginian planters, a surfeit of former servants posed considerable danger, as Governor Berkeley had put it at the time of Bacon's Rebellion against his authority: "How miserable that man is that Governs a People when six parts of Seaven at least are Poore Endebted Discontented and Armed." Given all that, when a new source of workers came on stream, when the African slave trade made slaves available in large numbers, planters increasingly adopted the new labor force. Workers who were permanently enslaved would, by definition, never become former slaves. If, moreover, their children were enslaved from birth, the new labor force could reproduce itself.

Throughout most of eastern Virginia, before the end of the seventeenth century, an exclusively Native American population was displaced by an overwhelmingly European one. That situation, even in 1700, was already shifting again, as Africans began growing toward numerical parity with

34

Europeans. Most of the seventeenth century was an in-between time, with Europeans numerically dominant. Virginia was, ever more as the years went by, what the newcomers from Europe, particularly the more wealthy and powerful among them, made of it. We now turn to what they made of it in the eighteenth century, they and a labor force more slave than either servant or free. What they made of it, however, never was entirely in their hands.

African Virginia

During the colonial era, two huge streams of humanity flowed west across the Atlantic, one from Europe, another from Africa, especially from among the Igbo people. In the aggregate, the African stream carried far more people from Old World to New, though to British North America the overall proportions were reversed. Virginia revealed an in-between pattern. Whether in the West Indies or in the Chesapeake region, workers were generally unfree, at first mostly white, but increasingly black. In ever-larger parts of North America, South America, and the Caribbean, the prospect of producing huge quantities of agricultural commodities for European markets brought together a vast acreage in the New World and a vast population resource in Africa.

Seventeenth-century Virginia led the way on race in England's North American colonies. By the 1620s, there were black Virginians as well as white Virginians, so in the Chesapeake region, sooner than anywhere else in the British colonies on the mainland, the two groups encountered each other, on whatever terms. These relations were not yet stenciled on stone, or even well defined, either at the time or for scholars now. Evidence as to their nature, albeit scant, is intriguing. Historian Ira

Had he been one before? What in this document might suggest similarities or differences in the lives of black and white unfree workers (all called "servants" here)—and the ratio of black servants to white ones—in early Virginia? One might consider, too, how this document relates to assertions (whether by academic historians or in the popular culture) as to whether slavery began in Virginia in 1619 or 1662.

In another such case from summer 1640, seven runaways—six of them white and one, Emanuel, described as "a negro of Mr. Reginolds"—were also captured and punished. Emanuel, like most of his comrades, was "to receive thirty stripes and to be burnt in the cheek with the letter R," but, in contrast to four of the others, no mention was made of additional time. Did he get off relatively easily, or should we conclude that he was already a slave?

FREEDOM AND POWER IN EARLY VIRGINIA

Over the years, whether on a military base in Korea or in a freshman survey course at Virginia Tech, I have often asked my students who they would want to be if they found themselves as settlers in colonial Virginia. For an overwhelmingly rural society, an overwhelmingly agricultural economy, I outline five choices:

1: Planter—own the land, own the laborers who work the land

2: Farmer—own yourself, your own labor, and the land you work

3: Landless but free—perhaps a former servant, free, but not independent

4: Indentured servant—unfree, working someone else's land, for a lengthy but fixed period

5: Slave—permanently unfree, even passing your unfree status to the next generation

My students divide between choices 1 and 2—never choosing 4 or 5. Once they have made their choices and explained them to me and their classmates, I urge them to consider the world they have sought to create for themselves. In theory, everyone could be a 2. But in no way can everyone be a 1, and there can be no 1 without somebody—preferably large numbers of somebodies—filling the roles, the unwilling roles, of 4 or 5. So how, I ask my students, should we recruit people to be 4 or 5, and

Berlin distinguishes usefully between the "charter generation" of African Virginians and the "plantation generation." The seventeenth century—the time of the charter generation—allowed a range of possibilities for relations between white and black Virginians. After a protracted struggle, by the 1650s a number of unfree black Virginians—among them Anthony and Mary Johnson, Francis Payne, and Emanuel Driggus—had obtained their freedom, and they raised free children, possessed land and livestock, and sometimes also had servants or slaves.

But if some of the possibilities that emerged early on appeared egalitarian in a seventeenth-century kind of way, they were soon sharply curtailed. A series of laws between the 1660s and the 1720s channeled social and economic change by barring free blacks from "purchasing christian [that is, white] servants," imposing greater taxes on free black couples than on their white counterparts, denying free black men the right to vote or to testify in court or to serve with arms in the militia—generally making it ever more difficult for Virginians with African ancestry to obtain their freedom and ever more difficult for their freedom to give them room to prosper. From time to time—as happened in the 1750s on the Eastern Shore, where a considerable proportion of black residents had long been free—their white neighbors made explicit a wish to exile "all free Negroes out of the Colony."

A settlement that started out in 1607 all male and all white became, within a century, a society nearly equally apportioned by gender and very much divided by race. A society that kept losing people through horrific mortality became a world in which natural increase—far more births than deaths—led to rapid natural increase, first by whites, the characteristic seventeenth-century immigrants, then by blacks, the characteristic eighteenth-century newcomers to eastern Virginia. A venture that began in the hopes of striking it rich did in fact generate enormous wealth, but the very possibility of riches led to the starkest distinctions of power, wealth, and liberty, as people did what they could to amass land and also the labor to make that land produce wealth. And a society that began with whites outnumbered by Indians gradually became a society dominated by black slaves and their white owners (see table on page 34). Black and white, Igbo and English, created—in a great many ways—a new society in eighteenth-century eastern Virginia.

One key way we can track the social history of black Virginians, and their relationships with white Virginians, is through the law—records of appearances in a court and statutes passed by the House of Burgesses. A case of three runaways in the summer of 1640 (see sidebar, page 34) offers a glimpse of Virginia's early labor situation, what workers might choose to do about it, and how the law might treat them when they tried to obtain their freedom sooner than their contracts said it was due.

As servitude persisted, and slavery emerged, slaves and servants continued to live together, work together, and sometimes run away together. Adding more time to a servant's indenture offered an obvious way to obtain repayment and was an obvious way to inflict punishment. How, though, could one obtain repayment or inflict punishment by the addition of time when a slave ran away? One answer: If a slave and a servant absconded together and were caught, the servant might get time added to his own period of service not only for himself but for his slave companion as well. Such an option, presumably known to both parties, had the added advantage of making it less

how should we try to keep them in those positions? And how would they feel, what might they do, if they found themselves there?

likely that servants would take on the additional risk—or the benefit from a pooling of strengths—of pairing up with a partner who happened to be a slave. Black and white might be divided in this fashion, and the House of Burgesses legislated just such an option in the 1660s (see sidebar).

It is usually understood that in colonial Virginia people were either black or white and either slave or free (or indentured servants). But the evidence points to a more complex social and legal reality, for many people were mixed-race, and people could be born into a servitude that lasted thirty or thirty-one years. A law that the House of Burgesses passed in 1662 addressed the status of mixed-race children who resulted from sexual behavior between white men and nonwhite women. No matter how a slave woman became pregnant—whether it was by her owner, his son, his overseer, a white neighbor, a servant, a slave, or indeed any-one—planters wanted assurance that the law considered the resulting child to be a slave as well. A law enacted in 1691 addressed the sexual behavior of nonwhite men with white women (see sidebar, page 42). Only white men should have access to white women, and white women who had biracial children should be punished. Moreover, those biracial children were condemned to three decades of servitude.

The children of an eighteenth-century mixed-race Virginia woman named Sarah Madden showed that, even after the American Revolution—under the series of laws that began in 1691 and continued through 1705, 1723, and 1765—long-term, mixed-race servants continued to be born to long-term, mixed-race, women servants. Moreover, even after the American Revolution, "white" people could be born into slavery. Sally Hemings, as the child of a white man and a woman whose mother was half-white, was "one-quarter black"—three-quarters white, the highest fraction white a person could be and not be classified white under Virginia law in the late-eighteenth century. Her children—also fathered

POPULATION FIGURES FOR
RED, WHITE, AND BLACK IN
EASTERN VIRGINIA, 1685–
1775

The painstaking efforts of historian Peter Wood to reconstruct the population numbers of colonial eastern Virginia, divided by racial identity, produced these figures:

	1685	1715	1745	1775
Red	2,900	1,300	600	300
White	38,100	74,100	148,300	279,500
Black	2,600	20,900	85,300	186,400
Total	43,600	96,300	234,200	466,200

by a white man, now widely thought to have been Thomas Jefferson, especially her youngest, Eston—would have been seven-eighths white, thus legally white. But their mother was a slave, so they were slaves.

Eighteenth-Century Tidewater and Piedmont Virginia

The seventeenth century belonged to the Tidewater, especially the areas of the lower York and James rivers. By contrast, the eighteenth century belonged increasingly to the Piedmont, the area between the fall line of the various rivers—where rocks and falls prevented upriver passage, and where such towns as Petersburg, Richmond, and Fredericksburg therefore developed—and the Blue Ridge. Reflecting the transition, Thomas Jefferson's father, Peter Jefferson, moved from Tidewater to Piedmont, where Thomas was born in 1743 in what is now Albemarle County. There he developed a farm that typified the agriculture of its time and place, on the Virginia frontier—or one of Virginia's frontiers, the western reach of eastern Virginia. During Thomas Jefferson's youth, the world around him developed into a plantation society, with ever-mounting numbers of slaves growing ever-mounting quantities of tobacco.

Black life in the Piedmont went through a series of stages. Backbreaking work generally had to be done to prepare new fields for cultivation, and doing it were mostly new hands recently arrived through the trans-Atlantic slave trade. Not only were living and working conditions often particularly crude, but family and community life was for a time truncated even for a slave society, as the newcomers had a sex ratio of roughly two men to one woman, quite aside from there being,

LAWS ON RACIAL IDENTITY AND SOCIAL PRIVILEGE IN SEVENTEENTH-CENTURY VIRGINIA

Approximately sixty years after the founding of Jamestown, the House of Burgesses enacted a series of laws that reflect the changing social, economic, and cultural circumstances of the colony. Typically asking a question and then offering an answer, these laws—taken from William Waller Hening's edited work *The Statutes at Large*—offer illuminating insights into the burgesses' conceptions of class privilege, racial identity, gender, and religion.

"ENGLISH RUNNING AWAY WITH NEGROES"

Bee itt enacted That in case any English servant shall run away in company with any negroes who are incapable of makeing satisfaction by addition of time, Bee itt enacted that the English so running away in company with them shall serve for the time of the said negroes absence as they are to do for their owne by a former act. (2:26 [1660–1661])

"NEGRO WOMENS CHILDREN TO SERVE ACCORDING TO THE CONDITION OF THE MOTHER"

Whereas some doubts have arrisen whether children got by an Englishman upon a negro woman should be slave or ffree, Be it therefore enacted and declared by this present grand assembly, that all children borne in this country [shall be] held bond or free according to the condition of the mother. . . . (2:170 [1662])

"AN ACT DECLARING THAT BAPTISME OF SLAVES DOTH NOT EXEMPT THEM FROM BONDAGE"

Whereas some doubts have risen whether children that are slaves by birth, and by the charity and piety of their owners made pertakers of the blessed sacrament of baptisme, should by vertue of their baptisme be made ffree; It is enacted and declared by this grand assembly, and the authority thereof, that the conferring of baptisme doth not alter the condition of the person as to his bondage or ffreedome; that diverse masters, ffreed from this doubt, may more carefully endeavor the propagation of christianity by permitting children, though slaves, or those of greater growth, if capable[,] to be admitted to that sacrament. (2:260 [1667])

for a time, few old people, few children, and few friends and relatives, or even countrymen from any local area of Africa. The second-generation black Virginians, born there, had a sex ratio that approached parity—and no direct knowledge of the continent of their ancestors—even as another new immigrant cohort coming in replicated the uneven demographic structure.

Increasingly, slaves and their owners, as well as the groups in between them in status and freedom, reproduced through natural increase, so black and white, and slave and free, began a rapid increase, regardless of whether newcomers were added to the mix. The social and cultural arrangements of eastern Virginia were constantly in tension and constantly in flux, but their center of gravity focused on slave labor and tobacco cultivation. In a grotesquely uneven struggle over work rhythms and family life, the people of Virginia's free and enslaved populations worked together as they created another new world. At the top of that social and economic world in Virginia were the great planter families.

The Virginia Gentry: George Mason I, II, III, and IV

A young man named George Mason, born in England in 1629, arrived in Virginia shortly after 1650. Previous arrivals had tended to cluster along the York and James rivers below the falls, but land in that area was becoming scarce, and Mason went instead to the Virginia side of the Potomac River, an area just getting settled by the English. There, in the years to come, he participated in Virginia's emerging hybrid economy and ecology, as he grew corn and tobacco, both of them American crops, and raised hogs and cattle, both of them European imports. By 1756 he possessed land that he had acquired by paying the passage to Virginia for himself and for seventeen other people, perhaps family, perhaps servants. In the 1650s he became a captain in the county militia, in the 1660s a justice of the county court and also sheriff. He and his wife Mary had at least one child, a son, George, born in 1660.

Upon the death of George Mason the elder in 1686, George Mason the younger took up his father's land—1,150 acres of it—and local political offices alike. Moreover, the freeholders of Stafford County elected him to the House of Burgesses. George Mason II built up the landholdings he had inherited, and he and his first wife had seven children, including, in 1690, George Mason III, to whom, when he died in 1716, he left the bulk of his holdings.

As a wealthy tobacco planter, George Mason III began with a lot of property, and he added to it. He also served as sheriff, commander in chief of the local militia, and member of the House of Burgesses. He became good friends with the colonial governor, Alexander Spotswood, and accompanied him in 1716 on a major expedition into the Shenandoah Valley, as elite Virginians began to look with greater desire on lands still farther west—and grew concerned that the French might hem them in. In 1721 he married a prominent widow, Ann Thomson, and the first of their three children was George Mason IV. As his father had, he owned numerous slaves, though he often preferred to take on indentured servants, many of whom, when they had served out their time, stayed on with him as tenants.

George Mason IV played a collection of prominent roles during the era of the American Revolution. More than two centuries later, people can visit his home, Gunston Hall, near the Potomac River, not far downstream from George Wash-

"NOE NEGROES OR INDIANS TO BUY CHRISTIAN SERVANTS"

Whereas it hath been questioned whither Indians or negroes manumitted, or otherwise free, could be capable of purchasing christian servants, It is enacted that noe negro or Indian[,] though baptized and enjoyned their owne ffreedome[,] shall be capable of any such purchase of christians, but yet not debarred from buying any of their owne nation. (2:280–281 [1670])

"FOR PREVENTION OF THAT ABOMINABLE MIXTURE AND SPURIOUS ISSUE" (1691)

Virginia's colonial legislature tried to regulate relations, including sexual and marital relations, between whites and nonwhites. In April 1691, the assembly passed a multipurpose law called simply "an act for suppressing outlying slaves." Here—with the italics removed, but the original spelling retained—are key portions of that act:

And for prevention of that abominable mixture and spurious issue which hereafter may encrease in this dominion, as well by negroes, mulattoes, and Indians intermarrying with English, or other white women, as by their unlawfull accompanying with one another, Be it enacted by the authoritie aforesaid, and it is hereby enacted, that for the time to come, whatsoever English or other white man or woman being free shall intermarry with a negroe, mulatto, or Indian man or woman bond or free shall within three months after such marriage be banished and removed from this dominion forever, and that the justices of each respective countie within this dominion make it their perticular care, that this act be put in effectuall execution. And be it further enacted by the authoritie aforesaid, and it is hereby enacted, That if any English woman being free shall have a bastard child by any negro or mulatto, she pay

ington's Mount Vernon. George Mason IV—like his father, grandfather, and great-grandfather—hardly typified all Virginia men, even of the planter class. But he certainly represented the great planters of eighteenth-century Virginia in their social and political prominence, their dependence on vast landholdings, and their enormous tobacco production. He represented that cohort also in being descended from a seventeenth-century Virginian, and more particularly someone who had arrived in the colony, not during the first generation, certainly not before 1620, but rather around midcentury.

The cohort of great eighteenth-century Chesapeake tobacco planters derived from ancestors who typically came to the area in the 1650s or 1660s and who—they and their first sons and in turn *their* first sons—held multiple political offices, worked servants and then slaves, grew tobacco and then more tobacco, consolidated their holdings through marriage with the daughters or widows of other planters, and navigated the twists and turns of the tobacco economy. Such names as Carter, Lee, and Randolph came down from the seventeenth century through the eighteenth, as each generation built on the accomplishments of its predecessor. Primogeniture—the practice according to which the eldest son inherits the bulk of the family estate—promoted these results. The family history of William Byrd I and William Byrd II supplies a variant story of how the great planters emerged in colonial Virginia.

The Virginia Gentry: William Byrd I and II, between England and America

William Byrd, the son of an English goldsmith, received a letter in 1670 from Virginia from his uncle

42

Thomas Stegge, who was "aged, lonely, and child-less." The letter promised young William that if he came to Virginia, Stegge would name him his heir, giving him land on the James River and a seat on the Virginia Council. At the age of eighteen, William Byrd arrived in the colony. A year later, his uncle died, and Byrd received all that had been promised to him. Byrd soon headed the office of receiver general for quitrents, which produced for him a portion of money from the annual rents of planters across the state. In 1673, Byrd married Mary Horsmanden Filmer, a young widow who brought to the marriage a family estate. William Byrd II was born a year later.

William Byrd I learned well from the year he spent with his uncle. Continuing the lucrative Indian trade his uncle had started, he expanded it to Carolina, swapping a wide range of English trade goods for furs and skins. Playing both the merchant and the planter, he continued to gain wealth through his seat in government, acquiring some 26,000 acres of land, and imported slaves and servants, both to work his estates and for sale to other planters. Having come a very long way since inheriting 180 acres from his uncle, he left a huge estate to his son William Byrd II.

Byrd the elder sent his son to school in England, where young Byrd embarked on the kind of education that would befit a gentleman and gain him access to the upper reaches of English society. He spent a year in the Netherlands to learn about business and then returned to London to study law. He also joined the prestigious Royal Society. William Byrd II, barely twenty when his father died, returned then to Virginia to take over his father's estates. He married Lucy Parke, and they had two daughters, Evelyn and Maria, and one son, who died as an infant.

William Byrd II kept secret diaries, in short-

the sume of fifteen pounds ster-ling, within one moneth after such bastard child shall be born, to the Church wardens of the parish where she shall be delivered of such child, and in default of such payment she shall be taken into the possession of the said Church wardens and disposed of for five yeares, and the said fine of fifteen pounds, or what-ever the woman shall be disposed of for, shall be paid, one third part to their majesties for and towards the support of the government and the contingent charges thereof, and one other third part to the use of the parish where the offence is commit-ted, and the other third part to the informer, and that such bastard child be bound out as a servant by the said Church wardens untill he or she shall attaine the age of thirty yeares, and in case such English woman that shall have such bastard child be a servant, she shall be sold by the said Church wardens, (after her time is expired that she ought by law to serve her master) for five yeares, and the money she shall be sold for divided as is before ap-pointed, and the child to serve as aforesaid. (In Hening, *Statutes at Large*, 3:86–88)

William Byrd II (1674–1744). Painting by Hans Hyssing, when Byrd was about fifty. Virginia Historical Society, Richmond, Virginia, gift of William Byrd.

Lucy Parke Byrd (1687–1716). She married William Byrd II in 1706. The couple's ten years of marriage was filled with tensions fueled in part by their conflicting conceptions of their respective realms of responsibility in the household and in Virginia planter society, in part by his liaisons with other women. Virginia Historical Society, Richmond, Virginia, A. C. Stewart Estate.

hand, that have been discovered, and published, only since the 1930s. They provide various glimpses of his life. In July 1709, for example—a few years after he married Lucy—Byrd sketched his day's routine: "I rose at 5 o'clock and read a chapter in Hebrew and some Greek in Josephus. I said my prayers and ate milk for breakfast. I danced my dance [exercised], and settled my accounts. I read some Latin. It was extremely hot. I ate stewed mutton for dinner. . . . In the evening we took a walk in the garden. I said my prayers and had good health, good humor and good thoughts, thanks be to God Almighty." Byrd left behind some memorable statements about his life—about love, sex, and religion (in particular, the published sermons of John Tillotson, archbishop of Canterbury), as they all came together. In July 1710, for example, he wrote: "In the afternoon my wife and I had a little quarrel which I reconciled with a flourish. Then she read a sermon in Dr. Tillotson to me. It is to be observed that the flourish was performed on the billiard table."

Byrd returned to London in 1715 to speak for more colonial rights in front of the Board of Trade, and while he was there Lucy died of smallpox in Virginia. He returned at last to Virginia in 1720, only to return to London the next year in search of a new wife, and in 1724 he married Maria Taylor. Byrd saw himself as rightfully a Londoner, and an elite Londoner at that, due to his education, his wealth, his many years living there, and his memberships in the Royal Society and Middleton Temple. His status as a Virginian, however, compromised his standing as a gentleman in English society. Cosmopolitan as he was, he remained a colonial.

Byrd went back to Virginia in 1726 and, though he had planned to return to England, remained in Virginia for the rest of his life. He had four children with Maria, including William Byrd III. He served in the House of Burgesses, often traveled to the capitol in Williamsburg, and was a colonel of the Virginia militia. Byrd helped finance and led the expedition of the "dividing line" between North Carolina and Virginia that began in 1725, and he is known as the founder of the cities of Richmond and Petersburg, both of them established in the 1740s—he identified their locations and suggested their names. Byrd became president of the Virginia Council in 1744 but died that year at the age of seventy. Half of his life he had spent in Virginia, and half on the other side of the Atlantic. From his travels, he often returned with the newest books, and when he died he had perhaps 4,000, one of the largest libraries in the British colonies.

Virginians of William Byrd II's generation gained the status of gentlemen in large part by the amount of land they owned and the kinds of houses they lived in. William Byrd I did not have a large brick home but lived instead, like many prominent men of the time, in a small wooden house without a foundation.

For the founding generation in the seventeenth century, the main concern of a gentleman was to work the land and develop an estate—a large house was not a consideration, and not until the 1730s did houses contain more than two bedrooms. In the eighteenth century, by contrast, the great planters typically set out to construct a country manor—George Washington at Mount Vernon, George Mason IV at Gunston Hall, and William Byrd II at Westover. Previously, the parlor had been the main area of entertaining, but the bigger houses included a dining room, where eating was combined with conversation, and big entrance halls that provided room for dancing. Brick replaced wood, and decorative walls and paneling replaced basic paint. The American gentry were establishing themselves as men of colonial authority through the construction of these magnificent homes.

William Byrd II began construction on his home in Westover after he returned from his expedition to North Carolina about 1730. Byrd set out to build his dream home in the baroque style that had become popular in Britain, also later known as the Georgian style after England's eighteenth-century kings: George I, George II, and George III. Byrd's manor house was distinguished by the unusual steepness of its roof and tall chimney pairs at each end. His plans based the inside of the home on the elegant manors in England's countryside. The fireplaces were made of marble and wood, and much of the fine furniture came from England. The main entry and the gates were elaborately decorated. Eagles on the gateposts played off the name "Byrd." Fashioned within the ironwork were such details as a pineapple to symbolize hospitality, a beehive for industry, and an urn of flowers for beauty.

A "Perfect Independence"—and Colonial Politics

William Byrd II once wrote in a letter: "Like one of the patriarchs, I have my flock and my herds, my bondmen and bondwomen, and every sort of trade amongst my own servants, so that I live in a kind of independence of everyone but Providence." His perfect independence could well be understood as an illusion, of course. The fact may be that he did not need to go to town, or anywhere off his plantation, to acquire much of what was needed on his place. But his independence was very much dependent on his numerous workers—as his letter made clear he understood—and in fact, because he possessed their freedom as well as his own, they subsidized him and his presumption. Moreover, his personal property—a great deal of it, vitally important to him and his image of himself—was imported from his other home, England. Finally, the independence of William Byrd II was such that he depended on the colonial government, which

Westover plantation house. In Charles City
County, on the James River downstream from
Richmond, built for William Byrd II in the
1730s. As photographed a century and a half
later. Virginia Historical Society, Richmond,
Virginia.

he and his peers largely controlled, not only to obtain vast tracts of land but also
to govern the vast numbers of people he considered his social inferiors.

Virginia's political leaders, including William Byrd II and George Mason IV,
combined a home-grown quality with a knowledge of the wider world, and an
aristocratic bearing with a reliance on election to office. Mason, it is true, was
a far more parochial being than was Byrd. One spent virtually every day of his
life in eastern Virginia, or just across the Potomac River, in Maryland. The other
spent half his life in England. Both, however, were well-read and current with
intellectual trends across the Atlantic, as they revealed when Byrd read Archbishop Tillotson's sermons or Mason drew on British political philosophy to
craft major documents of the American Revolution. Both participated in, and
contributed to, an Atlantic culture that cut across space and altered ideas and
institutions in their time.

George Mason II, George Mason III, and George Mason IV all served as justices on the Stafford County Court, where each in turn dealt with a broad range of judicial and administrative responsibilities. In that and other local offices, they served something of a political and governmental apprenticeship, demonstrated their growing competence, gained experience and maturity, and gained something else as well—the confidence of the local freeholders who would have to decide whether to vote for them and send them on to higher office. The county courts are sometimes referred to as "temples of democracy" and the like, although recruitment to them was not at all democratic, in that membership was appointive, not elective. Yet they operated in a fashion that gave formal democracy space to put down roots and grow. The only elective office to which Virginians could be elevated in the colonial era was burgess, and in the House of Burgesses they gained further experience and worked with new people on larger problems. George Mason II and William Byrd I both served in the 1680s, as did George Mason III and William Byrd II in the 1690s.

George Mason IV and George Washington both first served as burgesses at the same time, during the French and Indian War, and they served together for many years thereafter. Their interests in and involvement in lands to the west, and their elevation to positions of responsibility in the east, came together in the era of the American Revolution. The next chapter introduces the west and supplies backdrop to the Revolution.

Chapter 4

The West

....

Virginia's colonial history can be roughly divided into four quadrants—east and west (divided at the Blue Ridge) and seventeenth century and eighteenth. Characterizing the east in the seventeenth century were a predominantly white society (largely English), an unbalanced sex ratio, the Church of England, servant labor and tobacco cultivation, and a scrambling for power and land. The eighteenth century brought new social and cultural worlds. Characterizing the east in the eighteenth century were a rapid rise of black residents toward numerical parity with whites, a new configuration of slave labor and tobacco cultivation, a balanced sex ratio among whites but an unbalanced one among blacks, and a far more settled arrangement of social, economic, and political dominance. Characterizing the west in the eighteenth century was a population of former servants, largely deriving from Ireland and Germany, entering Virginia from Pennsylvania via Maryland. By the eighteenth century, the episodic violence that often characterized relations between Indians and settlers had moved with the frontier to the west. Concerns about Spanish forces coming by sea had been displaced by concerns about French activity in the mountains and beyond.

During the first century after the English launched a settlement at Jamestown, colonization was largely restricted to portions of the Tidewater area. The area of colonial settlement expanded gradually farther west up the James River as well as farther north along the Chesapeake and up other rivers. During the first half of the eighteenth century, William Byrd II helped found the cities of Richmond and Petersburg at the fall line on two rivers, and Thomas Jefferson's father farmed in the Piedmont. West of the Blue Ridge, settlers began carving out farms in the Shenandoah Valley, and social and cultural developments there diverged in significant ways from those in the east.

Euro-Virginians from the east explored the west seeking to expand their trading networks and land claims. Government policy sought to establish a buffer

A Map of Virginia Discovered to the Hills, by John Farrer, 1651, revised after his death by his daughter Virginia and published in this form in 1667. In this map (one change is that he had written "to the Falls"), Farrer characterized the region to the south of "Virginia" as "Ould Virginia" or "Rawliana." To the north, the map shows the recent emergence of the colony of Maryland—and a northwest passage, still assumed to be there, connecting the Hudson River with the Pacific. Even the Virginia Piedmont, the area between the fall line and the Blue Ridge, had yet to be settled by the English when Farrer drew this map. The area beyond the Blue Ridge remained unexplored by colonists before the 1670s and was little settled by them until well into the eighteenth century, so the New and Shenandoah rivers were invisible in this map. Virginia Historical Society, Richmond, Virginia.

zone in the west to protect the area east of the Blue Ridge. Although the western portions of Virginia offered new financial opportunities to prominent people from the east, most of the region's new settlers made their way southwest out of Pennsylvania rather than west from the older parts of Virginia. Whereas whites in the east were largely Anglican, those in the west were largely Presbyterian or Lutheran. Slavery spread to some degree everywhere colonial settlement did, but the western region remained overwhelmingly white.

The west in the mid-eighteenth century pointed toward three new arenas of conflict in Virginia. Native Americans had reason to feel threatened as whites moved on to additional, vast tracts of land. The French to the north and west also fretted about English incursions. And over the longer haul, the differences in economic and cultural patterns between the east and the west augured tensions between whites in the two regions.

Exploration West to the New River—and a Jamestown of the West

During the seventeenth century, some white men from eastern Virginia, seeking to trap for furs or trade with Indians, crossed the Blue Ridge not far from present-day Floyd. Not primarily interested in exploring or mapmaking, let alone establishing permanent farms and communities, they depended on friendly relations with Indians and profitable exploitation of fur-bearing animals.

Deliberate exploration parties pushed west across the Blue Ridge as early as the 1670s, long before the settlement of what is now Montgomery County, in the New River valley. Abraham Wood sent out a party of exploration in 1671 from a place that later became Petersburg. The party included Thomas Wood, Thomas Battes, Robert Hallom, and an Indian guide, Perecute. The men made their way up the Roanoke River to present-day Salem, across the Allegheny Ridge, and down a river—they called it Wood's River, though it later acquired the name New River—into present-day Giles County and beyond. The New River (after becoming the Kanawha River) joins the Ohio River, so the 1671 expedition to the New River provided one basis for England's claims to the Ohio River valley. The Wood expedition's explorations eventually led to the organization of the Wood's River Land Company, which surveyed land in the Blacksburg area and in the late 1740s established a settlement called the Patton Tract, some of which became known as Drapers Meadows.

Meanwhile, Governor Alexander Spotswood's trek into the Shenandoah Valley in 1716 had spurred development of that area, though again not right away.

He had dubbed his companions on that expedition the "Knights of the Golden Horseshoe." The House of Burgesses created a new county in the west—Augusta County, which at one time was larger than all of eastern Virginia—and, to encourage settlement, stated that settlers in the new region would be exempt from quitrents, or taxes.

At the time of the Drapers Meadows settlement in the New River valley, the area seemed empty. We could call it the Jamestown of the west, a new beginning, but this one, unlike the original in the east, suffered from no pestilential climate or polluted water. It was a healthy place to live, and it seemed a safe one as well. An archaeological dig in 1966 near Blacksburg revealed evidence of a palisaded Indian village from roughly the time the English landed at Roanoke Island or at Jamestown. But the village's residents had evidently left the area before the Wood expedition's arrival—the explorers mentioned no Indian activity, and the site revealed no European trade goods. Indians surely traveled throughout the New River valley, and they hunted in the area, but they seem not to have had villages near Blacksburg when white newcomers began to call the area home and to establish their own settlements.

The Eighteenth-Century West

People from England and other places in Europe settled along the Chesapeake Bay and the rivers, including the James, that flowed into the Chesapeake. Across the seventeenth century, they filled in much of the Tidewater region and began to push into the Piedmont. By the 1740s, they had settled much of the Piedmont, too, and people, including Thomas Jefferson, were born there who would call it home throughout their lives. By the time Jefferson drafted the Declaration of Independence in 1776, the children of Africa were as numerous as the children of Europe in much of eastern Virginia. During his childhood, few yet of either race lived west of the Blue Ridge or near the New River.

If the 1600s belonged to eastern Virginia, western Virginia claimed a share of the 1700s. The Wood expedition's trek west did not provide the model for most migration into the New River valley. Most settlers came neither directly across the ocean nor across the Blue Ridge. Rather, settlers headed south by southwest out of Pennsylvania, through Maryland, and into Virginia's Shenandoah Valley along the route that is today Interstate 81. The area around what became Winchester beckoned first, and later Staunton. As the land in the northern Shenandoah filled up and more families pushed south from Pennsylvania seeking land of their own, they had to go farther. By the 1750s, scattered settlements could be found in the New River valley. Especially after the American Revolution, some people continued on until they reached eastern Tennessee, where an old man named Scott McCollum declared in the 1920s that he lived in the house where he had been born, and his father before him, a house that his Scottish grandfather had built in 1792.

Landless and wealthy alike participated in the colonization of western Virginia. Most of the people who entered the region had first gone to Pennsylvania as servants, intent on coming to America but unable to pay their own way. The larger numbers embarked from the northern part of Ireland or from the German states, as did smaller numbers from England, Scotland, and elsewhere, and made their way to William Penn's colony. They worked off their time, gained their freedom, and went in search of the land that had drawn them to the New World in the first place.

David Ward's family illustrated this general migration pattern. His grandfather, a Presbyterian from Ireland, emigrated with his three sons to Pennsylvania in the early 1730s. He and his family later moved to Augusta County, in Virginia's Shenandoah Valley. Over time, as the Valley grew more populated and farmland there more expensive, local prospects diminished, and the next generation moved farther south and west. In the early 1770s, Ward moved with his family to a 400-acre farm in Ward's Cove in the Clinch River valley, in what was then Fincastle County but later became Tazewell County.

The Patton-Preston and Draper-Ingles Connections

Two names central to the early history of both the Shenandoah Valley and the New River valley are Patton and Preston. The Patton-Preston connection began in Ireland when Elizabeth Patton married John Preston in the 1720s. Their first four children—Letitia, Margaret, William, and Ann—were born in Ireland, but their last two, Mary and James, were born in Augusta County, Virginia, in 1740 and 1742, at the new family place a few miles south of present-day Staunton.

The family's move to Virginia derived from their connection to Elizabeth's brother, James Patton. Patton arranged with some of the leading men in Virginia to help develop a portion of the colony that lay west of the Blue Ridge. John Preston agreed to assist his brother-in-law, and thus he and his family accompanied Patton and his family on the ship *Walpole*, which arrived in Virginia in 1738. All of them moved to the frontier in the Shenandoah Valley and took up land there. John Preston established a farm and joined the Tinkling Spring Presbyterian Church. James Patton acted as military leader as well as land speculator, and he financed migration, sold the contracts of servants, and carved the land into farms. He signed the Treaty of Lancaster in 1745, which called for Indians to relinquish their claims to land in the area but also called for colonists to extend the Great Road southwest from the Staunton area as far as the New River.

Patton represented the Wood's River Land Company in the mid-1740s when he took possession of a large piece of land, the Patton Tract, in what later became Montgomery County. The Patton Tract, or Drapers Meadows, lay a few miles east of the New River, between Toms Creek and Price Mountain and between present-day Blacksburg and Prices Fork. Other families originally from Ireland settled there. Patton sold some land to George Draper, who helped build the road to the New River, and by 1748 the Thomas Ingles family settled there as well.

After John Preston died in the 1740s, his son William spent a great deal of time in the company of his uncle, James Patton. He accompanied Patton as his private secretary on a trip in 1752 near present-day Pittsburgh to make a treaty with Indians in that area. William Preston became deputy surveyor of Augusta County that same year; in 1755, a justice of the Augusta County Court and captain of a company of rangers; and in 1761, a trustee of the new town of Staunton.

In 1763 William Preston became colonel of militia and a burgess from Augusta County. After he acquired the beginnings of a plantation, Greenfield, in present-day Botetourt County, he entered the same offices for that county. Continuing to move south and west, in 1773 he bought several hundred acres of land at Drapers Meadows—land previously owned by John Draper and his brother-in-law William Ingles—where he established Smithfield Plantation and moved his family.

Patterns of Life in the Eighteenth-Century West

From time to time, outside events crashed in upon the residents of the New River valley, yet people focused most of their thoughts and their energies on making their lives, raising their families, and building their communities. In the early years, people had, of course, no central heating and no electric lights; no town water, sewage, or trash collection services; no telephone or television; and no indoor plumbing with hot and cold running water; no mosquito repellant or bottled water; and no Kenmore dishwasher, GE clothes washer, Jenn-Air cooktop, or KitchenAid refrigerator. They had no chainsaws or lawnmowers, no automobiles or paved roads, no Social Security or unemployment insurance, and no Wal-Mart or Seven-Eleven. Not only was there no Blacksburg Electronic Village, people had to physically convey a message to the recipient, in much the way they transported a bushel of corn or a collection of hides.

As far as Blacksburg's early residents were from the world of 2007, they found themselves far, too, from the world of their ancestors or even, for many, of their births. Diet offers one measure of how far from their ancestral homes the early settlers found themselves. At first they had few cattle or hogs to provide beef or bacon. Depending instead on venison and bear meat, they ate more like Indians than like Europeans. Their major crop was corn—Indian corn.

Later they would merge the two diets, American and European, and what they ate would more resemble what their counterparts in eastern Virginia ate. Whatever else they ate, easterners combined European pork with Indian corn. Westerners grew wheat as well as corn, their cattle multiplied in numbers, and milk and beef became important parts of the local diet, even as venison remained so. Settlers on both sides of the Blue Ridge thus created a hybrid menu and a hybrid civilization, one neither wholly European nor wholly Native American but clearly both.

Settlers would go still farther in their shift back toward the ways their grandfathers and grandmothers had known. Their gristmills, like the one William Ingles built in 1750, facilitated processing the grains they grew into the food they ate. Again, however, it was a hybrid civilization, for the preferred grain they processed was Indian corn.

George Washington and the Seven Years' War

John Lewis, able to finance his own transportation from Ireland, traveled aboard a ship captained by James Patton about 1730, and after getting established in the Shenandoah Valley, he sent for his wife Margaret and their five children, among them Andrew. John Lewis, whose Greenbriar Company was one of many land companies involved in settling the west, established the town of Staunton. Andrew, whose talents, like those of many young men of the new west, included surveying as well as hunting and farming, later made his way farther south, to the Roanoke River valley, near where the town of Salem would later grow. The Lewises filled a variety of military and political offices of the western counties, just as they helped carve the land into settlements and farms, and Andrew Lewis, like his male relatives, found himself occasionally going off to war, whether in the 1750s or the 1770s. So did men from the east.

Easterners like George Mason and George Washington had a great interest in western lands, and the French posed a serious threat to their claims. Westerners were routinely vulnerable to threats to their physical safety. Continuing trouble on the frontier between Indians and settlers, continuing jockeying between the British and the French, and continuing concern for control of lands in the west—all these combined to foster tremendous rivalry in the region, with

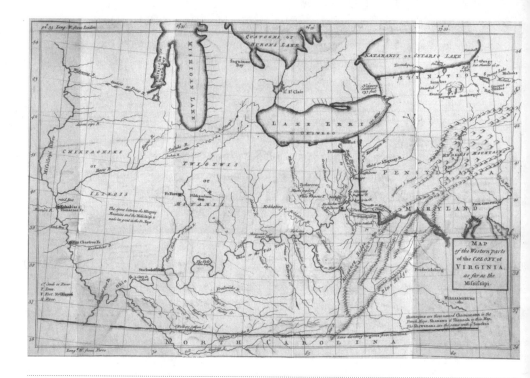

George Washington's map of the West. The vast Ohio River valley figured prominently in Washington's mind, and in the prospects of many other prominent Virginians, as suggested in this "Map of the Western parts of the colony of Virginia, as far as the Mississipi," in his journal in 1754. Virginia Historical Society, Richmond, Virginia.

Virginia leaders at the center of it all. The French and Indian War—the Seven Years' War—broke out, part of a huge contest between the superpowers of the time, the French and English empires. Significant fighting in the war occurred in the western fringes of Pennsylvania and Virginia, mostly beyond the settled areas, in the Ohio River valley.

Members of a number of leading families in eastern Virginia formed the Ohio Company and obtained approval at midcentury from the Board of Trade to gain control of hundreds of thousands of acres of western lands. The French responded by building new forts between the Great Lakes and the Ohio River, and in turn British authorities made their own moves. In 1753, Governor Robert Dinwiddie appointed young George Washington to take a letter to a French commander in the West to protest the French actions; it described the "lands upon the River Ohio" as "in the western parts of the colony of Virginia." The

French proved unreceptive to this assertion, and Washington learned that they planned to move farther south. The Virginia governor next sent Washington and some 200 men into the Ohio River valley to protect men who were building a fort near today's Pittsburgh. Meanwhile, the French built Fort Duquesne there. Washington attacked a contingent of French troops, then built Fort Necessity, but suffered a defeat in a subsequent engagement with the French.

This time the British government got involved. If the colonials could not get the job done, then British regulars would have to do it, though Washington returned to the region yet a third time, this time as a part of the British forces. But the French as well as the British threw large numbers of forces into the region. In July 1755, French soldiers and their Indian allies defeated and killed British general Edward Braddock as he led his British and colonial troops toward Fort Duquesne. War was on, and the English had proved vulnerable. In August 1755, Washington was appointed commander of a new Virginia Regiment, with more than 1,000 soldiers; he subsequently sought, but failed, to obtain an appointment as a regular officer in the British army. Word of the developments in 1755 in the west reached London, and England declared war on France in 1756. The French and British settled into a world war, known in the colonies as the French and Indian War but in Britain and France as the Seven Years' War. Increasingly, the action took place far from Virginia and far, too, from the Ohio River valley, so Virginia had less involvement as the war dragged on in the late 1750s and early 1760s.

Even before the formal declaration of war, in fact three weeks after Braddock's defeat and death, the war came to the New River valley, probably as a huge surprise, as a war party of Shawnee Indians attacked the Drapers Meadows settlement. When the war reached into the fringe settlements, Indian war parties had two objectives. Not only might attacks deter the settlements that intruded into Indian hunting territory, they might also supply captives who could replace lost members of an Indian community. Virginia folklore abounds with stories of terror and violence, as frontier women and children were attacked by Indians and taken into captivity. The story of Mary Draper Ingles, a young mother who was taken prisoner by the Shawnee in summer 1755, illustrates the resilience and resourcefulness of pioneer women, mostly of Scots-Irish or German descent, who lived in eighteenth-century Virginia's border country.

William and Mary of Drapers Meadows

In 1750, the son of Thomas Ingles, William, married the daughter of George Draper, Mary, uniting the families of two men who had left Ireland and made their way to Drapers Meadows by way of Pennsylvania. Mary Draper was born in Philadelphia in 1732 and participated with her family in the great migration into Virginia. She spent her childhood outdoors and developed athletic skills on a par with those of her older brother, John Draper. In the 1750s, newlyweds Mary and William Ingles resided for a time in the area where Smithfield Plantation sits today. The young couple—we could call them William and Mary of Drapers Meadows—had two young sons, Thomas and George. Mary's brother John married Betty Robinson in 1754, and they had a baby.

In July 1755 came a Shawnee attack. The dead included James Patton, who had stopped to visit; George Draper's widow, Eleanor; and her grandson, the Draper baby. Captured were Mary Ingles, her two young sons, George and Thomas, and her sister-in-law, Betty Draper. Survivors included John Draper and William Ingles, who were working in a field that morning, too far away to intervene. The four captives were all absorbed for a time into Indian life. Mary Ingles reportedly handled herself with sufficient courage and spirit to win the admiration of her captors, but she never stopped looking for an opportunity to escape. She convinced another prisoner, a German woman, to leave the camp one morning with her and never return. Without a map or compass, the two women followed the shores of the Ohio River upstream, and then eventually the New River, taking detours at every branch and tributary since neither of them had ever learned to swim. They completed their nearly impossible journey in a reported forty-four days, arriving half starved and nearly naked at a friend's cabin near present-day Eggleston, Virginia.

Meanwhile, William Ingles and John Draper had traveled to the Cherokee Nation, hoping to persuade the Cherokees to act as intermediaries and bargain for the release of their wives and children, but then, despondent, returned home— where Mary, having escaped, was waiting to greet them. The attack at Drapers Meadows resonates two and a half centuries after the events, as does the saga of Mary Draper Ingles's successful effort to escape and return home. George Ingles died in captivity, but his brother Thomas and his aunt Betty Draper were eventually ransomed. The Ingles family picked up where they had left off before that awful day in July 1755. Mary recovered her health and vitality, bore four more children, and lived to tell her remarkable story to her children's children and beyond before dying at age eighty-three.

Brief accounts of Mary Draper Ingles's escape were published in colonial and British newspapers within months of her return. More complete written narratives originated much later, after her death. John Ingles's 1830s manuscript about his mother, "Escape from Indian Captivity," seems accurate and authentic as far as it goes. A second line of literature stems in part from an 1843 letter by Letitia

Preston Floyd of Smithfield Plantation to historian Lyman C. Draper. Following that second line, James Alexander Thom, in his historical novel *Follow the River,* has it that Mary was pregnant when captured, gave birth along the trail, and later made the wrenching decision to leave her baby behind with her captors.

Peace and War

England and France finally made peace in 1763. Meanwhile, George Washington settled down as a civilian after his considerable involvement in the war, from which he came away with military experience and a name for himself, not to mention a sense of having been spurned as a colonial when he sought formal recognition from the British Empire for his military contributions. Washington's public and private lives moved on. By 1759 he had married the widow Martha Dandridge Custis and was serving in the House of Burgesses. He spent fifteen fairly quiet years at Mount Vernon, developing his landholdings in that area and to the west, and also occasionally riding down to the capital at Williamsburg to attend sessions of the legislature. Then war found him again. It found countless other Virginians, too, among them David Ward and Andrew Lewis.

In 1775, fighting began between American colonists and British forces in Virginia and Massachusetts, and Washington soon joined what unfolded as the American Revolution. During the previous year, though, in October 1774, a fierce battle between Virginia militia and Shawnee braves took place in western Virginia, near where the Kanawha River flows into the Ohio. A century after the mutual depredations and competition for land that had fueled Bacon's Rebellion, the settler community and the Indian people were fighting again, fighting still, this time far to the west of the Blue Ridge, rather than east of it.

The Battle of Point Pleasant

At Point Pleasant, hundreds of men under Andrew Lewis fought successfully to secure a region in the West for settlers to move in. The battle is said to have been fought between white men and Indians—which is true as far as it goes. Indians and whites frequently clashed on the moving frontier, and sometimes their encounters—when white women and children were seized, adopted, and retained for long periods—led to a radical shift in identity, as people became what historian James Axtell has termed "white Indians." David Ward's family supplies a compelling example. A cousin, James Ward—the son of one of the second-generation Wards from Augusta County—moved with his family in the early 1750s into what is now West Virginia. Indian raids forced him to retreat east, but in 1758, during the French and Indian War, Indians seized his three-year-old son, John. Young John Ward lived out his life with his new people, marrying an Indian woman and raising a family with her, and even, in battles from the 1770s on, fighting against settler armies that included members of his white family. He fought as a Shawnee brave in the Battle of Point Pleasant, in which his father was killed.

The Battle of Point Pleasant reflected relations between Indians and settlers in territory that Virginia claimed as its own—land in which Virginia's eastern gentry had a huge speculative interest through big land companies, land on which settlers in western Virginia wanted to establish secure and prosperous farms. At the end of the French and Indian War, the British government had established the Proclamation Line in the Ohio country, designed to keep settlers and Indians apart, prevent bloodshed, and guard against having another war erupt in the region; and any number of colonists had strenuously objected to the limits placed upon them. A decade later, on the banks of the Ohio River, Indians fought to secure the Ohio country as their homes and hunting grounds, while Virginians, together with Governor Dunmore, fought to secure the region for white settlement against Indian raids. Each side had ample reason to fear and fight the other. Colonists, by their presence and their behavior, shaped the Indians' world in ways large and small. Indians, by their presence and their behavior, shaped the universe in which Virginians plotted their economic, political, and military future. With the stakes extremely high, tensions on the frontier continued on past 1774.

As late as October 1774, the English governor of Virginia and the vast majority of white Virginians, in both the east and the west, still saw each other as fellow countrymen, colleagues in a common enterprise. Already under increasing strain, that condition soon came to an end. In the next chapter of Virginia's history, France became an ally and England the enemy, as Virginia's quest for control of the West continued and a struggle over political domination of the regions east of the mountains emerged as the most significant development.

The events in the aftermath of Point Pleasant took place in the late eighteenth century. Their commemoration extended far into the future, and spokespeople for Virginia and Massachusetts challenged each other for primacy in inaugurating the American Revolution, much as they did regarding the first settlement of the colonies that became a nation. More than a century after these events, in the 1890s, West Virginia newspaperwoman Livia Nye Simpson Poffenbarger campaigned to have Congress declare the Battle of Point Pleasant "the first battle of the American Revolution," having occurred six months before the fighting in Massachusetts at Lexington and Concord. Although her efforts were not successful, they induced the West Virginia legislature to obtain the site and establish Tu-Endie-Wei Park—"the point where rivers meet"—in the town of Point Pleasant; Congress appropriated funds to assist in erecting a monument. Dedicated in 1909, it includes a statue of Andrew Lewis and an engraving of the battle between white Virginians and Ohio Valley Indians.

Part II

1760s–1820s

POLITICAL INDEPENDENCE
AND POLITICAL SLAVERY

In England, during the run-up to the American Revolution, Dr. Samuel Johnson famously challenged the integrity of colonists who complained about British regulations. "How is it," he demanded to know, in his pamphlet *Taxation No Tyranny*, "that we hear the loudest yelps for liberty among the drivers of negroes?" Yet leading Virginians of the 1770s—among them George Washington, Thomas Jefferson, and Patrick Henry, substantial slaveowners all—perceived malevolent intent in British policy, an intent to reduce white colonists to slavery. Washington wrote in 1774: "The crisis is arrived when we must assert our rights, or submit to every imposition that can be heap'd upon us; till custom and use, will make us as tame, and abject slaves, as the blacks we rule over with such arbitrary sway." Henry, declaring that life for him had little value if he were subjected to "chains and slavery," cried out in 1775, as legend has it: "Give me liberty or give me death!" Jefferson wrote in the Declaration of Independence in 1776: "The history of the present King of Great Britain is a history of repeated injuries and usurpations, all having in direct object the establishment of an absolute Tyranny over these States."

White Virginians led the movement toward independence, and they led the war for independence. They sought freedom, they feared being treated as slaves, and they eventually found themselves declaring independence. What motivated them? The Virginians who crafted resolutions, gave speeches, and represented their constituents in Williamsburg, Philadelphia, and elsewhere placed the highest value on freedom, all the while, most of them, routinely denying it to considerable numbers of people they held in bondage. Dr. Johnson's statement makes them sound like hypocrites. That they were, one can readily say. Yet to understood what was going on, what was really being said, and what was feared, perhaps we should take the leading Virginians of the 1760s and 1770s seriously in their protests and their rhetoric.

Perhaps in their minds they really were vulnerable to enslavement. For them, the loss of freedom was no abstraction. The prospect of losing power over their lives brought horror. As the owners of slaves and the masters of servants, as the neighbors of slaveholders and slaves—even as former servants themselves or as the children or grandchildren of servants—they understood what it meant to lose one's liberty. More to the point, so did countless relatives, neighbors, voters, and potential soldiers throughout Virginia. In the west or the east, most Virginians were servants or slaves, or had been servants, or were descended from servants, and were not separated from them by many generations. A considerable number, as Johnson asserted, owned slaves or kept servants. Very few had no acquaintance with the ways in which unfreedom, whether under servitude or slavery, blighted people's lives, frustrated their dreams, denied them dignity, and withheld control over their work lives, their love lives, and their wish to form free families and farm their own land.

To be engaged in Virginia slaveholding, to become a Virginia revolutionary— these were related in multiple ways. The Virginia social structure and political system fostered a combination of aristocracy and democracy among white men, a political landscape that provided political experience and rewarded men by promoting them to leadership positions on the basis of their performance. The colony's most promising political leaders led the new state out of the British Empire and worked to form a new union.

But the inclination of those leaders to lead the colony out of the empire—the impulse to deploy their capable leadership in the cause they chose—related not only to the behavior of the British king, administration, or Parliament but also, very much so, to the world around them that shaped their views of liberty and freedom, their understanding of the significance of British behavior, in the ways it did. Virginia slaves, by their presence, animated and shaped the political behavior of their masters across the era of the American Revolution. Deny the planters their property, deny them their liberty, and the next step constituted enslavement, an utter loss of control over one's public life and private life. All was at risk, resistance imperative.

Essential to their happiness was a framework of government, subject to their own control, that might effectively look after their interests. If the British could not supply it, if the British set out to deny it, then they must create, or re-create, their own. And so they did. For most, the world they re-created supplied them much of what they had sought. For some, the experience led them to see anew the importance of freedom, not only for themselves but even for those whose freedom they had denied. As one great consequence of the Revolution, though hardly to have been predicted at its outset, thousands of black Virginians gained their freedom from slavery.

Chapter 5

Conservative Revolutionaries

Virginians and Independence

....

A legal matter related to religion launched the political career of one of Virginia's great leaders of the era of what became the American Revolution, and at the same time, it revealed tensions between the colony and the mother country. The Church of England, as the established church in Virginia, was supported through public revenues. The clergy were to be paid in terms of tobacco, but then bad crops in the 1750s made for tobacco shortages, high prices, and therefore an inflated value of the clergy's pay. When the market price had soared from a normal 1.5 cents to as much as 6 cents, and the Virginia legislature changed the terms in 1758 so clergy would be paid at the rate of two pennies per pound of tobacco, some clergy protested to England and sued in the courts. England took the clergymen's side. When one clergyman won his suit in the courts, a young lawyer named Patrick Henry stepped in to argue the case in the sentencing phase. So persuasive was he that the jury returned a verdict that the clergyman's compensation ought to be a single penny—not even tuppence.

The Two-Penny Case boosted Henry's legal career and launched his political career. It revealed a growing disenchantment among Virginians, especially people of dissenting faiths, with the established church. Moreover, it featured Henry's rhetoric, even before the political developments that followed the French and Indian War, suggesting that the English government had no authority over Virginia's internal affairs. All of these—Henry's mounting popularity and his political leadership, his voicing the notion of a limited British authority in the colonies, and the emerging opposition to the Church of England in Virginia—proved to be important characteristics of the next three decades.

British leaders, royal governors, and colonial politicians had their ups and downs, but across the first half of the eighteenth century, they routinely smoothed out their differences and avoided any crisis, and the Seven Years' War demonstrated that they could work effectively together. But the French and Indian War changed the British Empire, as an extraordinary success had extraordinary consequences. The war set in motion a series of events that nudged enough people ever closer to rebellion, so that what we know as the American Revolution came to seem unavoidable. Such a revolution was neither widely anticipated nor warmly welcomed, before suddenly it was upon everyone.

By the 1760s, Virginia had had a century and a half to develop its society, politics, and economy since the straggly beginnings at Jamestown. Its population was the largest of the thirteen mainland British colonies—by 1776 approaching a half million—and its political institutions and leadership were well in place. At home, it had developed the conditions that might, under the right circumstances, drive it to rebel against imperial authority and even permit it to win. Those circumstances could not have developed as soon as they did had it not been for a series of actions taken by the British government directed toward its North American colonies. Moreover, these developments unfolded in combination with a continuing struggle between England and France for global supremacy.

The events took place in another context, too—the multiracial social and military universe white Virginians lived in. Lord Dunmore, who arrived in Virginia as governor in 1771, made himself something of a hero to many white Virginians, especially in the west, in his warring in 1774 on Indians in the Ohio River valley. At the Battle of Point Pleasant, Virginia militia forces drove the Shawnee Indians west across the Ohio River and, as it turned out, freed Virginians to focus their attention on the English in the east. In mid-1775, a few months after "Dunmore's War" in the west, as tensions rose and colonists tilted toward independence, Dunmore attracted the wrath of many white Virginians, especially in the east, when he offered freedom to slave men, and servant men as well, who joined him in an effort to put down the rebellion. To a great many whites, it looked like the governor was inciting a slave insurrection, as he offered liberty to black Virginians who agreed to take up arms against white Virginians and to try to thwart *their* aspirations to liberty.

Virginians not only led their own colony out of the British Empire but also provided leadership as thirteen mainland colonies transformed themselves into the thirteen original states, part of a new union of independent states. In some key ways, the enterprise was radical—waging war against the mightiest military force in the world, and attempting to set up republican governments. And yet these were conservative revolutionaries. They responded to provocations, as they regarded the behavior of Lord Dunmore in Virginia and the empire's leaders in London. Their rhetoric revealed their fervent wish to maintain what they thought they had, to restore what they understood as normal relations with the empire, to leave things pretty much alone. Yet their actions, and their rhetoric, opened the gates first to independence and then to further change—including changes regarding race and religion.

From the French and Indian War to "Give Me Liberty!"

Major events during the decade after the Seven Years' War, revealing ever-more-serious stresses in the British Empire, constituted an extended prologue to the American Revolution. The Proclamation Line of 1763 declared land west of the Alleghenies to be off-limits to further white settlement, in hopes of preventing clashes between settlers and Indians. What, white Virginians wanted to know, had they been fighting for, if all that land to the west was going to be unavailable to them? Any free Virginian could cast a longing eye on the western lands, but the great leaders, involved as they were in land companies, speculating in land futures, took the lead in protesting.

Next came the Stamp Act of 1765, which imposed taxes on newspapers and legal documents. It was one thing for Parliament to regulate trade in the empire, but taxes imposed on colonists, as some people in Virginia and elsewhere asserted, were another thing, by no means acceptable. In the colonists' world, their legislatures set such taxes, and conceding a precedent threatened to undermine the self-government they had come to view as their birthright. Elected to the House of Burgesses, Patrick Henry arrived at his first session, in May 1765, just in time to participate in the response to the Stamp Act. He framed the Stamp Act Resolves that, broadcast from Virginia, invigorated resistance in other colonies as well. But when delegates from most of the colonies met in the Stamp Act Congress in October—to formulate a program of resistance, to voice their rationale for viewing a tax bill as a dangerous threat to their political liberties—Virginia did not send delegates, because the royal governor, Francis Fauquier, refused to reconvene the House of Burgesses, so they could not act.

Two years later, when the House of Burgesses opposed another such bill, the Townshend Acts, the new governor, Norberne Berkeley (baron de Botetourt), dissolved the assembly—whose members moved down the street to the Raleigh Tavern, where they voted to join the other colonies in a boycott of British imports. British merchants pressured the government to repeal the acts. And so it went, in fits and starts, sporadically over the next several years. England acted;

colonists reacted; England declared it had the authority to do what had been protested but—in the interests of peace and of keeping trade going—relented for a time, but only for a time.

The Boston Tea Party in 1773—with colonists protesting the Tea Act by throwing a ship's cargo into Massachusetts Bay—had enormous consequences. Parliament responded by passing what it termed the Coercive Acts, directed toward Massachusetts, where the Tea Party had taken place. The Massachusetts Government Act suspended the provincial government and even required localities to obtain permission before holding town meetings. The Boston Port Act closed the port until compensation had been made for the lost tea. These laws did not directly affect the other colonies, yet those colonies took them as an example of what could happen to them as well. Another of the Coercive Acts, the Quartering Act, provided for soldiers to be quartered in private homes in any colony.

Moreover, Parliament passed another act at the same time, one on its face having nothing to do with the dispute with Boston. The Quebec Act, designed to govern England's northern and western territories, was a belated attempt to address the acquisition of so much new territory from the French in 1763. How should the area be governed? What laws should prevail? The government of the region would be unelected, so the Quebec Act challenged Virginians' ideas regarding free government. French law would continue there—thus no trial by jury, a central part of an Englishman's procedural rights to protect his life, liberty, and property. Moreover, from a Protestant perspective, no good could come from—or could have been meant by—the apparent privileging of the adherents of Catholicism in the territory. Worse, these provisions all applied to a vast territory, as "Quebec" was redefined to reach south to the Ohio River, thus absorbing territory claimed by numerous colonies, including Virginia. In sum, Virginians looked west and saw, to their dismay, their land claims once again in doubt, their religious freedom in question, their customary rights to self-government challenged, and their rights as Englishmen compromised. The Intolerable Acts, as they were widely termed in the colonies, included not only the Coercive Acts but also the Quebec Act. They must be resisted.

Should the colony continue to pursue a peaceful resolution, or should it also prepare for war? More and more, especially during the first half of 1776, Virginia's leaders shifted away from the former and toward the latter. Virginians met in convention and sent delegates to a congress to meet in September 1774 in Philadelphia, what we call the First Continental Congress. Among the delegates was Patrick Henry. He also attended the Second Continental Congress, which first met in May 1775—shortly after fighting between colonists and English troops took place at Lexington and Concord in Massachusetts. Between the two meetings in Philadelphia, Henry was active in the second Virginia Convention, in March 1775, at which he gave his shrill call: "Give me liberty or give me death!" The next year, he was a member of the convention committee that drafted a declaration of rights and a state constitution. Virginia was declaring independence.

Meanwhile, black Virginians took Lord Dunmore up on his November 1775 offer, and white servants did too. Recruits for Dunmore's Ethiopian Regiment, as he called it, made up about half of the British force that Virginia militia attacked the next month at Great Bridge, a few miles from Norfolk. The militia's victory that day eased slaveowners' minds for a time. Soon, though, several of Washington's white servants absconded. So did his slave Harry. Before the Revolution was over—whether at the outset in 1775–1776 or later on, especially in 1781, when British troops returned to Virginia soil—several thousand additional slaves had departed the holdings of such other eastern Virginians as Jefferson, Robert Carter, Benjamin Harrison, and the widow of William Byrd III.

George Mason and the New State of Virginia's Founding Documents

In Philadelphia on May 15, 1776, the Second Continental Congress approved a resolution whose preamble, referring to Great Britain, declared: "The exercise of every kind of authority under the said crown should be totally suppressed." The delegates had determined that there was no going back, no chance or desire anymore for reconciliation with Britain. The time to talk, to hope, to fret, to negotiate was over. It was time to move to independence. Jefferson led the drafting of the Declaration of Independence.

Meanwhile, the Virginia convention acted as well, appointing a large committee to draft a declaration of rights and a constitution for the new state, and the committee began its work on May 15. George Mason IV played the lead role in drafting Virginia's Declaration of Rights and America's first state constitution. Thus he embodied Americans' growing conviction that it was far better to live with than without a written agreement about the structure of power and a written recitation of limits to public authority, of individuals' rights against their government. So important was a statement of individual rights, in fact, that Virginia's provincial congress first adopted that before moving on to a constitution that would outline the structure and functions of the new government. George Mason called the first document, when he presented his draft of a declaration of rights, "the Basis and Foundation of Government" (see sidebar). Once the declaration had been adopted in the convention, the committee set

THE VIRGINIA DECLARATION OF RIGHTS, WILLIAMSBURG, JUNE 1776

A DECLARATION OF RIGHTS made by the Representatives of the good people of VIRGINIA, assembled in full and free Convention; which rights do pertain to them and their posterity, as the basis and foundation of Government.

Section 1. That all men are by nature equally free and independent and have certain inherent rights, of which, when they enter into a state of society, they cannot, by any compact, deprive or divest their posterity; namely, the enjoyment of life and liberty, with the means of acquiring and possessing property, and pursuing and obtaining happiness and safety.

Section 2. That all power is vested in, and consequently derived from, the People; that magistrates are their trustees and servants, and at all times amenable to them.

Section 3. That Government is, or ought to be, instituted for the common benefit, protection, and security of the people, nation, or community;—of all the various modes and forms of Government that is best which is capable of producing the greatest degree of happiness and safety, and is most effectually secured against the danger of mal-administration;—and that, whenever any Government shall be found inadequate or contrary to these purposes, a majority of the community hath an indubitable, in-

George Mason IV (1725–1792), father of the Virginia Declaration of Rights and the Virginia Constitution of 1776. Painting by Louis Mathieu Didier Guillaume, copying a portrait by John Hesselius. Virginia Historical Society, Richmond, Virginia, gift of Thomas Tabb.

about drafting a constitution, and by June 29, that too had been approved. Back in Philadelphia, the Continental Congress declared independence on July 2 and approved a final version of Jefferson's language in the Declaration of Independence on July 4 (see sidebar, page 76).

Virginia's new government would include a legislature called the General Assembly. The old House of Burgesses would become the House of Delegates, and there would be a Senate as well. The General Assembly would choose a governor—his term would be a year, but he could serve three consecutive terms—and the state judges. The first governor, Patrick Henry, served three years, and Thomas Jefferson followed him. Together they served in that office for almost the entire time from the Declaration of Independence to the victory at Yorktown that signaled a successful end to military action. During that time, many men from Virginia—most of them white, some of them black—served in combat. Several proved particularly significant in their military leadership, among them George Rogers Clark, Daniel Morgan, and of course George Washington.

Fighting between Americans and the English began in 1775 in both Virginia and Massachusetts. After July 1776, the British continued to view Americans as colonists, but the former colonists, as Americans increasingly viewed themselves, were fighting for their political independence. Then, after a key victory in upstate New York, at Saratoga in October 1777, Britain's traditional rival France entered the war as an American ally. Fighting continued—in the West, the South, and the Middle Atlantic states—for several more years, until a major American military victory at Yorktown, Virginia, after which came British recognition of the new nation.

George Rogers Clark (1752–1818) and War in the West

Born in Albemarle County, as a young man George Rogers Clark headed west to Pittsburgh and then in 1772 moved on to Kentucky. Soon he accumulated land and then fought Indians in Lord Dunmore's war against the Shawnee. With revolutionary activity under way in the east, where Virginia's leaders had declared their new state's independence, Clark was named an emis-

alienable, and indefeasible right, to reform, alter, or abolish it, in such manner as shall be judged most conducive to the publick weal. . . .

Section 5. That the Legislative and Executive powers of the State should be separate and distinct from the Judicative; and, that the members of the two first may be restrained from oppression, by feeling and participating the burdens of the people, they should, at fixed periods, be reduced to a private station, return into that body from which they were originally taken, and the vacancies be supplied by frequent, certain, and regular elections, in which all, or any part of the former members, to be again eligible, or ineligible, as the law shall direct.

Section 6. That elections of members to serve as Representatives of the people, in Assembly ought to be free; and that all men, having sufficient evidence of permanent common interest with, and attachment to, the community, have the right of suffrage, and cannot be taxed or deprived of their property for publick uses without their own consent or that of their Representatives so elected, nor bound by any law to which they have not, in like manner, assented for the publick good. . . .

Section 12. That the freedom of the Press is one of the greatest bulwarks of liberty, and can never be restrained, but by despotick Governments. . . .

Section 16. That Religion, or the duty which we owe to our *Creator*, and the manner of discharging it, can be directed only by reason and conviction, not by force or violence; and, therefore, all men are equally entitled to the free exercise of religion, according to the dictates of conscience; and that it is the mutual duty of all to practise Christian forbearance, love, and charity, toward each other.

sary to Williamsburg. There he asked Governor Henry for gunpowder for a militia to repel the numerous Indian attacks on Kentucky's settlers, and also that the area be organized as Virginia's Kentucky County. He secured both. Back in Kentucky, as a major in the militia, Clark used his new ammunition to safeguard Kentucky from Indian attacks. These raids were a result of British and Indians working together to harass the American settlers in the West, and Clark resolved to put an end to the English military presence. He traveled again to Williamsburg, where Governor Henry authorized him to raise a force of up to 350 men and, in a secret mission, to try to take the Illinois country from the British.

Far fewer than 350 men accompanied Clark. Regardless, his first destination was Kaskaskia, a fort on the Mississippi River south of St. Louis where the British maintained a small garrison. During summer 1778, on the way, news reached him that only a small number of French soldiers actually garrisoned the fort—and that France had signed a treaty of alliance with the United States. Kaskaskia surrendered without a fight. Clark then took Cahokia, across the river from St. Louis, and sent a captain east to take Fort Sackville, near Vincennes. By this point, though, the British lieutenant governor, Henry Hamilton, was on his way to Vincennes to launch a counterattack on Clark and his newly acquired forts. In December 1778, Hamilton reached Vincennes and convinced the captain there to surrender without a fight. Instead of following up his victory with an attack on Clark, Hamilton decided to wait until spring. Word reached Clark, and he seized upon the notion that a daring and sneaky assault on Fort Sackville in the midst of winter could work.

In the cold of February 1779, Clark and his small band marched the 240 miles east to Sack-

Le General Washington. The painting by Noël Le Mire offers a French perspective of Washington in front of his military camp during the Revolution, with an African American holding his horse, after the Americans in 1778 had secured a treaty of amity and commerce as well as a treaty of military alliance with France. The general is holding iconic documents of the new order—the Declaration of Independence and the "treaty of alliance between his most Christian majesty and the United States of America"—while shredded at his feet are British documents that include "the bill to pardon the rebels of North America" and "protection to rebels on submission." The Colonial Williamsburg Foundation.

... We hold these Truths to be self-evident, that all Men are created equal; that they are endowed by their Creator with certain unalienable Rights; that among these are Life, Liberty & the Pursuit of Happiness:—That to secure these Rights, Governments are instituted among Men, deriving their just Powers from the Consent of the governed,—That whenever any Form of Government becomes destructive of these Ends, it is the Right of the People to alter or to abolish it, & to institute new Government, laying its Foundation on such Principles, & organizing its Powers in such Form, as to them shall seem most likely to effect their Safety and Happiness. . . . The History of the present King of Great-Britain is a History of repeated Injuries & Usurpations, all having in direct Object the Establishment of an absolute Tyranny over these States. To prove this, let Facts be submitted to a candid World. . . . For imposing Taxes on us without our Consent. For depriving us in many Cases, of the Benefits of Trial by Jury.—For transporting us beyond Seas to be tried for pretended Offences.—For abolishing the free System of English Laws in a neighbouring Province, establishing therein an arbitrary Government, & enlarging its Boundaries, so as to render it at once an Example and fit Instrument for introducing the same absolute Rule into these Col-

ville. Knowing his small force might not be enough in a battle, Clark created the impression that he had a far larger force than he actually did. Hamilton surrendered the fort. Without a casualty, Clark had taken most of the Ohio country back from the British. Had Clark waited until warmer weather to go on the offensive, as Hamilton did, the opportunity might well have been lost. In later years, such cities as Chicago and Detroit put up statues to commemorate George Rogers Clark and his exploits in the West.

George Washington (1732–1799) on the Main Front

By the end of the French and Indian War, George Washington had become something of a celebrity in the colonies. Tales of his exploits in battle and of his horses getting shot out from under him at Fort Duquesne delighted ordinary citizens. Washington settled down at Mount Vernon, yet he entered into the new revolutionary fervor that arose in the 1760s and 1770s. His county, Fairfax, was radical, and George Mason was a neighbor. He had always been a bit hesitant to speak in public, but as unrest heightened in Virginia and war seemed ever more likely, he took an increasingly active role. He, like Patrick Henry, was sent to both Continental Congresses.

Massachusetts delegate John Adams wanted a Virginian as commander of the Continental forces, as it seemed essential to link the leading colony in New England with the largest one in the South. So in 1775 the Second Continental Congress named George Washington commander in chief. Remarking, "I do not think myself equal to the command I am honored with," Washington nevertheless accepted the post.

The battles of Lexington and Concord had already been fought, and the British occupied Boston, when Washington arrived on the scene on July 3, 1775. Washington's first mission was to get the groups of militia surrounding Boston better organized. He placed cannons atop Dorchester Heights in the middle of the night and, having gained the high ground, eventually forced the British to retreat from Boston. Washington soon moved his forces to the Middle Atlantic states.

Washington had won a victory, yet he recognized that the British had better training, better equipment, and higher morale. If the war turned in favor of the British, many Americans would retreat from the revolutionary cause. But if Washington could avoid a direct, definitive conflict with the British, then perhaps he could hold his force together and sap the will of the British, who—partly because of distances, partly because of costs—would find it difficult to send sizable numbers of reinforcements.

Shortly after the capture of Boston, however, Washington's strategy was jeopardized by developments on Long Island, and he nearly lost the war there. Outnumbered and surrounded, only by a retreat across the East River to Manhattan did he save his army. Skirmishes at Harlem Heights and White Plains punctuated a long retreat that took Washington across the Hudson River and south through New Jersey. His forces fled into Pennsylvania demoralized and frustrated. Desperately needing a victory, he invaded New Jersey across the Delaware River on Christmas night, capturing almost a thousand Hessian (German) mercenaries, at a loss of two men. Shortly thereafter, he attacked the British at Princeton. Here, Washington directed his men masterfully, bravely risking his own life to ensure that the British line broke. The

onies.—For taking away our Charters, abolishing our most valuable Laws, & altering fundamentally the Forms of our Governments.— For suspending our own Legislatures, & declaring themselves invested with Power to legislate for us in all cases whatsoever.—He has abdicated Government here by declaring us out of his Protection & waging War against us.— . . . He has excited domestic Insurrections amongst us, & has endeavoured to bring on the Inhabitants of our Frontiers, the merciless Indian Savages, whose known Rule of Warfare is an undistinguished Destruction, of all Ages, Sexes and Conditions. . . . We, therefore, the Representatives of the United States of America, in General Congress assembled, appealing to the Supreme Judge of the World for the Rectitude of our Intentions, do in the Name, & by Authority of the good People of these Colonies, solemnly publish & declare, That these United Colonies are, & of Right ought to be Free & Independant States; that they are absolved from all Allegiance to the British Crown, & that all political Connection between them and the State of Great-Britain is, & ought to be, totally dissolved; & that as Free and Independant States they have full Power to levy War, conclude Peace, contract Alliances, establish Commerce, & to do all other Acts & Things which independant States may of right do. . . .

British won the initial skirmish, but Washington rallied his lines and won the day.

The war dragged on, and Washington managed to keep his force together. Battles at Brandywine Creek, Pennsylvania; Germantown, Pennsylvania; and Monmouth Courthouse, New Jersey, were all losses, but the end result was a British retreat to New York, a sign that the British army had made little progress after all. Washington's army had faced trials at Valley Forge during winter 1777–1778 but emerged loyal to Washington. His strategy had succeeded, and the focus of the war shifted south to the arena of Charles Cornwallis, Nathanael Greene, and Daniel Morgan.

Daniel Morgan (1753–1802) and the War in the South

In summer 1780, British general Charles Cornwallis was advancing through the South to great effect. Georgia had already fallen to his powerful force, and a royal governor sat in the capital. In battle after battle, in place after place, Cornwallis and British commander Banastre Tarleton crushed any resistance they encountered. Tarleton, head of the 550-man British Legion, was a brilliant military leader with a well-publicized cruel streak. In a victory at Waxhaws, his troops slaughtered Continental soldiers who had surrendered. Desperate to stop the British juggernaut, the Continental Congress called on a Virginian by the name of Daniel Morgan.

Morgan was a large man with a rugged physique, a shock of red hair, and a skill for instilling camaraderie with Continentals and militia alike. He had once been a wagoner delivering supplies to the British lines during the French and Indian War. When the Revolution came, he formed a local militia for the Continental Congress, with ninety-six of the hardiest men ever to fight for Virginia. Dressed in hunting shirts, buckskins, and coonskin caps and having been trained since they could walk to fire a gun, these men became famous both for their dress and for their deadly aim. In August 1775, Morgan marched his men into Cambridge, Massachusetts, where they put on a display by hitting seven-inch targets from 250 yards away. Morgan led his troops into battles elsewhere, including at Saratoga in upstate New York, where in September and October 1777 he and his riflemen played key roles in an American victory, which in turn led to the French decision to sign on as an ally. Despite his success, Morgan resigned, in part because of his failure to obtain a promotion. Retiring to his home in Virginia, Morgan had put the war behind him when Congress turned to him in summer 1780.

Daniel Morgan (1736–1802). Morgan played vital roles fighting the American Revolution in the North at Saratoga in 1777 and in the South at Cowpens in 1781. Portrait by Charles Willson Peale. Virginia Historical Society, Richmond, Virginia, gift of Percy Robert Blythe.

Morgan answered the Congress's call and, with the rank of brigadier general, began recruiting militia for a campaign in the South. This time, most of his fellow Virginians were away fighting elsewhere, and he found many of his men—militia and regulars—in Georgia and the Carolinas, some of them fresh from an important victory at King's Mountain, in upstate South Carolina, in October 1780. Tarleton, seeking to finish the war in the South by a direct attack, hurried toward Morgan's position, at a place known as Hannah's Cowpens, also in northwestern South Carolina. It was a hilly site, well suited to Morgan's long-range riflemen, but if the American line collapsed, the Broad River would be at their rear, making escape impossible. Morgan and his men would have to win, or they would be at the mercy of the infamous Tarleton.

The Battle of the Cowpens took place on January 17, 1781. When Tarleton's massive force, more than a thousand men, came into view, Morgan had placed his long-range militia at the front of the field. Behind them were the Continental soldiers, with a cavalry unit on a hill to the rear. Morgan's varied troops held their ground, then went on the offensive, and the British line crumbled. The Americans suffered 24 dead, half militia, half Continentals. The British suffered 110 dead and hundreds more taken prisoner. Tarleton fled back to Cornwallis, his army destroyed. British plans for domination of the South were in tatters.

Peace with Victory: Yorktown

British general Cornwallis headed north and, in desperate need of supplies, ventured to the Virginia town of Yorktown, at the mouth of the York River, to link up with the British Royal Navy. Here, an amazing confluence of events developed. A French fleet sailed up from the West Indies and defeated the British fleet in the Battle of the Chesapeake. A blockade from sea went into effect around Yorktown. Meanwhile, Washington marched his force from the north, and a combined French and American force surrounded the British general. His supply lines cut, and with no chance of escape, Cornwallis surrendered. Over a quarter of all British forces on the continent were captured at Yorktown, and this proved to be the decisive blow of the war, and its effective end, as it led to the fall of the government of Lord North, whose successors made peace with the United States.

In the West, George Rogers Clark may not have much altered the military course of the war, but he had made possible a far more favorable peace. He ensured that the Treaty of Paris in 1783 would end with the Ohio country in American hands. In the South, Daniel Morgan's small army of backwoodsmen had won a huge battle at Cowpens, as a Virginian perhaps turned the tide of the war. As for George Washington, his strategy in the New England and Middle Atlantic states had worked, and his forces converged at Yorktown for the final victory. There, the French shaped the outcome, not only by supplying troops and goods but also by bringing their navy.

The improbable had happened, and America was independent, thanks to Virginia and its conservative revolutionaries. Some Virginians—Patrick Henry, George Mason, Thomas Jefferson—participated in the political dimension of the war, crafting the documents that, on the one hand, articulated the need for political independence and, on the other, framed the ways the new state's government would operate. Others—like George Rogers Clark and Daniel Morgan—went off to war, fought for independence, and shaped the course, first, of the war and, then, of the peace that followed once the former colonies had won. Washington did both. With the help of his comrades, much good fortune, and the French, George Washington won the war, and when it was over he resigned from the army and headed home to Mount Vernon.

The peace treaty of 1783 not only recognized the political independence of the United States but also agreed to a western boundary along the Mississippi River. According to Great Britain, the thirteen former colonies were free to develop in whatever ways they chose, and also to expand their settlements west into the Ohio and Mississippi valleys. Virginia was free to make its own rules—revamp its government, set its taxes, refine its land policies, and do what it wished about racial regulations and slavery and also about the rules that governed the relations between church and state. The thirteen states were free to go their separate ways or to set up some umbrella government that would shape foreign relations or settle conflicting land claims or regulate interstate trade or even, in one sphere or another, govern internal policy. The British would not be sending troops anytime soon, either to enforce rules made in England or to protect the former colonies. Virginia and its sister states were on their own. They had gained their liberty, and with authority and responsibility alike, they had to govern themselves.

Chapter 6

Perfecting Independence (I)

Power and Policy in Postrevolutionary Virginia

....

Once the former colony of Virginia declared its political independence from Great Britain, Virginia's voters and leaders turned their attention to renovating the way their government, and therefore their society, operated. The Virginia Constitution of 1776 set up a new state government, working with generations of institutional experience and not only adopting a written constitution but also adopting a bill of rights that individuals were to be assured of against their state government. Beyond that, two major areas of life that the new government addressed—or, rather, Virginians with a political voice addressed through their new government—were race and religion.

These founding moments of life in an independent state were potentially as important in setting a new agenda as were the founding moments at Jamestown in establishing the colony in the first place. With regard to religion, the founding generation established a framework that Americans for centuries to come would reach back to as they made their own way through challenging issues in public and private life. With regard to race, much was contested in the first generation of political independence, and while change in that regard proved more finite, it was substantial.

Churches and the State

In fits and starts through the decade beginning with independence in 1776, Virginia took the lead among states with established churches in inaugurating freedom of religion. Key players—though they did not all pull in quite the same direction—were George Mason IV, Patrick Henry, Thomas Jefferson, and James Madison.

In May 1776, when the Virginia Convention met to draft a plan of civil government, George Mason was the primary author of the Virginia Declaration of Rights, but it underwent some changes along the way. In the amended form in which it was printed and distributed, not only in Virginia but elsewhere as well, the article on religion stated:

> That religion, or the duty which we owe to our CREATOR, and the manner of discharging it, can be directed only by reason and conviction, not by force or violence; and therefore, that all men should enjoy the fullest toleration in the exercise of religion, according to the dictates of conscience, unpunished and unrestrained by the magistrate, unless, under colour of religion, any man disturb the peace, the happiness, or safety of society. And that it is the mutual duty of all to practice Christian forbearance, love and charity, towards each other.

This version was subsequently modified. The language about "the fullest toleration," though itself an extraordinary advance, upset delegate James Madison. According to Madison, the term "toleration" suggested that the free practice of religion was a privilege that, if the state could grant it, the state could also revoke at any time. Holding instead that religion was an unalienable human right, he urged that the article be rephrased to state that "all men are equally entitled to the full and free exercise of [religion according] to the dictates of Conscience; and . . . no man or class ought on account of religion to be invested with peculiar emoluments or privileges; nor subject to any penalties or disabilities." The convention agreed to replace "the fullest toleration" with "the full and free exercise." Rejected, however, was Madison's effort to disestablish the Church of England. Thus the final Article XVI, as it went into the Virginia Constitution of 1776, reflected a middle ground, achieving substantial change even in Mason's original language, and greater change given Madison's amendment, but not as much change as Madison had proposed.

When the new state's General Assembly met for the first time, in October 1776, legislators were swamped with petitions from dissenters. A petition that came from Prince Edward County used characteristically colorful language: "The last Article of the Bill of Rights we also esteem as the rising Sun of religious Liberty, to *relieve* us from a long night of ecclesiastical Bondage; and we do most earnestly request and expect that you would go on to complete what is so nobly begun." Quakers, Baptists, and Presbyterians all used Article XVI of the Declaration of Rights to petition for the right to have their own clergy perform legal marriages, for looser regulations on their places of worship, and for the state to abolish the tax that was levied on all citizens and used to support the Church of England. The petitions to "abolish . . . spiritual tyranny," as Thomas Jefferson wrote, looking back near the end of his long life, made for a stormy session, and he recalled it all as "the severest contests in which I have ever been engaged."

In November 1776, the legislature approved resolutions calling for a repeal of laws punishing the failure to attend an Anglican church, together with a repeal of taxes to support the established church. No longer, according to the new dispensation, would tax money pay the salaries of Anglican ministers. But the Anglican church would retain undisputed use of the glebes—the land and home that Anglican ministers had long had for a residence and a support—as well as the church buildings. As enacted, the "Bill Exempting Dissenters from Contributing to the Established Church" did not go as far as Jefferson, Madison, or Mason wished—the very title made clear that there remained an "established church," and it suspended the salaries of Anglican churchmen, rather than abolishing them—but it was a substantial beginning. Jefferson went further and drafted a bill for full religious freedom, but the General Assembly was not buying what he wanted to sell.

Three years later, in 1779, with the Revolutionary War still in full swing, the General Assembly tackled the issue again. Anglican salaries were still suspended, but a multitude of Virginians pressed for full disestablishment of the Church of England, though many petitions argued against Jefferson's proposed bill. Jefferson was unavailable to press the case in the legislature for his bill, since he had been elected governor. The legislature chose not to act on two competing bills, one Jefferson's, the other calling for "support of religious teachers and places of worship" and declaring "the Christian religion" to be "the established religion of this Commonwealth." Mason proposed a bill to repeal all provisions for support of the Anglican clergy and to end all parish levies to support "the former established Church." The legislature enacted it.

The Church of England had been disestablished, had lost its uniquely privileged status, but the competing bills displaced by Mason's remained the major alternatives for a fuller settlement of church-state matters in Virginia. Year after year, session after session, neither of those bills gained sufficient support in the legislature to be passed. In one major related development, the Methodists broke away from the Episcopalians in 1784, so the Episcopal Church found itself in an even more weakened condition.

In late 1784, the General Assembly replayed its debate of 1779. Patrick Henry led the side seeking a general assessment, one in which taxpayers would specify the church they wanted to receive their payment. Numbered among his supporters were Washington and John Marshall. Jefferson was away in France, and Madison took the lead in promoting Jefferson's "bill for establishing religious freedom." Henry seemed to have more legislators on his side, but before a bill could be framed and acted on, Madison managed to maneuver Henry into the governorship, so this time around it was the other team without a key leader in the legislature. The General Assembly, deciding once again to postpone a final decision, put off a vote until late 1785.

In the meantime, Madison wrote a "Memorial and Remonstrance against Religious Assessments," a wide-ranging consideration of why any kind of establishment, multiple or singular, was a bad idea. Madison characterized Henry's bill as "a dangerous abuse of power." Yet many Virginians continued to be concerned about the state's moral future if the assessment bill failed. One of them saw the choices as either financially supporting the churches or finding Virginia divided between "immorality" and "Enthusiastic Biggotry." The petitions rolled in, and some 90 percent of them opposed assessment. So while Henry's supporters generated a good many signatures, Madison's supplied far more. It was a close call, and could have readily gone either way, but Henry's bill was abandoned, as the General Assembly gave its approval to the Virginia Statute for Religious Freedom. Jefferson's "bill for establishing religious freedom," after having languished since 1777, became law in January 1786. In so many ways, it had been a stunning decade since George Mason penned Article XVI in May 1776.

Virginia no longer had an established church—neither an established Church of England, nor the proposed substitute, a multiple establishment. Moreover, the very name "Church of England" carried baggage in an independent Virginia, baggage that had to be jettisoned. The former Church of England was incorporated in December 1784 as the Protestant Episcopal Church in Virginia, merely one of a number of denominations that also included the Baptists, Methodists, Lutherans, and Presbyterians. Even then some major pieces of unfinished business remained.

The evangelicals—especially the Baptists—had turned the tide on the question of establishment and assessment. They wanted no government interference in churches' internal affairs. That did not mean, however, that they wanted no governmental involvement in the life of the community; they had in mind no high wall of separation between religion and the state. Presbyterians called for "wholesome Laws." Baptists called on the legislature to do "its part in favour of Christianity." The same session of the General Assembly that passed the Statute for Religious Freedom also passed an act banning work on the Christian Sabbath, a law that lived on through the nineteenth century and most of the twentieth as well. On that bill, far more than on the other, evangelicals and Episcopalians saw eye to eye.

The Church of England had long carried out secular as well as religious activities. One major function of the established church across the seventeenth and eighteenth centuries had been to look after the poor. Who would now take on that responsibility? After the incorporation bill became law at the end of 1784, Virginians expressed considerable concern at the disappearance of the social welfare safety net. The end of church responsibility had left "the distressed" among "our fellow Creatures . . . destitute," said a memorial from Essex County in 1785. Please "make Provision for the Poor," urged a petition from Amherst County. At about the same time as the legislature was moving toward final approval of the Statute for Religious Freedom, it also enacted a bill to create for the counties of eastern Virginia the secular framework of support for poor people that had for a generation and more been the situation in non-Anglican areas west of the Blue Ridge.

The new Protestant Episcopal Church in Virginia retained the glebes—the enormous wealth that had been built up during the long period when the Church of England had been a tax-supported institution. To this remaining privilege the evangelicals—again, especially the Baptists—next turned their attention. Newly chosen by his fellow Episcopalians as Virginia's first bishop of the new church, David Griffith wrote in late 1786: "We shall again be warmly attacked in the present session [of the General Assembly]. The Presbyterians are Petitioning for a repeal of the incorporating Act, & the Baptists for the Sale of the Glebes & Churches. It would seem that nothing will satisfy these People but the entire destruction of the Episcopal Church."

The revolutionary settlement of church and state began with George Mason's call for toleration. It proceeded through a period of uncertainty that seemed for a time likely to end up with Patrick Henry's call for a multiple establishment but that turned instead to a different kind of equality among religious faiths, with none of them receiving direct financial support from the state. And then, pushing on to complete the job of disestablishing the old Church of England, the evangelicals saw to it that the Protestant Episcopal Church in Virginia lost not only its tax revenue but its ancient property as well.

The Great Glebe Grab

The Virginia Declaration of Rights in 1776, followed by the Statute for Religious Freedom in 1786, released dissenters from legally mandated demands on their church attendance or taxes to support any church. Their religious freedom of expression assured, they soon exercised their growing political clout to alter yet again the relationship between churches and the state. The great compromise over religion, leaving the Protestant Episcopal Church in Virginia in possession of church property while terminating its privileged position otherwise, came unraveled. The General Assembly repealed the glebe arrangement in 1799, and in 1802 it provided for the sale of glebe lands. Sales would take place not immediately but, rather, after a minister either resigned or died, so his successor to the ministry would not also succeed to the glebe.

Episcopalians counted on the state judiciary to protect their interests, but in a narrowly split decision in a case from Chesterfield County, *Turpin v. Lockett* (1804), the state's highest court approved the statute. Evangelicals marched into the nineteenth century triumphant, whatever nonevangelical colleagues had intended by the policy adopted in 1786. Episcopalian churchmen sometimes fought back—for example, concerning the Cherry Point glebe in Northumberland County, in the case of *Claughton v. Macnaughton* (1811). In *Terrett v. Taylor* (1815), a case from Alexandria County—thus in the District of Columbia—the U.S. Supreme Court declared the Virginia statute of 1799 unconstitutional. Later, the Loudoun County overseers of the poor seized and sold a glebe; and the vestry and minister challenged the action. They lost at trial, but they appealed the ruling, and in *Selden v. Overseers* (1840), the Virginia Supreme Court—noting that the Virginia Constitution of 1830 seemed to have assumed church ownership of the glebes was at an end, that "almost all the glebe lands" had been seized and sold, and that a multiplicity of new interests depended on clear title—ignored the U.S. Supreme Court's 1815 decision and declared itself bound by the 1804 *Turpin* precedent. In the twenty-first century, places like Glebe Road in Alexandria testify to the long-ago colonial religious establishment and its evolving Revolutionary denouement.

Race and Slavery

In addition to changes in the law of religion in Virginia, the decade after the Declaration of Independence brought important changes to the law of race and slavery. In 1778, during the American Revolution, the legislature of the new state of Virginia passed a law declaring that "no slave or slaves shall hereafter be imported into this commonwealth by sea or land"—that is, whether from outside the United States or from another state—and "every slave imported into this commonwealth, contrary to . . . this act, shall upon such importation become free." The children of slave women would continue to be born into lifelong slavery, but the only other way for new slaves to come to inhabit Virginia would be if their owners moved with them from another state.

People held as slaves could go to court to attempt to prove themselves wrongly held—"freedom suits" made up their main legal right. Nanny Pagee, who was held as a slave, as were her children, went to court and sued for her freedom, on the grounds that she had been brought illegally into Virginia from North Carolina as a slave after passage of the 1778 act and thus should be free and, moreover, that she was a white woman. Either argument might suffice, but the second one particularly attracted the court's attention. At trial, she was inspected—her hair, for example, was examined, as were her fingertips. Determining that she appeared to be white, and with no evidence introduced to show her to be the daughter of a slave woman, the court declared her free—after having been held as a slave for over thirty years—and that thus her children (though perhaps the mixed-race offspring of a slave father) were free as well. The appeals court upheld the trial court's reasoning and conclusion, so she—and, as the appeals court put it, "(and of course her children)"—gained her freedom.

In 1782, the Virginia legislature went beyond curtailing the growth of slavery through commerce and provided authority for slaveowners to free their slaves. Owners could, without restriction, emancipate slave women between the ages of eighteen and forty-five and slave men between the ages of twenty-one and forty-five, provided the newly freed people were "of sound mind and body." Other slaves, however, could be freed only if the former owners "supported" them, that is, saw that the people newly freed did not become charges upon the county. Washington, for one, provided for the freedom of all his many slaves after his death.

Beginning in 1782, therefore, slavery in Virginia was, in effect, redefined. Enslavement was still defined as lifelong, and it was still inherited from a slave mother, but owners could now (much more readily than before) free their slaves. Beginning in 1782, through manumission, the number of people in Virginia who were free even though nonwhite began rapidly to grow. Whether slavery proved to be lifelong had become contingent. Moreover, as had been the case ever since a 1662 law clarified matters, free nonwhite women would continue to bear free children. Because there had never previously been many free nonwhite women, few nonwhite children had ever been born free, but that began to change in the 1780s.

The 1782 manumission law held without material change until 1806, when the legislature mandated that, in the future, slaves who gained their freedom must leave the state within a year or forfeit their freedom. County officials could still permit newly freed people to stay, but the privilege of staying could be denied, and by that time the willingness of slaveowning Virginians to manumit some of their human property had receded. Special legislation sometimes permitted manumitted slaves to remain in Virginia beyond the standard year, provided they were never convicted of a crime. In 1827, for example the General Assembly passed such a law to benefit Joe Fossett, Burwell Colbert, John Hemings, Madi-

Life of George Washington—the Farmer.
This composite of farm activities and people at
Washington's home at Mount Vernon, painted
by Junius Brutus Stearns, was published in
France in 1853. Library of Congress, Prints and
Photographs Division, LC-USZ62-3912.

son Hemings, and Eston Hemings, all of them Hemings family members who had been freed according to Jefferson's will upon his death the year before.

The number of free nonwhites grew rapidly in the late eighteenth century. Some people were born to free mothers who were classified as nonwhite—"people of color"—whether they were black, Indian, or mixed-race. In the early years after 1782, far more Virginians gained their freedom from owners who, whatever their motivation, determined to manumit one or more of their slaves. And some had stolen their freedom during the Revolution and managed to maintain it in Virginia afterward. After growing rapidly between 1782 and 1806, Virginia's population of free nonwhites continued to rise each decade from the 1810s through the 1850s, though it did so at a much more modest pace.

The Revolution had other implications for some black Virginians than the legislative initiatives that expanded the number who gained manumission. By whatever means a black man came to be free in Virginia, some eventually obtained pensions from the state for military service during the American Revolution. An 1821 law provided sixty dollars, as well as a pension for life, to a man in Rockingham County, George McCoy, who was described as having been a soldier in the Revolution, severely wounded, and who had grown old, poor, and infirm. Other black veterans of the Revolution receiving financial assistance in their old age included Aaron Weaver, who had suffered serious wounds while serving in the navy, and Richard Nickens, who had enlisted for three years and had grown old and infirm.

During the last half century of Virginia slavery, approximately one in ten nonwhite Virginians were free. The number of free nonwhites grew by more than half in the 1790s to 20,124, and then by half again to 30,570 in 1810. The number of counties increased in which the number of free nonwhites made it possible for a majority of residents to be free even though only a minority of residents were white. By 1830, the Tidewater region as a whole displayed that pattern: 48.6 percent of all residents were slaves, and 7.6 percent were free nonwhites. So, in particular, did the cities of Richmond and Petersburg.

Two Tales of Freedom under the 1782 Law

Carter family members were among the great planters of colonial Virginia, and for many their wealth and prominence carried over through the Revolution. Robert Carter III, however, in taking advantage of the new authority he had over his enslaved property, manumitted hundreds of slaves—as many slaves as Jefferson and Mason, combined, owned and never freed. Sixty-three years old in 1791, and destined to live another thirteen years, this grandson of the great planter Robert "King" Carter recorded what he called a "Deed of Gift."

Carter eased his slaves into their new lives—and the plantation into a post-slavery status. The older slaves should have a small plot of land of their own. The more experienced and skilled—slave foremen among them—should continue some of their former tasks, even while they spent time on their new land, and they should take on others, field hands, as tenants. Work would continue, production would continue, but people who had been slaves would increasingly run their own lives. Some white neighbors expressed their displeasure at Carter's effrontery. One wrote him: "A man has almost as much right to set fire to his own building though his neighbor's is to be destroyed by it, as to free his slaves."

Another wealthy Virginian, Thomas Jefferson's cousin Richard Randolph Jr., made out a will in 1796 designed to make good on his conviction that his many slaves, inherited from his father, should be free. Randolph declared it "my will and desire, nay my most anxious wish," that they be free, "altogether as free as the illiberal laws will permit them to be." He meant to "yield them up their liberty, basely wrested from them by my forefathers."

Randolph died that same year, at the age of twenty-six. For another fourteen years, delays put off the manumission of his ninety slaves. Over the final half century before the Battle of Fort Sumter, however, Hercules White and his fellow slaves and family members created a community in Prince Edward County where they demonstrated, year in and year out and in a vast array of ways, that black Virginians could effectively make their way in freedom, and that black and white Virginians could interact effectively together.

The law of 1782 had made both actions possible, that by Carter and that by Randolph. True it was that black freedom in Virginia was not to be confused as identical with white freedom, that the state's "illiberal laws," as Randolph put it, would not permit but so expansive a definition of black freedom. True it was as well, however, that the law liberated white owners of slaves to emancipate their human property, and then it was up to the former slaves, and their children, to make their way as best they could. Randolph intended to ease their path, to make it more likely that their free lives would be good ones, and at the same time recompense them for their years of unpaid toil, by giving them absolute ownership of a 400-acre tract on which they could construct their free lives.

The actions of Carter and Randolph reflected some combination of changing religious ideas, changing political ideas, and changing laws that made a postrevolutionary Virginia potentially a very different place than the late colonial years. What Virginians, black and white, would make of their state's independent condition depended on them, and also on developments over which they had little control. The invention of the cotton gin, together with Indian removal and the growth of the demand for cotton fibers, generated a voracious demand in the Deep South for slaves from outside the region, and that meant mostly Virginia. The former slaves of Carter and Randolph—unlike their counterparts who remained in slavery—might escape being drawn into the vortex of the interstate slave trade. More than that, they built up communities, experience, literacy, and property holding that permitted them to provide leadership and assistance when a general emancipation came in the 1860s.

But these enticing prospects were anything but enticing to many white Virginians. Over time, especially as a small abolitionist movement emerged in the North after 1830, Virginia's propagandists for slavery responded to northern condemnation of enslavement by ignoring what Carter had done and publishing calumny about what Randolph's former slaves had accomplished. Most white Virginians never adopted the stance or took the actions that Carter and Randolph did, so most black Virginians could not experience the free life that Hercules White did. Nonetheless, those who freed their slaves, and those who thereby obtained freedom, together revealed one face of the American Revolution, carried out by Virginians, black and white, that seemed to promise a far different future than had come out of the colonial era.

Even while Virginians made their way through these years of changes in state law and private behavior, other states were blazing their own trails. Pennsylvania enacted a gradual emancipation law in 1780. In Massachusetts, people held in slavery went to court to argue in freedom suits that the language of the state's constitution of 1780—"all men are born free and equal," said its bill of rights—barred slavery, and the courts agreed. The 1790 census counted 12,866 free nonwhite residents in Virginia, but it also counted 292,627 slaves there, and no slaves whatever in Massachusetts. By 1804, every northern state had at least begun the process of ending slavery within its borders, and by 1830, the process was virtually complete everywhere in the North. The changes in Virginia between the 1760s and the 1790s were impressive, but they paled in comparison with the changes in the North. The North became increasingly different from any southern pattern.

Perfecting Independence in a New State

Together, these core changes—in church and state, in race and slavery, and in constitution making and a bill of rights—represented the policy options that a majority of politically active Virginians evidently desired in a world where they were not going to be overruled by an overseas authority. In the aftermath of a war for independence, in a society that had entered the Revolutionary era with all kinds of tensions and a wide range of possibilities, Virginians moved closer to their understanding of a republican state and society. That Virginians by no means spoke with one voice could be seen in the divergent ways in which they saw the role of the state in religion, and in the contested ways they navigated their way through matters of race and slavery.

The Revolutionary settlements on race and religion, when they were partially undone around the turn of the century, went in divergent directions. In religion, change accelerated; the process rumbled on toward total disestablishment. In race, change was curtailed, moves toward greater liberality were turned back—but by no means to the legal situation before 1782. The legislature had received petitions to end the permissive environment in which owners might free their slaves, but no such action was taken. There remained such a condition as black freedom, and additional residents of Virginia continued to move into it.

What the political leaders of the Revolutionary generation had attempted, and what they had achieved, would resonate down through the centuries—on race, on religion, and on government. Such matters loomed, almost immediately, on a larger stage, as Virginians participated in a move to amend the Articles of Confederation. In fact, at the very time the General Assembly was finishing up its work on the Statute for Religious Freedom, it was choosing delegates to go to Annapolis, Maryland, to discuss interstate trade.

During the American Revolution, the Articles of Confederation—which had been drafted shortly after the Declaration of Independence and finally ratified in 1781—had contributed toward, or at least had not prevented, the achievement of independence. Were they adequate to the needs of a postwar world? Like affairs within Virginia, perhaps the framework of national government stood in need of attention in the quest for perfecting political independence. Barely a decade after having worked out a written constitution for the state, Virginians went about the task of substantially revising the wartime framework of national government, even working out an entirely new constitution for a new nation.

Chapter 7

Virginia and a New Union

....

No longer a colony in the British Empire, Virginia emerged from the American Revolution a sovereign state and also a member state in a larger grouping under the Articles of Confederation. That document had been designed early in the Revolutionary War primarily as a means of coordinating the independence effort. With independence achieved, had the Articles of Confederation been successful to the point of no longer being important? Or might they become, instead, more important in providing a framework of national government for the thirteen independent states? Might the articles prove insufficient? If they should be strengthened, how much, and in what ways? Who might win, and who might lose, under a more powerful framework? Were they important primarily in safeguarding the thirteen states from outside political and military dangers, from internal social and political weakness, or from problems of facilitating trade among the former colonies up and down the East Coast? Through the rest of the 1780s and into the 1790s, these questions of postwar governance remained at the center of American politics, as the Founders found themselves called upon to help steer the thirteen states, the new federation, through the turbulent developments that followed the American Revolution.

The Annapolis Convention

James Madison, with his extensive experience in state and national politics, saw an urgent need for the national government to obtain greater power than the Articles of Confederation granted it. He supported two amendments, one to give Congress authority to regulate interstate commerce, the other to authorize Congress to levy taxes to finance the national enterprise. Efforts to amend the articles failed, however, to obtain what the articles required for amendment—

James Madison (1751–1836), fourth president of the United States (1809–1817). Even in his twenties he took a lead role in the new state's approach to religious freedom, and in the 1780s he became a force in the affairs of the nation as well as the state. This is a photograph of a miniature painting that dates from 1783, done in watercolor by Charles Willson Peale. Library of Congress, Prints and Photographs Division, LC-USZC4-4097.

the unanimous consent of the states—despite Madison's 1783 *Address to the States* and a companion call by Washington, *Circular to the Governors*, urging ratification.

In 1786 Madison attended the Annapolis Convention in Maryland, a meeting of delegates from several states. The Annapolis Convention called for a general convention of delegates from all thirteen states to meet in Philadelphia the next year. There, Madison hoped, a renovated framework of national government might be hammered out, one that would give the nation a more effective government and a greater chance of surviving in a dangerous world as an independent republic.

Returning from Annapolis to the Virginia legislature, Madison worked to secure his state's agreement to participate in such a convention. He himself was selected as one of Virginia's delegates. Seeking to enhance the convention's chance of success, he helped persuade Washington to participate as another Virginia delegate. If a man of Washington's political stature led Virginia's delegation, Madison thought, perhaps other states would also send their leading men. Before the convention met in May, Madison was also reelected to the Confederation Congress (which was meeting in New York), so he was able to work there to lay the groundwork for a successful convention in Philadelphia.

The Philadelphia Convention: James Madison, Father of the Constitution

The Philadelphia Convention met in 1787 from May to September. Madison was the chief author of a collection of resolutions introduced early on by Virginia delegate Edmund Randolph. The Virginia Plan, as those resolutions came to be called, provided the basis for discussion that led to the proposed Constitution of the United States to which the convention eventually agreed. The Virginia Plan proposed a complete renovation of the national government that had struggled along under the Articles of Confederation. Instead of having only a unicameral legislature, the new government would have two legislative houses, and it would also have independent executive and judicial branches. Instead of representation in Congress being identical for every state, it would be apportioned on the basis of state population, although the original plan was changed in convention so that only the House of Representatives would be apportioned by population, and each state would have equal representation in the Senate.

The new government, as proposed by the Philadelphia Convention, would have powers that had previously been denied. Whereas under the Articles of Confederation the national government had depended on the states to supply requisitions, the new government would have the power to tax citizens directly to secure revenue. Moreover, it would be authorized to regulate trade among the states and between the United States and other countries, so states could not put up their own tariff barriers. In these and other ways, the new national government would be far more than a committee of the states to deal with little more than war and diplomacy. In one key exception to the authority to regulate international commerce, the new government, as proposed by the Philadelphia Convention, would have no power to abolish the international slave trade for another twenty years.

Because the new national government would be far more than a committee of states, key questions to be addressed in its establishment under the Constitution had to do with representation and the apportionment of taxes—the distribution of power in the new nation and the apportionment of tax obligations to provide revenue for the new government. If taxes—and representation—were apportioned on the basis of population, should it be according to total population or just free population? If by total population, slave states would pay more than the other way, free states less, and if by free population, vice versa. And yet, if by total population, southern states would get relatively inflated representation, but if by free population, northern states would. The three-fifths clause addressed these dual concerns, splitting the difference. According to the scheme that was adopted, everyone, men and women, adults and children, blacks and whites, propertied and penurious, Protestants and Catholics, voters and nonvoters, everyone, would count at full value—everyone, that is, except slaves, who would be counted at three-fifths. These values would apply not only to taxes but also to representation in the lower house of Congress, the House of Representatives. The president would be chosen by the electoral college—where each state would get votes equal in number to its members of the House of Representatives plus its two members in the Senate—so the question applied directly to the executive branch as well as the legislative. And because the president would nominate federal judges, the question also applied to the judicial branch of the new federal government. Without agreement on a formula for determining representation and allocating taxes—without the three-fifths clause—there could have been no agreement at Philadelphia on the Constitution.

George Mason: A Minority Report

Madison did not speak for all Virginians, or even for all the Virginia delegates to the Philadelphia Convention. In early July 1787, Mason said that he "would bury his bones" in that city rather than see the convention fail, but by the end of August he declared (according to Madison's notes of the proceedings) he "would sooner chop off his right hand than put it to the Constitution as it now stands." And in mid-September, when the actual time came to sign the document, Mason refused. "As the Constitution now stands," he explained, "he could [give it neither his support nor his] vote in Virginia; and he could not sign here what he could not support there."

There are a number of misconceptions about George Mason. According to one, his consistent support of states' rights explains his concerns about the new federal government. But he rejected states' rights as far as South Carolina, Georgia, and the slave trade were concerned. Madison quoted him as saying at the Philadelphia Convention: "As to the States being in possession of a right to import [slaves], this was the case with many other rights, now to be properly given up. He held it essential in every point of view that the general government should have power to prevent the increase of slavery" via the slave trade into the United States.

Moreover, of considerable concern to Mason was the agreement at Philadelphia to grant the states, regardless of their population, equal representation in the Senate. In that respect, nothing of substance would have changed since the Articles of Confederation. Virginia delegates were unhappy about the potential mischief of states' rights in this sense, since the small states were chiefly in the

North. Mason saw the larger numbers of small northern states as threatening Virginia on everything from commerce to taxation.

Who would have the authority to regulate navigation was a vexing question. Navigation acts had a long and troubled history, as colonists experienced their costs and inconveniences and feared their potential. Who, for example, had the right to carry American shipping, and who might be excluded? The British government had previously supplied official answers to such questions, and under the proposed Constitution the new American national government would succeed to that authority. Already during the Confederation period—in 1786, only shortly before the Philadelphia Convention—a combination of northern states had appeared entirely prepared, with respect to Secretary for Foreign Affairs John Jay's negotiations with the Spanish over a commercial treaty, to spurn southern wishes and agree to give up rights to navigate the Mississippi River for the next twenty-five years or more. In illustrating the potential dangers that a more powerful national government posed to southern interests, southern spokesmen pointed toward the possibility that a congress dominated by northerners would vote to ban foreign vessels from carrying American exports. If northern shippers enjoyed a monopoly of the carrying trade, they might well raise their freight rates to their own benefit but to the great cost of southern planters.

So, as a Chesapeake planter, Mason feared the navigation acts that, with a simple majority in Congress and a complaisant president, might be enacted to serve the interests of northern shippers. In August 1787, Mason lost twice to what he saw as a terrible combination of the New England states and the Deep South. He wanted navigation laws to require supermajorities, two-thirds in each house, for passage. And he wanted an end to slave imports. New England delegates, insisting on greater freedom to enact commercial laws, sought to reduce the requirement to a simple majority. The Deep South states of Georgia and South Carolina were prepared to support such a change on condition that northern delegates agree to keep the new government from blocking slave imports during the next twenty years. Mason soon wrote in his "Objections to This Constitution of Government" that a two-thirds vote on "Commercial & Navigation Laws" would have "removed an insuperable objection to the adoption of this Government."

Mason here supplies a telling comment regarding his motivation for opposing the proposed Constitution. The plethora of small northern states, combined with Mason's opposition to slave imports and his concerns regarding navigation acts, drove him to his negative stance. In fact, historian Lance Banning explains Mason's emergent opposition to the new charter as preceding the slave-trade/

navigation-acts arrangement, noting that it began with his fear that Virginia might find itself beset by a national government controlled by the many small states of the North.

Richmond: The Ratification Convention—Madison versus Mason

Mason was nearly alone among the delegates at the Philadelphia Convention in opposing the document they had produced. Next came the fight over whether to ratify the Constitution. Mason grumbled and feared it would be ratified. Madison, by contrast, hoped it would be ratified, and he pushed hard to achieve that outcome.

Achieving agreement among most of the delegates in Philadelphia was a vitally important start, but it would avail little if the states did not ratify the proposed Constitution. To this effort, Madison next turned his vast ability to framing compelling political arguments and to writing them up for general distribution. Supporters of the proposed new constitution styled themselves "Federalists," so opponents of ratification became known as "Anti-Federalists." Madison joined Alexander Hamilton (who wrote most of the papers) and John Jay in writing *The Federalist Papers,* a series of essays in political theory and history that laid out the arguments for granting the national government greatly enhanced power. A republic was as well suited to a large territory as to a single state, Madison insisted, and the proposed constitution promised a successful conclusion to the Revolution, not a reversal of it.

In state after state, those arguments made the difference in convincing majorities, often by only narrow margins, to permit the new government to go into operation. As a member of the Virginia ratifying convention in 1788, Madison directly played that role. But it was a close call, from start to finish, and Patrick Henry and George Mason put up the greatest opposition.

During the ratification debates in Richmond, as Mason sought to attract delegates to his side and against ratification, he demanded specific changes in the Constitution before, he said, he could approve it. On June 4, he declared: "An indispensable amendment in this case, is, that Congress shall not exercise the power of raising direct taxes till the States shall have refused to comply with the requisitions of Congress." This matter dealt with neither a Bill of Rights, as we know it, nor the slave trade. Speaking of prior requisitions and the taxing power, Mason continued: "On this condition it may be granted, but I see no reason to grant it unconditionally; as the States can raise the taxes with more ease, and lay them on the inhabitants with more propriety, than it is possible for the General Government to do. . . . Should this power be restrained, I shall withdraw my

GEORGE MASON, SLAVERY, AND THE INTERNATIONAL SLAVE TRADE

George Mason argued the short-comings of the Constitution on June 11 and again on June 17, 1788, during the great debate in Richmond over whether Virginia should ratify the Constitution or, instead, insist that it be amended first. Mason's language demands careful reading, for it is central to understanding his stance on slavery in the states, on the one hand, and the international slave trade, on the other. To conclude from his strong opposition to the slave trade that he had a similar aversion to slavery fundamentally confuses his personal situation and his public positions on the great questions of the time. Yet writers have often said about Mason that he insisted on the abolition of slavery—and even that, had he had his way, slavery would have been abolished and there would have been no Civil War. Here is what Mason actually said:

The security of our liberty and happiness is the object we ought to have in view in wishing to establish the union. If instead of securing these, we endanger them, the name of the Union will be but a trivial consolation. . . . There ought to be a clause in the Constitution to secure us that property, which we have acquired under our former laws, and the loss of which would bring ruin on a great many people.

objections to this part of the Constitution: But as it stands, it is an objection so strong in my mind, that its amendment is with me, a *sine qua non*, of its adoption. I wish for such amendments, and such only, as are necessary to secure the dearest rights of the people."

Such amendments, it turns out, related to questions of federal taxation, navigation acts, the federal judiciary, and various other matters, including possible attacks against slavery. Mason spoke at the Richmond convention about the dangers posed by the proposed new federal judiciary, which might, he said, "destroy the State Courts," even "destroy the State Governments." Speaking on June 17 on the power to tax, Mason remonstrated that though the proposed Constitution specified a formula for allocating the federal direct-tax burden among the states (the three-fifths basis, under which slaves counted three-fifths, while all other people counted full value), it offered no guidance on the nature of the tax: "But the General Government was not precluded from laying the proportion of any particular State on any one species of property they might think proper. For instance, if 500,000 dollars were to be raised, they might lay the whole of the proportion of the Southern States on the blacks, or any one species of property: So that by laying taxes too heavily on slaves, they might totally annihilate that kind of property" (see sidebar). In a similar fashion, Patrick Henry had just finished expressing a fear that Congress was being given power to interfere with property in slaves "by laying a grievous and enormous tax on it, so as to compel owners to emancipate their slaves rather than pay the tax."

By a convention vote of 89–79, Virginia nonetheless ratified the new Constitution, and Madison and Washington were elected in 1789 to help launch the new national government—Washington as the first president and Madison to the first session of Congress. President Washington consulted with Congressman Madison on a wide range of matters. Madison drafted not only Washington's inaugural address but also the House's response to the president. Madison also did much to shape protocol in the new regime. Calling for a democratic etiquette, for example, Madison helped defeat a proposal according to which the president would have been addressed as "Your Highness" rather than "Mr. President." Madison also led the way on policy matters. Consistent with his experience throughout the 1780s, he fostered passage of a revenue bill, the first federal tariff law.

As for the international slave trade into the United States, Congress, at the earliest time permitted under the Constitution, placed a ban on it, effective in 1808. By that time, even South Carolina and Georgia had determined that they could live better without than with large numbers of newly imported slaves; that natural increase, together with the interstate slave trade, would suffice to generate the numbers required; and that people born to slavery in America were safer to have around. An illegal trade persisted for the next half century, bringing perhaps 1,000 new slaves per year. Devastating as it was for Africans ensnared by it, the continued slave trade into the United States had virtually no demographic significance for the new nation. The interstate slave trade, the primary means of supplying the Deep South, proved to be another matter.

James Madison, George Mason, and the Bill of Rights

It is often said about George Mason that his problem with the proposed Constitution was that it

The augmentation of slaves weakens the States; and such a trade is diabolical in itself, and disgraceful to mankind. Yet by this Constitution it is continued for twenty years. As much as I value an union of all the states, I would not admit the Southern States [South Carolina and Georgia] into the Union, unless they agreed to the discontinuance of this disgraceful trade, because it would bring weakness and not strength to the Union. And though this infamous traffic be continued, we have no security for the property of that kind which we have already. There is no clause in this Constitution to secure it; for they may lay such a tax as will amount to manumission. And should the Government be amended, still this detestable kind of commerce cannot be discontinued till after the expiration of twenty years.—For the fifth article, which provides for amendments, expressly excepts this clause. I have ever looked upon this as a most disgraceful thing to America. I cannot express my detestation of it. Yet they have not secured us the property of the slaves we have already. So that "they have done what they ought not to have done, and have left undone what they ought to have done."

had no bill of rights—and that his insistence on a bill of rights qualifies him as "Father of the Bill of Rights." Certainly his 1776 Declaration of Rights at the state level served as a model for the federal Bill of Rights. Yet the conventional characterization of Mason misstates his opposition in 1787 and 1788. His concerns, as he expressed them at the time, provide insight into Virginia's political culture, at the time of the debates over the Constitution and also for at least the next three-quarters of a century.

James Madison understood, of course, that the new Constitution must be subject to amendment, but he himself had at first resisted calls for amendments that would serve as a bill of rights. To overcome enough resistance to win ratification, however, Federalists had promised to seek guarantees of various rights, and Madison had repeated the promise in his campaign for election to Congress. For one thing, making concessions of this sort decreased the likelihood that calls would be successful for a second constitutional convention, where the new national government might be severely weakened. Moreover, although Madison had pushed throughout the 1780s for a stronger national government, he understood that one too strong was also a danger.

Madison therefore pushed for various amendments to the document that the Philadelphia Convention had produced and that the states, as he had urged, had ratified. Congress considered a large number of proposals during 1789 and, in September, shortly before the first Congress's first session came to an end, approved twelve. One proposed amendment, building on Virginia's achievement in its constitution of 1776 and then in legislation in the 1780s, would deny Congress the power to deny citizens their freedom of religion.

Congress was wrapping up action before sending the proposed amendments out for ratification by the states, when George Mason wrote, as he is often quoted, "With two or three further Amendments . . . I could cheerfully put my Hand and Heart to the New Government." But Mason's list of "further amendments"—and not just "two or three"—did not include what we think of as civil rights or civil liberties. They did not relate to freedom of the press, freedom of religion, or trial by jury. Rather, they related to election laws, a council to the president, the jurisdiction of the federal judiciary, and control by a two-thirds majority rather than a simple majority over commerce (Mason's "insuperable objection" at Philadelphia in 1787), though Mason did not now specify a change in the imposition of federal taxes (his "sine qua non" in Richmond in 1788).

Mason's Anti-Federalist colleagues in Virginia, too, viewed Madison's handiwork as inadequate. U.S. Senator William Grayson wrote Patrick Henry that Madison's proposals "effect personal liberty alone, leaving the great points of the Judiciary, direct taxation, and etc., to stand as they are." As for Henry, he worked mightily in the General Assembly to galvanize opposition to the proposed amendments. Although the amendments were designed to place limits on the new national government, the politics of ratification in Virginia had the proponents of the new government supporting the amendments, while legislators concerned that the Constitution had created a machine too powerful opposed them.

With both houses of the General Assembly narrowly divided, Virginia failed to ratify the proposed amendments in late 1789. Two years passed. Ten of the original thirteen states had ratified at least ten of the twelve amendments, but Connecticut and Georgia had rejected them, and their fate rested with Virginia. In December 1791, when the General Assembly finally acted, it actually ratified all twelve, and ten of the twelve, having obtained the approval of three-fourths of the states, became part of the Constitution. The ten came to be known as the Bill of Rights, and James Madison came to be known not only as "Father of the Constitution" but also as "Father of the Bill of Rights."

Genuine as George Mason's commitment was, and his contribution, too, in 1776 to the idea and practice of a written list of rights to be protected, he is often credited with more than he deserves regarding the first ten amendments to the U.S. Constitution. Mason was late to declare the need for a bill of rights to the 1787 Constitution to parallel his own Declaration of Rights in the 1776 Virginia constitution. Nor was he satisfied with Madison's handiwork. Rather, Mason expressed early on a fear that Madison would offer up only "some Milk & Water propositions"—no "important and substantial Amendments"—and in the end, to Mason's mind, Madison offered nothing more.

Alexandria, D.C.

After the first session of the first Congress looked after organizing the executive branch and the judiciary, and framed a bill of rights and a revenue bill, the second session faced two remaining major issues: what to do about the states' debts left over from fighting the American Revolution and where to situate a permanent home for the new national government. For a national capital, New York or Philadelphia (or an alternative site nearby) might suffice, but proponents of a site farther south—especially Thomas Jefferson, James Madison, and George Washington—pushed successfully for a location on the Potomac River. What is sometimes termed the Compromise of 1790 determined that the nation would have a southern capital and that the federal government would absorb the states' debts from the Revolution. A federal debt was born. And according to the agreement, the federal government would operate out of Philadelphia for the next decade but in 1800 would settle into new facilities in a new town.

Washington's second inaugural, 1793, Phila-
delphia, painting by Jean Lyon Gerome Ferris.
Virginia Historical Society, Richmond, Virginia,
Lora Robins Collection of Virginia Art.

When surveyors in the 1790s traced the boundaries of the new District of
Columbia, which straddled the Potomac River and contained portions both
from Maryland and from Virginia, it had two towns—George Town, formerly
in Maryland, and Alexandria, which had been in Virginia. By 1810, the new city
of Washington had a population (8,208) that exceeded either Alexandria (7,227)
or George Town (4,948), and enough people lived in the district but not in any
of those three towns to bring the total population to 24,012.

Had the nation's capital district retained its original diamond shape, then
workers at the Pentagon two centuries later or visitors to Arlington National
Cemetery would have found themselves inside it. But the Virginia portion was
given back in 1846. During the Civil War, after Virginia's secession ordinance was
adopted in 1861, a government of Virginia loyal to the United States set up shop
in Alexandria, and it could do so and still represent Virginia because Alexandria
had once again become a city in Virginia.

Somewhere no doubt there are letters carrying the postmark "Alexandria,
D.C.," revealing a time when such a place existed. The term "Washington, D.C.,"

denoting a new city that grew up in what had been swampland in 1790, also reflected a vanished world, when Washington was a minor part of the nation's capital district, not synonymous with it.

The American System—and the Unintended Emergence of Two-Party Politics

During Washington's first term as president, Secretary of the Treasury Alexander Hamilton proposed a series of measures to bolster the economy and the federal government. In particular, Hamilton proposed that the U.S. Congress charter a Bank of the United States, but other leading politicians opposed that charter, chief among them Jefferson and Madison. The new Constitution, they argued, nowhere granted the federal government the power to charter corporations. Hamilton held that unless the Constitution prohibited an action, the action was constitutional. Madison argued that, to the contrary, unless the Constitution expressly authorized an action, it was unconstitutional. Thus arose the controversy over whether it was better to follow a "strict" or "loose" construction—that is, interpretation—of the Constitution.

The Founding Fathers did not anticipate the emergence of a two-party system in U.S. national politics. In fact, they resisted the idea as a bad one. Yet during the first few years after the Constitution was ratified, a two-party system began to emerge. The two national parties came to be known, for a time, as the Federalists and the Democratic-Republicans.

Madison's political biography demonstrates that the Federalists of the struggle over whether to ratify the Constitution were by no means identical to the Federalists of the two-party system that emerged in the 1790s under the Constitution. Hamilton and Madison had served as the leading proponents of ratification. For a time, they worked together to achieve a goal they shared. Soon, however, they became political opponents. Their views of just what the Constitution permitted grew very different, so they clashed. Those who resisted ratification in 1788 are known as Anti-Federalists. Those who opposed Hamilton's economic policies a few years later were known as Democratic-Republicans, or simply Jeffersonians.

Not only did the two parties oppose each other's interpretation of the Constitution, but they also contested each other's power in national politics. Jefferson ran against John Adams, of Massachusetts, in both 1796 and 1800. Jefferson lost in the first contest over who would succeed Washington and become the nation's second president, but he won the rematch. Meanwhile, Madison declined to run for reelection to Congress in 1796 and instead retired to Montpelier, his plantation home in Virginia.

The "Principles of 1798"

Between the elections of 1796 and 1800, the nation found itself caught up in European politics and war and in an undeclared war with France. Democratic-Republicans opposed administration policies in international affairs as well as domestic matters, and Federalists responded by passing the Alien and Sedition Acts in 1798 to muzzle the opposition party's leading politicians and journalists. In what became known as the Kentucky and Virginia Resolutions, Jefferson and Madison denied that Congress had the authority to pass such measures, which were therefore illegitimate.

Madison wrote in the Virginia Resolution that the Alien and Sedition Acts were "unconstitutional." In violation of the Tenth Amendment they trampled, he said, on "the authorities, rights, and liberties reserved to the states, respectively, or to the people." The Sedition Act, in particular, exercised "a power not delegated by the Constitution, but, on the contrary, expressly and positively forbidden by one of the amendments thereto"—the First. Madison urged that "necessary and proper measures" be taken to prevent the enforcement of the offending laws.

The crisis passed, however, when Jefferson defeated Adams's bid in 1800 for reelection. The Federalists relinquished the presidency and allowed the political opposition to take power. Despite the anger and fear associated with the political turmoil of the late 1790s, the new nation demonstrated that a peaceful transfer of power was possible. It was a gift of tremendous magnitude.

Chapter 8

Mother of Presidents,
Mother of States

....

For eight of the first nine terms under the U.S. Constitution, for all but four years of the period from 1789 to 1825, the president of the United States was a Virginian. George Washington served two terms. Then in 1796, in a close defeat for Thomas Jefferson, John Adams of Massachusetts won. Four years later, in another very close election, the results were reversed, and Jefferson defeated Adams, and the presidency was back in Virginians' hands. Jefferson served two terms, then James Madison served two and, finally, James Monroe served two. If John Adams served as one of the bookends bracketing twenty-four consecutive years of Virginia administrations, his son John Quincy Adams, elected to a single term in 1824, became the other.

Not only was Virginia the mother of presidents, it was also the mother of states. In multiple ways, an independent Virginia created a greatly expanded America. During the Revolution, the exploits of George Rogers Clark in the Ohio River valley made far more likely, when the time came to frame a peace treaty ending the war, the concession by the British of all non-Indian claims to a vast hinterland into which the new nation might grow. In 1781 the state of Virginia relinquished its claim to the territory north of the Ohio River. Under the terms of the Northwest Ordinance of 1787, that area was organized as the Northwest Territory, with slavery forever prohibited, and from it were organized the states of Ohio, Indiana, Illinois, Michigan, and Wisconsin. South of the Ohio River, Virginia organized Kentucky County and then gave its blessing to a new state of Kentucky, open to slavery, established in 1792. Native Virginians helped substantially to populate not only all these states but also the vast area south and west of Kentucky—all the more so after President Jefferson acquired the vast Louisiana Territory in 1803.

Thomas Jefferson (1743–1826), a philosopher-statesman and the third president of the United States. Born in Albemarle County, he graduated from the College of William and Mary in 1762 and, having trained as a lawyer, first entered the House of Burgesses in 1769. One of the young men of the Revolution from Virginia, Jefferson filled a wide range of offices in state and national government, in America and in France. But he wished most of all to be known for the Declaration of Independence, the Virginia Statute for Religious Freedom, and the University of Virginia—and, at his request, his tombstone at Monticello specified those three accomplishments. In addition, his legacies include the "Principles of 1798" and the Louisiana Purchase. This is a Gilbert Stuart portrait. Library of Congress, Prints and Photographs Division, LC-USZ62-117117.

The Virginia Dynasty—Republicans in Power

Thomas Jefferson, in winning the presidency, celebrated what he called, then and afterwards, the "revolution of 1800," according to which the rejection of John Adams and the Federalists in 1800 was "as real a revolution in the principles of our government as that of 1776 was in its form."

Yet Jefferson in power proved hardly the same as Jefferson in opposition. As president, he, like Adams, had to navigate the turbulent waters of strident conflict at home and persistent danger abroad. He, like Adams, lashed out at the political opposition—revealing what historian Leonard W. Levy called the "darker side" of his presidency. And with the presidency in what he understandably perceived as good hands, he felt few compunctions about acting in ways that reflected a centralization of power, regardless of whether he had the express support of the Constitution—in no way more clearly than in the Louisiana Purchase.

All that lay in the future, however, when Jefferson was inaugurated in March 1801, the first such ceremony to be held in Washington, D.C., the new nation's even newer capital. When Jefferson sent his inaugural message to Congress, it was a conciliatory address, one phrased in vintage Jeffersonian language and precepts, in which he called for his "fellow-citizens" to "unite with one heart and one mind." He went on: "Let us restore to social intercourse that harmony and affection without which liberty and even life itself are but dreary things. And let us reflect that, having banished from our land that religious intolerance under which mankind so long bled and suffered, we have yet gained little if we countenance a political intolerance as despotic, as wicked, and capable of as bitter and bloody persecutions." Americans knew very well that they often differed in their opinions, but he insisted, "Every difference of opinion is not a difference of principle," and indeed, "We are all Republicans, we are all Federalists." Jefferson was positing here what he believed, or hoped, to be a key feature of American political culture, that despite their differences Americans shared a fundamental set of values and attitudes about their social and political systems.

Jefferson knew that neither peace nor prosperity, abroad or at home, came with guarantees, but he voiced at the outset of his presidency the core principles that he wished the nation to know that he planned to follow to the best of his ability. He called for "a wise and frugal Government, which shall restrain men from injuring one another, which shall leave them otherwise free to regulate their own pursuits of industry and improvement." He called for "peace, commerce, and honest friendship with all nations, entangling alliances with none; the support of the State governments in all their rights, as the most competent administrations for our domestic concerns," and "the preservation of the General Government in its whole constitutional vigor, as the sheet anchor of our peace at home and safety abroad."

The Louisiana Purchase

In 1803, the United States obtained a vast territory between the Mississippi River and the Rocky Mountains. President Jefferson first sought France's guarantee that Americans could use the port at New Orleans. He wanted assurance that farmers in the Tennessee and Ohio river valleys could ship goods down the Mississippi River and on to Atlantic basin markets. Instead, Napoleon Bonaparte offered the United States all of France's North American holdings, the western half of the Mississippi River valley. Napoleon concluded that, in view of France's waning fortunes in a war to suppress a slave uprising in St. Domingue (later known as Haiti), he no longer needed Louisiana as a military post or breadbasket and that, in view of an imminent return to war with England, it would be better to convert the territory to cash.

If Jefferson accepted the offer, the United States would double its territory, with both banks of the Mississippi River under American control. As he pondered a constitutional amendment to authorize the purchase, he gave as a major justification the prospect of clearing Indians from land east of the Mississippi by offering them lands in the West. Yet given the dim prospects of timely ratification and the unlikelihood that Napoleon's offer would wait, he decided to go ahead without express constitutional authority. The river and the territory became America's, though the potentially immense trade advantages were briefly jeopardized late during the War of 1812, when English forces attacked New Orleans. Indian Removal, largely accomplished by 1840, facilitated the Cotton Kingdom's expansion through Alabama and Mississippi. Trans-Mississippi lands from the Louisiana Purchase permitted slavery's expansion farther west.

Indian Removal and the Old Southwest

When people in general, and scholars in particular, think of the Louisiana Purchase, they generally emphasize the vast area west of the Mississippi River. But it was the area east of the river that had Jefferson's attention, and we might want to revisit his perception of the true immediate value of that grand land transaction. In part, of course, he had in mind that the tens of thousands of American farm families already in the Old Southwest and the Old Northwest—areas that extended north from the Spanish possessions along the Gulf coast to the Ohio

River, plus the Northwest Territory—should have a waterborne way to ship to distant markets whatever surpluses they could grow on their land. But he also had in mind the vast tracts of land that, as of 1803, were not yet available for settlement by American farmers. The bonanza of land farther west permitted him to see a way to clear the land less far west, to rid it of the human obstacles to white settlement. The Indians might be persuaded to abandon their lands east of the river in exchange for lands west of it.

President Jefferson spoke often of this notion. As early as November 1802, he wrote to Georgia governor John Milledge: "The acquisition of Louisiana will, it is agreed must, put in our power the means of inducing all Indians on this side to transplant themselves to the other side of the Mississippi before many years." The Georgia governor had a profound interest in seeing large numbers of Creeks and Cherokees make such a move. When Jefferson drafted a constitutional amendment, one that would expressly give him the authority to acquire foreign territory, he included language directed to the Indians' future in his grand vision. Responding to General Horatio Gates's congratulations for the successful negotiations to acquire Louisiana, Jefferson spoke of his hope that Congress would make the region "the means of tempting all our Indians on the East side of the Mississippi to remove to the West."

Every U.S. history textbook contains a map of the evacuation of Indians during the presidencies of Andrew Jackson and Martin Van Buren—especially in the Old Southwest but also in the Old Northwest—with colored areas depicting the sizable chunks of territory that became open to settlement by American farmers once the original occupants were forced out, especially along the Trail of Tears, the forced relocation of Native Americans from the southeastern states and the Old Southwest to Indian Territory, west of the Mississippi River. But the process began on Jefferson's watch. By the time Jackson assumed the presidency in 1829, Indian occupancy east of the Mississippi was already substantially reduced from what it had been just a quarter century earlier. Jackson himself said to the southern Cherokees, when he offered them "a country beyond the Mississippi," that it was something "Mr. Jefferson promised you." Jackson and Van Buren accelerated the process, made it more coercive, and largely completed it, but it had been building for years, and the Louisiana Purchase was key to it.

The Lewis and Clark Expedition, 1804–1806

Even before acquiring Louisiana for the United States, President Jefferson had conceived a "Voyage of Discovery" into and beyond the Louisiana Territory, beginning at the mouth of the Missouri River and heading upstream to the Rocky

Mountains and then on to the Pacific Ocean. Many members of this voyage were born in Virginia or Kentucky. Leading it were the president's personal secretary and neighbor from Albemarle County, Captain Meriwether Lewis of the army, and William Clark, younger brother of Revolutionary hero George Rogers Clark. Initially inspired by his learning about Alexander Mackenzie's trip west from Canada a decade earlier, Jefferson's vision—for which he sought and obtained congressional support in January 1803—had Americans traveling through Spanish territory to the Rockies. But just as the American expedition got under way, word came that Spain had transferred the territory to France, and France had sold it to the United States. Traveling downstream on the Ohio River, then up the Mississippi to St. Louis, the expedition began the trip up the Missouri in May 1804. The group reached the Pacific in November 1805, wintered there, and arrived back in St. Louis in September 1806.

The Voyage of Discovery did not find a waterway connecting the Missouri and Columbia rivers, nor did it return with agreements regarding peace or trade with Indians. The expedition did bring back, however, a tremendous fund of knowledge regarding the geography, minerals, fauna, and human residents of the vast region. Lewis and Clark each not only played an essential role as co-leader of the expedition but also kept a journal, so accounts of their movements and discoveries can be read two centuries later. Also important were people not on the roster as full members, whose presence eased the expedition's acceptance along the way. One, Sacagawea, was a young Indian woman whose key role was less as guide than as interpreter and as an indication that this was not a war party. Another, Clark's personal servant York, inspired awe among Indians because of his very dark color, but in addition his skills were important, and he enjoyed a greater freedom than he had previously known, until he returned to Virginia and resumed his status as a slave. According to historian Thomas P. Slaughter, who relied on Indian oral tradition, York managed eventually to escape slavery and return west, where he became a chief among the Crow Indians.

The Second War of American Independence

Soon after the purchase of the Louisiana Territory and the launching of the Lewis and Clark expedition, England and France continued their on-again, off-again war between the superpowers of the age, and the United States tried to continue trading with both—U.S. farmers and merchants depended on it—while at the same time staying free of the war. Such could not be done forever, because neither France nor England wanted to see its enemy benefit from trade with the United States. Each side seized U.S. vessels, and the United States responded by attempting to use trade embargoes and other measures to repel such activities. Particularly notable from Virginians' point of view was the incident of the *Chesapeake*, an American war vessel that had been constructed at Norfolk and was pushing out of the Chesapeake Bay in June 1807 for deployment in the Mediterranean. A British vessel stopped it to inquire about deserters from the Royal Navy and ended up firing on it, killing several crewmen, and putting it out of commission.

That the new nation was hostage to the good behavior of the great powers was true during Jefferson's second term in office, and it remained true when Madison succeeded Jefferson as president in 1809. Great Britain's navy kept taking sailors off American ships, arguing that these were British sailors who had absconded, though in fact they were often American citizens. Moreover, Great Britain continued, from Canada, to supply Indians in the Old Northwest and encourage their resistance to U.S. expansion into that area. A group of so-called War Hawks in Congress argued forcefully that England was not treating the United States as a sovereign nation—that the nation's political independence was in doubt and had once again to be secured. The combination of actions by the British, in the Old Northwest and on the high seas, led Madison finally to ask Congress to declare war in June 1812.

Later in 1812, Madison was elected to a second term in the White House, with the new nation once again at war with England, just as had been the case when Madison entered public life back in the 1770s. In the earlier war, Americans had managed to win their political independence; in the latest war, that independence was very much in jeopardy. In New England, ships rotted in Boston harbor, penned in by another in a series of embargoes. In the West, Indians threatened all along the frontier. In the South, before hostilities ended, the British attacked New Orleans; had the attack succeeded, it might have undone the Louisiana Purchase in making every westerner dependent on the British to permit him to move his shipping surpluses down the Mississippi and off to market, whether along the eastern seaboard or in foreign ports.

During the war, British forces even invaded Washington, D.C., in August 1814 and forced President Madison to flee the nation's capital. New England Federalists, meeting at a convention in Hartford, Connecticut, muttered secession. Times were difficult and dangerous. England finally defeated France, however, and therefore no longer had so great a need to interfere with U.S. shipping. A peace treaty in December 1814 brought a conclusion to the war but no express resolution of the many issues that had led to the war in the first place. The nation had survived, and, with the war over, President Madison and the Congress could turn to peacetime policies.

THE HARTFORD CONVENTION
RESOLUTIONS

The Hartford Convention's resolutions all targeted the Republican
Party and its power base in Virginia.
Were new states being constantly
admitted into the Union, bringing
additional votes in the electoral
college for Republican candidates
for the presidency? Make it harder
to admit new states. Should war
be declared with merely a simple
majority in Congress? Change that
fraction, too, to a supermajority
of two-thirds. Were Republican
victories hatched from the three-
fifths clause? Fix it, by eliminating
slaves from the population count
for purposes of apportioning representation. Did Virginia manage
to send one leader after another
off to govern the nation? Tie Virginia up, in multiple ways. Here are
some of the resolutions—constitutional amendments demanded
by the convention's delegates:

First. Representatives and direct
taxes shall be apportioned among
the several states . . . according to
their respective numbers of free
persons . . . and excluding . . . all
other persons.

Second. No new state shall be
admitted into the Union by Congress . . . without the concurrence
of two thirds of both houses.

Third. Congress shall not have
power to lay any embargo on the
ships or vessels of the citizens of
the United States, in the ports or
harbours thereof, for more than
sixty days. . . .

Attack from New England— the Hartford Convention

As the War of 1812 dragged on, the Massachusetts
legislature called in 1814 for a regional convention
to fix the new nation's broken politics. Delegates
appointed by the legislatures of Massachusetts,
Connecticut, and Rhode Island met in Hartford,
the Connecticut capital, in December 1814. In the
face of grave challenges in national and international politics, New Englanders would save, if
they could, the Federalist Party, the New England
region, and the American nation. New western
states had already been admitted to the Union,
states whose votes supported the Virginia Republicans in national politics against New England
Federalists, and any number of additional states
seemed on the way. Desperate over the loss of political power in the nation, military costs incurred
during the War of 1812, and economic losses suffered because of a trade embargo, the Hartford
Convention delegates resolved to address all these
unhappy developments.

Urging adoption of several constitutional
amendments, the convention insisted that henceforth it should take a two-thirds supermajority
rather than a simple majority in each house to pass
a measure admitting a new state, declaring war, or
placing an embargo on foreign trade. The three-
fifths clause should be amended so that slaves
would no longer count in determining power in
the U.S. House of Representatives or in the electoral college. Given that Jefferson had served two
terms as president and James Madison was in his
second term, another proposed amendment took
two additional thrusts at Virginia's dominance:
No president should serve more than a single
term, and successive presidents should not come
from the same state (see sidebar).

The convention did not call for secession but left that option open, so its actions might appear moderate although its demeanor was threatening. If the war persisted, and the proposed amendments were not adopted, the delegates vowed to meet again. In short, Hartford Convention delegates acted as did the delegates to the First Continental Congress of 1774, which urged adoption of various measures by Great Britain. When they were rebuffed, the Second Continental Congress followed and ended up declaring independence. As for the First Continental Congress, that had been a response to the Intolerable Acts, one of which had closed Boston port in response to the Boston Tea Party. An embargo by Virginia Republicans, or an act of Parliament—no matter who closed the port, or why, its closure brought economic damage and social hurt and had political consequences.

As the convention wrapped up its deliberations in January 1815, however, word was on the way across the Atlantic that a peace treaty had been signed in Europe. The war had ended, and the convention's proposals went nowhere. Widely viewed as treasonous, the convention went far to destroy the Federalist Party. By the winter of 1860–1861, New England had long since forsaken secession and would not brook it among southerners.

One-Party Politics—and the American System, Revised

During the era of the War of 1812, as in the 1780s, Madison had seen the dangers of a weak national government. Despite his reservations in the 1790s about the constitutionality of the first Bank of the United States, he came to see that the nation had accepted the chartering of the bank as a legitimate

Fifth. Congress shall not make or declare war . . . without the concurrence of two thirds of both houses.

. . . .

Seventh. The same person shall not be elected president of the United States a second time; nor shall the president be elected from the same state two terms in succession.

Resolved, That if the application of these states to the government of the United States, recommended in a foregoing resolution, should be unsuccessful and peace should not be concluded, and the defence of these states should be neglected, as it has since the commencement of the war, it will, in the opinion of this convention, be expedient for the legislatures of the several states to appoint delegates to another convention, to meet at Boston . . . with such powers and instructions as the exigency of a crisis so momentous may require.

The redoubtable Dolley Madison (1768–1849), at the end of her tenure as first lady, in 1817. She served as first lady for sixteen consecutive years, as she performed the role not only during her husband's administration but also during widower Thomas Jefferson's two terms, when James Madison served as secretary of state. Portrait by Joseph Wood. Virginia Historical Society, Richmond, Virginia, gift of Katherine W. Davidge.

function of the federal government. Seeing the necessity as well as the constitutionality of federal measures to promote economic growth and development, he now called for a new Bank of the United States, a tariff law that provided protection for U.S. manufacturing in addition to federal revenue, and a bill to promote road construction and other internal improvements. Thus did a leading strict constructionist of the 1790s call in late 1815 for a revised combination of federal policies that would later be hailed as the "American System."

As with Madison's reversal on a Bill of Rights, his reversal on a national bank reflected a combination of changing constitutional priorities and a changing political environment. Seeking to navigate a middle way, he continued to display concern about too strong a national government and too weak a one, too broad an interpretation of the Constitution and too narrow a one. Congress enacted all three of his proposals in 1816, but he vetoed the internal improvements bill in the absence of a constitutional amendment that would authorize such a measure.

In 1817, yet another president from Virginia—the Hartford Convention delegates had been right, not only that Virginia could keep getting its leading men elected to the presidency, but also that it had a seemingly inexhaustible supply of them—James Monroe took office. Monroe was a transitional figure. Younger than either Jefferson or Madison, unlike them he had not been a major player in the events of the Revolution and the first years of nation building, though he had played lesser roles. But he, like Jefferson and Madison before him, served two terms.

With the apparent demise of the Federalist opposition, the Republican Party dominated in what seemed to be a one-party system. Many people no doubt felt relief that the time of a two-party political system, which seemed to have slipped into the past, might have been an aberration after all. Some historians have labeled the late 1810s, or indeed Monroe's entire two terms in office, as "the era of good feelings." A Boston newspaper, the *Columbian Centinel*, coined the term to capture the outpouring of national feelings when New England gave a warm welcome to the new president from Virginia as he toured the country during his first year in office. But if such an era of good feelings had a beginning then, its end came very soon, for good feelings characterized neither the hard economic times that unfolded after the Panic of 1819 nor the acrimony associated with the Missouri Crisis of 1819–1821.

An End to the Virginia Dynasty

Dozens of presidential elections have come across the years, but never again since the campaign of 1820, Monroe's second, has a native resident of Virginia been elected president of the United States. From an almost perfect score of eight terms out of nine, Virginia presidents fell to a score of zero terms out of the next forty-six, a string that remained unbroken in 2007. To be sure, an occasional native of Virginia has served as president since Monroe left office. But William Henry Harrison, well before he was elected president in 1840, had moved his residence, and his political base, west to Ohio. Similarly, Zachary Taylor moved away from his native Virginia long before being elected to the presidency in 1848. Finally, Woodrow Wilson, a Virginia native, went to the White House in 1913 from the governor's mansion in New Jersey. As for John Tyler, he was both a native of Virginia and a resident of that state when he became president in 1841, but the nation's voters had chosen him only for the vice presidency.

Nor is that an end to the evidence of a dramatic decline in Virginia's influence and in the presence of Virginians in the nation's councils. Consider the U.S. Supreme Court, where at least one justice came from Virginia, with hardly a break all the way from 1789 to 1860—including most of all Chief Justice John Marshall. When Justice Peter V. Daniel died in 1860, some Virginians spoke of a "Virginia seat," but not until the 1970s would another Virginia native and resident, Lewis F. Powell, take a seat on the nation's highest court.

Why? It's not that Virginia grew barren, no longer a fertile source of potential leaders. One possible explanation is that political jealousy, such as that exhibited

The Ruins of Jamestown, Virginia, America.
John Gadsby Chapman, a native of Alexandria, did this somber painting of Jamestown's church ruins in 1834 (Virginia Historical Society, Richmond, Virginia, First Settlers Fund Purchase). In the years after the Virginia dynasty, numbers of Virginians revealed a longing for a lost past, a sense that Virginia's best days might already be over, as reflected in the founding in the early 1830s of the Virginia Historical Society. A key organizer was Jonathan Peter Cushing, president of Hampden-Sydney College. The society's constitution listed among its objectives "to discover, procure, and preserve whatever may relate to the natural, civil, and literary history of this state." Supposing the society "should last but some six or seven years," Cushing observed, "it will in that time have done a great deal of good." The Virginia Historical Society—"the Center for Virginia History"—celebrated its 175th anniversary in 2006.

at the Hartford Convention in the midst of the Virginia dynasty, put an end to Virginians' ability to gain the highest national offices. A better explanation is that Virginia's share of the national population rapidly shrank across the nineteenth century. The fact that William Henry Harrison was elected from Ohio rather than Virginia suggests that many native Virginians—voters and political candidates alike—no longer lived in Virginia. They lived and voted and ran for office elsewhere, and they reflected the interests of their new homes, not their old. William Leigh, a Southside delegate to Virginia's constitutional convention of 1829–1830, would ask and answer the question: Where "has the genius of Virginia fled? Of all the old States, none has contributed more to the peopling of the new States than Virginia."

Virginia had a great deal to say about the public events of the age of the American Revolution and the early American republic. Thereafter, Virginians continued to be powerfully connected to events outside the state but had far less control over those events.

The Legacies of President James Madison and Chief Justice John Marshall

At the end of his second term as president in 1817, Madison retired from public life once again. In the years to come, he continued the struggle to find a middle way for ordered liberty to thrive between an overgrown national power and an exaggerated states'-rights orientation. He objected to the broad constitutional interpretations of the U.S. Supreme Court under Chief Justice John Marshall. He had occasion to reconsider his conservative republican stance in the face of the democratic tendencies that, as in the Virginia constitutional convention of 1829–1830 (which he attended, the only delegate left from the 1776 Virginia Convention), increasingly called for an extension of voting rights to all white men. He worried about the security of southern interests in the face of an emerging northern majority that threatened a diminished security for property in slaves, but he worried, too, about the South Carolina nullifiers' use of the states'-rights concepts and language that he and Jefferson had voiced in the Kentucky and Virginia Resolutions.

Madison died in June 1836, just before the sixtieth anniversary of the Declaration of Independence. During his long public life, Virginia and the United States had undergone various transformations. He had played central roles in political developments across the era of the American Revolution, the framing and ratification of the Constitution and the Bill of Rights, through the War of 1812, and even beyond.

Madison left another legacy as well. At the Philadelphia Convention in 1787, he had kept extensive notes regarding the proceedings. He declined to permit those notes to be published until after his death, but they finally appeared in print in 1840. Therefore, scholars and citizens since then have been able to know much of what went on during the convention.

Never was there solely one template according to which political Virginians were cut in the early national era. The Madison-Jefferson wing of the political opposition that developed in the 1790s dominated the state's politics, and the nation's as well, for many years. Yet the chief justice of the Supreme Court from 1801 to 1835, John Marshall, was also a Virginian, and he outlasted the final years of the Virginia dynasty. Not only did his extraordinary performance as chief justice mold the nation's high court as an institution, but it also produced decisions that reflected a far more centralized vision of the new nation than either Jefferson or Madison ever supported. In such decisions as *Martin v. Hunter's Lease* (1816) and *Cohens v. Virginia* (1821), the U.S. Supreme Court ruled in ways that limited the authority of state legislatures and state judiciaries alike—and both these decisions overruled the Virginia Supreme Court. These rulings also left the U.S. Supreme Court as the chief arbiter of the Constitution's meaning in any dispute. The conflict from the Marshall years would resonate in Virginia politics down through the state's secession in 1861, indeed into the 1950s and Massive Resistance—and, more broadly in American politics, into the twenty-first century.

Human Harvest, Black and White, West from Virginia

Into the nineteenth-century American West went numberless Virginians, of every station and into every region. Jefferson's Louisiana Purchase soon made the Old Southwest, in particular, far more effectively available than before for American settlers to begin to call home. Such settlers, a great many of them, left homes in Virginia to find their new land in that vast area. But not all Virginians who left the state of their birth set a southwesterly course. A great many—year after year, from Jefferson's presidency on down through the 1820s, 1830s, and 1840s—moved west by north across the Ohio River, into territory to which Virginia had relinquished all claim back in the 1780s.

Some migrants took slaves with them, some were the slaves taken or sold there, and some were neither slaves nor slaveowners. Each among the tens of thousands of migrants left for good reason, someone's reason, and every departure had an impact, on both the society being left behind and the society being

John Marshall (1755–1835). Marshall served in the military during the American Revolution, in the Virginia convention that ratified the U.S. Constitution in 1788, and in various other positions in state and national government. But he had much his greatest influence and significance as chief justice of the U.S. Supreme Court, from his appointment by John Adams in 1801 until his death thirty-four years later. Marshall played the leading role in establishing the Constitution's supremacy over state law, as well as in solidifying the Supreme Court's role as the arbiter of the Constitution's meaning. Thus he embodied a political antonym to the "Principles of 1798," which Jefferson and Madison had espoused that year and which provided the sacred political text that did much to guide Virginia's political orientation for long afterward. Painting by James Reid Lambden. Virginia Historical Society, Richmond, Virginia.

Rockbridge County native Cyrus McCormick (1809–1884) developed a mechanical reaper, applying new technology to crop harvesting, in Virginia's Shenandoah Valley. In the 1840s, McCormick began large-scale production in Chicago, thereby helping foster the agricultural development of the Midwest. This print, dating from the late-nineteenth century, shows the reaper being successfully tested in a Virginia oat field. Virginia Historical Society, Richmond, Virginia.

joined. When Virginians moved, Virginia changed, in a myriad of ways, and so did the places Virginians moved to.

Census figures from 1850 show where free Virginians, when they moved out of state, went. The largest numbers went to Ohio (19 percent of that year's total), Missouri (13 percent), Kentucky (11 percent), Tennessee and Indiana (9 percent each), and Illinois (8 percent). Most of those six states had boundaries on the Ohio River; the only exception among them, Tennessee, left the Union in 1861. Next up were northern states Iowa (4 percent) and Pennsylvania (3 percent). By contrast, a mere 2 percent each moved to Alabama, Mississippi, or Texas in the Deep South, and even fewer moved to Georgia, Louisiana, or Florida. More particularly among free migrants, black Virginians, whether born free or manumitted, often moved to Ohio.

A good example of Virginia migrants to Ohio is Benjamin Adair, who owned no land in Virginia but obtained more than 200 acres in Ohio. From his Virginia home in Rockbridge County, Adair arrived in Ohio in 1805 and bought land in Ross County, across the river from his son Philip. Philip Adair was married to Elizabeth Tudor, and Elizabeth's father, John Tudor, like Benjamin Adair, came in hopes of helping his children settle on their new land and keeping the family together as he aged. Traveling in multifamily groups, as the Adairs and Tudors did, provided protection on the frontier and made the move as well as the settling easier. Nine of Benjamin Adair's ten children settled with their families near him in Ohio.

Whites also moved from Virginia to the Deep South, though in far fewer numbers than to states farther north. The following three families exemplify the shift of plantation operations south and west out of Virginia in the last generation before the Civil War. Isaac Otey lived in Bedford County, his slaves numbering 33 in 1830. Three of Otey's sons moved out of Virginia, including Walter, who in 1860 owned 43 slaves in Phillips County, Arkansas. William Irby, whom census after census listed with more than 40 slaves in Nottoway County, had three sons, Edmund, John, and Freeman, and all three moved in the 1840s to Panola County, Mississippi, where in 1860 Edmund's slaves numbered 31; John's, 13; and Freeman's, 36. John Tayloe III owned hundreds of slaves when he died in Virginia in 1828. In 1860, Tayloe's five surviving sons all had large holdings in Alabama—Benjamin, William, George, and Henry in Marengo County, and Edward, with 104 slaves, in Perry County.

Two of the small number of white Virginians who moved to Texas became giants in the history of that state. Sam Houston and Stephen F. Austin were both born in Virginia in 1793. Houston made his way from Rockbridge County by way of Tennessee, Austin from Wythe County by way of Missouri. Far more black Virginians ended up in Texas. Black or white, slave or free, migrants from Virginia did much to shape the social and political history of territories a great distance from their native state. Whether reflected in such public events as the Louisiana Purchase or such private occurrences as migration, Virginia was the mother of states as well as of presidents. In multiple ways, Virginia continued to be cradle to America.

Part III

AFTER JEFFERSON'S LOUISIANA PURCHASE

Virginia and the nation faced a crisis, from 1819 to 1821, when a portion of the Louisiana Purchase sought to become the state of Missouri. In the past, Congress had authorized the creation of new states as routine business, but this time was different. A congressman from New York, James Tallmadge Jr., attempted to impose a condition. New York had recently set slavery on the path to disappearance by declaring that all slaves born there after a certain date would, when they reached adulthood, become free. Tallmadge wanted the same to happen in Missouri. Perhaps nobody who is a slave today will ever become free, he conceded, but eventually slavery will be over.

Thus, in 1819, sixteen years after the Louisiana Purchase, former president Thomas Jefferson heard with horror that intense political conflict had emerged over the western territories. "Like a firebell in the night," Jefferson wrote, the news of Tallmadge's proposal and its testy aftermath alarmed him. Might the Union break up over slavery in those western lands? The consequences of Jefferson's stunning diplomatic success in 1803 suddenly threatened to undo a lifetime of work, jeopardizing his political legacy harking all the way back to the Declaration of Independence.

North or South: Who Gets the West?

Southern members of Congress saw as a big problem the very idea that the national government might take any action against slavery. Then too there was a belief, stated by many and believed by some, that the only way for slavery to come eventually to an end in places like Virginia was for the percentage of slaves in the slave states to become smaller, and the way to accomplish that was for slaves from Virginia to be sent to work in other places, such as Missouri. If Virginia came to look enough like New York, then Virginia, too, some thought, could make slavery go away.

Perhaps it is easier to understand the Missouri Crisis by distinguishing between economic and political considerations. Northerners wanted room for their system of family farms to grow. But southern slaveholders wanted more land for slaves and their owners to farm. Which system would get to spread to new areas like Missouri? And northerners wanted more power for themselves in national politics, but southerners resisted relinquishing such power as they had and in fact wanted more for themselves. Which way would voters in Missouri lean in presidential elections? Which way would their congressmen and senators vote on legislation being considered in Congress? Whether in economics or politics, the question was much the same: Which region would get Missouri—the North or the South?

In the end, North and South compromised. The South could have Missouri, but the new state's two votes in the Senate, as well as its votes in the electoral college, would be offset by the votes of a new nonslave state, Maine, which would be detached from Massachusetts. And the territory in Missouri that the southern system would get for expansion would be offset by the promise that much of the rest of the Louisiana Purchase would be forever closed to slavery. A further advantage, to both sides, was that Congress would have already decided, in advance, how to treat the question of slavery in other areas of that region that might later want to become states. Congress would not have to face that crisis again. Or at least that was the hope. Yet in the 1850s the Kansas-Nebraska Act—designed to revisit the question of slavery in the areas of the Louisiana Purchase not yet organized into states—led to the rise of a new Republican Party, one that insisted on the exclusion of slavery from all western territories. Just west of Missouri, warfare in the Kansas Territory over the extension of slavery presaged the Civil War.

Maine and Massachusetts: Land, Schools, and Roads

Another set of questions proved very important in American life in these years. It was a question of land but not one of slavery or national politics. How, Americans asked themselves and each other, can we have schools and roads, more and better than we have, and how can we pay as little as possible for them? Beginning in the 1810s and 1820s—at about the same time as the Missouri Crisis—people in the northern states and the southern states alike asked these questions.

The Missouri Compromise illustrated the answers they came up with. In order for the Missouri Compromise to be possible, Maine and Massachusetts first had to reach their own compromise. The state of Massachusetts owned vast amounts of land in the Maine District. The people of Massachusetts hoped to sell that land off to citizens and, in the process, obtain large amounts of money to spend on education and transportation. They could have better schools and better roads and still avoid higher taxes.

Massachusetts agreed to let Maine go on one condition. As the land in Maine was sold off, half the proceeds would go to each state. And that is what happened. But what happened to the money? Massachusetts divided its half into two shares. One of those shares went to the support of education, and the other half to transportation. One share supplied the money that Horace Mann used to build up the Massachusetts system of public schools. The other went to finance a railroad across the state, from Boston, Massachusetts, to Albany, New York.

Nineteenth-Century Virginia, Nineteenth-Century America

Two central themes across the nineteenth century, both of them visible in this pair of scenes from the Missouri Compromise, framed developments in Virginia as they played out in state affairs and in national affairs. For one, education and transportation alike often loomed large in Virginia's political and social development. For another, matters of race and slavery could not be put to rest—before, during, or after the Civil War.

And although white Virginians might often find themselves hostage to developments elsewhere regarding race and slavery, Virginians themselves contested the key issues of their time. Political controversies regarding race or slavery never required that outsiders always take the leading roles, for Virginians themselves could act the parts that John C. Calhoun, William Lloyd Garrison, and Frederick Douglass played on the national stage. Across the nineteenth century, Virginia proved to be the home of a three-way struggle over the future of slavery, racial identity, race relations, and black opportunity.

Whatever else might be said about the territory that Jefferson acquired from France, it made possible the land-grant college system established under the Morrill Land-Grant College Act of 1862. By the late nineteenth century, moreover, the region became one of the world's great producers of grain and meat alike. Farmers in Iowa produced corn and hogs, while those in the Dakotas raised cattle and wheat. Oklahoma became an important source of crude oil. The Louisiana Purchase, which had been envisioned to secure the political unity of the new nation, endangered it as well, but in the longer run it helped the United States become an agricultural and industrial superpower.

Chapter 9

Perfecting Independence (II)

Power and Policy in Early National Virginia

....

Between the 1810s and the 1850s, Virginia acted in various ways to improve both its economy and its society. Doing so, it went beyond the concerns addressed during the first decade of statehood, when terminating the international slave trade and establishing a new foundation for church-state relations seemed so important. Older matters having been more or less settled, the state went on to other things, some of which required resources that had never before been available for mobilization. Education, inadequately addressed in the 1780s, came up for recurrent reconsideration, as new resources opened up new possibilities or new needs arose. Concerns about race and slavery veered off in new directions. In the early nineteenth century, various Virginians pushed to initiate or implement ambitious new programs in state policy. Among these was Charles Fenton Mercer.

The Multifaceted Schemes of Charles Fenton Mercer

Charles Fenton Mercer, a key player in Virginia politics in the years of the early republic, grew up on an estate near the Rappahannock River, spent time as a child in Richmond in the 1790s while his father served on the Virginia Supreme Court, and further expanded his horizons by later attending college in Princeton, New Jersey. From 1810 to 1817, Mercer represented Loudoun County in the Virginia House of Delegates, before serving for eleven terms in the U.S. House of Representatives. In a letter he wrote in 1825, Mercer spoke of the "three great objects" of his public career—"Colonization, Internal Improvement and public education"—that is, transportation, education, and the deportation of free black residents. All three were designed to promote the social or economic betterment of Virginia society, as Mercer and other leaders understood it and tried to foster it. Two were spurred by the War of 1812. All three received support from the new state government to promote the improvement of a politically independent Virginia.

Virginia entered the nineteenth century with no more system of public education than it had enjoyed during the colonial period. In fact, it had less, if one considers the College of William and Mary a public institution in the years after its founding in 1693, for the college lost any such status after the Revolution. After the Revolution, as before, the wealthy employed tutors or supported academies to train their sons. For the children of families of lesser means, opportunities were spotty, indeed scant. There had been talk of more, including proposals by Thomas Jefferson in the 1780s, but little or nothing had come of it all.

In 1810, however, at Mercer's urging, the General Assembly established the Literary Fund, to begin supplying state funds for education. In early 1816, with the federal government owing Virginia a large sum for money loaned by the state during the War of 1812, Mercer introduced legislation into the House of Delegates to apply those funds, when they were repaid, to the Literary Fund, and thus finally to begin to make available enough money to do something with. Caught in a crossfire of partisan and sectional hostilities in state politics, the Literary Fund was derailed. Mercer was a Federalist in a state largely Republican. His understanding of the wave of the future—the prospect that far more white men would be permitted to join the electorate—drove him to seek to tame them by exposing them to a few years of public schooling. Though an easterner, Mercer identified to a large degree with the aspirations of western Virginians, who had relatively few votes in the legislature. From the perspective of Tidewater planters, the world already operated as it ought, for they had their academies and their tutors, and why should they help pay for schools for the children of westerners?

Thomas Jefferson continued to show a great deal of interest in promoting education, but he preferred that the Literary Fund support a single university to be established near Monticello, rather than a statewide system of primary schools. In no way did the Literary Fund's early operations suggest that, even had it met with enthusiastic legislative support, the state could have provided anything approaching enough money to promote education at three levels—primary schools for basic schooling; academies for more advanced preparation; and one college or university, let alone more than one. To Jefferson's delight, the new University of Virginia, established in 1817 and opened in 1825, absorbed much of the Literary Fund's annual allocations. At lower levels, private academies continued to provide most schooling down through the Civil War.

Charles Fenton Mercer's plantation, Aldie, with its ample fields and large mill, neighbored James Monroe's in Loudoun County. Virginia inaugurated the practice of installing historical markers in 1927, and the Department of Historic Preservation continues to add new ones. Courtesy of Jason O. Watson.

More effective, but far more expensive, was the impulse to promote transportation improvements. In late 1812, Mercer proposed that the General Assembly create a Board of Public Works. That early proposal failed, but in 1816, after the War of 1812, the legislature established it. The new board, its members appointed by the legislature, would coordinate transportation improvements throughout the state. Since it would need technical advice, the board would employ a civil engineer. With technical as well as political input, the board would vet proposals for roads and canals—and, later, railroads as well—and make recommendations to the legislature as to which ones merited state financial assistance, whether those only in the planning stages or those already under way.

The funding to be made available to the board would be made up of all the stock in Virginia's two main banks, and it would be used to supplement private investment. Once private funding to the amount of three-fifths of projected costs were in hand, the state would contribute the other two-fifths. This mixed system, combining public funds with private investment, was designed to mobilize sufficient capital and to coordinate developments so that Virginia might eventually have a statewide system of transportation. Sectional tensions would always shape decisions, for western areas were especially interested in construct-

ing improvements, while rivers already went a long way toward satisfying eastern planters' needs. But canals looked essential even in the east, for example near
the fall line at Richmond, and eastern cities looked for ways to enhance their
commercial reach and industrial growth. The state invested enormous amounts
of money in a wide array of ventures, with implications that continued to play
out down through the Civil War and beyond.

Colonization Equals Deportation

Mercer came to the third of the three great ventures—colonization, that is, the
deportation of free black residents—by accident, but the idea fell on fertile
ground and quickly grew into a national program for addressing what many
white Americans viewed as otherwise intractable race problems. For Mercer, the
question was simple: How could Virginia be rid of a perceived surfeit of people
who were neither white nor enslaved? Mercer was perhaps neither more nor less
tribal in his racial orientation than were other white Virginians in particular or
white Americans in general. He saw that Virginia's growing population of free
African Americans faced severe limitations in their opportunities and, therefore,
that black pauperism would be a growing problem. England had, generations
before, found a solution to a comparable difficulty by shipping its least-wanted
people to America; Virginia might take a similar approach and ship free black
residents off to some other place, any other place.

Mercer was ambivalent about slavery, but he was no abolitionist. Freeing
slaves would release additional people into the ranks of those already living in
the narrow confines of black freedom, and Mercer wanted to reduce those ranks,
not increase them. In late 1816 he proposed to the House of Delegates a resolution asking the federal government to designate a foreign place to which might
be sent such free blacks as chose to go there. By a wide margin, the resolution
was adopted. At the same time, in a related development, a group of men organized what soon became known as the American Colonization Society (ACS).

As regarded colonization, America was Virginia writ large. During the next
dozen years and more, the ACS represented the dominant approach of the nation's elite to resolving problems of race and slavery. Free black northerners
overwhelmingly rejected the idea of their own deportation, or at least they did
so until the 1850s, when the situation grew so bleak that some changed their
minds. In the South in general, and Virginia in particular, some free blacks did
opt for the chance to try out their freedom in an environment that might leave
them more room to grow. In the dominant white perspective in Virginia, deportation offered a possible solution to a complex of seemingly insoluble problems.

Proslavery people heralded the exile of free blacks as a means to strengthen slavery. Antislavery whites saw it as a means of encouraging slaveholders to grant freedom to some of their property, provided that the newly freed would enjoy their freedom somewhere else, preferably in Africa. Among the emigrants from Virginia to West Africa was Lott Cary. Born a slave in Charles City County about 1780, Cary was hired out in Richmond, where he bought his freedom about 1813, learned to read, and became a Baptist minister before embarking for Liberia as a Baptist missionary in 1821. When he died in 1828, he was acting governor of the colony.

Joseph Jenkins Roberts, another African American who moved to Africa, has been called "Virginia's ninth president." A native of Virginia, he became the president of his adopted country, Liberia, and thus might be included along with the four men of the Virginia dynasty plus William Henry Harrison, John Tyler, Zachary Taylor, and Woodrow Wilson. Born in Virginia to free black parents in 1809, Roberts emigrated in 1829, following the death of his father, from his home in Petersburg, Virginia, to Monrovia, Liberia, with his mother and younger siblings, under the auspices of the ACS. There he went into business, held public office, and in 1841 became the first black governor appointed by the ACS. When Liberia declared its independence in 1847, he was elected the new nation's first president and is thus sometimes also called "the father of his country." He served in that office from 1848 to 1856 and again from 1872 to 1876, and he also served for many years as president of Liberia College, before he died in 1876. Petersburg has a Joseph Jenkins Roberts Monument, and outside Monrovia is the Roberts International Airport.

White Women in Political Life—A Political Voice without the Vote

"We mean to be counted," wrote Lucy Barbour in a letter to the editor published in the *Richmond Whig* in 1844. Elite white women could and did count, playing varied political roles in a presuffrage world. Within the limits imposed by a political culture in which men did most of the public speaking and all of the voting and legislating, women crafted their own responsibilities. Rejecting the notion that women had to safeguard their purity by abstaining from politics, many involved themselves in ways that might perfect society or purify politics. Women circulated petitions, wrote letters to editors and politicians, published novels with political messages, established and ran various organizations, attended campaign debates or barbecues, and assembled to monitor the proceedings of Virginia's 1829–1830 constitutional convention and the 1861 secession convention.

Public policy revealed no change that might give women a formal say in public events, but women acted in ways that gave them some say anyway.

From the early republic to the Civil War, generations of women engaged in Virginia politics. Women found that they could participate in public activities, so long as their involvement was understood as benevolence, not politics; mediation, not conflict; persuasion, not coercion. From the nineteenth century's first decade, some of Virginia's women applied the notions of republican motherhood to establish and run charity boarding schools to assist poor young white women, who themselves had to be prepared to carry out their adult duties of raising men for citizenship in the new nation. Among their many public activities, white women organized the Female Colonization Society of Virginia.

Higher Education

The University of Virginia opened its doors in 1825. Making that event possible were the political leadership of Thomas Jefferson and the financial support of the state legislature. The new institution took up the role in the nineteenth century that the College of William and Mary had played during the eighteenth century: training new generations of Virginia's professional and political leaders. Its students—all of them white and male—generally came from the private academies that had sprouted across Tidewater and Piedmont Virginia. A great many attended for a session or two and then left to pursue other ventures. But by the 1840s one could stay at the university and earn a medical degree, a law degree, or a master's degree.

Meanwhile, a very different institution emerged on the other side of the Blue Ridge. The geography of higher education in Virginia can be seen as an ellipse, with the University of Virginia (UVA) at one focus and the Virginia Military Institute (VMI) at the other. VMI, which began classes in 1839, was also launched with financial support from the state. The new school trained soldiers, engineers, and teachers, and its students were far less likely to come from plantation families or the private academies. Yet, as at the university, the students and their teachers were white men. Not until after the Civil War would the state undertake to provide any sort of higher education for people who were not white as well as male.

So the new state of Virginia did not make the College of William and Mary a public college; rather, it established two new institutions. Yet citizens did not depend on the state for all opportunities in higher education. Most institutions of higher education in Virginia in the half century before the Civil War were private, not public. Typically affiliated with one Protestant denomination or an-

The University of Virginia in 1856, Thomas
Jefferson's "academical village," which had
been in operation by then for thirty-one years.
Virginia Historical Society, Richmond, Virginia,
Frank G. Bynum Fund and Carrie Wheeler Buck
Fund Purchase.

other, they served different purposes and constituencies. Among men's schools,
Hampden-Sydney College was founded by Presbyterians in 1776. Founded as
Methodist schools in the 1830s were Emory and Henry College and Randolph-
Macon College. Richmond College, which grew out of the Virginia Baptist Sem-
inary, dates from 1840. Roanoke College originated in the 1840s as a Lutheran
school, the Virginia Institute.

White women, categorically denied access to government-supported institutions, sometimes found their way instead to a female seminary. The Buckingham Female Collegiate Institute received a charter in 1837 and operated briefly,
and the first edition of what is now Longwood University was founded in Farmville two years later and lasted far longer. Mary Baldwin College, which originated as the Augusta Female Seminary, began operations in the 1840s, as did the

school that is now Hollins University. Averett University was founded in 1859 as a Baptist school, Union Female College.

Claudius Crozet and an Activist Southern State

Claudius Crozet came from outside Virginia, even outside the United States, but the undertakings that drew him to Virginia were very much homegrown. Shortly after the French Revolution broke out, and just about the time George Washington began his first term as president under the new U.S. Constitution, Claudius (or Claude) Crozet was born in France. He graduated from the Ecole Polytechnique and, after service as an officer with a battalion of bridge builders, participated in Napoleon Bonaparte's 1812 invasion of Russia, where he was captured and spent nearly two years as a prisoner of war. Subsequent to his release and his return to France, he resigned from the army in 1816, married, and soon departed France with his bride for the United States, where he spent the rest of his life, mostly in Virginia.

In September 1816, Crozet began teaching engineering at the U.S. Military Academy at West Point, New York. The academy, founded in 1802 during Thomas Jefferson's first term as president, was still a young institution, and Crozet had a profound influence on its engineering curriculum. He brought to it the best civil and military engineering known then in Europe. He introduced the study of descriptive geometry, the basic language of engineering, and he also taught such courses as artillery and topography. He taught cadets, many of them destined for the U.S. Army Corps of Engineers, how to build bridges, buildings, fortifications, canals, and roads.

Virginia attracted Crozet's attention, however, as a better place of employment. Hearing about the new University of Virginia, he wrote Thomas Jefferson in 1821 to inquire about a professorship there but was told that no school existed yet. Another opportunity arose, however, when the recently established Virginia Board of Public Works developed a vacancy for a principal engineer, and from 1823 to 1832, Crozet filled that position. His assignments included not only surveying routes for possible roads, canals, and eventually railroads but also rendering technical advice on how to choose among and then execute various projects. In particular, he came to favor a water route from Richmond west to Lynchburg but a railway from there through western Virginia to the Ohio River valley. Eastern interests, with no particular wish to see the western area thrive, dominated the legislature to which he reported. Local rivalries and legislative interference led him to resign his position and look for a more promising place

The Virginia Military Institute, Virginia's second state institution of higher education, in 1853. Virginia Historical Society, Richmond, Virginia.

to deploy his talents and experience. He left for Louisiana, where he served first as state engineer and then as president of a state-supported college.

In 1837 Crozet accepted an invitation to return to his old position as principal engineer for the Virginia Board of Public Works. For a time he made headway in promoting turnpikes, waterways, and railroads in the Old Dominion, but in 1843 the legislature terminated his position. In the meantime he had taken a major role in developing the new Virginia Military Institute. He served as president of the board of visitors, the governing board of the institution, from 1837 to 1845 and greatly influenced its curriculum, which, from the beginning of its operations in 1839, emphasized military and engineering studies. From 1845 through 1849, he served as principal of another school, the Richmond Academy.

In 1849 Crozet returned to engineering. That year the legislature incorporated the Blue Ridge Railroad and the Virginia and Tennessee Railroad, both of them lines that Crozet had championed during his tenure as the state's principal engineer. Certain that he wanted to direct the construction of one of the two lines, he

Claudius Crozet (1790?–1864). Crozet was a leader in Virginia's state ventures in transportation improvements and higher education. Painting by William Garl Brown. Courtesy Virginia Military Institute Museum.

obtained appointment as chief engineer of the Blue Ridge Railroad Company. That line would traverse the Blue Ridge between Charlottesville and Staunton and would require tunnels, cuts, and an iron bridge through extremely difficult terrain. Eight years later, the project successfully completed, Crozet moved to the District of Columbia, where he worked from 1857 to 1859 with Montgomery C. Meigs on the Washington aqueduct, a system designed to supply Georgetown and Washington—the twin cities of the District of Columbia—with water from the Great Falls of the Potomac River. Crozet's final position, in 1860 and 1861, was as chief engineer of the Virginia and Kentucky Railroad, a line intended to push west from a point in southwestern Virginia.

Crozet's career displayed the close relationship between civil engineering and military affairs in the nineteenth century, and it also displayed the significant state sponsorship, in the South as much as in the North, of education and transportation improvements in the pre–Civil War years. After his death he was honored for his work in both education and transportation. A building at Virginia Military Institute was named after him, and a station, later a town, on the Blue Ridge Railroad (later the Chesapeake and Ohio) was named for Crozet in 1876.

A School for Deaf or Blind White Children

In view of how little support the state gave education at any level, certainly aside from the University of Virginia and VMI, it is not surprising that Virginia lagged behind many states in initiating schooling for deaf or blind children. A private school for deaf children ran for a while in the 1810s, but occasional calls to establish a permanent institution with state support went largely unheeded, with opposition voiced largely in terms of there being so few people in need of such schooling, and with Governor Littleton W. Tazewell observing in 1834 that any such citizens might best be sent to schools in other states. In 1825 the legislature had sent a committee to visit such schools in Connecticut and Kentucky, and leading proponents later had deaf people put on exhibitions to show what an education could mean for them.

In 1838 the General Assembly provided funding for such a school and the next year specified that it would be located at Staunton. At the Virginia School for the Deaf and Blind (its later name), children of poor families would be supported with state funds, and other children might pay to attend. Seventy years later, the state established an additional institution, the Virginia State School for Colored Deaf and Blind Children, at Newport News.

Perfecting State Government

Proposals to establish a basis for supporting elementary schools or a state university, like those for inaugurating a massive program of internal improvements, met with more or less favorable outcomes depending on how many votes they could muster in the General Assembly. That support did not depend solely on how many Virginians favored or opposed an idea, because not all people could vote. And among those who could vote, their votes did not count equally. Those two questions, of suffrage and representation—always very much involved in questions of race and of region within Virginia—came up repeatedly, including at a state constitutional convention held in 1829–1830.

Chapter 10

Collision of Three Virginias

....

Giant fractures in Virginia society and politics came vividly into view in the early 1830s. The dual legacies of the Revolution, liberty and equality, were seen once again to clash. So were the most basic of contradictions, between slavery and equality, between white property and black freedom. First, in a state constitutional convention that met in 1829–1830, whites from the east and the west jousted over the distribution of political power—voting rights and legislative apportionment. Then a slave uprising, in summer 1831 in the southeastern part of Virginia, suggested a simmering hostility to slavery, a profound fracture between whites and blacks in the eastern half of the state. And the uprising led directly, at the next session of the General Assembly, to another clash between whites of the east and the west, over a proposal to phase slavery out. At stake was the very future of Virginia society and politics. Three key sets of players—two with varying degrees of formal political rights, the third with none at all—contended to secure their place or enhance their position.

Richmond (I): The Virginia Convention of 1829–1830

The Virginia Constitution of 1776, although widely revered as the product of the Revolutionary founding generation, came under attack in many quarters as inadequate and undemocratic. Thomas Jefferson gave his blessing in 1816 to a convention that would revise the constitution, and he suggested apportionment in the House of Delegates based on white population, voting rights extended to all white men, and even popular election to fill local offices and the governorship. Thus the ancient system of recruiting members of the county courts through appointment—which had always been undemocratic and was increasingly anomalous in nineteenth-century America—would be significantly changed. Disenfranchised white men not only in the west but also in the growing cities as well as in the rural areas of the east wanted the vote. The great sticking point for eastern legislators was the system of apportionment that safeguarded their control of state government, from the selection of state governors and U.S. senators to such key substantive issues as state aid to education and transportation. In the late 1820s, some of the leading opponents of change acted on the perception that the 1830 census would probably show that the west was pulling away from the east in total white population, so it would soon become even harder to contain change in a convention. Therefore, approval to call one was finally gained—with four delegates elected from each of the twenty-four senatorial districts.

The convention that met in Richmond in October 1829 had as its task modifying the original Virginia Constitution of 1776. Reformers had met with sustained resistance over many years, but now they had an opportunity to address key questions of political power, whether and how it might be redistributed by class and by region. The right to vote had remained so restricted that perhaps one-third of all white men had no formal role in politics. Regardless of who could vote, western whites saw their vote devalued in a system of legislative apportionment that left most members of both houses of the legislature representing eastern constituencies, and the General Assembly was the key to control of public affairs in Virginia.

The right to vote, especially in the west, was a matter of political symbolism—the value of a white man—and of political power. How high should taxes be, who should pay them, how should the proceeds be spent, and who should decide these matters? Indicating what was at stake, eastern delegates worried that westerners intended that "the poor of the West are to be educated at the expense of the East." Chapman Johnson, a delegate from Augusta County in the west, made the statement, characterizing a dominant perception among eastern delegates even as he tried to reassure them, but the concern was real. Just as important was the issue of spending, in one section rather than another, on roads and other internal improvements.

Former president James Madison reported the recommendation of the Legislative Committee: "Resolved, that in the apportionment of representation in the House of Delegates regard should be had to the white population exclusively." The reaction was immediate and direct, as John W. Green, a planter from Culpeper County, sought to replace the word "exclusively" with the phrase "and taxation combined." Political and economic power should, in this view, continue to be closely related. More particularly, property in the form of slaves should continue to be a significant consideration in determining the number of representatives from each section, east and west.

The west might or might not be hostile to slavery in the abstract, but if empowered sufficiently, western delegates might well shift more of the tax burden to the owners of slaves. In short, said an eastern spokesman, a shift in power to the west could lead to "the plundering of their property by raising their taxes and emancipating their slaves." The regional distribution of wealth, of slaves, and of slaveholders was only half the problem. Easterners recognized that the future would bring ever greater relative numbers of white residents in the west. The formula reported by Madison would, according to John Scott Jr.—a planter in eastern Fauquier County, the owner of more than fifty slaves—"give to the people west of the Blue Ridge, if not immediately, in a very short time, a majority in the Legislature." According to Southside delegate Benjamin Watkins Leigh, any shift to an exclusively white basis of legislative apportionment would be the "most crying injustice ever attempted in any land." Leigh warned that if such a proposal were adopted, representation would "rise in the Mountains," and as it did, taxation would rise "in the Lowlands," and the proceeds would "flow to the Mountains." In turn, should the west lose its bid for this fundamental change in the constitution, Philip P. Doddridge, representing far-northwest Brooke County in the Ohio panhandle, spoke favorably of forming a separate state.

In the end, the convention provided for periodic reapportionment—but only within each of four regions. The Piedmont garnered more power, and so did the Shenandoah Valley, where slavery was becoming increasingly important, but most importantly, the Tidewater preserved its strength. Under the Virginia Constitution of 1830, no matter what happened to the distribution of population—white or black, slave or free—the west could never gain control of the state. Eastern spokesmen felt relief at their narrow success; western spokesmen perceived a galling failure.

Meanwhile, as whites in the west jousted with whites in the east over the place of slavery in the social, economic, and political life of the Commonwealth, whites were not the only Virginians unhappy with the way things were or might become. Black Virginians, those people over whom whites were arguing, had far more to lose—or gain. One was Gabriel, a slave belonging to Thomas Prosser and then to his son, also Thomas. Born a few miles north of Richmond in the year of the Declaration of Independence, Gabriel worked as a blacksmith in Richmond as a young man, and in 1800 he participated in a grand conspiracy to mount a slave insurrection, centered in the Richmond area but reaching beyond to Petersburg and Norfolk. When his plan was betrayed by another slave, he was executed, along with twenty-six colleagues and followers. Another, three decades later, was Nat Turner.

Southampton County: Nat Turner's Uprising

Nat Turner was born in Southampton County, Virginia, in October 1800, days before the election that gave Thomas Jefferson the presidency. His parents, at least one of them born in Africa, were slaves belonging to Benjamin Turner. Nat Turner changed owners a number of times in the next thirty years, but he spent his entire life in his native county and so did not experience the disruption of being shipped south to the Cotton Kingdom. He nonetheless experienced separation from all the people who mattered most to him. Separated while very young from his father, who reportedly escaped to the North, he was raised by his mother and paternal grandmother. In 1809, Benjamin Turner loaned Nat and his mother, along with some other slaves, to his son Samuel Turner. The next year, Benjamin died, and Samuel inherited both mother and son. At the age of twelve, Nat was put to work as a field hand. By 1822 he had married a slave named Cherry, but that year he was separated from his wife and his mother when, following the death of Samuel Turner, each was sold to a different owner. Nat Turner became the property of Thomas Moore, but Moore died in 1828. Turner then became the legal property of Thomas Moore's nine-year-old son, Putnam Moore, whose mother married Joseph Travis in 1829, and thus Joseph Travis gained control of Nat Turner, who continued to be the property of the child Putnam Moore.

Whites and blacks alike recognized Turner's exceptional intelligence even as a child, so much so that it was widely said of him that he "would never be of any service to anyone as a slave," that—as his parents had drummed into him—he was "intended for some great purpose." As a child he learned to read. In his teens he began preaching at slaves' clandestine religious meetings, and in 1827 he even baptized a white overseer, Etheldred T. Brantley. All through his teens and twenties he worked as a field hand—and found himself separated from one family member after another. He had to live apart from his wife and their children. As he approached thirty years of age, standing about five feet seven inches, weighing 150 pounds, very dark skinned, wearing a mustache, often projecting a commanding presence, he belonged to a little boy. None of his owners had been particularly cruel or unkind, but each had presumed to be his master.

Turner was proud, brooding, austere, and deeply religious, and he saw slavery as a great and terrible serpent, Satan institutionalized. On May 12, 1828, he experienced a vision that led him to believe that God had chosen him to lead a great uprising of blacks against whites. As he was later reported to have recalled, he "heard a loud noise in the heavens, and the Spirit instantly appeared to me and said the Serpent was loosened, and Christ had laid down the yoke he had borne for the sins of men." The Spirit went on to declare that Nat Turner should take that yoke on "and fight against the Serpent, for the time was fast approaching when the first should be last and the last should be first." Turner must watch the heavens for signs that would tell him when, and then he "should arise" and "slay [his] enemies with their own weapons."

Turner recruited four slave men to work with him—Nelson, Sam, Henry, and Hark, each a field hand and active in a slave church—and in the summer of 1831 he set a date for action, the Fourth of July, later postponed to August 21, a Sunday. The rebellion began in the early hours of August 22. The Travis place was the first stop, and the first to be killed were young Putnam Moore, his mother Sally, and her husband Joseph. "General Nat" swung first at Joseph Travis, and Will, a member of the small army, finished him off. More than fifty more whites died at the hands of Turner and his men during that Monday and Tuesday.

Supported by forces ranging from the local patrol and vigilante groups to units of the U.S. Army and Navy stationed at Fortress Monroe, Virginia militia captured or dispersed Turner's comrades. Dozens of his followers were tried, convicted, and either executed or transported out of Virginia to slavery elsewhere. Scores more among slaves and free blacks in other communities were also tried or were killed without the formality of a trial.

Turner himself was found on Sunday, October 30, hiding in the woods less than two miles from the Travis place. Brought to trial on November 5 in Jerusalem (later Courtland), he was convicted of "conspiring to rebel and making insurrection." He was hanged six days later from an oak tree. While in jail awaiting trial, Turner granted an interview to Thomas R. Gray, a white lawyer Turner's age, and the result of their collaboration continues to supply much of what is known about Turner and the rebellion, as within days of Turner's execution, Gray published "The Confessions of Nat Turner, the Leader of the Late Insurrection in Southampton, Va., as Fully and Voluntarily Made to Thomas R. Gray." Various southern states responded to the events of August 1831 by tightening their laws against slaves and free blacks alike. Moreover, in private imagination and in the discourse of political debate, the rebellion supplied the ominous image of a slave rebel as a stark alternative to that of the contented slave.

Richmond (II): The Great Debate over Slavery

In direct response to Nat Turner's uprising, a far-reaching debate on slavery occurred in the Virginia House of Delegates in early 1832. The 1831–1832 legislature convened three months after Turner led his rebellion, and only a few weeks after

Turner's capture, trial, and execution. White Virginians sought security against a recurrence, and many—even some leading slaveowners in eastern Virginia—were prepared to consider an end to the institution Turner had rebelled against. Governor John Floyd, who hailed from the west's Montgomery County, hoped that a program might be launched during his administration that would bring an eventual end to slavery in Virginia and, in the meantime, greater control over all black Virginians and the expulsion of free blacks.

The legislature's lower house appointed a select committee to consider the removal of free blacks from the state and a program of gradual abolition. Mecklenburg County's William O. Goode, however, introduced a resolution stating that it was "not expedient to legislate" on the subject of emancipation. Albemarle County's Thomas Jefferson Randolph, grandson of Thomas Jefferson, countered with a resolution calling for gradual emancipation. According to Randolph's measure, all children born to slave mothers after July 4, 1840, would, if still in Virginia, become the property of the state, women when they reached age eighteen and men at age twenty-one. They would then be hired out until their labor had raised funds sufficient to pay for their transportation out of the United States. Young female slaves would begin obtaining their freedom in 1858, as would their brothers in 1861.

Half a century earlier, the state of Pennsylvania had taken the first action of any legislature in the New World to undo slavery when it passed a gradual-emancipation act in 1780. By the time of Turner's uprising, every northern state had acted to end slavery, but no state south of Pennsylvania had gone any further than Virginia, which, in 1782, merely eased a restriction that had previously kept slaveowners from manumitting their slaves.

Only in its broad outlines did Randolph's 1832 proposal resemble Pennsylvania's. Pennsylvania's law terminated slaves' bondage at birth but required them to work for the mother's master until adulthood. It postponed final freedom for slaves yet unborn to the age of twenty-eight. But that law also granted free blacks all the rights that their white neighbors enjoyed, including the right to remain in their home state and the right to vote, and it sought to protect black Pennsylvanians from being sold out of state. Virginia's proposal did nothing to expand the definition of black freedom, and its supporters anticipated that slaveowners, acting to protect their investment, would seek a market in the Deep South.

Two weeks of intense debate followed the introduction of competing proposals in the 1832 Virginia legislature's lower house. A western representative, William Ballard Preston of Montgomery County, proposed an amendment to easterner Goode's resolution, to declare it "expedient" that the legislature enact an emancipation measure. Hanover County delegate William Henry Roane, grandson of Patrick Henry, unapologetically rejected the notion of the "natural equality of man" and explained, "I am not one of those who have ever revolted at the idea or practice of slavery." Rather, Roane said, "I think slavery as much a correlative of liberty as cold is of heat." Similarly, Alexander G. Knox of the Southside's Mecklenburg County declared slavery to be "indispensably requisite . . . to preserve the forms of a Republican Government."

By contrast, proponents of some action to curtail slavery, or at least its continued growth in Virginia, condemned the "evil" of slavery—sometimes because it injured slaves, always because it damaged the prospects of white Virginians. Buckingham County delegate Philip A. Bolling conceded that slave labor might be defended, but no such allowance might be made, he insisted, for the slave trade, "dividing husbands and wives, parents and children." Most of the rhetoric in support of taking some action, however, emphasized slavery, not the slave trade, and the damage slavery did to whites, not blacks. Slavery retarded the growth of education, the development of industry, and the spread of internal improvements; it imposed on nonslaveholders the task of manning the patrols that safeguarded slavery; and it drove nonslaveholders out of the state.

Reformers challenged the sanctity of property as it applied to slaves; their opponents insisted on their property rights and attacked as impractical every proposed remedy for slavery. The two groups agreed only that free blacks should be expelled. George W. Summers—who, though a native of the east, resided in and represented the west's Kanawha County—stated the central postulates of the reformers' approach to the question of property: that the right to own property was contingent, not absolute, especially when it fundamentally threatened society's well-being, and that owners of slaves had fewer, if any, claims on property they did not yet possess, slave children not yet born: "Sir, all property is held subordinate to, and only as it promotes the general welfare of, the community in which it exists. . . . Mr. Speaker, by emancipating the *post nati* [slaves not yet born], the interests of the present owners are but little affected."

No one in the debate advocated any proposal to end slavery soon—or to permit a significant continued black presence in Virginia after an end to slavery. As William H. Broadnax of Dinwiddie County declared: "No emancipation of slaves should ever be tolerated, unaccompanied by their immediate removal from among us."

Thomas Jefferson Randolph understood that his Virginia depended for its well-being on a continued "exportation" of surplus slaves, else the number would, he estimated, exceed 1 million by 1860 and approach 3 million by 1900. White Virginians still had some control over the outcome, but Nat Turner's uprising pointed up a "despairing future," and slavery must end, said Randolph—

"Whether it is effected by the energy of our own minds, or by the bloody scenes of Southampton and St. Domingo, is a tale for future history!" In a variation on that theme, James McDowell, of the Shenandoah Valley's Rockbridge County, denied that it was the news of Nat Turner's actions in faraway Southampton County that so disturbed white Virginians across the state. Rather, it was "the suspicion that a Nat Turner might be in every family, that the same bloody deed could be acted over at any time in any place."

Another apocalyptic vision was also voiced. Charles J. Faulkner, from Berkeley County in the west, saw his part of the state vulnerable to a flow of the east's surplus slave population, and he attacked such an outcome: "If we are to remain united, we must have some guarantee, that the evils under which you labor shall not be extended to us," to the white Virginians "west of the Blue Ridge." He rejected a future in which "the bold and intrepid forester of the west must yield to the slothful and degraded African—and those hills and vallies which until now have re-echoed with the songs and industry of freemen, shall have become converted into desolation and barrenness by the withering footsteps of slavery." Brunswick County's John E. Shell would not suffer such an attack in silence. Faulkner, he said, "in order, I suppose, to stimulate us to action, told us that his course in relation to a *division* of *the State*, would depend on future events. By this declaration, we are left to infer, that should his efforts in the cause of abolition fail, then he will go for division. . . . But I take this opportunity to say, in the language of truth, that if this question be carried against us, it will immediately be met by a proposition to *divide this State*." Thus some easterners, too, would split Virginia rather than lose this debate.

Members of the Virginia House of Delegates divided into two main groups of roughly the same size. One group supported some immediate action toward the eventual abolition of slavery; the other stood opposed. A small but crucial swing group favored eventual emancipation but resisted any specific action at that time. Preston's amendment, declaring that abolition was "expedient," lost, 58–73. The vehemence of proslavery spokesmen had paralyzed enough wavering delegates that a majority refused to take any action against slavery in 1832.

Two years earlier, in the state constitutional convention, easterners had rejected calls from western delegates for greater representation, legislative apportionment according to white population. Had the Virginia Constitution of 1830 granted westerners' wish for greater power in the legislature, the 1832 vote on slavery would have been closer, though the reformers might still have lost; and had a gradual-emancipation measure won in the House of Delegates, it would have faced tremendous opposition in the Senate. The next Virginia constitution, in 1851, offered concessions to western Virginia on voting and apportionment. It also empowered the legislature to remove free blacks. But it curtailed slaveowners' right to free their slaves, and—eliminating any possible repeat of the 1832 debate—it expressly barred the legislature from acting against slavery.

The Resolutions of 1830 and 1832

At the end of two years of concentrated political turbulence, Virginia politics and policy appeared to have changed little, if it all. The eastern elite had made the scantest of concessions in either the franchise or the system of legislative apportionment. Having blocked a redistribution of legislative power, they turned back a challenge by other white Virginians to the very system of slavery. Even after the Nat Turner Uprising and the Great Debate over slavery, matters of race and slavery looked as if they might well flow on into the future without any changes in direction.

Appearances deceived. All sides felt vulnerable, under attack, on the defensive. Political leaders on each side had threatened that if the other side won, separation must follow. It wasn't just the west saying the east must not dominate, it was also the east replying that, if its dominance were lost, the east would have to separate. With so much at stake, matters might be resolved for a time on one issue or another, but they could not be relied upon to stay resolved, either as to which white social group should rule or as to whether slavery should persist—most of all when the two issues were so intertwined.

Three major social groups—eastern whites, western whites, and eastern blacks—had been heard from. Such a triangular configuration was by its nature unstable. How the three would play off each other would remain a central issue in Virginia society and politics through the remainder of the nineteenth century. The slaves would no doubt have much more to say, as certainly would their owners. Meanwhile, spokesmen for the west and spokesmen for the east had in turn spoken publicly of the prospects of dividing the state. Yet to be fully heard from was the largest group of Virginians—whites who, whether from east or west of the Blue Ridge, owned no slaves, people who were neither slaves nor slaveowners.

Between 1830 and 1832, at the very time Virginians were arguing so stridently among themselves over race and slavery, John C. Calhoun of South Carolina was clarifying his call to protect the interests of slaveowners in a world increasingly dangerous for slavery, and William Lloyd Garrison of Massachusetts was launching his newspaper the *Liberator,* with its unambiguous call for an end to slavery in the South and a beginning of racial equality everywhere in the United States. Developments and personalities in the Boston area, and those as well in the Deep South, continued to affect developments in Virginia. Outside voices were critical to the unfolding struggle throughout the American nation. But Virginians demonstrated during these episodes that the struggle over the future of slavery in Virginia was not just an external matter, and they showed that they could mount the main arguments without help from outside. The struggle within Virginia was homegrown. The questions had not gone away, and other crises soon offered new occasions for those questions to be addressed.

Chapter 11

Race and Slavery, 1820s–1850s

....

During the generation after the triple events of 1830–1832, racial identity and chattel slavery remained at the heart of public events. Every decade, tens of thousands of Virginia slaves made their way to the Cotton Kingdom, whether sold south to new owners or taken south by current owners, especially during the 1830s, when Virginia's slave population actually declined despite continued strong natural increase. By the thousands, white Virginians left the state as well, whether to other slave states or to places without slavery. Free blacks left the state, too, seeking a more generous definition of black freedom than could be found in Virginia. Only to a tiny degree were these emigrants from Virginia offset by newcomers, among them immigrants from Ireland or Germany who found their way to Norfolk or Richmond in the late 1840s or the 1850s. This chapter explores change and continuity regarding slavery in Virginia society and politics; the experiences of black Virginians, slave and free; and the varied attitudes and behavior of white Virginians toward these black residents.

Virginia, West and East

The migration of native Virginians out of Virginia—and into territory that either had once been part of a greater Virginia or became available for settlement by Americans in the aftermath of the Louisiana Purchase—constitutes a hugely important chapter in the social and political history of pre–Civil War America. Yet an associated matter bears exploration as well. Had Virginia in the 1790s already been defined in terms that came true in the 1860s, the state's history might have taken a very different turn. Developments in western Virginia, including migration into the region, profoundly affected the state's political history. Meanwhile, the exodus of eastern Virginians affected both the east and the political rivalry between east and west.

Populating the Shenandoah Valley in the half century before the American Revolution were people moving southwest out of Pennsylvania. They shared the experience of great numbers of eastern Virginians in having begun their lives as indentured servants, but they typically did so at a later time, and when they headed south out of Pennsylvania seeking land of their own, they brought other languages, other religious persuasions, other national origins than had their eastern Virginia counterparts. When they moved into or through the Valley, they were coming south, not west across the Blue Ridge. The world they created was not a western variant of Virginia so much as it was a southern variant of Pennsylvania, not so much an extension of England as it was a transplanted version of Germany or the northern part of Ireland. Their identities as Presbyterians or Lutherans predisposed them to maintain identities different from easterners, especially from Anglicans/Episcopalians.

Whether in the Shenandoah or, even more, farther west and southwest, western Virginians developed priorities that distinguished them from eastern Virginians. For an extended period—before, during, and after the Revolution—their vulnerable position on the military frontier left them skeptical that they could count on eastern politicians. Later, from the 1810s through the 1840s, they perceived the people of eastern Virginia as arrogating more power in the state legislature than they deserved and, as a consequence, denying the west the public funds needed to promote improvements in transportation and education.

In areas even farther west, another trajectory brought settlers to their new homes. The Virginia panhandle, jutting up between eastern Ohio and western Pennsylvania, was a tremendous distance, and not only in terms of miles, from Richmond. Proportionally more settlers there in the 1840s and 1850s came from other states, even other countries, than from other places in Virginia. Much of western Virginia was more like Ohio than like eastern Virginia. Slaves were few, and the owners of slaves were few. The need to safeguard slavery from northern interference was not a consuming consideration.

The west was not all of a piece, though. By the 1830s, the Shenandoah Valley was in transition toward a greater reliance on slave labor in agriculture. Moreover, it became ever clearer that slaves could be profitably engaged in nonagricultural activities, as historian Charles Dew has shown about iron manufacturing at Buffalo Forge in the Valley. By the 1850s, as a railroad made its way through southwestern Virginia, connecting east with west, economic and political ties developed between the east and that part of the west. These various patterns, overlays on the eighteenth-century origins of the western settlements, pointed toward western Virginia's becoming a separate state in the 1860s—configured to exclude both the Shenandoah Valley, where slavery had become more prominent, and the southwest, through which the Virginia and Tennessee Railroad passed.

Meanwhile, eastern Virginia, though it had been changing as well, continued in many ways to resemble the eighteenth-century colony, based on plantation slavery. In 1830, both the Tidewater and the Piedmont had more slaves than whites. East of the Blue Ridge, county populations ranged from 24 to 69 percent white, and few were as low as 30. Between the Blue Ridge and the Ohio River, counties ranged from 2 to 31 percent slave, and few were as high as 20. Despite continued high natural increase, Virginia's slave population actually declined in the 1830s as migration to the cotton country of Alabama and Mississippi surged. Exports of the most valuable commodity grown on eastern Virginia's plantations, new slaves, helped keep the overall eastern population from growing very much, while the west kept up a rapid growth, and westerners could look forward to a time when white residents in their section would outnumber those in the east.

For many years after the Louisiana Purchase, tobacco and slaves continued to dominate the rural economy of much of eastern Virginia. Yet Virginia slaves always had worked—and increasingly did work—at other tasks than growing tobacco. Across the eighteenth century, hundreds of slaves worked on the Northern Neck, along the Rappahannock River, for John Tayloe I and then John Tayloe II, many of them in tobacco, but others in other crops, at an ironworks, as domestics, as gardeners, or as carpenters. By the nineteenth century, the hundreds of slaves working for John Tayloe III grew no tobacco. Rather, the field hands among them concentrated on wheat and corn as the major cash crops, while they also raised hogs and corn for their own meals.

Slaves also worked in tobacco factories in Richmond, and many slaves worked near or on waterways, whether moving goods along rivers or the coast or loading ships at the docks. Slaves in cities, such as Richmond and Norfolk, often had somewhat greater control over their work lives and their personal lives than did most rural slaves. They also had greater access to means of escape from slavery, especially by boat from either Richmond or Norfolk. George Teamoh, born a slave in Norfolk in 1818, learned somehow to read and write, and he worked as a caulker and carpenter in the U.S. government's Gosport Navy Yard, among many other jobs, until his wife and children were sold away in 1853. Then he made his way to freedom by way of a merchant ship carrying tobacco out of Virginia's port city to Germany.

Picture of this memorable Country.
May. 26th. 53.

The Virginia and Tennessee rail-road through Montgomery Co.—
An awful and magnificent appearance, rocky fine stones ascend out
of deep and gloomy—Vallies, or are Surrounded by dark gulfs and
bottomless abysses in which water is roaring,

The Virginia and Tennessee Railroad. Sketch by Lewis Miller (1796–1882), a Pennsylvania carpenter, who had a lifelong hobby of sketching scenes everywhere he went. Several times he visited Christiansburg, Virginia, home of his cousin Charles Miller. There, in 1853, Lewis Miller sketched a railroad being built through Montgomery County. Constructing a railroad through mountainous terrain required a tremendous investment of labor, capital, and engineering expertise. As the Virginia and Tennessee Railroad pushed through southwestern Virginia in the 1850s, it fostered—as eastern politician Henry A. Wise, for one, had hoped—the emergence of a more commercial agriculture in the region, together with a greater incidence of slaveholding, as well as closer economic and political ties to the east, ties that helped keep that part of the state in Virginia when a third of the counties broke away and formed the new state of West Virginia. Abby Aldrich Rockefeller Folk Art Museum, The Colonial Williamsburg Foundation, Williamsburg, VA. Gift of Dr. and Mrs. Richard M. Kain in memory of George Hay Kain.

Slavery and the Slaves

The vast majority of African Americans in Virginia in the 1850s had been born into slavery and would remain slaves all their lives—or, as it happened, into the 1860s. The narratives of former Virginia slaves, based on interviews conducted and written down in the 1930s, can take us back to those times, whether through people's direct memories or through stories their parents and others told them, and thus hearsay testimony rather than direct experience. Mrs. Patience Martin Avery, for example, was born in Richmond in 1863 and was interviewed in Petersburg in 1937. Mrs. Avery had her own vivid recollections of an event that took place in 1870, but she was reporting what she had heard from others when she observed in response to questions about the slave trade that "Richmond was a great slave market."

One feature that suffuses the narratives of former slaves is whipping. Arthur Greene, replying to a question on the subject, agreed—as his language was transcribed—to "tell you how dey uster whup slaves. Um! Um! Um! Hit makes me shudder when I draw dat pitcher 'fo' you." But even if there had never been a whipping, the terrors of the slave trade were omnipresent. Greene also spoke on that painful subject: "My brother was sold at one dem sales to South Caroliny when he was 'bout nine years old. Dr. Minnifield bought him. Dat doctor said all dem old white folks down south was mean to slaves. Brother came back home de third yeah after de surrender."

Indeed, the slave trade, particularly the interstate slave trade, pervades the Virginia slave narratives. Market forces extracted many tens of thousands of enslaved Virginians from the Upper South to the Deep South. Slave families were not recognized under Virginia law, but slaves themselves often had very close emotional ties to their parents, siblings, and children, as well as to other community members. And the interstate slave trade put slave families and communities in constant jeopardy. Mrs. Fanny Berry, interviewed in Petersburg in 1937, was in her twenties when she moved to Petersburg in "the first year of the Civil War" from her slave home in Appomattox County. Prompted by a question, she began: "Now, you want to know how slaves were sold. Um, um, um, sad, sad times. . . . Child, it makes me shudder when I hear talk of dat cotton country. I ain't never seen dar an' I don't wanta!"

Families and communities experienced separation because of their slave status. Black families were divided among heirs in the white family, individuals were hired out, and the slave trade was a core feature of slavery times. Moreover, owners and overseers frequently invoked the prospect of being shipped farther south as a weapon to secure compliant behavior from the slaves in their charge.

Reverend Israel Massie, who had been a teenager during the war, spoke with black interviewer Susie Byrd at length and with passion from the City Home in Petersburg about his recollections of long-ago slavery: "Lord chile, ef ya start me I kin tell ya a mess 'bout reb times, but I ain't tellin' white folks nuthin' 'cause I'm skeer'd to make enemies. Lord chile, dar wuz mo' grievin' and mo' crying over de family partin'—jes like de grief when ya sister or brother dies. Pew! Pew! Pew! Speculatin' on us humans! God's gwine punish deir chillun's chillun, yas sur! Dem wuz terrible times! I had two brothers sold away an' ain't never seen 'em no mo' 'til dis day." Anna Harris, born in 1846, recalled a great many years later: "No white man ever been in my house. Don't 'low it. Dey sole my sister Kate. I saw it wid dese eyes. Sole her in 1860, and I ain't seed nor heard of her since. Folks say white folks is all right dese days. Maybe dey is, maybe dey isn't. But I can't stand to see 'em. Not on my place." More than seventy years after the searing event, Anna Harris was still in pain, still in fury—she was not reconciled; that crucial piece of the past could not be fixed. And about "brother John," said Mrs. Louise Jones, who was about ten when the war ended, "Um! Um! He was sol', den I los' track o' him. De man dat bought him took his slaves 'way down South. Dat's right fer, ain't it?"

Though only a small proportion of white Virginians migrated to the Deep South, a large majority of black migrants did so, taken by their owners or sold off to slave traders. Virginia slaves, when they moved south and west, mostly left tobacco country for a land where they would work cotton or sugar. Former slaves' narratives from Gulf Coast states in the twentieth century point back toward that migration out of Virginia. Ellen Betts, for one, recounted in 1937 how her master and his hundreds of slaves migrated from Virginia to Louisiana around 1853. Sarah Allen moved with her family (except her father, a white man) and her owner from a small holding in the Blue Ridge to Texas in the 1850s. Henry Baker, who was born a slave on a small holding some six miles south of Richmond, reported being taken, along with his mother and siblings—but not his father, who lived on a neighboring farm—by his owner to Texas early in the Civil War. Virginia Bell was born on a Louisiana plantation near Opelousas, but both her parents were Virginia natives, brought from different places in Virginia to Louisiana by slave traders; her father had had a wife and five children back in Virginia, before he was sold away from them.

Fannie Brown, born on a farm near Richmond, "wuz sol' from my mudder w'en I wuz 'bout five years ole" and taken to Texas. Isabella Boyd remembered smatterings of her early childhood in rural Virginia. She also remembered being separated from her parents and journeying by boat from Richmond—"ev'y time we look back an' t'ink 'bout home it mek us sad"—all the way to Galveston.

Slave Trader, Sold to Tennessee. In 1853, folk artist Lewis Miller sketched this depiction of the sights and sounds of a coffle of slaves making their involuntary way from Augusta County to Tennessee. Miller recorded the words he heard these slaves sing or chant—like the title of the sketch, a composite—describing on the one hand the misery of their enslavement and their forced removal, and on the other hand the prospect of heaven, that "happy shore" where they would be separated from loved ones no more: "Arise! Arise! and weep no more, dry up your tears, we shall part no more. Come rise we go to Tennessee, that happy shore. To old Virginia, never—never—return." Abby Aldrich Rockefeller Folk Art Museum, The Colonial Williamsburg Foundation, Williamsburg, VA. Gift of Dr. and Mrs. Richard M. Kain in memory of George Hay Kain.

Some of Virginia's so-called slave narratives came from people who never were enslaved. Census figures tell us, and the narratives reflect this, that roughly one in ten black Virginians on the eve of universal emancipation was already free— although what free black Virginians experienced in the 1850s was a black south- ern variant of freedom during slavery times. George Lewis, who was born in 1859 in Richmond and grew up there, explained in a 1937 interview with Faith Morris, a black woman far younger than he, that both his parents had been free: "My mother was set free by her young mistress two years before I was born." She and her sister both came to Richmond, he explained, where they soon mar- ried young black men. His father, Lewis reported, was a black businessman who hired out boats on the James River. Because his mother was free by the time he was born, young George was born free. Born about the same time in Petersburg was Mrs. Octavia Featherstone, who said of her siblings and her mother, Mary Tinsley, "No, none of us was ever slaves." Mrs. Sarah Wooden Johnson told Susie Byrd that although at least one of her grandfathers had been a slave, her parents had both been free, and "I ain't no slave—ain't never bin one."

One story of race in Virginia is that of John Mercer Langston. Langston's father, Ralph Quarles, had once owned Lucy Langston, but they became lov- ers. He had in mind freeing her at some point, but when the legislature enacted the 1806 law requiring newly freed slaves to leave the state within a year of their manumission, he rushed to free her before it could go into effect. Whether she was slave or free, they could not marry, because of the Virginia law against in- terracial marriage. Banned from marrying, at least they could live out the rest of their lives together in Louisa County. John Mercer Langston, the youngest of their three sons, born in 1829, was still a child when both his parents died, and he and his brothers were packed off to Ohio, where they had people to look af- ter them. Langston went to school, graduated from Oberlin College, became a lawyer, and went into public life. Ohio gave Langston advantages he could not have experienced in Virginia.

Beginning in 1831, a Virginia law declared it a crime for anyone to conduct a school attended by African Americans. In the early 1850s, Margaret Douglass, a white woman, was teaching such a school in Norfolk, attended by children who were free but also black. Arrested and convicted for this crime, she went to jail for a month in 1854. In Ohio, the working definition of black freedom, though hardly identical with white freedom, was far more expansive than in Virginia. In both states, the biracial young man John Mercer Langston was defined as black, but in Virginia, the law would have forbidden him from attending even a primary school. In Ohio he could go to college.

Thomas Roderick Dew

Margaret Douglass was hardly typical of white Virginians. Thomas Roderick Dew, born in 1802, grew up in a planter family in Tidewater Virginia, taught at the College of William and Mary from 1826 until his death in 1846, and gained wide influence with his essays on public issues. He gained particular notice in the early 1830s with his essays on slavery, in which he proclaimed the institution's merits and rejected as impractical the Virginia General Assembly's enacting any kind of legislation designed to end slavery in the Old Dominion.

In the 1831–1832 legislative session, the Virginia House of Delegates had conducted its searching debate as to whether, in the wake of Nat Turner's slave uprising, the state should gradually emancipate and then deport all its slaves. Dismayed by the debate, Dew rushed a lengthy essay, "Abolition of Negro Slavery," to publication in the *American Quarterly Review* of September 1832. He also published an expanded version, *Review of the Debate in the Virginia Legislature of 1831 and 1832* (1832). That work reached a wide readership at the time and was selected after Dew's death for inclusion in *The Pro-Slavery Argument as Maintained by the Most Distinguished Writers of the Southern States* (1852).

Dew lectured in *Review of the Debate* against "the crude, undigested theories of tampering legislators." Politicians' "passion for legislation" against slavery, he warned, intruded upon "dangerous and delicate business" and threatened to do "irretrievable" damage to Virginia. Dew sought to demonstrate why no good, and much evil, would come from legislative interference.

Dew demonstrated "the impossibility of colonizing the blacks." How could deportation be financed, he asked, and where would the emigrants go? Drawing on historical analogies, such as Europeans migrating to the Caribbean or to North America, he contended that African Americans, if they went to Africa, would die in droves of disease and would create great hostilities with their neighbors. No matter how conceived, the costs of forced colonization would be too great for everyone affected.

Nor could emancipation be accomplished without deportation. Virginia's slaves, whether from nature or nurture, were unfit for freedom in Virginia, Dew claimed. They would work only under compulsion. And white Virginians, with their customs and prejudices, would not permit much black freedom in Virginia. Dew rejected, as irrelevant to Virginia, the models of the successful abandonment of slavery in Europe or the North. The North had had few slaves to free, and European societies had developed a middle class that could gradually absorb slaves as free people. The South had far too many slaves for its middle class to absorb and, unlike European societies, had an unfree population that differed in physical appearance: A black southerner, said Dew, "forever wears the indelible symbol of his inferior condition."

Having disposed of the arguments for emancipation, whether with or without deportation, Dew proceeded to adopt a proslavery stance—"to demonstrate . . . the complete justification of the whole southern country in a further continuance of . . . slavery." He denied that most slaves suffered from either discontent or poor treatment: "A merrier being does not exist on the face of the globe than the negro slave of the United States." For Dew, Nat Turner better symbolized why whites should desist from collective action than why they should feel an urgency to act: "But one limited massacre is recorded in Virginia history; let her liberate her slaves," and it "will be almost certain to bring down ruin and degradation on both the whites and the blacks."

As one support for his position, Dew reached for a biblical justification for slavery. In the Old Testament the "children of Israel were themselves slave-holders," he wrote, and in the New Testament, though slavery in the Roman Empire was "a thousand times more cruel than slavery in our own country," Christ himself never challenged slavery. In addition, slavery, for Dew, rather than being incompatible with republican liberty, was basic to it, for slavery fostered "the perfect spirit of equality so prevalent among the whites of all the slave-holding states." Even more important, Dew could not compromise on the sanctity of property, regardless of whether that property was slaves. He called on "Western Virginia and the non-slave-holders of Eastern Virginia, not to be allured" by arguments that the state could properly interfere in such property holding. For Dew, the French Revolution demonstrated why no legislature should be so wantonly foolish as to "tamper" with "the fundamental relations of society."

Then, however, Dew's rhetoric veered from explicitly proslavery to implicitly antislavery. If only the legislature would leave slavery alone—and especially if it would foster improvements in transportation, whether roads, canals, or railroads—Virginia would emulate Maryland in gradually abandoning slavery through social and economic evolution. Towns would emerge in rural eastern Virginia, and plantations would become farms. Let the slave trade to the Deep South continue. Free labor would replace slave labor in Virginia, as white immigrants displaced black emigrants. Looking far down the road, Dew could envision an all-white, free-labor Virginia. Not only was a legislative emancipation scheme incapable of accomplishing such an outcome, it would make things far worse for everyone rather than any better for anyone. "In due time," Dew forecast, "abolitionists will find" that this natural process was "working to their heart's content, increasing the prosperity of Virginia, and diminishing the evils of slavery without those impoverishing effects which all other schemes must *necessarily* have."

The political economist Dew, a devotee of free trade but not of laissez-faire, assigned government at each level, national and state, a particular role in regard to slavery. He blamed the federal government and its high tariffs on imported goods, not slavery, for the South's economic malaise. The federal government's tariff policies damaged Virginia, he wrote, and a state-sponsored emancipation-ist scheme would damage Virginia even more. The state government should protect, not challenge, wealth invested in slaves, and its actions should foster economic growth and development through banking and transportation im-provements.

Dew died young, in the 1840s, so he did not live to observe or write about later developments in the struggle over slavery. The challenges to legislating the system away had led Dew to conclude that the system must persist for the fore-seeable future. Subsequent proslavery theoreticians built on Dew's work, but they ignored his words on "the evils of slavery." Similarly, historians have tended to characterize Dew as proslavery, when in fact his writings reveal a powerful ambivalence regarding the institution. His was a contingent commitment to the institution. He could imagine Virginia without slavery, but he could not imagine a postslavery world in which large numbers of black Virginians lived, let alone lived on terms of freedom and equality.

Thornton Stringfellow

Thornton Stringfellow was perhaps the leading proslavery spokesman in the Old South to base his arguments on the Bible. Born in 1788 in Fauquier County in Virginia's northern Piedmont, he lived there or in neighboring Culpeper County most of his life. The population in his part of Virginia was majority slave—Culpeper County's population in 1850 was 42 percent white, 54 percent slave, and 4 percent free black. Stringfellow himself, the son of a slaveowning family, owned about sixty slaves. He was also a Baptist minister.

In the realm of reformers in pre–Civil War America, Stringfellow resembled his northern counterparts in many of his ideas, but not in his defense of slavery. While he involved himself in temperance and in domestic and foreign missions, he also committed himself to the South's proslavery crusade. In the 1840s, when northern churches determined to exclude slaveowners from Baptist missionary activities, he convinced his fellow Baptists in the South to separate themselves and organize a Southern Baptist Convention—an important early indication of the growing political rift over slavery between northerners and southerners.

As a proslavery spokesman, minister, and planter, Stringfellow contributed a scriptural variant to the proslavery writings of the South in the 1840s and 1850s. The Bible offered a sure guide to "the true principles of humanity," he wrote in *A Brief Examination of Scripture Testimony on the Institution of Slavery* (1841). He demonstrated that God in the Old Testament ordained slavery and that Christ and the apostles in the New Testament, never challenging the institution, directed all Christians to accept their stations in life, whether as servant or as master. How could it be, Stringfellow demanded of abolitionists in the North, that "God has ordained slavery, and yet slavery is the greatest of sins"? Stringfellow's writings made it easier for his fellow white southerners to view the institution of slavery as consistent with their understanding of Christianity.

Neither corporal punishment nor the breakup of slave families gave Stringfellow pause—these, he held, were supported in scripture. Nor did it trouble him that Abraham relied on an army of 300 of his own slaves—that so many Old Testament "servants" might "bear arms"—although America's variant of slavery displayed nothing of the sort. The "essential particulars" of slavery in the Old Testament and in the Old South, that it was "involuntary" and "hereditary," were what mattered. But then there was race. "The guardianship and control of the black race, by the white," he argued in *Scriptural and Statistical Views in Favor of Slavery* (1841), "is an indispensable Christian duty, to which we must yet look if we would secure the well-being of both races."

Henry "Box" Brown

Henry "Box" Brown, born a slave in the Piedmont's Louisa County in 1815, was fourteen when his elderly master died. Then the Brown family was divided, occasioning what Brown later called "the most severe trial to my feelings which I had ever endured," when he was sent alone to work in Richmond. At about age twenty he married another Richmond slave, Nancy, and they lived as happily as possible under slavery for perhaps twelve years. In August 1848, she and their three children were suddenly sold to a Methodist preacher from North Carolina. The vagaries of slavery had once again intruded upon Henry Brown and utterly separated him from his family.

No longer deterred from seeking to escape slavery—"my family were gone," he later explained—he conceived an approach that, though dangerous, might work. He had a carpenter make a wooden box, 2 × 2½ × 3 feet, and took it to a white friend, Samuel A. Smith, a shoe dealer, and Smith's free black employee,

James Caesar Anthony Smith. Asked what the box was for, Brown exclaimed, to "put Henry Brown in!" The two Smiths marked the box "right side up with care"; addressed it to William A. Johnson, Arch Street, Philadelphia; and on March 29, 1849, shipped it by Adams Express.

Brown took with him a container of water and had three small holes for air, yet he thought he would die when, for parts of the journey, he traveled in the crate upside down. But the trip ended at last, after twenty-seven hours, and like Lazarus from the dead, Brown rose from the box when four men (including William Still, a black abolitionist, and James Miller McKim, a white one) from the Philadelphia Vigilance Committee (a group associated with the Underground Railroad and the Pennsylvania Anti-Slavery Society) collected the box and opened it. As for Samuel Smith, he went to the Virginia penitentiary for attempting in May 1849 to ship two more boxes, each containing a slave man, north to freedom.

Henry Brown took the name Henry "Box" Brown and, after moving to Boston, became active in the abolition movement as a witness to the horrors of slavery even at its best. He told crowds his tale, and the abolitionist Charles Stearns published Brown's narrative, *Narrative of Henry Box Brown* (1849), "written from a statement of facts made by himself." In January 1850, Brown attended a giant antislavery convention in Syracuse, New York. Also at the Syracuse meeting was James Caesar Anthony Smith, who, having made his way north after Samuel Smith's conviction in Richmond, assumed the moniker "Boxer" for his role in boxing up Brown. Some people in Boston painted a panorama, *Mirror of Slavery,* that depicted scenes from slavery and Brown's flight, and Box Brown and Boxer Smith toured the Northeast with the panorama and the famous crate.

On August 30, 1850, slave catchers nearly kidnapped Brown. In order to put himself beyond their reach and that of the new Fugitive Slave Act—necessitated by the actions of people like Henry Brown—he left for England, where in subsequent years he continued to tell his compelling story. In England he also published another version of his story, *Narrative of the Life of Henry Box Brown, Written by Himself* (1851, republished 2002). Slavery in Virginia came to an end in 1865, but Brown continued to perform on stage in England and Wales until as late as 1875, when he returned to America.

Virginia at Midcentury

At midcentury, as before, Virginians were deeply divided in the futures they wished for themselves and for others. The shoe dealer Samuel A. Smith and the schoolteacher Margaret Douglass approached their worlds—their local worlds

Virginia Planter's Family, painted by Augustus Köllner in 1845. Read one way, the painting's title reflects a young white nuclear family, with the planter about to leave to look after his family's public business, representing them in the wider world. Read another way, domestic slavery incorporated the slave, as a "servant," into the "planter's family." Virginia Historical Society, Richmond, Virginia.

and the wider world—in ways that profoundly diverged from Thornton Stringfellow's way or Thomas Dew's. Henry Brown, to obtain his freedom, had to leave the state. John Mercer Langston, to experience a far richer array of opportunities for one who never was a slave but had a black mother, had to leave the state. Slavery challenged the liberty of Samuel A. Smith and Margaret Douglass, as well as the freedom of Henry Brown and his wife and children and of John Mercer Langston and his parents and siblings. Slavery required of Thornton Stringfellow and Thomas Roderick Dew that they strive mightily to square the circle and make sense of their world, impose intellectual and political coherence on their surroundings, and navigate through a democratic world contorted by the enslavement of hundreds of thousands of fellow Virginians.

Dew's image of a free Virginia, a white Virginia, was by no means yet coming into view when he died in 1846. Three years later, Henry Brown could not wait for an end to slavery, and in any case Dew's utopia had no place for him, slave or—especially—free. The vast emigration, slave and free, from Virginia to the Deep South meant that the center of power in the South kept shifting ever southward. The vast immigration across the Atlantic to the cities and farms of the North meant that the center of political gravity in national politics kept shifting northward. Moreover, the tremendous numbers of native Virginians, white and black, who headed to free states further reduced Virginia's relative numbers. As the mother of states, Virginia saw its former lands, and other lands that its leadership had brought within effective settlement by American citizens, filled by people whose interests might not be at all identical to those of Virginia's political leadership. As the mother of migrants to those lands, Virginia assisted in its own relative decline in power, as both the North and the Deep South grew ever greater in population. As one index, Virginia—where 42 percent of all slaves in the new nation resided in 1790—still held 23 percent of the expanding nation's slaves in 1830, but by 1860 that proportion had dropped to 12 percent, barely ahead of second-place Georgia or other Deep South states.

Increasingly, Virginia was hostage to events outside its borders. It remained to be seen in what ways and how soon those events might shape the future, might foster or deny the freedom of black Virginians, the liberty of white Virginians. Yet as Henry Brown showed, when he became Henry "Box" Brown, even the least powerful Virginians could force the issue upon the more powerful, could help shape developments, could contribute to the emergence of one future rather than another. Not only did people beyond the borders of their state increasingly set the agenda, as the most powerful Virginians came to see. Even the slaves within their state might.

Chapter 12

The Compromises of 1850–1851

Twin volcanoes threatened Virginia in 1850. One, focused on national politics, related to territorial expansion and slave property. The other, a matter of state politics, had been building ever since the convention of 1829–1830 did so little to provide for greater political power for the western half of the state. At mid-century, Virginia and the nation each came to some resolution of a collection of dangerous outstanding differences. Each such resolution bought time for those hoping to find greater political serenity.

The national crisis, though it had roots far and wide, can be said to have originated in Texas, and much of the story of Texas can be told in terms of several native Virginians. Stephen Austin was a central figure in the migration of Americans into what was then Mexican territory, beginning in 1823, and Sam Houston was a key figure in the movement that gained Texas its independence from Mexico in 1836. Houston, as president of the independent Republic of Texas, sought annexation by the United States. The Democratic presidents Andrew Jackson and Martin Van Buren, though they looked favorably on such action, bided their time, knowing it would be controversial and intent on obtaining other objectives first. Van Buren lost his bid for reelection in 1840, and two Virginia natives were elected on the Whig ticket. Ohio resident William Henry Harrison, the new president, died one month into his term, and John Tyler moved up, the first vice president to do so on the death of a president. Despite his Whig identity, Tyler was anything but a supporter of the American System, an approach to economic policy that included substantial tariffs, a national bank, and federal aid to transportation improvements. Rather, he opposed the other major political party, the Democrats, out of disgust with some of President Andrew Jackson's actions in the 1830s.

As president, John Tyler quickly alienated Henry Clay—a native of Virginia who had much earlier moved to Kentucky—and the rest of the Whig Party. In

Sam Houston (1793–1863). A native of Rockbridge County, Virginia, Houston served first as commander in chief (1835–1836) of the army that gained Texan independence from Mexico and then as president of the Republic of Texas (1836–1838 and again 1841–1844). As U.S. senator from Texas (1846–1859), he opposed the Kansas-Nebraska Act, and as governor of Texas from 1859 until he was deposed in March 1861, he opposed his state's secession. Library of Congress, Prints and Photographs Division, LC-USZ62-110029.

no way did Tyler reflect mainstream Whig tendencies, either in resisting territorial expansion or in promoting the American System. Following his own political instincts and seeking a new political alignment with southern and northern Democrats in an improbable bid for reelection in 1844, by late 1843 Tyler was publicly urging annexation of Texas. In charge of crafting a treaty of annexation was Secretary of State Abel P. Upshur—also a Virginian, and an avid proponent of states' rights and of slavery, as well as of annexation. Upshur died in February 1844 when a warship he was a guest on exploded, and Tyler appointed South Carolina's John C. Calhoun secretary of state. Calhoun proved far more overt in justifying annexation on the basis of the needs of the slave South than had earlier proponents, who had stressed broad national interests. With the Texas annexation issue, sectionalism began seriously to trump party differences in national political life.

The Senate failed in April 1844 to supply the two-thirds supermajority required to ratify the treaty—in fact, the Senate voted decisively against the treaty, 35–16. In December, nearing the end of his presidency, Tyler changed tactics and sought a simple joint resolution, a maneuver that required only a simple majority in each house of Congress. Before he left office, the House passed such a resolution, 120–98; the Senate passed it, 27–25; and the president signed it.

All Virginia Whigs in both houses opposed the resolution; Virginia Democrats mostly supported it. Days later, the newly elected president, Democrat James K. Polk, took office. Polk, committed to Texas annexation, was fully prepared to go to war with Mexico to achieve it, and indeed war soon came. The Mexican War brought into the American empire a vast new area that included California and the vast expanse of territory between it and Texas.

The series of expansionist victories—the joint resolution, the annexation of Texas as a state, the defeat of Mexico—in turn brought the threat of catastrophe. Most notably, when a northern congressman, David Wilmot of Pennsylvania, proposed the Wilmot Proviso, according to which any territory gained as a consequence of the war with Mexico would be closed to slavery, the issue of slavery in territories—long since resolved in the Missouri Compromise—surfaced again as a vital issue. National politics increasingly operated less along a Whig Party–Democratic Party split and more along a North–South sectional alignment. The Virginia General Assembly voted unanimously for the "Virginia Resolution" that denounced the Wilmot Proviso.

The Compromise of 1850

The first of the twin compromises at midcentury came on the floor of Congress. California sought statehood, and crisis loomed again, as it had when Missouri knocked on the door back in 1819. One source of the crisis was the Mexican War, which had led to Mexico's relinquishing California to the United States. Another was the discovery of gold in California in 1848, the same year that the Treaty of Guadalupe Hidalgo was signed ending the war with Mexico. Gold! People from across the country and around the world raced to California, whose population soon appeared sufficient to warrant statehood. But that raised the inescapable question: slave state or not? Surely not, said the North in general and Californians in particular, and thus southern leaders objected.

For many months, members of the U.S. House and Senate wrangled over the question. Nor was it only the question of California, for that question could not escape entanglement with other issues associated with slavery or the western territories. Some northern congressmen called again for ending slavery in the nation's capital, or at least for ending the slave trade there and ending the interstate slave trade as well. Their counterparts from the South thought it time to strengthen the Fugitive Slave Act and thus make it easier to recapture runaway slaves—white Virginians had in mind the likes of Henry "Box" Brown and his famous escape in 1849. In sum, North and South geared up to battle over the meaning of the Constitution as it related to the retrieval of runaway slaves, the sale of surplus slaves, the expansion of slavery into new territories, and the numbers of states with and without slavery and what that portended for power and policy in the American nation.

Both sides looked to federal power to answer the needs of the hour. Antislavery spokesmen sought congressional action to restrict slavery. Proslavery spokesmen—wishing, on the contrary, to deploy federal power to strengthen slavery—opposed states' rights in the North, where some legislatures had enacted laws making enforcement of the old Fugitive Slave Act more difficult. Despite the enormous differences in their approaches, most people on both sides agreed that any solution would be better than the alternative of secession, as threatened by South Carolina, although some Virginia leaders sided with South Carolina. Concerned that Congress would sell out Virginia's interests, the *Lynch-*

burg Republican wrote that if it did, "southern rights will be a mere empty name, and southern property in slaves a thing that *has* been but *is* not."

In the end, both sides came away with something. On the lesser issues, Congress acted to end the slave trade in the District of Columbia—thus forcing the trade across the Potomac River to Alexandria, Virginia, a former part of the District of Columbia that had just recently been given back to Virginia—but Congress also declared that slavery itself should not be ended in the District without the approval of slaveowners there, and it declared inappropriate any congressional action to restrict the slave trade from one slave state to another. On the main issue, California entered the Union as a free-labor state, a victory for the North, and Congress enacted a stronger Fugitive Slave Act, a victory for the South. Following the pattern of the so-called compromise—in which different portions passed with the support of different coalitions—Virginia's congressmen and senators did not vote for all the provisions. Rather, most of them voted against California statehood and the District of Columbia slave-trade provisions. The only Virginia congressman to vote for all five pieces of the Compromise of 1850 was a Whig from the northwestern corner of the state, Thomas S. Haymond. Both senators from Virginia—Robert M. T. Hunter and James Murray Mason, grandson of the American Revolution's George Mason—were states'-rights Democrats, and though they opposed most of the compromise, they voted for the new Fugitive Slave Act, which Mason had drafted.

Whigs and Democrats, congressmen from the North and the South alike, looked upon the Compromise of 1850 as offering a respite from the dangerous bickering over slavery. Maybe now that this most dangerous issue had been once again resolved, or at least once again pushed off the table, the nation could go about its business. Nonetheless, reflecting the emerging dominant opinion among white Virginians, *Southern Literary Messenger* editor John R. Thompson, who rarely spoke out on political matters, insisted: "The continued existence of the United States as one nation depends upon the full and faithful execution of the Fugitive Slave Bill." Both political parties ran for the presidency in 1852 on platforms approving the compromise as a "final" solution to the nation's most urgent political problems. Through the decade, though, the Second American Party System—revolving around Whigs and Democrats, with substantial support for both parties in North and South alike—fell apart. Rancor over slavery had killed it. Southern Democrats came to dominate their home states, including Virginia, and the nation's highest offices as well. To represent Virginians' interests, Virginia voters sent mostly Democrats to the U.S. House of Representatives as well as to the General Assembly, and the General Assembly sent states'-rights Democrats to the U.S. Senate.

The Virginia Constitution of 1851

In Virginia, the constitutional convention of 1829–1830 had left a great deal undone, to the relief of many in the east and the dismay of many in the west. Two decades later, in 1850–1851, delegates came to Richmond again. Again the great questions were, in terms of process, what changes might be achieved or blocked in the rules of the political game and, in terms of substance, what might be the outcome regarding slavery, on the one hand, and taxes and spending, on the other. The new constitution, ratified in 1851, looked, on its face, to be a far cry from the one it replaced.

The traditional rulers of Virginia stepped out of the way of Jacksonian democracy. The property requirement, which had kept many thousands of white men from voting in the past, vanished. Universal white manhood suffrage, the symbol of the age and the badge of citizenship, finally came to Virginia. More important, the east conceded its control of the House of Delegates, and another reapportionment, scheduled for 1865, would surely, it seemed, give the west a majority in the Senate as well. In another significant change, the state governor would henceforth be elected to a single four-year term by the voters, so the newly reconfigured electorate could control the executive branch in addition to the legislature. Thus did the white population of western Virginia, where small farms were the rule and slavery the exception, wrest control of the machinery of state government. Now, surely, they could control public policy in the Old Dominion—except that eastern slaveholders managed nonetheless to do much to safeguard the peculiar institution from any potential rash action by a nonslaveholding majority.

The key interest remained slavery. Remembering the close call back in the legislative debate of 1832, planters of the east stipulated in the new constitution that the legislature, no matter who controlled it, had no authority to free any slaves, whether before or after they were born. Intent on making it clear, however, that the legislature could take action to control the size of the free black population in Virginia, the makers of the new constitution declared that the legislature could prevent slaveowners from freeing slaves, could seek the reenslavement of slaves who gained their freedom but remained in the state more than a year, and could force the removal or reenslavement of any or all free blacks living in Virginia.

The tax system underwent some change, yet little more could take place under the new constitution. Property would henceforth be generally taxed according to its value. But taxable slaves would be taxed as if they were worth only $300 each, and no slave under the age of twelve would be taxed at all. All white men were to pay an annual poll tax, equal in amount to the tax on $200 worth of real estate, and half that tax would go to a fund to help pay for public schools. The constitution did not attempt to specify what the tax would be on each $100 worth of property—that decision was left to the judgment of legislative majorities—but it did hem in legislators' discretion. Given the linkages among the taxes on polls, land, and slaves, if legislators decided to increase the tax on slaves, they would at the same time be jacking up the poll taxes and the tax on land. The only way to get eastern planters to pay more, then, would be to increase the taxes on western men and on their landed property by an identical percentage.

These were the results of the convention's deliberations. More telling is the key role played by Henry A. Wise, delegate from the Eastern Shore, who argued with force and effect that eastern delegates must ease their parochial concerns with local issues. He urged concessions to the west as the best means of shoring up eastern interests. According to Wise, the "protection of slavery, not the liberalizing of Virginia's constitution," was "the most significant business before the convention," and he explained that the two were the same, not starkly at odds. If easterners continued to insist on "black slaves" as the basis of apportionment, "the foundation of power," then westerners would increasingly see slavery as their enemy. The only way for Virginia to project its will in national politics as it had in the glorious days of the Virginia dynasty, according to Wise, was to be united at home, and the only way to do that was to pull the west into a united vision of what Virginia was and should be. Enough easterners bought into this approach, when coupled with the tax safeguards, to carry the day.

If the years 1850 and 1851 appeared to resolve the great questions of mid-nineteenth-century politics in Virginia and the nation, the appearance faded in the next few years. In Virginia, the new popular majority in state politics came to recognize the implications of the bargain of 1850–1851, as slave values rapidly rose but taxes on slaves remained stuck at a low figure. Ten years later, in the secession winter and spring of 1861, many westerners became so angry about the tax on slaves they couldn't see straight.

Resolutions Undone—Anthony Burns

Even sooner came a broad realization that the national Compromise of 1850 had lost its ability to save the nation. News from Boston sounded distinctly unpromising: Anthony Burns, a Virginia slave, had taken matters into his own hands and stolen himself. Or so his putative owner alleged at a hearing in Boston, where the federal magistrate, of the kind provided for under the new Fugitive Slave Act, determined him to be a runaway, as they claimed.

Anthony Burns ranks near Frederick Douglass and Harriet Tubman among the famous fugitive slaves in U.S. history. Born in the early 1830s in Virginia's Stafford County, where he had a hand mangled in a sawmill accident, he learned how to read and write and in his teens became a Baptist preacher. Employment in Richmond in 1853 offered him a realistic opportunity to escape, and in February 1854 he stowed away on a ship bound for Boston by way of Norfolk.

On May 24, eleven weeks after arriving in Massachusetts, Burns was on his way home from his job at a clothing store when he was arrested on a false charge of robbery, taken to the federal courthouse, and confronted by his Virginia owner, Charles F. Suttle. The next morning, Burns was taken before the fugitive-slave commissioner, Judge Edward G. Loring, for what was intended to be a quick hearing under the Fugitive Slave Act of 1850 and a quiet return to slavery in Virginia. But a failed rescue effort on May 26 led to the death of a jailer. Continued intervention by Burns's black pastor, Leonard A. Grimes, a white lawyer, Richard Henry Dana, and other Bostonians drew the procedure out until June 2. Judge Loring then determined that Burns was indeed the fugitive slave being sought. Hundreds of state militia and more hundreds of federal soldiers ushered Burns to the docks for his return to Virginia.

At enormous cost, the federal act had been enforced, a situation that inflamed passions over slavery on both sides. Northerners who had considered slavery a distant phenomenon saw the system's political power reach into their own region—and just when a furor over the Kansas-Nebraska Act was erupting as well. Opposition toward slavery grew along many dimensions, whether because of what it did to so many blacks or what it did and threatened to do to whites. White northerners, that is, even if they had little interest in or concern for the enslaved in the South, might respond, as did one Massachusetts newspaper, "We are the slaves and vassals of the South." Yet proslavery southerners could see that the Fugitive Slave Act might not be worth much; as the *Richmond Enquirer* put it, "A few more such victories, and the South is undone." The Anthony Burns case helped to propel the nation toward secession, Civil War, and emancipation.

As for Anthony Burns himself, in despair after his capture, he had regarded quiet cooperation with the slave catchers as the safest way to behave, but the fracas associated with his being sent back to slavery also led to his eventual freedom. For months following his return to Richmond on June 12, 1854, he was kept manacled in a filthy jail cell, until Suttle sold him to David McDaniel, a slave trader and planter from Rocky Mount, North Carolina. Burns managed to write letters to Boston, so black Bostonians learned of his new whereabouts, and they took action. McDaniel agreed on a purchase price that would permit Burns to return to the North, this time as a free man. Burns arrived back in Boston one year after he had stepped off the steamer that carried him out of slavery the first time.

Resolutions Undone—The Kansas-Nebraska Act

At the same time that the Burns imbroglio in Boston was unfolding, headlines told of another struggle, this one in Congress. In 1854, both houses of Congress passed the Kansas-Nebraska Act, a measure that divided the vast unorganized remainder of the Louisiana Purchase into two territories, Kansas and Nebraska, with voters in each territory empowered to determine whether slavery would be permitted. The Missouri Compromise had once seemed to settle the question of whether slavery would be allowed there, but with the Kansas-Nebraska Act it was opened anew. The security of a settled agreement gave way to uncertainty as to the outcome, for popular sovereignty would determine the outcome there. Since the question would be settled on the spot, enormous violence developed as both sides sought to win a war. There seemed little likelihood that slavery would spread into Nebraska, the more northern of the two territories, but Kansas became a battleground. Men and weapons from both sides, South and North, proslavery and antislavery, surged into Kansas.

The very idea of a southern assault on the Missouri Compromise led to the organization of a new political party, the Anti-Nebraska Party, soon to become known as the Republicans. A direct response to the Kansas-Nebraska Act, the Republican Party had its origins in a commitment to prevent the expansion of slavery to new territories. On that it would not compromise, not in 1856, not in 1860. In 1856 it ran a candidate for the presidency, John C. Frémont, who came in second to the Democratic winner, James Buchanan. Four years later, even more powerful and no less committed to containing the growth of slavery, the party nominated a man from Illinois named Abraham Lincoln.

In 1854, therefore, not only did the Compromise of 1850 come unglued, but the sacred Missouri Compromise, from a generation earlier, came apart as well. Voters in Virginia, already anxious over the consequences of the state Constitution of 1851, could see that no resolution of outstanding problems—including the Missouri Compromise and the Compromise of 1850—seemed any longer to supply assurances that the world would remain a safe place to live. Everyone's interests were at risk.

Dred Scott's Freedom Suit

Like many other native Virginians, Dred Scott spent much of his life in the western part of the United States. Sometimes he was in a slave state, Missouri, and sometimes in a free territory, Wisconsin. In view of the Northwest Ordinance, Wisconsin Territory was closed to slavery. Under the Missouri Compromise, the state of Missouri was open to slavery, though the vast area of the old Louisiana Territory north of Missouri was not. Scott sued for his freedom, as Americans held in bondage had been doing since before the American Revolution—in Massachusetts, in Maryland, in Virginia, and in Missouri. Whether he should have his freedom—and whether his wife and their two daughters should as well—depended on how the courts interpreted the law. For years, his case was in the courts, first the state courts of Missouri and then the federal courts.

In 1857, Chief Justice Roger B. Taney, a native of Maryland, wrote the principal opinion of a deeply divided U.S. Supreme Court. Should Dred Scott be permitted to sue for his freedom? And should his freedom be granted? No, and no. At great length Taney worked out his argument. He concluded that Scott, as an African American, had no right to bring the case into federal court. Having done so, however, Scott occasioned a ruling by the nation's highest court that Congress had no authority under the Constitution to have enacted the Missouri Compromise—that Congress could not prevent the expansion of slavery into new territories.

The Republican Party, having organized in the North in response to the Kansas-Nebraska Act of 1854, pounced on the *Dred Scott* decision of 1857 as yet another example of public policy gone awry, of southern power run amok, and of the North and freedom trammeled at the hands of the "slave power," and as showing the urgent need to put the nation's politics under new management. Yet the Court had ruled in such a way as to undermine the Republicans' core issue. Much as Anthony Burns had, by stealing himself and getting to Boston, Dred Scott—another native of Virginia, another man held in perpetual bondage—raised a question, forced an issue, that made even more irreconcilable the positions held by many northern politicians and their southern counterparts in the 1850s.

The Slave Power—and the Preponderance of Immigrants

From an antislavery perspective, slavery had shown its true colors in the 1850s. Supporters of slavery might talk the language of states' rights, but such talk was camouflage, as became clear when they insisted on strengthening federal power

Dred Scott (c. 1800–1858). Born a slave in Virginia, Scott brought the freedom suit in Missouri that led to the U.S. Supreme Court's divided and divisive 1857 ruling. Wood engraving in *Century* magazine, published in 1887. Library of Congress, Prints and Photographs Division, LC-USZ62-5092.

to facilitate the return of runaway slaves to bondage. The Kansas-Nebraska Act represented the duplicitous willingness of proslavery politicians to discard a sacred compact like the Missouri Compromise. In 1857 the Supreme Court, in the *Dred Scott* decision, ruled that Congress never had authority to restrict slavery's expansion in the first place.

From a proslavery perspective, the North had begun ever more clearly to demonstrate hostility to slavery and to the interests of white southerners. The case of Anthony Burns demonstrated how little faith could be placed in northerners' willingness to abide by the law. Slaveowners began with the premise that one ought to be able to take his property anywhere in the Union, but they saw that any number of northerners were prepared to use violence, at least in Kansas, against that right.

A great many northerners grew ever more disenchanted as the South seemed to dominate national politics and policymaking. At the same time, the North was pulling ahead in a variety of ways, not least of all manufacturing capacity, but perhaps most of all in terms of population. Partly, the shift resulted from a migration out of the South and into the North and West. Partly—in fact to a huge degree—it resulted from mass migration from Europe to America. Immigrants stepped off ships where the ships docked. Ports of entry included Baltimore and New Orleans; to a lesser extent Norfolk, Charleston, Savannah, and Mobile; but most of all Boston, New York, and Philadelphia. Immigrants in New

York State alone, where 24 percent of the nation's total lived in 1860, outnumbered those across the entire slave South.

Soon the men among the nation's newcomers were voting. Regardless of whether immigrants voted, or how they voted, their numbers counted, because every ten years, a federal census counted the returns. Every ten years, Congress was reapportioned to reflect the shifting patterns of residence, and every ten years, the North gained more power in the House of Representatives and in the electoral college, at the South's expense. Neither Congress nor the presidency could be guaranteed to the South forever. Lose the presidency and the Senate, and the South was bound to lose the Supreme Court as well. Whatever some northerners might say in complaining about "the slave power," people who did not share their interests and perspectives knew that what the South as a region had was not too much power but too little, and prospects for the future grew ever less promising.

The North was developing an identity as not-South. And the South was developing a regional identity—a southern nationalism—that rejected the northern variant of a national identity. In the 1840s, the Baptists divided over slavery, and the Methodists did too. In the 1850s, so did the Whig Party. Replacing the Whig Party was a new Republican Party, with scant support anywhere in the South. At the end of the 1850s, among the nation's leading religious or political institutions that had transcended the boundary between North and South, the Democratic Party remained.

At midcentury, Virginia and the nation had each settled the most dangerous issues, or so it seemed, so people could hope. In both cases, the hopes proved illusory, the serenity unachievable. Just as white Virginians had contested each other in 1829–1830, in 1831–1832, and again in 1851–1852, they contested each other in 1860–1861. Never had the stakes been higher.

Chapter 13

Virginia's Road to Secession and War

....

In one sense, the Civil War began in the western territory of Kansas in the mid-1850s, where a northern white man named John Brown cut his teeth in a contest over the expansion of slavery. Antislavery people shipped in men and weapons—the rifles were referred to as "Beecher's Bibles" in honor of the abolitionist preacher Henry Ward Beecher (brother of writer Harriet Beecher Stowe), who raised funds for the weapons, characterizing them after passage of the Kansas-Nebraska Act as more effective moral agents against slavery in the territories than Bibles. Large numbers of so-called "border ruffians"—proslavery men from neighboring Missouri, illegitimate voters, not actual settlers in Kansas—slipped across the border and voted in favor of making Kansas a slave state. Each side formed a state capital. Each claimed to be in authority, and each did what it could to stop the other side, including carrying out violence against people and property. Brown, who referred to himself as an avenging angel of the Lord, murdered five white southern settlers in Kansas in May 1856.

Surely the secession of Virginia became more likely after John Brown brought his war against slavery to a slave state in the East. A chilly drizzle fell on the evening of October 16, 1859, as nineteen men—fourteen white and five black—crossed a bridge over the Potomac River from Maryland to the small town of Harpers Ferry, Virginia. They despised slavery and followed Brown, with his apocalyptic vision that the time had come for an attack on slavery in the South. From taking an active antislavery stance in Kansas—seeking to prevent slavery's expansion—Brown moved on to act the abolitionist in Virginia, seeking an end to slavery where it already was.

Brown dreamed of beginning a slave insurrection. The place he chose to begin his uprising, Harpers Ferry, sits on a narrow neck of land where the Shenandoah and Potomac rivers merge. Located in the northern part of Virginia, surrounded by mountains, it was home to a federal armory. He planned to seize the

John Brown (1800–1859). A white abolitionist from the North, Brown led the October 1859 raid at Harpers Ferry, Virginia. Photo by Black and Bachelder, Library of Congress, Prints and Photographs Division, LC-USZ62-2472.

armory complex and rifle works, barricade the two bridges leading into town, and rally the slaves on nearby farms. The raiders brought a wagonload of pikes to hand out to slaves, who might not be experienced with guns. From Harpers Ferry, raiders and slaves alike might head into the hills—hills that could take them north to freedom, or instead through south Appalachia into the Deep South. War against slavery would "destroy the money value of slavery by rendering it insecure." Believing that God would "guard and shield him," Brown did not plan an escape should things go awry. Things quickly went awry.

President James Buchanan, after hearing the incorrect news that "700 whites and negroes" were attempting to seize Harpers Ferry, dispatched federal troops under the command of a colonel named Robert E. Lee. Lee captured Brown and his men, and the invasion ended, a day and a half after it had begun. Ten of Brown's eighteen followers died in the raid, including two of Brown's sons. Others, including Brown, were put on trial and sentenced to death. A few disappeared into the mountains.

Virginia governor Henry A. Wise decided to try Brown in a Virginia court rather than turning him over to federal authorities. A jury in Charlestown (now Charles Town, West Virginia) found Brown guilty of treason, murder, and conspiring with slaves to rebel. Before the jury announced his sentence, Brown justified his actions as being consistent with God's commands. As for his future, he said: "If it is deemed necessary that I should forfeit my life for the furtherance of the ends of justice, and mingle my blood with the blood of millions in this slave country whose rights are disregarded by wicked, cruel, and unjust enactments, I say let it be done." The jury sentenced Brown to death, and he was hanged December 2, 1859, surrounded by a throng of spectators. As his body went slack, Colonel J. T. L. Preston from the Virginia Military Institute shouted: "So perish all such enemies of Virginia! All such enemies of the Union! All such foes of the human race!"

Virginian fire-eater Edmund Ruffin—a retired eastern planter, influential agricultural reformer, and committed southern nationalist—was in the crowd watching Brown's execution. Earlier, upon hearing news of the raid, he had welcomed it, hoping Harpers Ferry could be tied to northern abolitionists, and he told his diary: "Such a practical exercise of abolition principles is needed to stir the sluggish blood of the South." Ruffin obtained one of Brown's pikes, marked the handle "samples of the favors designed for us by our Northern Brethren," and took it over to Washington, D.C., where he showed it off to southern members of Congress. Gratified at the response, he secured more of the pikes, labeled them too, and shipped one off to each southern governor.

John Brown, having earlier taken violent action to prevent the expansion of slavery into the territory of Kansas, had acted violently in October 1859 against slavery in a state where the institution had long been very much entrenched. James L. Kemper, Madison County's representative in the House of Delegates, warned: "All Virginia should stand forth as one man and say to fanaticism, in her own language, whenever you advance a hostile foot upon our soil, we will welcome you with bloody hands and hospitable graves." The *Richmond Enquirer* declared: "The Harper's Ferry invasion has advanced the cause of Disunion more than any other event that has happened since the formation of the Government."

John Brown Goes to Congress—as a Republican

Most northerners disapproved of Brown's action, but some prominent abolitionists hailed him as a martyr. White southerners understood the words of praise as threats to their freedom and safety. Moreover, shortly after Brown's hanging, they faced an election for speaker of the House of Representatives in which one leading candidate was John Sherman, who had, along with many of his Republican colleagues, endorsed *The Impending Crisis of the South*, a recent book by Hinton Rowan Helper attacking slavery.

Hinton Helper was from North Carolina. Antiblack in his bones, he nonetheless appeared in the guise of an abolitionist. Had he lived in the Midwest, he might have been an avowed antislavery Republican, seeking to keep slavery—and black people—away from his region. But where he lived, slavery surrounded him, so containment of slavery could hardly suffice. Helper attacked slavery as an institution, arguing that it impeded economic growth in the South, blighted the lives of white nonslaveholders, and had to go if white southerners were to be free.

To white southerners it seemed as though, right after John Brown died, he had made his way to Congress. Brown and Helper were often linked, as when a Virginia legislator spoke in February 1860 of "admirers of Brown and endorsers of Helper." The events at Harpers Ferry in late 1859 reverberated down to the presidential election a year later. Northern abolitionists spoke glowingly of the martyr John Brown; Republican leaders endorsed Hinton Helper; northern voters chose Abraham Lincoln. True, the Republican platform voiced a commitment to antislavery, not abolition. Nonetheless the association, in the minds of many white southerners, was clear: Antislavery—abolition—Republicans. John Brown—Hinton Helper—Abraham Lincoln. Most southerners voted in late 1860 not for secession but for any alternative to Lincoln. To their consternation, Lincoln won.

In December 1859, on the day after John Brown's death, Lincoln observed in a speech at Leavenworth, Kansas: "Old John Brown has just been executed for treason against a state. We cannot object, even though he agreed with us in thinking slavery wrong.... So, if constitutionally we elect a President, and therefore you undertake to destroy the Union, it will be our duty to deal with you as old John Brown has been dealt with. We shall try to do our duty."

The Presidential Election of 1860 and the First Wave of Secession

In the 1860 presidential election, the political parties were by no means what they had been two or three campaigns earlier. Differences over slavery had divided the Whig Party into its northern and southern halves, and then the party disappeared. One northern response to the Kansas-Nebraska Act was to organize the Anti-Nebraska Party, soon named the Republican Party, which ran a strong second in the 1856 election. When the Democratic Party met in Charleston, South Carolina, it could not agree on a candidate or a platform, and the last major organization to survive the rancor over slavery divided over whether the party should commit to a federal slave code for the territories. Stephen A. Douglas ran as the northern Democratic candidate, and John C. Breckinridge as the southern Democrat. John Bell of Tennessee also ran, on a Constitutional Union platform that, pursuing peace at all costs, avoided the pressing issues.

John Bell carried the popular vote in Virginia by a mere 156 ballots, the close election hinting at how divided Virginia was, and at how divided was the nation. A vote for Bell was a vote to preserve the Union, but by no means can votes for the other candidates be assumed to have been against such preservation. As for Abraham Lincoln, he collected a mere 1,887 votes in Virginia and none at all in most other southern states. Yet such was his support in northern states that, had his three opponents combined their votes against him, they could not have defeated him in the electoral college.

The Republicans, in their party platform (see sidebar, page 182), had declared their opposition to such violence as had been visited either upon Kansas Territory by the Border Ruffians or upon Virginia by John Brown and his band. More than that, they had declared that they were no party of national abolition, for the federal government had no authority to tamper with slavery in those states where it existed. The Republican platform disappointed abolitionists, as it seemed to them tepid, even avowedly proslavery in its hands-off posture toward the South. But the Republican Party was expressly antislavery, in the sense of being committed to preventing the extension of slavery into new territories in the West. And the Republicans had declared themselves categorically opposed to any state's secession.

Some leaders in the region, especially in the Upper South, argued that such a momentous action as seceding should await Lincoln's taking direct action, as president, against southern slavery—and he was not even scheduled to take office until early March. Other spokesmen, especially in the Deep South—refusing to distinguish between the party's antislavery stance and true abolitionism—argued instead that the Republicans had made it plain that they were sufficiently hostile toward slavery that secession should not wait, as Lincoln's election promised nothing but danger for slavery and for the South's system of race control.

On December 20, 1860, a convention in South Carolina voted to take that state out of the Union. By February, six other states had followed: Mississippi, Florida, Alabama, Georgia, Louisiana, and Texas. A convention in February of those seven states in Montgomery, Alabama, drafted a constitution and organized a provisional government for a new nation, the Confederate States of America. Virginia's fire-eater Edmund Ruffin, to avoid living "for even an hour"

3. That to the Union of the States this nation owes its unprecedented increase in population, its surprising development of material resources, its rapid augmentation of wealth, its happiness at home and its honor abroad; and we hold in abhorrence all schemes for Disunion, come from whatever source they may; and we congratulate the country that no Republican member of Congress has uttered or countenanced the threats of Disunion so often made by Democratic members, without rebuke and with applause from their political associates; and we denounce those threats of Disunion, in case of an overthrow of their ascendancy, as denying the vital principles of a free government, and an avowal of contemplated treason, which it is the imperative duty of an indignant People sternly to rebuke and forever silence.

4. That the maintenance inviolate of the rights of the States, and especially the right of each State to order and control its own domestic institutions according to its own judgment exclusively, is essential to that balance of powers on which the perfection and endurance of our political fabric depends; and we denounce the lawless invasion by armed force of the soil of any State or Territory, no matter under what pretext, as among the gravest of crimes. . . .

in a country with a Republican president, fled to South Carolina before Lincoln's inauguration in March.

Some states having seceded and declared themselves members of a new breakaway nation, Virginia, the southern state with the largest population and the greatest wealth, faced a wrenching decision—to stay in the Union or join the Confederacy. Beset by abolitionist Yankees, antislavery midwesterners, and fire-eaters from the Deep South, the state of Virginia twisted and turned.

The Virginia Secession Convention

Beginning in December 1860, Virginians sought to head off the emerging crisis. Virginia congressman Alexander Boteler initiated a call that led to what became known as the Crittenden Compromise, a proposal named after U.S. Senator John J. Crittenden of another Upper South state, Kentucky. The key component would revive the old 36° 30′ line of the Missouri Compromise, the latitude of the southern border of Missouri, and would bar actions by the federal government to interfere with slavery in federal territories south of that line. Republicans would not budge, however, on the extension of slavery, the central provision in the party's 1860 platform.

Next, Virginia proposed a peace conference in the nation's capital. The conference, held in February and headed by former president John Tyler, failed when delegates from only twenty-one out of thirty-four states showed up. The seven seceded states were all absent (those states convened the same day in Alabama); missing also were Arkansas, three states from the Midwest (Michigan, Minnesota, and Wisconsin), and California and Oregon. So the Republicans rejected the Crittenden Compromise, and the Deep South rejected the peace conference. What else could Virginia propose? Meanwhile, on January 14 the General Assembly voted to hold a constitutional convention in Richmond on February 13, and delegates were quickly elected to it. Of the 152 delegates, no more than a third were considered hard-core secessionists. Most, however, came to the convention believing in Virginia's right to withdraw from the Union. Many favored secession if war came.

According to historian Ralph Wooster's analysis of the Virginia convention, data from the 1860 federal census showed that 78 percent of the 152 delegates were slaveholders, with 42 percent owning at least twenty slaves. On the surface, the debate seemed to be about coercion and the value of the Union, not about slavery, yet the more slaves a delegate owned, the more likely he was to vote for secession. The elected delegates came in three main categories. The unwavering Unionists typically came from overwhelmingly white counties of the northwest. Most of the committed secessionists came from the east. In between were the contingent Unionists, and in their hands lay Virginia's course in 1861.

Connecting the three groups in some fashion were their memories of the Virginia dynasty—the leadership role Virginia and Virginians had played in the past, especially in establishing the nation in the first place. In 1861, however, decisions made elsewhere were controlling Virginia. Delegates could hope—hope that the Republicans would accept the Crittenden Compromise, which included restoring the Missouri Compromise line and extending it to the Pacific; hope that the Deep South would give up the Confederacy. Neither was likely.

There was one other consideration. Over the major issues of the time—certainly on slavery, certainly on secession—Virginia continued to be

7. That the new dogma that the Constitution, of its own force, carries Slavery into any or all of the territories of the United States, is a dangerous political heresy. . . .

8. That the normal condition of all the territory of the United States is that of freedom; That as our Republican fathers, when they had abolished slavery in all our national territory, ordained that "no person should be deprived of life, liberty, or property, without due process of law," it becomes our duty, by legislation, whenever such legislation is necessary, to maintain this provision of the Constitution against all attempts to violate it; and we deny the authority of Congress, of a territorial legislature, or of any individuals, to give legal existence to Slavery in any Territory of the United States. . . .

conflicted. When eastern Virginia's leaders peered anxiously out at the wider world, they saw the Deep South steering in its own direction. And they saw the North pulling away from the South—its population pulling ahead in terms of numbers, and its society and politics diverging in terms of increasing differences in opinions and values. They recognized a similar ominous pair of trends inside Virginia. Thomas Roderick Dew may have had it right, back in the 1830s, when he projected that Virginia would gradually move away from slavery. As planters gradually lost their numerical dominance in Virginia, especially in view of the growth in the western half of the state, and as their power looked less certain even within Virginia, the prospects for secession down the road dimmed as well—which made it all the more important to move now if secession was to be achieved.

A substantial bloc of eastern delegates were committed to secession. To come to their conclusion, they had no need to await further developments. But they could not act alone.

Commissioners from the Confederate States

The Confederate states sent three commissioners to Virginia in hopes of influencing the minds of the forty-three delegates who appeared moderate on secession. The convention gave the commissioners—Fulton Anderson of Mississippi, Henry Lewis Benning of Georgia, and John Smith Preston of South Carolina—permission to speak at noon on Monday, February 18. The day before Preston planned to deliver his oration, he had warned, in a letter to South Carolina governor Francis W. Pickens: "Virginia will not take sides until she is absolutely forced." Yet all three commissioners knew full well why their own states had seceded, and each arrived in Richmond convinced that a strong expression of similar reasoning would bring Virginia around.

The next day, Anderson of Mississippi delivered his speech to what a diarist called an "immense crowd" inside the Mechanics' Institute Hall. The victorious Republican Party, he warned his audience, desired "the ultimate extinction of slavery and the degradation of the Southern people." John Brown's raid at Harpers Ferry foretold Virginia's fate at the hands of the party of Lincoln, as Republicans had embarked, Anderson cried, on "a holy crusade" to destroy slavery, the institution that lay "at the very foundation" of southern society and politics.

Benning then took the stage. He began his lengthy speech by explaining that Georgia had seceded because "a separation from the North was the only thing that could prevent the abolition of her slavery." He laid out a nightmarish scene of the South as it would become if Republicans had control over it. "We will be overpowered," he said. Describing "the fate which Abolition will bring upon the white race" in the South, he went on: "Our men will be compelled to wander like vagabonds all over the earth," and "as for our women, the horrors of their state we cannot contemplate in imagination." Urging Virginia to emulate Georgia and secede, he concluded: "We have a cause—the cause of honor, and liberty, and property, and self-preservation."

The day grew late as Benning finished, so delegates voted to postpone the last speech until the next day. Then it was Preston's turn. Born in Virginia, Preston had become wealthy as a sugar planter in Louisiana and had then taken up residence in South Carolina. Why had South Carolina chosen to secede? Since the early 1830s, he explained, northerners had "assailed the institution of African slavery." Not many months ago, he reminded his audience, John Brown had gone to Harpers Ferry, having "proclaimed the intention of abolishing slavery by the annihilation of the slaveholders." So "the conflict between slavery and non-slavery is a conflict for life and death." The North had voted for Lincoln, had given him a "decree" to annihilate white southerners, who must protect themselves. "The South cannot exist without African slavery," he insisted. So, he wanted to know, what would Virginia do? Would Virginians "skulk for protection beneath the crumbling fragments of an ancient greatness," or would they "step forth," he asked, and "keep the ancient glory" of their name? Preston had assured his fellow Confederates, he told his audience, that "before the spring grass" had time to grow, the South would comprise "a mighty host of men." And leading that host, he went on, would be a "banner whose whole history is one blaze of glory, and not one blot of shame"—"and on that banner" would be written "the unsullied name of Virginia."

With his call to Virginians' pride, with reference to their "ancient greatness," Preston brought his audience to their feet in what a diarist called "uncontrolled applause." A Richmond paper observed that Preston had moved his audience to "tears." Nevertheless, on April 4, the delegates voted against secession, 88–45. Still, they recognized that the vote did not bring the story to a conclusion. Those for whom Preston's arguments were perhaps right on target were already committed to secession. Many others would not budge from their Unionist stance. But the wavering delegates—and they were many—might still be persuaded.

Virginia Is Forced to Choose

On March 19, 1861, five weeks into the proceedings of the Virginia convention that had been called to consider secession, its Committee on Federal Relations reported a series of proposed amendments to the U.S. Constitution. One was to revive and extend the old 36° 30' line, as had been proposed in the Critten-den Compromise, already rejected. Another would bar state action in the North designed to prevent enforcement of the Fugitive Slave Act. According to yet another, "The elective franchise and the right to hold office, whether Federal or Territorial, shall not be exercised by persons who are of the African race." The final proposed amendment would require unanimous consent of all the states to change the current three-fifths clause, the current fugitive-slave clause, or any of these proposed new amendments, once Congress had approved them and the states had ratified them. That was the plan anyway.

Charleston, South Carolina, had been heard from when the Democratic Party broke up there in May 1860, and again in December when a convention there voted in favor of secession. Yet a third piece of front-page news, this one in April 1861, completed the triptych. Edmund Ruffin, as a temporary member of a South Carolina militia unit, had the privilege of firing one of the opening shots on a fort controlled by Union forces in Charleston Harbor. On April 13, after the men wearing Union blue had fought for thirty-three hours against forces of the Confederate States of America, Major Robert Anderson lowered the U.S. flag and surrendered the pile of bricks that had been Fort Sumter. The Confederacy took over the last U.S. installation in South Carolina.

When news from Fort Sumter arrived in New York, the *New York Times* wrote in "The Course of Virginia" (April 15): "Everybody here sees that now war has commenced, the question which the Virginia Convention has to decide is simply whether Virginia will declare war against the United States or stand by the Government; whether she will invite the battle upon her soil to her utter ruin, or aid in bringing the fratricidal strife to a speedy termination by sustaining the Government and Union" (for a related *New York Times* statement, see sidebar, page 188).

On April 15, two days after Fort Sumter fell, Abraham Lincoln called for 75,000 troops from the states still loyal to the Union to help put down the rebellion in the seven states that had seceded. Lincoln's request for troops forced Virginia to choose sides. John Minor Botts, a staunch Unionist convention delegate from Richmond, said that in Virginia after Lincoln's call for troops, "the union feeling almost entirely swept out of existence." Patrick County delegate Samuel Staples declared: "Ten days ago, I was known as a Union man," but Lincoln's call for troops changed that, and the convention, "having exhausted all peaceable measures to save the Union and avoid a resort to arms, has no alternative left but to adopt an ordinance of secession."

When asked to turn around and fight their neighbors in the Deep South, the states of Virginia, Tennessee, North Carolina, and Arkansas no longer had the op-

Prince George County native Edmund Ruffin (1794–1865). Taking on the task of redressing the depleted soils of Tidewater Virginia, Ruffin became a soil chemist, agricultural reformer, and editor of the *Farmers' Register*. Never much directly involved in politics as an office-holder, Ruffin grew ever more committed to a larger politics of southern nationalism, expressly based on racial slavery, and emerged as one of the leading southern "fire-eaters" of the late 1850s. Present at the hanging of John Brown after the Harpers Ferry raid, after President Lincoln's election the next year Ruffin left Virginia for South Carolina, where he was given the honor of firing the first shot at Fort Sumter. Within days of Virginia's secession Ruffin returned home, where he joined in the fighting at First Manassas. Over the next four years, Federal troops pillaged Ruffin's estates, slavery was abolished, and Ruffin's economic independence vanished, as did his dreams of an independent southern nation. This illustration from South Carolina dates from April 1861. National Archives and Records Administration.

The Old Dominion has reached the crisis of her existence. She stands upon the very verge of her fate. She must choose instantly and forever between the American Union and the New Confederacy. She has lost what she has long been striving for, the ability to control the conduct and decide the policy of either. South Carolina has snatched the decision from her hands, and plunged the Southern Confederacy into War with the United States. The Federal Government has accepted the issue, and it only remains for Virginia to decide *on which side she will range herself* in the coming contest. Her decision will be of momentous interest to the country and the world—but of infinitely greater importance to herself than to anybody else.

Virginia cannot prevent war—but she can determine its character, and limit both its area and its duration. If she decides to stand by the flag of the American Union, she will limit the struggle to the Gulf States, withhold from them the ability to make it protracted, and convert the whole war into a simple blockade of the Southern ports. If she decides to join the South, she will elevate the great rebellion into something like dignity from its magnitude, advance it 500 miles further north, to the very gates of the capital, make her own soil the scene of its greatest and its fiercest conflicts and

tion of staying neutral. Rather than join in a fight against the states of the Confederacy, on April 17 the Virginia Convention voted 88–55 in favor of an ordinance of secession (see sidebar, page 190). For the delegates who had been neither committed Unionists nor committed secessionists, Fort Sumter and Lincoln's call made the difference, and they shifted the vote from a large majority for staying in the Union, at least for a while longer, to one for leaving the Union right away. On May 23, Virginia voters ratified the secession ordinance, and the cradle of America was no longer in the Union.

Religion and Secession in Virginia

Churchmen in Virginia, like their counterparts in the Deep South, gave vigorous and sustained support to slavery before the war and to the Confederate cause throughout the war. But evangelical Virginians made their way, their very reluctant way, according to historian Charles Irons, to a last-minute commitment to secession. In the 1840s, when many in the North had moved against slavery, Baptists and Methodists alike broke ecclesiastical ranks with their northern brethren. But they did not then adopt a stance that called for a political break as well. They distinguished between the break in church organization, which they insisted on, and a break in political union, which a great many of them opposed, then and through the 1850s and even after the election and inauguration of Abraham Lincoln as president.

Virginia was not the Deep South. Churchmen in Virginia avowed God's approval for slavery but, at the same time, were convinced that God demanded faithful support for civil political institutions. Breaking with northern Baptists or Methodists could not be avoided. Breaking with the United States had to be avoided if at all possible. In January 1861, shortly after South Carolina had made the decision to secede, a representative Virginia statement had it that "any resistance to the Federal authority we regard as rebellion," and therefore unacceptable. At about the same time, a Presbyterian spokesman wrote his mother: "As for South Carolina, the little impudent vixen . . . is as much a pest as the Abolitionists." Jeremiah Jeter, one of Virginia's leading Baptist ministers, wrote in December 1860: "Will it not be sad, if between Northern fanaticism and Southern rashness the best government that the world has ever seen, the work of our revolutionary fathers, the admiration of the friends of freedom in all nations, and the last refuge of republican liberty, should perish?" "My only hope," Jeter went on, "is in God."

A great many Virginians' commitment to the Union was conditional, and their stance left them hostage to developments that South Carolina had precipitated and continued to cause. After the firing on U.S. troops at Fort Sumter, the U.S. Constitution—which evangelical Virginians had insisted must be obeyed—in their minds vanished the moment Lincoln called for troops to put down what he termed a rebellion. It was one thing for Virginians to perceive South Carolina as in rebellion. It was another for them to be called on by the president to supply troops to put down that rebellion. At that point, they must rebel themselves, and yet now it was in self-defense, as they saw it, and thus just and necessary. A great many Virginians abruptly changed direction, embraced a new loyalty, and became avowed secessionists and avid Confederates. In Nelson County, an Episcopal minister wrote in his diary, "Lincoln having ordered up . . . troops to coerce the seceding states I this day change my position and am for opposing him to the bitter end. . . . May the god of battles be with us!"

give it a vitality which may protract it for years.

What, moreover, would be the effect upon her internal interests of secession from the American Union? The first effect would be the division of the State into two distinct communities, from the same antipathies that have parted the North and the South.

AN ORDINANCE

To repeal the Ratification of the Constitution of the United States of America, by the State of Virginia, and to resume all the rights and powers granted under said Constitution.

The people of Virginia, in their ratification of the Constitution of the United States of America, adopted by them in Convention, on the 25th day of June, in the year of our Lord one thousand seven hundred and eighty-eight, having declared that the powers granted under the said Constitution were derived from the people of the United States, and might be resumed whensoever the same should be perverted to their injury and oppression, and the Federal Government having perverted said powers, not only to the injury of the people of Virginia, but to the oppression of the Southern slave-holding states:

Now, therefore, we, the people of Virginia, do declare and ordain that the ordinance adopted by the people of this State, in Convention, on the 25th day of June, in the year of our Lord one thousand seven hundred and eighty-eight, whereby the Constitution of the United States of America, was ratified—and all acts of the General Assembly of this State ratifying or adopting amendments to said Constitution—are hereby repealed and abrogated; that the Union between the State of Virginia and the other

Troops Gather in Richmond

No state was more important to the Confederate cause than Virginia. As both sides could see, the Confederacy stood far less chance in a conflict without Virginia's manpower, agricultural and industrial resources, wealth, and prestige. No longer important enough to control the onset of war, Virginia might still be important enough to control the outcome.

In spring 1861 a great many white Virginians rushed to defend their land against any invasion. Even before the ordinance of secession was ratified, they began to gather in Richmond, filled with excitement and the anticipation of future glory. Wealthy sons with new rifles and sharp uniforms arrived from the Tidewater, and mountain boys dressed in deerskin filed in from the hill country. Semi-organized companies marched from college campuses, among them the Sons of Liberty and the Southern Guard from the University of Virginia. As men from all over the state put down their schoolbooks or farm tools, those who already lived military lives faced the hard decision of which army to pledge their alliance to. Regular army officers from Virginia divided fairly evenly between those who chose to remain with the Federal army and those who enlisted with the Confederate forces.

The men who gathered in Richmond had no lack of enthusiasm or ambition, but they had very little experience. They supplied the makings of an army, but an army by no means prepared for a battle, let alone a war. General Robert E. Lee took charge of mobilizing the forces in Virginia. He quickly organized Camp Lee, a basic-training camp for infantry, at the old fairgrounds on the western edge of Richmond. To act as instructors, he summoned former U.S. Army officers and the

Virginia Military Institute's corps of cadets. Soon other camps sprang up around Virginia. In a matter of weeks the Confederate army in Virginia had evolved from a massive gathering to an army of 40,000 troops, with field and staff officers, and with every regiment at least partially armed.

The politics of slavery had long divided northern voters and united southern ones. The issue of secession, by contrast, tended far more to divide southerners and unite northerners. War, when it came, united southerners again—but only up to a point.

Two States and Two Nations

People in the eastern and western portions of Virginia had long threatened each other with dividing the Commonwealth over their differences. When legislators held their great debate over slavery in 1832, each side, those insisting on action against slavery and those insisting there be no such thing, spoke of going its own separate way should the other side win. Three decades later, such tensions persisted. When the Virginia convention shifted direction in April 1861 and opted for secession, there was little chance the northwestern part of the state would not try to break away.

In the northwestern third of Virginia, whites constituted 94 percent of all residents. In the convention vote that took Virginia out of the Union, delegates from what later became West Virginia voted against secession, 32–11. In the referendum to ratify the convention results, voters in the region voted "no" by nearly two to one. East and west were pulling in very different directions.

A mass meeting, held in Clarksburg on April 22, 1861, five days after the convention vote, led to the First Wheeling Convention, in mid-May. Steps to seek separate statehood were postponed

States under the Constitution aforesaid is hereby dissolved, and that the State of Virginia is in the full possession and exercise of all the rights of sovereignty which belong and appertain to a free and independent State. And they do further declare that the said Constitution of the United States of America is no longer binding on any of the citizens of this State.

This ordinance shall take effect and be an act of this day when ratified by a majority of the votes of the people of this State, cast at a poll to be taken thereon on the fourth Thursday in May next, in pursuance of a schedule hereafter to be enacted.

Done in Convention, in the City of Richmond, on the seventeenth day of April, in the year of our Lord one thousand eight hundred and sixty one, and in the eighty-fifth year of the Commonwealth of Virginia.

until the referendum results came in, but then a Second Wheeling Convention met in June 1861. That convention declared all state offices vacant, set up in Wheeling a Reorganized Government of Virginia, and selected Francis H. Pierpoint (later Pierpont) governor. It also appointed John S. Carlile and Waitman T. Willey to the U.S. Senate seats from Virginia previously held by James M. Mason and Robert M. T. Hunter.

Federal military power in the region reinforced the sentiments of a majority of its residents, and a movement for separate statehood proceeded. The U.S. Constitution requires that, before a new state can be formed from an existing state, the current state's legislature must give its consent. The state government in Richmond was not about to approve such a step, but the Wheeling government, claiming to act as the legitimate government of Virginia, signaled its approval. A referendum on the question had already gained overwhelming support in the northwestern counties, and the Wheeling legislature passed, and Governor Pierpont signed, a bill to approve separate statehood.

In June 1863, Congress passed and President Lincoln signed a bill recognizing West Virginia as the nation's thirty-fifth state. The reorganized pro-Union "government" of Virginia moved east from Wheeling to Alexandria, where it continued to act and to be recognized by the Union government in Washington as the legitimate government of Virginia. War raged on.

Chapter 14

Virginians at War

....

Confederate president Jefferson Davis determined before April 1861 was over that the new nation's capital should be moved from Montgomery, Alabama, in the Deep South, to Richmond, the capital of Virginia. A large city, Richmond was home to the Tredegar Iron Works and much more of the Confederacy's manufacturing capacity. South Carolina may have been the Confederacy's birthplace, and Alabama its cradle, but Richmond would be its capital. As had been predicted in the spring of 1861, much of the fighting during the Civil War took place in Virginia—in large part because the Union was fighting to secure the Confederate capital, 100 miles south of Lincoln's White House.

Four years separated Virginia's secession at the convention in Richmond in April 1861 from Robert E. Lee's surrender at Appomattox Courthouse in April 1865. By war's end, Virginians of all descriptions—black and white, slave and free, men and women, eastern and western—had perhaps had their fill of glory and of gore, of honor and of horror. Like Americans everywhere, Virginians variously brought their own fears and hopes, and their own predictions of what a war, if it came, might bring. The War between the States, as many southerners would long call it, or the War of the Rebellion, as the Union officially termed it, was also—in Virginia and elsewhere—a war within the states. The war intruded everywhere and surprised everyone.

First Manassas

The Union army first targeted the railroads at Manassas Junction in northern Virginia, some forty miles west of the U.S. capital. There, on July 21, 1861, the First Battle of Manassas (as the Confederates called it, after the nearby town)—also known as the First Battle of Bull Run (as the Yankees called it, identifying it by the name of a nearby waterway)—ended in a Union loss. Federal casualties—

Tredegar Iron Works, 1865. The Tredegar enterprise, led by Joseph Reid Anderson, represented the high level of industrial development in Virginia by the 1850s, one major reason for Virginia's great attractiveness to the Confederacy in February and March 1861 and for the continuing importance of industrial Richmond after the war. Lithograph by Edward Sachse, based on a drawing by F. Dielman, shortly after the fall of Confederate Richmond. Virginia Historical Society, Richmond, Virginia.

killed, wounded, or missing—were numbered at 2,708. Confederate losses numbered 1,982. The battle told the Confederacy that indeed the Union would fight. But its outcome suggested that the Union might not fight very well, so it bolstered Confederate confidence—and the hope that victory might come quickly. Confederate men had shown that they were going to fight, and fight well.

During the 1850s, Kansas and Harpers Ferry pointed toward a war. In April 1861, Fort Sumter and Lincoln's response to it guaranteed there would be war. With Bull Run, war had begun. Little military action took place in its immediate aftermath, however, so it was hard to guess the magnitude of what was to follow. First Manassas was the largest battle ever fought in Virginia—indeed the largest ever fought on North American soil—up to that time. Within four years, far larger battles made the casualties at First Manassas appear light by comparison.

From a great many Virginians' perspective, the entire Civil War was fought on Virginia soil, except when General Lee and the Army of Northern Virginia

General Winfield Scott (1786–1866). Born near Petersburg, Virginia, Scott attended the College of William and Mary. His half-century-long military career included service in the War of 1812 and in the Indian wars of both the Old Northwest (the Blackhawk War) and the Old Southwest (campaigning against the Creeks and the Seminoles). A hero of the Mexican War—where his subordinate officers included Robert E. Lee—he ran for the presidency on the Whig ticket in 1852. He remained loyal to the United States following Virginia's secession, and thus one Virginia native and career army officer led the Union's military effort, while another led the Confederacy's. Having conceived the "anaconda" strategy that eventually proved successful against the Confederacy, Scott retired in late 1861 at the age of seventy-five. Library of Congress, Prints and Photographs Division, LC-MSS-44297-33-138.

moved north into Maryland or Pennsylvania and fought huge battles at Antietam in 1862 or Gettysburg in 1863. Indeed, an enormous amount of the fighting took place in Virginia. But there was another war, west and south of Virginia, and it was hugely important too. One example is the fighting along the Mississippi River, including the Union's occupation of New Orleans in 1862 and General Ulysses S. Grant's siege of Vicksburg in 1863. Another is the everlasting fighting that took place in central and eastern Tennessee, followed by Union general William Tecumseh Sherman's unstoppable movement south to Atlanta in 1864 and then on to Savannah.

A key southern officer who stayed with the Union, General Winfield Scott—a native of Southside Virginia, veteran of the War of 1812, and hero of the Mexican War—advised President Lincoln in 1861 to follow a so-called anaconda policy, taking command of the Mississippi River, blockading coastal cities, and squeezing the Confederacy like a boa constrictor. That broad policy put pressure on multiple points throughout the Confederacy, and it led to successful efforts to divide the would-be nation into smaller and smaller fragments to defeat it.

Robert E. Lee and Stonewall Jackson

After a year of fighting, Robert E. Lee took charge of the Army of Northern Virginia. Much of the war in Virginia can be told in the stories of Lee and, while he lived, Thomas J. Jackson. Lee, born in 1807, and Jackson, born in 1824, had both graduated from West Point and had both fought in the Mexican War. At the time of secession, Lee was in the U.S. Army, Jackson a professor at the Virginia Military Institute. Both men had some involvement in the Harpers Ferry affair in 1859, as Lee headed up the troops who captured John Brown, and Jackson attended Brown's hanging. Lee, when asked by President Lincoln and General Scott to lead the Federal forces in putting down the rebellion, chose instead to side with his home state and later to go with the Confederacy. As Mary Custis Lee said about the general: "My husband has wept tears of blood over this terrible war, but as a man of honor and a Virginian, he must follow the destiny of his State." Jackson—even though his sister Laura in western Virginia, his only remaining close blood relative, was a staunch Unionist—said much the same thing: "My first allegiance is to my State, the State of Virginia." Jackson picked up the sobriquet "Stonewall" at First Manassas when a general from South Carolina rallied his troops with the shout, "Look, men, there is Jackson standing like a stone wall!"

Lee gave Jackson's troops, the Stonewall Brigade, two assignments. One was to prevent substantial numbers of Union troops, recruited in western Virginia,

Stonewall Jackson (1824–1863). Painting by William Garl Brown, 1866, based on a wartime photograph. Virginia Historical Society, Richmond, Virginia.

from entering the struggle farther east. The other was to protect the Shenandoah Valley, Virginia's breadbasket, from Union control or depredations. These tasks Jackson and his men carried out magnificently, as well as a third, helping to prevent Federal troops from massing near Richmond. But for only so long. On the occasion of an extraordinary victory by Lee at Chancellorsville in May 1863, Jackson was mistakenly shot by Confederate troops and soon died. And still the war was, as it turned out, only half over.

Toward Petersburg

Union troops targeted Richmond far more than Confederate forces aimed at Washington, D.C., although John Singleton Mosby—who fought at both First and Second Bull Run, scouted for J. E. B. "Jeb" Stuart, and then secured permission to organize the Partisan Rangers—ran his guerrilla operations all over northern Virginia. Farther south, the two main armies, like sumo wrestlers trying to take each other down, struggled over who would control Richmond. When General Grant took over command of Union forces in Virginia in 1864, he determined that the main objective of his Army of the Potomac was Lee's Army of Northern Virginia, not the city of Richmond. With his superior numbers, equipment, and supplies, he opened up multiple lines of attack.

Fredericksburg ruins after the fighting in December 1862. This Mathew B. Brady photograph shows damaged buildings in a place that lies midway between the capital city of the United States and the capital city of the Confederate States. Virginia Historical Society, Richmond, Virginia.

Fighting was renewed in the Shenandoah Valley. In May 1864, 247 cadets at the Virginia Military Institute marched from Lexington north to New Market. General John C. Breckinridge ordered the VMI cadets to join him, and Commandant Scott Ship (later Shipp) led them. The cadets included Samuel H. Letcher, son of the former Virginia governor, and George T. Lee, a nephew of General Lee. Others were nephews of General Jubal A. Early and Secretary of War James Seddon, as well as cousins of General Breckinridge. On May 15, the cadets went into battle. They suffered ten dead and forty-seven wounded. But they helped win the day, as Confederate forces repulsed a large Union force, a vital outcome at the time, preventing further control by Union forces in the Valley and greater pressure on Lee to the east. By October, though, the Valley was under Union control.

Farther east, the horrors of the fighting in the Wilderness Campaign, west of Fredericksburg, unfolded in May 1864, where Grant lost some 18,000 troops, and Lee some 10,000. Grant secured replacement soldiers. Lee could not. And some of Lee's finest officers fell as well: Stonewall Jackson having died in May 1863, Jeb Stuart died in May 1864.

Increasingly, Petersburg appeared to be the place to force the question of military supremacy, and action there was also an alternative way to gain control of Richmond, for, barely twenty miles south of the Confederate capital, Petersburg provided Richmond's rail connections south and west. At Petersburg in July 1864, coal miners from Pennsylvania dug a 500-foot-long tunnel toward Lee's troops, with the intent of bringing explosives in. An enormous explosion took place, and some 15,000 Union soldiers, black and white, raced through the smoke toward Lee's troops. But the Confederate forces repulsed the Union men, in the so-called Battle of the Crater, with losses of about 1,500 Confederate soldiers and 4,000 Union men. There were many Confederate heroes, and General William Mahone made his name that day.

Through the summer and fall and on through the winter, fighting continued throughout much of the Confederacy. In Virginia, the main focus was at Petersburg. Lee's troops continued to dwindle, partly from combat deaths and partly from desertion, whether just to check in on their families or to give up the fight for good. At the end of March, Grant jacked up the level of attacks, throwing all his mighty forces at the men in gray. By April 2, it was clear that the Confederate troops could no longer hold on.

Battlefront and Home Front: War Comes to Virginians

Billy Yank and Johnny Reb chased each other all across Virginia and across much of the rest of the Confederacy, as well as in New Mexico Territory and the states of Missouri, Kentucky, Maryland, and Pennsylvania. Hundreds of thousands of Union soldiers and their Confederate counterparts camped and fought in Virginia—along the Chesapeake Bay, up the James River, in the Shenandoah Valley, and, it seemed, everywhere else. General Lee and his horse Traveller headquartered for a time in Culpeper County. So did General Grant and his horse Cincinnati. Big armies had to be supplied, and where they were was where they looked for food and other necessities.

The war could not be contained; it never affected only soldiers; it refused to be restricted to the battlefields. War took place on the home front, too, so it reached civilians everywhere as well. It was not for nothing, for example, that a Richmond resident observed at one point about wounded Confederate soldiers: "We live in one immense hospital." Federal incursions acted, on the one hand, to stiffen resistance. They also acted, on the other, to destroy the material basis for continuing the war and, finally, to wear down resolve by demonstrating, un-remittingly, that the war for Confederate independence could not be won. And the war often pounded people regardless of their loyalties. Said one farmer in Culpeper County: "I hain't took no sides in this yer rebellion, but I'll be dog-garned if both sides hain't took me."

After West Virginia separated, what remained of Virginia was more than 40 percent black, with nine out of ten blacks enslaved. With most white men of military age in the war, society on the home front was mostly made up of every-one else: white women of all ages, white children, elderly white men, and slaves of every description. The men might return—wounded, sick, or just to look af-ter farm and family—but they usually went away again, leaving everyone else to look after things in their absence. White folks on the home front had loneliness and terror as their constant companions. Concerned about the well-being of their loved ones in the field, they shipped food and clothing to the men. But vol-unteer efforts of individuals and families were never remotely enough to supply the soldiers. That task took collective work, efforts organized through volunteer societies and local governments. Nor were supplies of bread and other necessi-ties sufficient to meet the needs of civilians, and what goods were available could only be had at greatly inflated prices, a condition that led to a bread riot by white women in Richmond in April 1863. The Virginia General Assembly took on far less of the responsibility for such matters than did its counterparts in such Deep South states as Georgia and Alabama.

One way to gain access to the war and its multiple meanings is to glimpse the experience of two black children in Petersburg, as they remembered it all a great many years later. Octavia Featherstone, who was just five years old when the war ended, recalled Union soldiers in her neighborhood late in the war. "Yes," she told her interviewer, "de Yankees come to Petersburg, down a hill an' camp on Farmer Street in front of our house. I use to go to de camp ev'y day in de af-ternoon an' git hard tacks." Sarah Wooden Johnson, who also had been a young child during the war, recounted of Petersburg: "Yes, I was big 'nough to see de Yankees come through here. I picked hard tacks off of de ground. We chillun would say to de soldiers, 'Mr. gimme some bread. Mr. gimme some meat.'" But of the noise of battle she had less fond memories, though just as vivid: "De fust gun 'po't I heard gal, hit just skeered me to death! I tracts I was standing in de middle of de flo' and, honey, I jes flew to my muma."

Another comes from the diary of a white woman, Mrs. Cornelia Peake Mc-Donald, in the Shenandoah Valley. She spoke at one point of her terror for the welfare of her children, when having let them go off a way, she heard the thun-der of cannon and knew the war had sneaked up on their home. Another time she wrote: "My heart sinks at the idea of having the enemy again this winter and seeing all hope cut off of seeing my husband again before Spring, if then." In the war's final weeks, deserters in tattered gray filed past her house, often begging food from her scant supplies, and she felt a loss of all hope, and a twinge of scorn, yet thought too that she "could not wonder that they did desert" Lee's dwindling army: "The conscription had forced many unwilling ones to go to the army, leaving unprotected wives and children in lonely mountain huts to abide their fate whatever it might be, freezing or starvation."

Region, Race, Slavery, and War—Why the Confederacy Lost

The ratio of needs and assets ebbed and flowed through the four years of war. At the start of the war, the Union had far more of everything. Yet to defeat the Confederacy, the Union needed far more troops, and far more of everything else, for all the Confederacy had to do was outlast the Union's will to fight, which nearly seemed to happen in 1864.

White southerners contributed to the Union side in ways that Lincoln understood as absolutely essential to his cause. Fighting in blue, not gray, were perhaps 25,000 white troops from western Virginia and another 25,000 white troops from eastern Tennessee. Every such soldier can be understood as subtracting from the Confederate strength one soldier, unavailable for wearing the gray, and as neutralizing another soldier, required to offset the one so lost. Moreover, Lincoln counted on keeping on his side the slave states of the Border South—Delaware and Maryland, Kentucky and Missouri. Although those states supplied manpower for the Confederacy as well as for the Union, far more of their men went to the Union, and every soldier in blue was another addition to the ranks of the Union, and each also offset a soldier in gray.

Yet another southern source of Union manpower, often unrecognized despite its tremendous importance, was the Midwest, a region from which numerous natives of Virginia returned to Virginia in the 1860s, wearing blue, as did their sons as well. Had all the white sons of Virginia fought on the side of the Confederacy, they would have made a mighty difference as the war weighed in the balance. But they did not, and Virginia and its sister states in the Confederacy could not win the war without them.

Not even every white man from eastern Virginia who trained at West Point went with his state. A leading example, standing at counterpoint to Robert E. Lee, is George Henry Thomas, a native of Southampton, the county made famous by the slave rebel Nat Turner. Thomas graduated from West Point in 1840, entered the army, and soon served in the Second Seminole War and in the Mexican War. When Virginia seceded, Thomas did not go with his state. Instead he remained in the Union army throughout the Civil War. He fought briefly in Virginia, but most of his Civil War service came in Kentucky, Tennessee, and Georgia, including at Chattanooga and at Atlanta. General Sherman characterized his fellow Union general as "splendid, victorious, invincible in battle." General Thomas's leadership in the Union cause, and absence from the Confederate forces, contributed twice over to Union victory.

Early in the war John Mercer Langston, a mixed-race native of Virginia living in Ohio, approached the governor of that state, David Tod, with an offer to organize units of black troops. He was told, "Do you not know, Mr. Langston, that this is a white man's government; that white men are able to defend and protect it. . . . When we want you colored men we will notify you." Langston may not have been surprised by the response, but he was surely disappointed. Restricted from fighting, free black northerners like Langston and former Maryland slave Frederick Douglass sought to transform the war into a war of universal emancipation. Not only did they hope that the Union would adopt abolition as a war aim, as eventually came to pass, but they also hoped that the war might lead to a more expansive definition of black freedom for all African Americans, northern and southern, both those currently enslaved and those already free, and this too came to pass.

From the first skirmish to the last, black southerners made absolutely vital contributions to the Confederate war effort. These contributions are best divided into three groups. Lincoln came to see that it was slaves who grew the corn that fed the Confederacy's troops, and slaves who grew the cotton that clothed them. As was clear too, slaves—in Virginia and elsewhere—did much of the combat-support work for Confederate forces, work that white Union troops had to do for themselves; so did free black southerners, who were impressed in large numbers because they too could assist and because they had no owners to object to their conscription. Moreover, one by one, by the thousands, slaves went to war as personal servants to their masters. Each of these people functioned, at least for a time, as a black Confederate, though few ever wore soldier gray.

Changes in the Union's wartime policy regarding emancipation and black troops were a direct result of Lincoln's perception of the potential that black northerners had for helping the war effort, as well as of the vital roles played by black southerners in prolonging the Confederacy's ability to wage its war for independence—thus the announcement of the Emancipation Proclamation, as well as the decision to recruit African Americans into the Union army and navy. After the change in policy in 1863, Governor Tod, getting back to John Mercer Langston, authorized him to organize units of black men from Ohio.

Powhatan Beaty (1837–1916), a native of Richmond who enlisted in the U.S. Colored Troops in Ohio in June 1863. Thousands of black native Virginians fought as soldiers and sailors on the Union side in the last two years of the Civil War. Some received a Medal of Honor, which the wartime U.S. Congress had recently established. Virginians receiving naval Medals of Honor included "contraband"—that is, a slave who entered Union lines—Robert Blake for his bravery in an action near Charleston, South Carolina. Receiving army Medals of Honor—for valorous conduct at the Battle of Chaffin's Farm (also called Fort Harrison or New Market Heights), southeast of Richmond, in September 1864—were former slave Miles James, free black Charles Veal, and two other black Virginians, probably slaves until sometime during the war, Edward Ratliff and James Gardiner. Beaty also received a Medal of Honor, for his actions at Chaffin's Farm. His citation reads: "Took command of his company, all the [white] officers having been killed or wounded, and gallantly led it." Library of Congress, Prints and Photographs Division, LC-USZ62-118556.

THE UNION PARTY ON SLAVERY AND UNION, 1864

1. *Resolved,* That it is the highest duty of every American citizen to maintain against all enemies the integrity of the Union and the paramount authority of the Constitution and laws of the United States; and that, laying aside all differences of political opinion, we pledge ourselves, as Union men, animated by a common sentiment and aiming at a common object, to do everything in our power to aid the Government in quelling by force of arms the rebellion now raging against its authority, and in bringing to the punishment due to their crimes the rebels and traitors arrayed against it. . . .

3. *Resolved,* That as slavery was the cause, and now constitutes the strength, of this rebellion, and as it must be, always and everywhere, hostile to the principles of republican government, justice and the national safety demand its utter and complete extirpation from the soil of the republic; and that while we uphold and maintain the acts and proclamations by which the Government, in its own defense, has aimed a deathblow at this gigantic evil, we are in favor, furthermore, of such an amendment to the Constitution, to be made by the people in conformity with the provisions, as shall terminate and forever prohibit the existence of slavery within the limits or the jurisdiction of the United States. . . .

Scholars and buffs alike continue to argue about the roles that African Americans, men in particular, played in the war: how they shaped its conduct, how they may have altered its outcome, and how their contributions should be understood to illuminate the nature of the war, the motivations for fighting it, and what that all says about white Confederates, black southerners, black northerners, and white northerners. On one side, it is reliably said that roughly 200,000 African Americans—born slave and born free, from the slave states and the free states—joined the Union army or navy, and without them the Union would probably have lost. On the other side, it is said that some number of black southerners—the figure 100,000 is voiced—fought in support of the Confederacy, proving, it is said, that the Confederate war effort was not founded on race or slavery.

Such numbers are worth reconsidering. To rebut the neo-Confederate claims, it is said that few men of African ancestry willingly helped the Confederacy, and virtually all the men included in the count not only were involuntary recruits but also were in combat-support roles. In turn, a rebuttal to that claim could observe that considerable numbers among the Union's 200,000—though the number declined over time—were themselves playing combat-support roles. Yet by the tens of thousands, African American men were Union combat troops. Moreover, slaves provided valuable information to Union sailors making their way along the coast and up the rivers, as well as to the army in maneuvering through unfamiliar territory.

What is not subject to serious controversy is that the Union transformed its war aims before 1864. The war itself may have been at bottom a struggle between one group of whites and another group of whites over America's political future and the destiny of African Americans, but black southerners and black northerners had much to say about the course of the war between the Union and the Confederacy. In no way was this more evident or more decisive than in the incorporation of black soldiers into the Union's military forces during the second half of the war.

An old man, a Civil War veteran, Cornelius Garner peered back from the 1930s into his recollections of the 1860s. Born a slave in Maryland in 1846, he was fifteen years old when the war broke out. In 1864 he turned eighteen, made his way to Norfolk, and enlisted in the Union army. The next spring, he recalled, "Our regiment was de fust into Richmond." Regarding black soldiers more generally, he claimed: "Dey won de war for de white man. Yessuh." More precisely, Cornelius Garner and his black colleagues helped win the war for the Union side, not for the Confederacy.

Slavery and Independence

A great many free Virginians had a tendency to conceive of their independence, their freedom to be who they wished to be, as including the right to own other humans—to exercise their own liberty and that of other people too. When the political turn of events in mid-nineteenth-century America seemed increasingly to threaten their personal independence, they collectively declared their political independence.

The Confederate experiment had to do with far more than slavery. But at its core it had to do precisely with slavery. Soldiers fought for all kinds of reasons, but most of all they fought because there was a war. South Carolina, followed by six other states, seceded to protect slavery from an antislavery national government, under new man-

5. *Resolved,* . . . that we approve, especially, the Proclamation of Emancipation, and the employment as Union soldiers of men heretofore held in slavery. . . .

STATE AND CONGRESSIONAL APPROVAL FOR RECRUITING BLACK CONFEDERATE SOLDIERS

Should the Confederate Congress give its approval to black soldiers wearing gray? A declaration from the Deep South's *Charleston Mercury* in January exclaimed: "*We want no Confederate Government without our institutions*." In Virginia, however, in early March the General Assembly finally gave its support to the innovation:

Resolved, That the General Assembly of Virginia do hereby authorize the Confederate authorities to call upon Virginia, through the Governor of the Commonwealth, for all her able bodied male free negroes between the ages of eighteen and forty-five, and as many of her able bodied male slaves between the ages aforesaid, as may be deemed necessary for the public defense, not exceeding twenty-five per centum of said slaves, to be called for upon the requisition of the General-in-Chief of the Confederate Armies, as he may deem most expedient for the public service. . . .

That our senators are hereby instructed and our representatives requested to vote for the passage of a law to place at the disposal of the Confederate authorities. . . .

A companion law repealed the state's ban on arms in the hands of black Virginians:

agement as Republicans defeated Democrats for control of the presidency. War came after Lincoln, determined to put down the Rebellion, called up troops and sent them off to do battle. Slavery led to secession, which led in turn to war.

The Civil War followed secession, which in the Deep South in particular had been intended more than anything else to safeguard slavery and the accompanying racial regime. If slavery constituted the core cause of the war, then slavery could not be unaffected by a war that raged on year after year. Lincoln's approach to slavery changed with the war, as the Emancipation Proclamation and black recruitment in 1863 showed. Beyond that, the Republican Party, having run on a platform in 1860 that, though clearly antislavery, was avowedly antiabolitionist, adopted a revolutionary platform four years later and won again. The 1864 platform committed the Republican Party to a constitutional amendment that would abolish slavery throughout the nation, however far that stretched (see sidebar, page 204). The promise, once Lincoln had been re-elected, led to congressional approval of the Thirteenth Amendment in early 1865 and, after Union victory, subsequent ratification by the states. The Union, fighting a war to keep the nation together, not to end slavery, ended up finding that the war could not be won without an attack on slavery, the root cause of the war.

Nor did the Confederacy manage to negotiate four years of war without having to reconceive its commitment to slavery. Though—back in 1860–1861, when the first seven states had seceded—the preservation of slavery had been the objective, and secession the means to that end, much had changed by the winter of 1864–1865. The Confederacy found itself running out of time, space, soldiers, and options. The Confederate Congress enacted a law in early 1865 to recruit slave men to fight for the Confederacy. By that time, it was too late in the game to make a difference.

Means and ends had switched places, so that slavery—some portion of it, at any rate—might be offered up as a sacrifice to achieve political independence. No greater measure of change in the South could be seen than the sight of black men in Richmond, the capital of the Confederacy, drilling for war as part of the Confederate military effort. And yet, desperate as was the gesture, and extraordinary as was the sight, not a lot had changed regarding the Confederate policy on slavery. Freedom was barred "except by consent of the owners and of the States" (see sidebar).

Lee's Church in Richmond

Civil War historian Emory M. Thomas tells an enchanting story of a deeply troubled General Lee who in December 1863 found his distress interrupted by a sprightly letter from two young ladies urging Lee to let one of his soldiers, Cary Robinson, leave the lines so they could spend Christmas with him. "If you will grant him a furlough for this purpose," they wrote, "we will pay you back in thanks and love and kisses." They signed themselves "your two little friends." Lee wrote back in a similar spirit and granted their request. Lee's "two little friends" included Lucy Minnegerode, the teenaged daughter of Dr. Charles Minnegerode, the rector at St. Paul's Episcopal Church in Richmond, where Lee worshipped when in town. Lucy was, we can surmise, no stranger to the general, and she wrote him in the spirit of a favorite niece to a cherished uncle.

At St. Paul's Episcopal Church in Richmond, the capital of the Confederacy, Minnegerode continued, as he had for some years and would for many more, to serve as rector. Minnegerode was a

Be it enacted by the General Assembly, That it shall be lawful for all free negroes and slaves, who may be organized as soldiers, now, or at any time hereafter by the State or the Confederate Government, for the public defense during the present war with the United States, to bear arms while in active military service, and carry ammunition as other soldiers in the Army. . . .

Having been instructed to change their votes and support the Confederate bill, Virginia's senators did so, and the measure passed in the Confederate Senate 9–8 and went into operation. Here is the language of "An Act to Increase the Military Force of the Confederate States," with the first section authorizing black soldiers and section 5 specifying that black soldiers would not necessarily get their freedom:

The Congress of the Confederate States of America do enact, That in order to provide additional forces to repel invasion, maintain the rightful possession of the Confederate States, secure their independence, and preserve their institutions, the President be, and he is hereby, authorized to ask for and accept from the owners of slaves, the services of such number of able-bodied negro men as he may deem expedient, for and during the war, to perform military service in whatever capacity he may direct. . . .

Sec. 5. That nothing in this act shall be construed to authorize a change in the relation which the said slaves shall bear toward their owners, except by consent of the owners and of the States in which they may reside, and in pursuance of the laws thereof.

Approved March 13, 1865.

According to section 5, any offer of freedom to slave men who would join the Confederate military—in combat roles—was expressly contingent on approval by the slaves' owners and by the states as well.

fixture at public events in the community as well as at Sunday services at the church. During the war, Minnegerode presided over baptisms, weddings, and funerals—far more funerals than if there had been no war. In 1862, Jefferson Davis was baptized at that church. In 1863, at St. James Episcopal Church in Richmond, Minnegerode was one of the ministers who conducted the funeral service for Stonewall Jackson. In January 1865, he married General John Pegram and Miss Hetty Cary—as one Richmonder later put it, "One of the handsomest and most lovable men I ever knew" and "the handsomest woman in the Southland . . . the most beautiful woman I ever saw in any land." Three weeks later, Minnegerode presided over General Pegram's funeral.

At St. Paul's Church on a communion Sunday, the first Sabbath in April 1865, the congregation reflected the time, late in the war, when most white men of military age were off at war. So women predominated in the church that day—though there were some old men, civilians, and some soldiers in uniform, off duty as they recovered from wounds. Also in attendance were a number of high officials of the Confederate government, among them President Jefferson Davis, as well as Virginia governor William Smith. During the service that April 2—before communion—someone brought in a message to the president, as had often happened at other such events. Davis hurried out, as he had at times before. But this message was from General Lee, advising that his lines were broken. To save what remained of his army, he must retreat. And it was time, that very night, to evacuate Richmond. What had seemed first impossible but then increasingly inevitable had come to pass. Even after Davis and other officials left the church, the service continued.

President Abraham Lincoln in Richmond, April 1865. With son Todd in hand, Lincoln makes his way through downtown Richmond, the day after Union troops entered the capital of the Confederacy. Black Virginians, as shown here, were jubilant; Confederate supporters, like the city, were devastated. This engraving by J. C. Buttre was based on a sketch by Lambert Hollis. Virginia Historical Society, Richmond, Virginia.

Lee had watched as the Confederacy won battle after battle in Virginia, and yet its manpower was further depleted in each encounter. Increasingly, the population advantage on the Union side, backed up by its superior manufacturing capacity, negated the Confederate advantages of fighting on the defensive, fighting on familiar ground, and fighting to protect their property and their communities from what they saw as an invading force that kept coming. And keep coming it did, especially after President Lincoln finally found his general, Ulysses S. Grant. In early 1865, Grant pounded Lee's forces around Richmond and Petersburg. Lee tried to slip away, but on April 9 he surrendered to Grant. The ceremony took place at the home of Wilmer McLean, who had moved to Appomattox from Manassas after the First Battle of Bull Run in order to get away from the war. Four years had passed, and the war washed up again on McLean's front step, but then it receded, this time for keeps.

Let Us Have Peace, a painting by Jean Lyon
Gerome Ferris of the meeting at Appomat-
tox between Union general U. S. Grant and
Confederate general Robert E. Lee. Courtesy
Virginia Historical Society, Richmond, Virginia,
Lora Robins Collection of Virginia Art.

The Killing Fields

The war killed roughly 300,000 men on each side, Union and Confederate, all Americans. More of the dead, on each side, died in Virginia than anywhere else. Rather than America's cradle, Virginia became for a time America's graveyard.

Virginia entered the war with the most white residents of any Confederate state. Even after West Virginia went its separate way, Virginia's white population, roughly 700,000, remained the Confederacy's largest. Most white men of military age spent at least some time in the military, and many served for the entire four years, from spring 1861 through spring 1865. Many returned from service maimed or in poor health, and many never returned at all. How might we tally up the human losses?

If every tenth Confederate death was a resident of Virginia, the number came to approximately 30,000, quite aside from the white Virginia Unionists and black Virginians who died. If one-quarter of the 700,000 white Virginians during the war—or 175,000—were men of military age, or became so during the war, then every sixth white man of military age in Virginia lay among the Confederacy's war dead. Those men never returned to their parents, wives, or children, to their mills, shops, or farms.

Death of the Confederacy, Death of Slavery

Confederate southerners had gambled that if they could obtain national independence, they could secure slavery. As the war continued, the preservation of slavery came to depend on their success in their bid for independence. In the end, failure in one meant failure in the other. When the war was finally over, it was black southerners who had enhanced their chances of greater personal independence, though how that might work out remained to be seen.

Had the Union not fought in 1861, the Confederacy would have gone its separate way, perhaps without Virginia. Had the Union won much sooner than it did—as it might very well have had Virginia not joined the Confederacy—slavery might have survived the War of the Rebellion. Had the Confederacy held out longer—had Virginia's contributions been even more effective than they were—the Union's military effort might well have collapsed and the bid for independence might have succeeded.

As it was, however, April 1865 brought the end of the Confederate experiment in Virginia. Secession as a political option died on the battlefield. With Union victory, slavery came to an end wherever in Virginia it had persisted that long—it had faded around Union-occupied Norfolk early in the war. Slavery, secession, and the Confederacy died, as did some 600,000 men. In Washington, D.C., Abraham Lincoln died on April 15 from the bullet of a pro-Confederate assassin.

The war was over. Many died, but most lived. Theirs would be the hard task of rebuilding personal lives, forging new ground rules, creating a new society. A new Virginia—but how new?—would take the place of the old Commonwealth.

The U.S. government—under a new president, Andrew Johnson, a Unionist Democrat from eastern Tennessee, but elected with Republican Abraham Lincoln in 1864 on a so-called Union Party ticket—had huge decisions to make as to how the states that had seceded might be restored to their normal political membership in the nation. Especially in the early stages of peace, the Freedmen's Bureau worked to keep people alive during desperate times in the South and to begin a transition to a new social order without slavery. Created by Congress early in 1865 even as the war ground on, the Freedmen's Bureau was a twin to, or arm of, the Union army, with peacetime responsibilities that included distributing emergency rations to needy white and black southerners alike and supporting schools for the freedmen. Those would be places to begin.

Chapter 15

Reconstructing Virginia—
After War and Emancipation

....

Edmund Ruffin's younger son, Julian, died in battle at Drewry's Bluff, south of Richmond, in May 1864; within a year, the rest of Ruffin's hopes had died. At home in Amelia County in June 1865, the staunch Virginia secessionist finished his breakfast one day, returned alone to his room, finished the last of a very long entry in his diary and, under the words "The End," signed his name. After wrapping himself in a Confederate flag, he pointed his musket at himself and pulled the trigger. His family found him dead next to the diary, which lay open to the last page, where he tried to explain: "I hereby declare my unmitigated hatred to Yankee rule—to all political, social & business connection with Yankees." He could only hope, he had written, for eventual "vengeance" on the "perfidious Yankee people" for "the now ruined, subjugated, & enslaved Southern States!" Edmund Ruffin had never been struck by a Yankee bullet or maimed by a Union bayonet. His remaining son, Edmund Ruffin Jr., nonetheless wrote in a letter to his own sons: "The Yankees have just as certainly killed your Grandfather as they did your beloved uncle."

The end of the Civil War and of the Confederate experiment variously brought deep despair, utter exhilaration, and tremendous uncertainty. As one white Virginia woman, Loula Grimes, wrote in May 1865, she found it "so humiliating to be under Yankee domination after all our hard fighting" that she was "nearly crazy" to escape to Europe. By contrast, people who had been living as slaves in Virginia often expressed ecstasy.

Robert E. Lee (1807–1870), after the Civil War. Mathew B. Brady had a number of photographs done of Lee at his home in Richmond in April 1865, right after the war. Later that year, Lee became president of Washington College, which, after his death in 1870, was renamed Washington and Lee University. This image, an engraving published in *Harper's Weekly* in 1869, was based on an earlier Brady photograph. Library of Congress, Prints and Photographs Division, LC-USZ61-1117.

Day of Jubilee

Slave narratives reflected the joy that came to their quarters when the news of freedom came. For years to come, African Americans in Virginia divided the history of the world at General Lee's surrender at Appomattox. Charles Grandy, who had been born in 1842, recalled in 1937, as his language was transcribed:

> Slaves was some kind o' glad when dey 'mancipated, all dey sing was:
>
> > Slavery chain is broke at las'
> > Broke at las', broke at las'
> > Slavery chain is broke at las'
> > Praise God 'till I die.

Georgianna Preston, born about 1855, recalled the first night of freedom:

> Us young folks carried on somep'n awful. Ole Marse let us stay up all night, an' didn't seem to mind at all. Saw de sun sot an' befo' we know it, it was a-risin' again. Ole folks was shoutin' an' singin' songs. Dar's one dey sung purty nigh all night. Don't know who started it, but soon's dey stopped, 'nother

one took it up an' made up some mo' verses. Lawdy, chile, I kin hear dat song a-ringin' in my haid now:

Ain't no mo' blowin' dat fo' day horn,
Will sing, chillun, will sing,
Ain't no mo' crackin' dat whip over John,
Will sing, chillun, will sing.

Louise Bowes Rose, born in 1853, recalled a certain baptism into a new life of freedom on the day word came to her Ashland plantation that slavery had ended: "Daddy was down to de creek. He jumped right in de water up to his neck. He was so happy he jus' kep' on scooping up han'fulls of water an dumpin' it on his haid an' yellin', 'I'se free, I'se free! I'se free!'"

Allen Wilson, who turned twenty the year the Civil War ended, reported having grown up in Brunswick County, together with his mother and siblings, and "right many" other slaves. But then Wilson's owner, Benjamin Myrick, made him a present to Myrick's son, who took him in 1862 to Petersburg, where young Wilson was hired out to work in a tobacco factory. Meanwhile, Allen Wilson's father, Edward Wilson, who belonged to another master in Brunswick County, Braxton Wilson, "ran away a slave and got with the Yankees in Grant's army." After leaving the army in 1867, Edward Wilson brought the three wings of the family together when he "moved to Petersburg, taking mother and all her children. We worked and bought a home on Dunlop Street and I've been living here every since."

An end to enslavement brought an end to the whipping of slaves—"no mo' crackin' dat whip over John"—and an end to the slave trade. Realizing the import of an end to slavery was precisely why, of course, the end brought such exhilaration. Moreover, the dawn of universal freedom fostered the possibility of reunifying families, as when Arthur Greene's brother made his way back from South Carolina to his family in Virginia (see chapter 11), or when Allen Wilson's father and mother moved in with their children to their own place in Petersburg—though Anna Harris, for one, never did see again her sister Kate who had been sold away, nor did Israel Massie ever see his two brothers again.

But change did not end in 1865. The unfolding process of emancipation led in the next few years to black voting, and black office holding too, and to black public schools, soon with black teachers. The legislative effort back in 1832 to inaugurate gradual emancipation, had it not failed, would have provided for slaves in Virginia to begin obtaining their freedom by 1861. Instead, Virginia seceded and joined the Confederacy that year. In the Civil War, slavery was ended suddenly, and without the deportation of all free blacks or freed slaves, as had been contemplated in 1832. In 1866, black residents of Virginia, numbering at least 600,000, were granted citizenship; in 1867, they received political rights.

Black Schools—From Crime to Norm

Even the narratives of black Virginians who had been born free reflected the transformation in public policy and private opportunity that emancipation brought to all black Virginians. Into the 1860s, a state law had made it a crime to hold a school that black Virginians—free or slave—attended. George Lewis and Octavia Featherstone, both born free, each turned age six the year slavery ended throughout Virginia, and both reported their experiences attending school that same year.

The schools were sponsored by the Freedmen's Bureau or by various northern missionary societies. Teachers of the freedmen were white and black, men and women, from Virginia and the North, but freedmen often reported them as white women from New England. As crucial to the new schools as their teachers were the black churches—some having originated during slavery times, some newly established—where they often met.

George Lewis recalled, in his earnest fashion: "Immediately after the War the Yankees from the New England states sent teachers down to the South to teach the children of ex-slaves." Such schools in Richmond in the postwar 1860s were located, he said, "in the different colored churches of the city, . . . First Baptist, 3rd Street, Second Baptist, and Ebenezer Baptist." As for himself: "The first school I entered during this era was Second Baptist Church between First and Second Streets on Byrd Street. I remained there for about four years. Then I entered Dills' Bakery; this was also a school conducted by Yankees. The next school I attended was Navy Hill and then to the Old High and Normal. I graduated in 1877 from this school." Not only that, Lewis went on to recount that, beginning in 1878, he became a teacher himself, a black teacher in a black school. So very much had changed, and just in time for him as he grew up. Moreover, in 1886 he entered law school at Howard University, in Washington, D.C., 100 miles to the north of Richmond—a school that had been established, also as a consequence of the end of slavery and the beginning of black citizenship in the 1860s, at the very time that George Lewis had been an elementary school student at Second Baptist Church.

Twenty miles away in Petersburg, Octavia Featherstone and her family had attended Third Baptist Church in the 1860s, and that was where she began school, too: "De first school after de war was in Third Church. I went dare to school an' was taught by a white northern woman, I forgit her name. Four or five teachers was sent dare from de North to teach colored people. . . . Dis school didn' last long fo' de public schools was opened. At dat time de ole an' de young folks flocked to de public school tryin' to learn to read an' write."

Allen Wilson, too, recalled the school that was held in Third Baptist Church—that was the church his family had joined when his father, mother, and siblings first came to Petersburg—but he also remembered the name of the white teacher, Miss Kate Brown. And he reported: "The very first colored school in Petersburg after the War was taught by a Mrs. Elam at the Freeman's Bureau at the Oak Grove on West Street between Farmer and Rome Streets." In fact, "my youngest brother and youngest sister attended dis school—Jeff Wilson and Lucy A. Wilson." As for himself, though, he "never had a chance at schooling."

A Radically New Dispensation?

Ask any Virginian, white or black, at the end of the war. According to any of their varied scenarios, little or nothing about Virginia in 1865 resembled what should have happened. White Virginians, in particular, had differed among themselves over many things in the generation before the Civil War, but few if any anticipated the scene in 1865. Black Virginians came to see, ever more clearly as the returns came in, that despite their celebrations of Union victory and emancipation, despite their defining history as divided at Lee's surrender, the contrast between slave times and what followed was far less than they wished. Whites tended to see far too much change. Blacks saw too much continuity.

Slavery had ended. But, as white Virginians saw, free black Virginians abounded—there was no colonization, no exile, no mass migration by people who, if they were to retain their freedom, would have to do so elsewhere. Free Virginians, white and black, would have to contrive new terms on which to live in a world without slavery. Some agreement would have to be found on what an end to slavery meant. Now that black Virginians were no longer slaves—or, as roughly one in ten had been, free blacks during slavery times—what could they expect to be? Might they have only black freedom, as it had been previously defined under Virginia law? Or might they have a chance at white freedom—voting rights, access to schools, and all the rest? Might it turn out to be something in between?

These legal and political questions were central to postwar deliberations. Key to the economic well-being of whites and blacks were the matters of who would control the land and whether a family would work their own land or someone else's. Landownership had never been universal among white families, and in the generations after slavery, various forms of tenancy and sharecropping mired many white Virginians and larger numbers of black Virginians. Former slave-owners lost their customary command of their labor force, and they also lost the property—the slaves—that they would have once used as collateral for loans or as the basis of transfers of wealth from one generation to another. Slaves had comprised the bulk of many planters' estates, but such a form of property no longer existed, as former slaves came to own themselves.

In politics, western whites had finally taken control of the House of Delegates under the state Constitution of 1851, and they had expected to take the Virginia Senate, too, after the next reapportionment, in 1865. In 1865, instead, the western half of the state was truncated, the numbers of western whites vastly diminished, because West Virginia had become a separate state. Political power in the state of Virginia, to the extent that it divided between eastern whites and western whites, appeared to shift back across the Blue Ridge to its traditional home in the east.

Unlike the other former Confederate states, whatever the new political geography, Virginia came out of the war with a loyal state government already in place, housed in Alexandria. That loyal government from the war years moved to Richmond, replaced the rebel government, and took up operations as though it represented the state. For a time, it did.

President Andrew Johnson placed two main conditions on the former Confederate states before political restoration could be completed, before southern voters could again go to the polls and elect officeholders, before southern men could return to the vacant seats in the U.S. Senate and House of Representatives. The losers in the war must accept the death of slavery and the death of secession. After the great gamble of secession, after the catastrophe of war, slavery and secession would die together. On their own, the former Confederate states crafted legal changes they saw as necessary to accommodate the end of slavery. Congress soon demanded additional conditions for political restoration and further consideration of how a general emancipation of slaves should unfold.

Congressional Reconstruction and Virginia

By early 1866, each state of the former Confederacy had enacted new laws to reflect the general emancipation of its black residents, but none of those Black Codes appeared, in many northerners' eyes, to go far enough in securing freedom to former slaves. Mississippi's, for example, which barred landownership by black farmers, seemed designed to keep black laborers from escaping the need to work on white planters' lands—seemed designed, in short, to prevent black residents from ever obtaining economic independence, from truly escaping slavery. Virginia took no such action on landownership, and yet its new laws, too—those preventing black testimony in court cases involving whites, for example, or appearing to put freed people at a disadvantage in seeking better working arrangements—gained a hostile reception by many northern observers, who saw them as reflecting too little change. And anyway, all the former Confederate states' actions were lumped together in the perception that perhaps slavery in the South was not yet sufficiently a thing of the past. Mainstream public opinion in the North demanded that slavery be in fact dead, with no potential of ever again becoming a major political issue.

Congress passed a civil rights bill in 1866. It declared African Americans to be citizens, and it stipulated basic rights that freedmen, as American citizens, must be accorded, including the right to buy and own land. President Johnson vetoed the bill, however. Congress enacted the bill over Johnson's veto, but northern Republicans, in and out of Congress, knew that a change in power could lead to its repeal and that an attack in the courts might lead to its being declared unconstitutional. To give greater permanence to the Civil Rights Act of 1866 appeared to require a constitutional amendment that would put the essence of the act beyond the reach of congressional majorities or federal judges.

Yet even had there been no concern about the civil rights of former slaves, Congress would have felt compelled to address the death of slavery along another dimension. Had President Lincoln lived to serve out his second term, he, like other Republican leaders, would have had to address an unexpected complication, a largely unanticipated political consequence of emancipation. The old three-fifths clause was still in the Constitution, but it meant something vastly different in the postwar, postslavery world. With slavery abolished, former slaves automatically changed categories and assumed full value. Thus, after the next apportionment, following the 1870 census, southern states would garner many more seats in Congress than they had before and, therefore, many more votes in the electoral college.

If white men across the South maintained a monopoly on voting, and if most voted Democratic, then, Republican northerners pondered, look at how bleak the future had become. As a consequence of defeating the Confederacy, dragging eleven southern states back into the Union, and bringing an end to the great divisive issue, slavery, southern Democrats would regain power in the reunited nation. Such wartime legislation as the Homestead Act and the Morrill Land-Grant College Act, not to mention the tariff and banking and currency legislation of the war years, would be in jeopardy. And no Republican member of the House or Senate could look with any confidence on his chances of election to the presidency. The consequence of victory and abolition would be the utter defeat of Republicans' policy initiatives and their presidential candidates.

So in death as in life, southern slavery roiled national politics. Republican leaders found utterly unacceptable the prospect that their wartime enemies might secure additional power as a consequence of having been defeated in their bid for independence. Congressman Roscoe Conkling of New York demanded: "Shall the death of slavery add two-fifths to the entire power which slavery had when slavery was living?" Senator John Sherman wrote his brother, Civil War general William T. Sherman: "Who shall exercise this [additional] political power? Shall the rebels do so?" At another time, Senator Sherman thundered: "But one thing I know, . . . that never by my consent shall these rebels gain by this war increased political power and come back here to wield that power in some other form against the safety and integrity of the country." The old "slave power" of the 1850s might have to be called something else, then, but unless something were done to address the core problem the Republicans saw, the white South would return to participation in the political life of the nation with far more power than before secession.

Quite aside from the question of civil rights, in other words, Republicans pondered the question of power, of policy, of political control of a reunified nation. And thus they crafted a constitutional amendment that would address both dimensions of public life in the postwar world, both implications of the death of slavery.

The Fourteenth Amendment, approved by both houses of Congress in June 1866, had two major provisions. Section 1 recognized as citizens "all persons" born in the United States, clearly including African Americans, and it guaranteed all citizens against actions by their state governments that threatened to deny them "the equal protection of the laws." The Civil Rights Act of 1866, passed in response to the Black Codes enacted by the former Confederate states in 1865 and 1866, would have a permanent home, enshrined in the Constitution—at least, that is, if the Fourteenth Amendment gained ratification.

Section 2 restated the old three-fifths clause, but deleted the phrase about slaves, and then proceeded to give the white electorates of southern states, together with their white representatives in southern legislatures, a hard choice. Counted at five-fifths, black southerners would inflate the congressional power of southern states, but only if black men were permitted to vote. Whites could retain a monopoly on political power if they wished, but if they did so they would have to accept the consequence, a proportional reduction in representation. If, that is, black residents were to count full value, they must be permitted to vote for their own representation; if they could not vote for their representation, no one could. If they voted, of course, it could be assumed that they would vote overwhelmingly for Republicans, the party of Lincoln and emancipation, not for Democrats, the party of slavery and secession. And in that case, black southern voters would largely offset white southern voters, and the world would once again be safe for the national Republican Party and the interests it represented. Moreover, black southerners could then look after their own interests in their states, under governments they helped elect.

Republican leaders, and mainstream voters across the North, did not enter the postwar era any more committed to black citizenship, let alone black suffrage and black office holding, than they had entered the war committed to an end to slavery. After the war, however, they needed assurance that slavery was indeed dead and that former slaveholders would have less capacity for political mischief. So they earnestly addressed black citizenship, with "equal protection of the laws," and black suffrage and representation. These two concerns, and these two emerging commitments, appeared in the Fourteenth Amendment. Once restoration was complete, it would be far too late to renegotiate the terms of readmission. So until this monumental concern was resolved, the former Confederate states could not be restored, their congressional delegations readmitted to their seats.

Toward the Resolution of 1870

Virginia governor Francis H. Pierpont urged Virginia legislators to vote to ratify the Fourteenth Amendment. Almost none did. Among all the former states of the Confederacy, only Tennessee accepted the new terms, voted to ratify the amendment, agreed to accept a reduction in representation if it failed to enfranchise black Tennesseans. That left ten states rejecting the terms. Requiring approval by three-fourths of all states for ratification, the Fourteenth Amendment could protect no interests, solve no problems, unless at least some among the ten intransigent states could be turned around.

Could Congress find a means to turn those states around? In the midterm elections of 1866, all members of the House of Representatives were up for re-election; President Johnson roamed the nation, haranguing voters to support Democratic candidates and reject the Republicans and their notions of a Fourteenth Amendment to the Constitution. When the results came in, northern voters had sent to Congress even larger majorities of Republicans than before.

Congressional Republicans took control of political restoration and converted it into political reconstruction. In March 1867 they enacted—over the president's vetoes—a series of laws. The new civilian governments of ten southern states were suspended. Virginia's new political identity was "Military District No. 1." Federal troops would take power and monitor a new set of elections.

In those elections, black men and white men alike would vote to choose delegates to new state constitutional conventions. Those conventions must write new state constitutions, each of which must provide for two things: the enfranchisement of black men (thus black residents would indeed henceforth count as five-fifths) and the establishment of a public school system with space for black children as well as white.

With black men as well as white men participating, the Old Dominion held new elections in 1867 to a constitutional convention, and the convention met in Richmond, with Republicans outnumbering Democrats by sixty-eight to thirty-six, with twenty-four black delegates among the Republicans. Among the new black politicians was George Teamoh, who had fled slavery in 1855 after his family was sold away, but who had then returned to Virginia in 1865, reunited with his wife and one of his children, returned to his work as a caulker in Norfolk, become involved with local politics, and gained election to the convention. White Republicans at the convention included John C. Underwood, a New York native who had migrated to Virginia in the 1840s to promote a shift from slave to free labor, had become active in Republican politics in the 1850s, and had been appointed a federal judge in the 1860s. The Republican majority chose Underwood to preside over the convention. As directed, the new Underwood constitution, as it was framed, contained provisions for black suffrage and public schools, with the schools to be supported in part by a poll tax on men. A great deal of uncertainty and delay, however, accompanied provisions that called for disenfranchising many whites for their wartime disloyalty to the Union. The delay postponed Virginia's political restoration beyond the 1868 presidential election. A compromise called for separate balloting on the constitution as a whole and on the disfranchising provisions. Under those rules, in 1869, voters overwhelmingly approved the constitution while rejecting the disfranchisement measures. Virginia's black men would be voting; Virginia's white men would as well. It was time to elect a governor and a legislature.

In the postwar world, political alignments were unavoidably uncertain, as prewar Whigs jockeyed with prewar Democrats, whites contested with blacks, and all factions looked to the nation's capital for guidance as to what would be required or permitted. The Democrats themselves had been divided in the 1860 presidential election; former Whigs had to find a new political home; and there was a new game in town, with the Republicans in the mix and a substantial black majority the cornerstone of their base. Therefore white voters, even had they been united, and they were anything but, found it necessary to invent new terms. Many, even most, white voters identified for a time as Conservatives, in opposition to the "Radical" Republicans.

Blanche K. Bruce (1841–1898). Bruce was among the former Virginia slaves serving their constituents in postwar politics. The son of a slave and her owner in Prince Edward County, Virginia, Bruce also worked in Mississippi and Missouri before escaping slavery early in the Civil War. Elected by the Mississippi legislature during Reconstruction, Bruce served a full term in the U.S. Senate, 1875–1881. Another former Virginia slave, George Teamoh (1818–1883?), was elected to Virginia's constitutional convention of 1867–1868 and then to the Virginia Senate, where he served from 1869 to 1871. Bruce and Teamoh each returned to a place of his former enslavement to make public policy in a postslavery world. Library of Congress, Prints and Photographs Division, LC-BH832-30088.

Two Republican candidates ran for the governorship in 1869, the hard-liner Henry H. Wells and the moderate Gilbert C. Walker. With the Republicans divided, the moderate wing, with substantial Conservative support, elected Walker. Conservatives, however, with broad-based white support in a majority-white state, gained a majority in the legislature. The outnumbered Republicans included six black members in the Senate and twenty-three in the House of Delegates.

Quickly ratifying the Fourteenth Amendment, the General Assembly satisfied the formal requirements for restoration. Members of Congress expressed concern, however, that once readmitted, Virginia would drop key provisions of its new constitution. Thus restoration was made contingent on leaving intact the two major innovations of the new regime, political rights for black men and a public school system open to children of both races. On that basis, Congress passed, and President Ulysses S. Grant signed, a measure restoring the "mother of states" to the status it had abandoned back in the secession spring of 1861. The Resolution of 1870, as we could call it, appeared to secure a new foundation for politics in Virginia.

Once again, Virginia voters elected members of Congress, and once again the legislature chose two U.S. senators. Moreover, Virginia would be participating in the 1872 presidential campaign when that time came. In that sense, restoration was complete. Reconstruction was over. In another sense, too, Reconstruction was over in Virginia, in that the Republicans had already lost control of the machinery of state government. In fact, their only time of dominance during the first postwar decade came in the constitutional convention of 1868–1869, so—in contrast to the ten other former Confederate states—there never was a time in Virginia during that decade when Republicans controlled both the governorship and the legislature.

In other ways, however, Reconstruction was by no means over. The new rules that the new constitution voiced remained in effect. Black men continued to vote, and black legislators continued to win election and serve their constituents. Among the issues to be faced, one involved creating a public school system, something quickly accomplished in 1870—with the proviso, however, that black students would be strictly segregated from white students. Another issue involved higher education.

War of the Colleges—and the Resolution of 1872

During the Civil War, while Virginia was in the Confederacy, the U.S. Congress had enacted a law that soon began to transform higher education across the nation. After Virginia was restored to the Union, the benefits of the Morrill Land-Grant College Act of 1862 became available to the Old Dominion. Each state was granted a large chunk of land in the trans-Mississippi West, to be sold, the proceeds invested, with the interest available to support one or more colleges, at which training in agriculture and engineering would be offered, whatever other courses were as well. During 1870, 1871, and early 1872, the legislature spent many days of animated oratory and frenetic maneuvering in an effort to determine what institution or institutions would receive the Morrill Act endowment.

Legislators in the 1870–1871 session argued on and on about the land-grant money. No decision seemed in sight when the *Richmond Dispatch*, in its head-

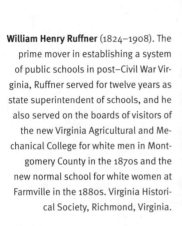

William Henry Ruffner (1824–1908). The prime mover in establishing a system of public schools in post–Civil War Virginia, Ruffner served for twelve years as state superintendent of schools, and he also served on the boards of visitors of the new Virginia Agricultural and Mechanical College for white men in Montgomery County in the 1870s and the new normal school for white women at Farmville in the 1880s. Virginia Historical Society, Richmond, Virginia.

line for yet another story on the inaction, used the phrase "War of the Colleges." No school found sufficient support in the legislature—including Washington College, just then changing its name to Washington and Lee University to honor Robert E. Lee, its postwar president who had recently died. The legislators went home without reaching a conclusion. Congress had extended to ten years the length of time states had for acting under the 1862 Morrill formula, but the ten-year limit was fast approaching.

When the General Assembly convened in December 1871, Governor Walker reminded members that they had to take some action. He urged that the endowment be split, with one portion going to a school that black Virginians might attend. As in the previous session, every school in Virginia seemed to put in a bid for some share of the Morrill Act funds. The University of Virginia sought mightily to secure at least a portion of the bounty. The Virginia Military Institute, which had been savaged by Union forces late in the war, offered to move lock, stock, and barrel to Richmond as a condition of getting the money. William Henry Ruffner, state superintendent of public schools, and William T. Sutherlin, delegate from Pittsylvania County, continued to push for a school unconnected with any existing candidate. As a spokesman for the State Agricultural Society, Sutherlin had urged legislators the year before to establish a new school, one that would grow into whatever Virginians might find they needed, a "purely

1. Be it enacted by the general assembly, That the annual interest accruing from the proceeds of the land scrip donated to the state of Virginia by act of congress of July [1862] . . . shall be appropriated as follows . . . : One-third thereof to the Hampton Normal and Agricultural Institute, in the county of Elizabeth City, and two-thirds thereof to the Preston and Olin Institute, in the county of Montgomery.

2. The said annuity to the Preston and Olin Institute shall be on these express conditions:

First. The name of the said institute shall be changed to the Virginia Agricultural and Mechanical College.

Second. The trustees of the said institute shall transfer . . . the land, buildings, and other property of said institute, to the Virginia Agricultural and Mechanical College.

Third. The county of Montgomery shall appropriate twenty thousand dollars, to be expended in the erection of additional buildings, or in the purchase of a farm for the use of the said college.

Fourth. A number of students, equal to the number of members of the house of delegates, to be apportioned in the same manner, shall have the privilege of attending said college without charge for tuition, use of laboratories, or public buildings, to be selected by the school trustees of the respective counties, cities and election dis-

agricultural and mechanical" institution at first, yet "a nucleus around which the accretions of time would gather a really great institution."

White legislators cared little where a black share went, just as black legislators cared little where the white share went. Samuel Chapman Armstrong, a wartime general in the U.S. Army, served shortly after the war as an agent of the Freedmen's Bureau and played a central role in establishing a school at Hampton for black Virginians, women as well as men. Armstrong, as the founding superintendent at the Hampton Normal and Agricultural Institute, and R. W. Hughes, a trustee of the school, wrote to the appropriate committee chairmen in the legislature on behalf of Hampton. Both wanted to be sure that black Virginians secured a portion of the fund and that Hampton was a recipient.

As the deliberations unfolded, one school after another fell out of the running for the white share. The University of Virginia and the Virginia Military Institute kept in the hunt until near the end, but in the end they canceled each other out. The legislature, when the final decision came down in 1872, divided the proceeds between a black school in the east, at Hampton, and a white school in the west, near Blacksburg. One-third of the money was allocated to the Hampton Normal and Agricultural Institute. The other two-thirds went to a school in Montgomery County previously known as the Preston and Olin Institute, a Methodist academy for white boys, which now took on a new identity as the Virginia Agricultural and Mechanical College (VAMC). The trustees of the old institute had had to make a difficult decision, for as good as they thought their school was, it was in dire straits, so they sought to obtain Virginia's share of the Morrill Act money by offering to let the state take it over and give it a new life as a land-grant school. Most roads during the debate had led somewhere else, but eventually the legislature took a primary route that led to Blacksburg, with an important secondary road to Hampton.

Governor Walker signed the measure into law in March 1872 (see sidebar). Ruffner became a member of the white school's board of visitors. A military college that trained farmers, engineers, and teachers, VAMC resembled VMI far more than it did UVA. It resembled Hampton in some respects, but not at all in terms of who could enroll there, other than that the new law provided for free tuition for 100 "state students" at each of the two schools. VAMC in 1896 took the name Virginia Polytechnic Institute (VPI). Hampton retained the land-grant designation until 1920.

With the end of slavery, the old ban against schools for black Virginians vanished, and with the enfranchisement of black men, black Virginians sent black legislators to Richmond to look after their interests. Black legislators, arguing that Virginia's population was more than 40 percent black, pushed for five-twelfths of the Morrill Act money, but one-third was far more, symbolically and substantively, than none at all. Black Virginians had successfully made a claim in state politics on public money—albeit federal money, not state—to support an institution of higher education, as well as state and local money to support black elementary schools. Many people, white and black, perceived that the federal mandate, under the conditions prevailing after the war, did not permit complete exclusion of black Virginians from the benefits of the Morrill Act. Moreover, white legislators assumed that black Virginians, if they could benefit from the fund at a black institution, would be easier to exclude from the white one.

VAMC's early students included Claude A. Swanson, who went on to be congressman,

tricts for said delegates, with reference to the highest proficiency and good character, from the white male students of the free schools . . . or, in their discretion, from others than those attending said free schools. . . .

3. The curriculum of the Virginia Agricultural and Mechanical College shall embrace such branches of learning as relate to agriculture and the mechanic arts, without excluding other scientific and classical studies, and including military tactics. . . .

13. The said appropriation to the Hampton Normal and Agricultural Institute shall be on the following conditions, namely: That the trustees of the same shall, out of the annual interest accruing, as soon as practicable, institute, support and maintain therein, one or more schools or departments wherein the leading object shall be instruction in . . . agriculture and the mechanic arts, and military tactics; and the governor . . . shall appoint five persons, three of whom shall be of African descent, citizens of the commonwealth, to be curators of the fund hereby set apart for the use of the said institute. . . .

And the trustees of said college may select not less than one hundred students, with reference to their character and proficiency, from the colored free schools of the state, who shall have the privilege of attending the said institute on the same terms that state students are allowed to attend the Agricultural and Mechanical College. . . .

AN 1878 LAW REDEFINES INTERRACIAL MARRIAGE AND INCREASES THE PENALTIES FOR IT

Historians often argue about when legally mandated racial segregation began, and why. "When" is difficult enough. Those who look for their evidence on trains and streetcars generally find that the first laws mandating segregation date from around the year 1900. Education reveals a very different time line. The public school system in Virginia, as almost everywhere else in the South, was born segregated. As regards the new land-grant institutions, the same was true of higher education. In both cases, segregation replaced simple exclusion and therefore constituted an advance. The famous phrase "separate but equal," from the Supreme Court decision *Plessy v. Ferguson* (1896), came long after 1870 or 1872—and it applied to transportation, not education—but separate schools emerged soon after the death of slavery. In yet another realm of life and law, segregation also applied to marriage, as a Virginia statute passed in 1878 made clear:

3. If . . . any white person and negro, shall go out of this state for the purpose of being married, and with the intention of returning, and be married out of it, and afterwards return to and reside in it, cohabiting as man and wife, they shall be as guilty, and be punished as if the marriage had been in this state.

governor, U.S. senator, and secretary of the navy. Hampton's included Booker T. Washington, who, having been born a slave in Franklin County in about 1856, first enrolled at Hampton in 1872, subsequently taught there, and in the 1880s began his life's work at Tuskegee Institute in Alabama.

The Resolutions of 1870 and 1872

In 1870, Virginia was restored to the Union—its voters could once again send representatives to Congress, and the legislature could send senators. A new state constitution guaranteed that black men as well as white would be numbered in the electorate. It also directed the legislature to establish and maintain a public system of elementary schools. By 1872, the state had awarded the annual proceeds under the federal Morrill Act to a new institution for white men as well as to the most significant institution yet established for the education of black Virginians.

The two legislative acts were closely related, in that the land-grant money was going to institutions that would be training some of their students to teach in the new segregated system of public schools. In important ways, the world of the 1870s contrasted sharply with the world of the 1850s. Former slaves were attending schools and teaching in those schools. The federal government had made funds available for higher education in Virginia, and former slaves were among the black legislators who sought to assure that a black institution received a share of those funds.

Black Virginians and white Virginians were stumbling toward a new set of social and political rules to govern life in a world without slavery (for another dimension, see sidebar). Such a new world without slavery was hardly expected before the war, certainly by no means so soon, and in fact white Virginians—many or even most of them—had always envisioned that whenever an end to slavery did unfold, it would be accompanied by an end to a significant black presence in Virginia. The war, together with its tremendous consequences, had surprised everyone. The postwar world was taking shape.

The fact of their cohabitation here as man and wife shall be evidence of their marriage....

8. Any white person who shall intermarry with a negro, or any negro who shall intermarry with a white person, shall be confined in the penitentiary not less than two nor more than five years....

Chapter 16

Railroads, Schools, and Readjusters

It is hard to know what might have been met with more astonishment at the time Virginia ratified the U.S. Constitution in 1788—a railroad train belching smoke and thundering east toward Norfolk hauling endless cars filled with coal, a public college attended by black students and taught by black teachers near Petersburg, or a black–white political coalition taking charge of the state government in Richmond. Less than 100 years later, all three were very much in evidence.

In post–Civil War Virginia, railroads were not new, but Republicans were, public schools were, and black political power was. The new combination transformed politics in Virginia, just as the railroad continued to transform social and economic patterns. For a time the iron horse proved a dead weight, in that an enormous public debt, dating from the state's prewar efforts to promote transportation improvements, hovered over all postwar decisions about taxes and spending. As the prewar public debt became the greatest postwar political issue, it led to an extraordinary interlude in postwar political developments. Meanwhile, the railroad continued to push into new parts of Virginia, bringing social and economic transformation.

Historian Horace Mann Bond observed many years ago about Reconstruction in the Deep South's Alabama that, although all the fuss and feathers revolved around matters of race, the key to the political struggle in that state revolved around railroad finance, competing interests of an economic and business nature far more than of a racial and social nature. His insight has application to Virginia, an Upper South state, as well—a state where access to government could make a huge difference in corporate wealth, much as in the colonial era it had been the means of acquiring landed wealth and with it the labor to work that land. Much of the postwar struggle pitted the Baltimore and Ohio Railroad, followed by the Pennsylvania Railroad, against the railway ambitions of William

Mahone for control of the major freight transportation lines. All of the legislative maneuvering took place against a backdrop of a massive state debt and a decrepit Virginia economy.

John Mercer Langston and William Mahone

John Mercer Langston left Virginia as a child in the 1840s and moved to Ohio. There he enjoyed a much broader definition of black freedom than Virginia offered. He graduated from Oberlin College, became a lawyer, taught school, and won election to public office. During the Civil War, he recruited black soldiers for the Union army. After the war, he established the law department at Howard University, one of the black southern institutions of higher education—along with Fisk University, Atlanta University, and Hampton Institute—that originated in the late 1860s. He tried to make Howard a school for both races and both sexes—much like Oberlin, except that Howard was largely black, Oberlin predominantly white. After seven years as a U.S. diplomat in Haiti, Langston returned to his native state in the 1880s and served for two years as president of a new public institution at Petersburg for the higher education of black Virginians.

William Mahone appeared a mere wisp of a man with a long white beard, but he towered over Virginia politics in the 1880s, when he served in the U.S. Senate. A native of Southampton County, and an 1847 graduate of the Virginia Military Institute, he became a railroad executive and then served the Confederacy as a general. After the Civil War, he became a leader in the railroad industry in Virginia, seeking for a time to consolidate a railroad line—the Atlantic, Mississippi, and Ohio Railroad—that would run from Norfolk through Petersburg all the way to Bristol and beyond. But his dream evaporated, a victim in 1876 of the Depression of 1873 as well as of state legislative politics, and he moved more directly into politics himself. He sought the governorship in 1877, and he finally broke with the Conservatives in 1879 to lead the Readjusters. Whatever other hats he wore in his illustrious career, he led a biracial group in the late 1870s and early 1880s that transformed the political and educational landscape in the Old Dominion. From the vantage point of the 1850s and 1860s, two people like John Mercer Langston and William Mahone seemed the most unlikely of allies, but such, to a degree, they became in the 1880s.

Virginia history's central theme of the early 1880s was political turbulence associated with race, education, and public finance. As Readjusters and Democrats took turns running the state, an extraordinary political conflict framed developments that strengthened elementary education and renovated higher education. Mahone's opponents found one voice when the writer George W. Bagby,

William Mahone (1826–1895). A native of Southampton County and an 1847 graduate of Virginia Military Institute, Mahone became chief engineer and then president of the Norfolk and Petersburg Railroad in the 1850s. When the Civil War began, he served in the Norfolk area, participating in the Confederate seizure of the Gosport Navy Yard. Wounded at Second Manassas in 1862, he made his greatest military mark at the Battle of the Crater in Petersburg in July 1864. After the war, he headed what for a time was styled the Atlantic, Mississippi, and Ohio Railroad, but he lost control of it in the 1870s depression; it eventually became the Norfolk and Western. Then he led the black-and-white-coalition Readjusters to power in state politics and served a term in the U.S. Senate. Library of Congress, Prints and Photographs Division, LC-BH832-2462.

ignoring Mahone's heroics as a Confederate general and seeking to render him illegitimate in voters' eyes, wrote a pamphlet, *John Brown and William Mahone*, in which he characterized Mahone's "raid" in 1879 as "less bloody" but nonetheless "more dangerous than that of John Brown" at Harpers Ferry twenty years earlier.

Prewar Debts, Postwar Schools, and the Readjuster Revolution

State school superintendent William Henry Ruffner's efforts to build up a school system in the 1870s lost steam in the later years of the decade. The Virginia economy suffered from economic depression, and Virginia politicians made fateful decisions about what to fund and what to let slide. In education, growth faded into decay, optimism into pessimism.

Virginia suffered under an enormous public debt in the 1870s. Not a product of the war years or of Reconstruction, the debt had originated before the war and resulted from investments in railroads, canals, and other transportation improvements. Not only did the war interrupt payments on the debt while unpaid interest mounted, but it also savaged the wealth that might have serviced the debt and paid it down.

After the war, virtually everyone in Virginia was cash poor. When evaluating the operations of their state government, residents found taxes high but benefits scant. The Funders—Democrats who insisted on paying the public debt in full, even if doing so left nothing for the new public schools—diverted money from the schools to service the debt. The 1869 constitution directed that the new school system be developed gradually with a "full introduction" by 1876, and one might have assumed that expenditures would, at worst, plateau at that level, not slope back down. Instead, the number of public schools in Virginia, never robust, fell from 3,442 for whites and 1,230 for blacks in 1877 to barely half as many in 1879.

In other states of the former Confederacy, Democrats could flog dissident whites with the notion that Republicans had brought high postwar taxes and public debt, but no such charge was available in Virginia, where Democrats had controlled the General Assembly ever since the war. Moreover, because the Republicans had not controlled state politics in Virginia after the 1867–1868 constitutional convention, there had been less occasion for the Ku Klux Klan or other white vigilantes to take the kind of violent action that so decimated black electorates in a number of Deep South states. Black political activity continued across eastern Virginia through the 1870s, ready for a more promising political environment, and this the Funders supplied.

Not only did the Funders slash spending on schools to service the ancient debt, but they also raised taxes on land. Acting against schools affected huge numbers of families, whether black or white. Taxes on farms did as well, but the property tax burden mostly hit white farmers, far more of whom owned land. As a consequence, Funders faced opposition throughout Virginia. Hence a biracial coalition challenged the Funders for control of the state. Large numbers of white voters in the west, like black voters in the east, supported a Readjuster ticket in the 1879 state elections. Readjusters demanded a fiscal "readjustment"—a reduction in debt service and an increase in spending on schools. Moreover, black Virginians called for a public institution of higher education that they might attend.

The Readjusters and the Schools

The Readjusters, a biracial and bipartisan alliance, defeated the Funders and took control of both houses of the state legislature in the 1879 elections, but the governorship remained in Democratic hands, so not a lot could yet be accomplished. In 1881, the Readjusters retained control of the legislature and also won the governorship, and they thus controlled the state's fiscal affairs. As one of their first items of business, they neutralized an 1876 law enacted by the Conservatives that had made payment of a poll tax a prerequisite to voting. They did not, as is often said, repeal the tax (the constitution continued to call for a poll tax to help fund public schools); rather, they passed a new law to cut the poll tax's linkage to voting rights. While in power, the Readjusters scaled back the debt, as they had said they would, reducing debt service by more than half. They cut property tax rates by one-fifth, yet the reduction in interest payments permitted a substantial treasury surplus that they channeled into education.

During the 1880s, therefore, Virginia embarked on a crusade all its own to spend more state money on education—elementary schools and higher education alike. Reversing the sharp decline in the late 1870s in state spending on public schools, the Readjusters built the elementary schools to a stronger position than at any previous time. Moreover, the state inaugurated support of one institution of higher education for white women and another for black men and black women.

The Virginia constitution of 1869 directed the legislature, "as soon as practicable," to establish "normal schools" to train teachers. Yet the legislature failed to find much money to promote the state's new "system" of public schools, and it ignored school superintendent William Henry Ruffner's campaign to secure one or more state-supported normal schools. In lieu of normal schools, the State Board of Education called for teacher institutes to be held every year beginning in 1872, and training sessions took place for a day or so or sometimes, as "Summer Normal Institutes," for a month or longer. These sessions helped upgrade teachers' effectiveness, but they hardly matched what might be done in an entire year or two at a teachers' college.

In 1879 a state senator introduced a resolution pointing out the legislature's constitutional obligation to establish a normal school, and, going farther, he urged consideration of "how far such schools might be made use of in promoting the higher education of women generally." Ruffner weighed back into the discussion, outlining three options for addressing the educational needs of white Virginia women as well as the professional training of white Virginia teachers: coeducation in current state institutions (at Virginia Agricultural and Mechanical College or the University of Virginia), a female state college, or (his preference) normal schools. The legislature did not act.

The Readjusters, wishing to appoint their own man, replaced Ruffner in 1882 with Richard R. Farr, a three-term member of the House of Delegates from Fairfax County who served as superintendent of public instruction for the next four-year term. Farr continued Ruffner's fight for normal schools and urged such training for black teachers and white teachers alike. Tallying the state's teachers and the places where they had trained, he reported that Virginia's only normal school, the private one for black teachers at Hampton, had supplied 174 teachers. Among the remainder of the 5,078 teachers on his roster, 45 had studied at the University of Virginia, 30 at Virginia Agricultural and Mechanical College, and 13 at Virginia Military Institute.

The growth in elementary schools in Virginia—first in the early 1870s and then in the early 1880s—created a great demand for teachers and, therefore, for schools to train teachers. To prepare teachers for black schools, the Readjusters established an institution near Petersburg. To prepare teachers for white schools, the legislature subsequently established a school in Farmville for white women and, before the decade ended, began to provide funds for the College of William and Mary to train white men.

Virginia Normal and Collegiate Institute

The Readjuster legislature established Virginia Normal and Collegiate Institute, a public school for the higher education of black Virginians. The nation's first fully state-supported school for the higher education of African Americans, it was also the Old Dominion's first institution designed specifically to train teachers. The new school was located just outside Petersburg in the heart of Southside Virginia, in as central a place as might have been found for black Virginians.

For land, buildings, and other start-up expenses, the legislature appropriated $100,000 from the proceeds of the sale of the state's holdings in the Atlantic, Mississippi, and Ohio Railroad. It also provided $20,000 in annual support. Before the school could go to work, it had to defeat a court challenge, brought by die-hard Funders, against the appropriation.

As Readjusters redeemed their promise to establish such an institution, a black legislator strove successfully to give the new school its shape. Alfred William Harris was born in Virginia to free black parents in 1854. The new educational opportunities that the 1860s brought African Americans led to Harris's earning a law degree from Howard University and setting himself up as an attorney in Dinwiddie County. He served four terms in the Virginia House of Delegates, from 1881 to 1888.

The legislature specified that the faculty would be African American, as would six of the seven members of the board of visitors. It also directed the school to offer a collegiate course as well as a three-year normal program for training teachers. Just as Virginia Agricultural and Mechanical College found it necessary to offer secondary or even elementary courses to prepare white students for more advanced study, Virginia Normal and Collegiate Institute maintained a preparatory program.

Like UVA and VMI, the new school distinguished between "pay students" and "state students." As many as 50 state students, between the ages of sixteen and twenty-five and of "good moral character," might enroll each year; they paid no tuition provided they contracted to teach for at least two years after completing their studies. To assure geographical distribution, state students were apportioned on the same basis as the state Senate. The legislature subsequently increased the number of state students to 200, two for each district in the House of Delegates, and directed school superintendents to select them.

The school began operations in October 1883 with 62 students, a number that rose to 131 before the end of the year—numbers that resembled those at Virginia Agricultural and Mechanical College when it opened in 1872. Alfred William Harris served on the new school's first board of visitors and thus—like William Henry Ruffner at VAMC—continued actively to shape the institution's faculty and curriculum. The first two officers in charge of the school were called principals, and neither lasted long in his post, but at the beginning of 1886, Harris and his colleagues brought in John Mercer Langston as the school's first president. Langston therefore headed the school when it graduated its first class of teachers, four men and four women, in June 1886.

John Mercer Langston (1829–1897).
Son of a former slave and her former
owner, Langston moved from Virginia
to Ohio in the 1830s and then back to
Virginia in the 1880s. A half century after having left a state that criminalized
holding any school for black Virginians,
he became president of the all-black
Virginia Normal and Collegiate Institute. In a district formerly represented
by committed advocates of slavery, he
gained election to Congress. Yet within
a decade of his death in 1897, disfranchisement would push the black vote
back near the vanishing point, public
transportation would be segregated,
and Virginia Normal would be stripped
of its collegiate program. Virginia Historical Society, Richmond, Virginia.

A "Race Riot" in Danville on the Eve of the 1883 Election

In 1883, the Southside city of Danville had a Readjuster-dominated government,
including the mayor, a white man. Two of the nine policemen were African
American, as was one of the five members of the police court. In October, white
Democrats issued a pamphlet that carried the title *Coalition Rule in Danville*
but came to be known as the Danville circular, a plea for help from white voters
throughout western Virginia, asking that they abandon the Readjuster Party and
vote Democratic in the upcoming state election. Unless Democrats were elected
to the legislature, it cried, "*we are doomed.*"

As historian Jane Dailey explains, what was really at stake in Danville was
that blacks insisted that there be equality of treatment, and most whites insisted

that there not be. In its "Litany of Shame" the Danville circular claimed there were four black policemen—twice the actual number, but the core complaint was that there were any—and it also asserted that on sidewalks, "*Negro women* have been known to *force ladies* from the pavement." In this charged atmosphere, each side viewed the other as aggressive. On Saturday, November 3, 1883, when a minor altercation took place involving a black man and a white man on a downtown street, it quickly grew into something far less routine, as whites formed a mob and fired weapons into a crowd of blacks, ending with five men dead, one white, four black.

Having by force of arms taken control of the city's streets, white Democrats also took control of the interpretation of the events of that evening, representing the affair as self-defense against black men they portrayed as not only assertive but also armed and the aggressors. Like the circular, the news was broadcast as a call to action, an election-eve bulletin. According to a report from one western county, Funders—not only demagogic but simply mendacious—"made passionate appeals to the white people to rescue their brothers of the east from the terrible consequences of negro rule, mixed marriages, and mixed schools." In the statewide election three days later, Democrats took back control of the General Assembly. The Readjusters garnered 13,000 more votes than two years earlier, but Democrats picked up 44,000, most of them in the west and many of them, thanks to the Readjusters against whom they were voting, from white men newly freed of the poll tax requirement for voting.

A Monument to the Readjusters

The Readjusters set tremendous change in motion. Yet weakened by extreme racial tensions in the electorate, they lost the elections to the legislature in 1883, and they lost the governorship in 1885. Though the Readjusters vanished from power, their fiscal innovations persisted. No longer calling themselves Funders, the regular Democrats intended not only to retrieve political power but also to maintain it. To do so they made concessions, more or less recognizing not only the debt settlement but also such legislative initiatives as the establishment and annual funding of Virginia Normal and Collegiate Institute. Yet they changed the composition of the school's board of visitors to majority white and Democratic.

Institute president Langston, frustrated by what he saw as hostile intervention from the new board, resigned in 1887 and ran for Congress the next year from his political base in Southside Virginia. Though his victory was disputed and his seating delayed until September 1890, he served for part of one term in

MAKING THE VIRGINIA TWIST.

Making the Virginia Twist. This painting by John Durkin for an 1887 article in the *Atlantic Monthly* about Virginia's tobacco manufacturing in Danville and Richmond depicts black workers employed making chewing tobacco twists in one of Virginia's leading industries. Just a few years earlier, events in the streets of Danville in 1883—the contrivance of those events, and their interpretation—had helped drive the Readjusters from power in the legislature in Richmond. Virginia Historical Society, Richmond, Virginia, gift of The Pinkerton Group.

the U.S. House of Representatives, Virginia's only black congressman until more than 100 years later.

Democrats reduced the school's annuity to $15,000 in 1888, but the school continued its work—its collegiate curriculum as well as its normal program—long after the Readjusters fell from power. It stood as a monument to that brief time in Virginia history when a biracial coalition took power and transformed the way the public business was done. The new president, James Hugo Johnston, served from 1888 until 1914. From among the new school's graduates in the 1880s and 1890s came many of the people who became the teachers in Virginia's black elementary schools. From among them, too, came a number of the people who became lawyers and other professionals in the world that emerged in Virginia after the end of slavery, for example attorney J. Thomas Newsome in Newport News.

Farmville and William and Mary

The Readjuster revolution had transformed the educational and fiscal environment. The rapid rise in state money going into elementary schools, white schools and black schools alike, generated an acute need for—and an obvious shortage of—teachers to staff the new schools. No doubt the establishment of a school to train black teachers encouraged white Democratic legislators to think more favorably about providing similar facilities for white Virginians. Moreover, readjustment of the Old Dominion's finances turned loose some money that might be put to such a use. The legislature quickly established a teachers' school for white women.

In 1884 the legislature created the State Female Normal School in Farmville and gave it $5,000 for equipment and $10,000 in annual support. The institution did not start from scratch. Much as had been done to secure land and a building for Virginia Agricultural and Mechanical College a dozen years before, the legislature in 1884 required Farmville to deed the property of the Farmville Female College to the state. This approach gave new life to a dying institution; otherwise another community, one that conveyed "suitable grounds and buildings," would have obtained the school. The former state superintendent of public schools, William Henry Ruffner, after striving for so long to foster the public schools and secure a normal school, became the new institution's first principal. In return for its $10,000 annuity, the Farmville school admitted "state students" tuition free if they pledged to teach in the public schools upon graduation. Over the years the annuity grew and the curriculum expanded, but the school enrolled only white women well into the twentieth century. It grew into Longwood University.

Four years after the Old Dominion established the school at Farmville, it provided similar training for white men. The College of William and Mary came on such hard times after the Civil War that it quietly suspended operations in 1881. The buildings were dilapidated, the student population had wilted away, and the school had no funds. Officers of William and Mary had not wished to alter the college's classical curriculum, but they came to see no alternative to obtaining a state subsidy to inaugurate a teacher-training program. Among the college's small faculty was the son of former president John Tyler, Lyon Gardiner Tyler, who held bachelor's and master's degrees from the University of Virginia. Even before the college closed, Tyler left to find a more adequate and reliable salary, though he turned up again later to assist his father's alma mater. Elected to the House of Delegates in 1887, Tyler was on hand to push the William and Mary initiative at the 1888 session.

Given the earlier decisions, in 1882 and 1884, to establish normal schools at Petersburg and Farmville, spokesmen for William and Mary were able to argue to good effect that, while the state had undertaken to support schools at which white women, black women, and black men could obtain training to become teachers, nothing of the sort was available to white men. They argued, too, that the Tidewater region ought to obtain benefits from state spending on higher education, as did every other area of the state—Southside (Farmville), the southwest (VAMC), Shenandoah Valley (VMI), and Piedmont (UVA).

Tyler and the college were successful. The legislature supplied William and Mary a stipend of $10,000 per year, and in return the college resumed operations and added a teacher-training curriculum. Of the 102 students who attended the school's first session after it reopened in 1888, half were "state students," who could enroll in the college without charge for tuition on pledging to teach for at least two years in the Virginia public schools. That year, the board of visitors appointed Tyler the school's new president, a position he held until he retired in 1919.

William and Mary was neither a state institution nor completely private, and was neither completely a college with a classical curriculum nor only a vocational school for training teachers. A hybrid, it limped along with chronic budgetary uncertainty. Yet the state subsidy enabled the college to survive, and each year it supplied dozens of new teachers to staff Virginia's public schools.

The Hatch Act of 1887 and the Morrill Act of 1890

Some years after Virginia's initiatives on higher education in 1872, in which the state funneled federal funds to VAMC and Hampton Institute, federal policy embellished the beginnings brought by the 1862 Morrill Act. In 1887, in the Hatch

Act, Congress added a significant research function to the land-grant mission by funding agricultural experiment stations. Farm groups lobbied Congress for support of applied research, as farmers, regardless of whether they ever enrolled at a land-grant college, needed practical help with immediate problems. Congress specified the kinds of issues that the additional money might be employed to address, among them plant physiology and disease, soil analysis, crop rotation, and the production of butter and cheese.

Teaching and research at institutions of higher education have often ridden together during the past 100 years, but teaching typically rode alone during the first quarter century after President Lincoln signed the 1862 Morrill Act. At first, the faculty at land-grant colleges taught students mostly in classrooms and sometimes in laboratories. The Hatch Act redirected their activity beyond the classroom or the campus. Over the years, the research done at experiment stations transformed American agriculture; a tremendous variety of farm products, raised with great efficiency in enormous quantities, embodied huge twentieth-century scientific improvements on nineteenth-century nature.

In 1890, a new Morrill Land-Grant College Act provided "for the more complete endowment and support of colleges for the benefit of agriculture and mechanic arts." Unlike the Morrill Act of 1862—enacted before emancipation and silent on race—the 1890 act offered additional money on the condition that black students benefit as well as whites. The 1890 Morrill Act permitted segregation so long as a state "equitably divided" its land-grant funds between "a college for white students" and an "institution for colored students." Every southern state divided the money in some fashion between a black school and a white one. Virginia divided the new money between VAMC and Hampton Institute according to the same two-thirds, one-third formula as it continued to use with the 1862 funds.

A Time for Reconstruction

Historians often say that Reconstruction ended in 1877. By that, they mean that Republicans controlled all eleven states of the former Confederacy for some period between 1867 and 1877 but not later. The Republican-dominated governments of those states had all fallen to Democratic regimes by 1877, with the dates in some states coming well before that. The Compromise of 1877, moreover, included a pledge that federal troops would end their presence in those states and any role in southern elections.

In some ways, however, the political changes of the early postwar years persisted until late in the century. Indeed, popular discourse has often hailed particular twentieth-century political events as the "first since Reconstruction" even

when the last previous example of such an event—for example, a black candidate serving in a state legislature, a city council, or even the U.S. House of
Representatives—may have been as late as the 1880s or 1890s, as was the case in
Virginia. When a black city councilman, Oliver Hill, was elected in Richmond
in 1948, he was the first since the defeat of Henry Moore in a bid for reelection
in 1898, and surviving to see the day was ninety-year-old Edward R. Carter, who
had served in the 1890s, late during a quarter century that had seen black membership without a break ever since 1871.

A perspective emphasizing 1877 supplies a definition and time line that apply poorly to Virginia. Republicans controlled the constitutional convention of
1867–1868, and they elected the first governor under the new charter, but they
did not control the legislature. In one sense, therefore, Reconstruction never
came to Virginia, or it ended before 1870. In another sense, it came to Virginia
only some years after 1877. Virginians participated in the 1880s in as vibrant an
example of biracial reform politics as the nineteenth-century South—for that
matter, the nineteenth-century American nation—ever produced. Yet regardless of when one dates the end of Reconstruction, black political power largely
vanished from the "reconstructed" states, especially in the Deep South but even
in Virginia. The revolution went backward.

Railroads, Coal, Timber, and the Transformation of Appalachia

Perceptions of Appalachia underwent a transformation around the turn of the
twentieth century. Since before the American Revolution, the mountains had
posed obstacles to settlers' westward migration. Beginning not long before 1900,
by contrast, the region changed from obstacle to bonanza, a place with great natural resources that, with burgeoning demand and new transportation capabil-
ity, suddenly became accessible and therefore greatly coveted. Some places had
huge coal reserves and most were forested, and railroad construction permitted
access to both mines and forests, resulting in a transformation of the economy
and the environment.

Before 1890, the timber industry in Appalachian Virginia was small, with
farm families engaged on a part-time basis in the off-season. When harvesting
timber, people sometimes used teams of oxen to bring selected trees down the
mountains, but they preferred taking the prime trees along the riverbanks. Either way, they sent tree trunks downstream to mills. Families often ran the mills
and sometimes specialized in woodworking skills.

Then came railroads. Railroads allowed lumbermen to go farther into the
mountains, and mills were built closer to the forest supply. During the great

timber boom between about 1890 and 1920, land was snatched up, railroads penetrated the mountains, sawmills were constructed, and logging towns emerged, as the industry became a large-scale operation with full-time employees systematically cutting across big areas. Timber went into local railroad construction, into coal-mining operations, and to users far outside the region. Among the larger developers, the Douglass Land Company of New York was founded in 1893 and controlled over 100,000 acres in southwest Virginia. Also in the 1890s, a group from Wisconsin began developing the timber from some 26,000 acres in Giles County. Later, the Clinchfield Timber Corporation developed a similar tract in Scott and Wise counties, and the Mount Rogers area was also extensively logged during the boom.

The coal industry told a similar tale. Beginning in the 1880s, magnates sought railroad connections between the coal reserves of Appalachia and, on the one hand, the cities of the Midwest and, on the other, the textile mills of the Southeast as well as the port facilities at Charleston, South Carolina. Meanwhile, the Norfolk and Western Railroad sought to keep the coal coming, in growing quantities, east to Norfolk. Key actors in the coal industry in southwest Virginia early in the twentieth century were George L. Carter and his bankers in New York, James A. Blair and Company, which controlled the Seaboard Air Line Railway. Together they constructed the South and Western Railroad, to fetch coal from Russell County; organized the Clinchfield Coal Corporation, which acquired vast coal lands and consolidated scattered mining operations; and constructed the Clinchfield Railroad across the Blue Ridge, to connect with the Seaboard Air Line.

The vast bulk of coal in Virginia came from the Clinchfield coal district, which lay between Tazewell and Wise counties in the southwest, including the counties of Russell, Dickenson, and Buchanan. In 1920, Virginia's coal industry employed 14,000 miners and produced an annual 45 million tons of coal. Wise County, where production began in the 1890s, generated half that total and employed half the miners. Many of the workers in coal, as in timber, were local, and many miners in West Virginia were Virginians—black and white—tracking job opportunities there. Many other resident workers in the coal company towns of Wise County and elsewhere in southwest Virginia were immigrants, drawn from Italy and elsewhere by the jobs, despite the danger. Unlike the timber industry, which tended to scalp a mountain of its forest and then move on, coal companies kept taking coal out of the mines, year after year. Mountaintop removal—scalping the landscape in quest of coal—came much later.

The tensions associated with the vast sudden changes taking place in the coal and timber country of western Virginia—the coming of the railroads, the eco-

nomic transformation, together with an influx of black workers, in particular—
sometimes led to lynchings. The most notable white-on-black mob violence
took place in the burgeoning towns of the region, especially in the early 1890s.
In October 1891, a white mob hanged—and then shot hundreds of times—four
black miners in Clifton Forge in Alleghany County. By contrast, east of the Blue
Ridge, where fifteen times as many black Virginians lived, two lynchings took
place that year. In February 1893, a white mob hanged five black railroad workers
in Richlands, in Tazewell County and then put up signs warning all other blacks
to leave the county or face a similar fate. Other lynching victims in the region
included two black men in the new city of Roanoke, William Lavender in February 1892 and Thomas Smith in September 1893.

Coal, a Railroad, and the City of Roanoke

In 1892, the town of Roanoke celebrated its tenth anniversary. Permeated by a
patriotic and prosperous spirit, the celebration marked an exciting decade of economic success, population expansion, and urban development. For two days, a
large audience saw and heard classical concerts, athletic competitions, and con-
gratulatory speakers. Such newspapers as the *Baltimore Sun* and the *Philadelphia
Herald* reported on the grand parade, held on the second day, featuring a marching band, cadets from VMI and VAMC, and laborers from the Roanoke Machine
Works, the heart of Roanoke's railroad complex. The celebration culminated a
decade of hard work and a century of technological innovation, it produced an
instant surplus of funds, and the publicity bolstered the city's image.

In the late nineteenth century, railroads made their way into Appalachian
coal country and hauled countless cars of coal out of the mountains, and railroads and coal combined to transform life in many communities. In 1882, a
junction had been completed connecting the Shenandoah Valley Railroad with
the Norfolk and Western Railroad at a rural community called Big Lick, population less than 1,000, and a new town had been established, on the Roanoke
River—Roanoke. Even the timing of the tenth anniversary celebration revealed
Roanoke's history to be defined by the railroad. Roanoke had received its charter
as a town on February 3, 1882, but the completion of the railroad junction came
June 18 that year, and the decennial celebration was kicked off on June 18, 1892.

The story of the Norfolk and Western Railway had begun two generations
earlier, when a much smaller incarnation of the line served as an agricultural
carrier with little influence and significance beyond the region it slowly traveled.
Coal changed that. In the 1880s and 1890s, no other commodity was as valuable
to the Norfolk and Western as coal. Just as Roanoke depended on the railroad,

the railroad depended on maximizing its coal transportation potential. Much of the Norfolk and Western's expansion, innovation, and financial consolidation came in an effort to maintain a significant hold on the coal transportation market in the face of larger competitors from the North. Sustained dominance over a significant portion of the coal market would not have been possible without the unique presence of the Roanoke Machine Works, commonly referred to as the Roanoke Shops, which quickly became the primary employer in the Roanoke River valley. They were essential to the railroad's success, as they supplied the in-house facilities and skilled laborers to manufacture and maintain high-quality steam locomotives. This system of interdependent relationships allowed for greater success for all three major players—coal, railroad, and city. Based on coal and a railroad, Roanoke had a population that ranked third among Virginia's cities for much of the first half of the twentieth century.

East and West, Black and White, at the End of the Century

By the end of the century, both the western and the eastern portions of Virginia had changed a great deal since 1861, but in very different ways. The separation of West Virginia left the region west of the Blue Ridge far less populous, no longer in a position to take over control of the state unless in combination with some large group of easterners, who in the Readjuster crusade turned out to be black voters. Division of the state, emancipation of slaves, and expansion of railroads, together with the postwar controversy over the prewar debt, all worked together to create the unstable series of postwar power combinations in the Commonwealth. Competing railroad forces did much to shape the struggle among white easterners, and with it the alignment of the other political forces in the state.

Defeat of the Readjusters signaled an end of substantial black political power, though black voters continued to elect a few black officeholders through the 1880s and even into the 1890s. White westerners could find no political partners that would return them to power. Eastern whites retrieved control. In some regards, though on very different terms, the same social group that governed Virginia in the 1840s and 1850s was back in the saddle a half century later. The constitutional convention that met in 1901 strived to put a permanent end to significant black political power and, though promising to safeguard white enfranchisement, cheerfully did much to curtail voting by the other wing of the old Readjuster coalition as well.

Census figures track another development that followed the defeat of the Readjusters. As late as 1880, the largest numbers of black native Virginians who were living in other states—Mississippi and Alabama—reflected the pre–Civil

War migration of slaves to the Deep South. Those elderly former slaves gradually died off, and a postwar migration took black Virginians north to the cities of Baltimore, Philadelphia, and New York. By 1900, the largest concentrations of native black Virginians outside Virginia were in Pennsylvania, Washington, D.C., New York, and Maryland.

The direction of the new migration was clear; so was the timing. The Great Migration from the Deep South began during World War I, but from Virginia it began in the 1880s, as the number of black native Virginians living in Pennsylvania doubled in the 1880s and doubled again in the 1890s. The proportion of the nation's black citizens living in Virginia dropped from 10 percent in 1880 to 7 percent in 1910; during that thirty-year period the percentages showed no drop in any state across the Lower South from South Carolina to Texas. The black proportion of Virginia's population dropped during those thirty years from 42 percent to 33 percent. Then came World War I, and Virginia's variant of the Great Migration continued as the Deep South's began. The black proportion of Virginia's population dropped another 3 percent in the 1910s and 3 more in the 1920s. Between 1880 and 1930, the total black population in Virginia edged up 3 percent, while the white population doubled.

The early years of the twentieth century brought formal disfranchisement and racial segregation that went far beyond what had been the case in the 1880s or 1890s. Very large numbers of white Virginians concerned themselves with the very large numbers of black Virginians, even as many black Virginians—proportionally more than their white neighbors—left the state in search of new lives elsewhere.

Part IV

1890s–1940s

THE POLITICS OF MIGRATION AND THE WINDS OF CHANGE

Black migration from Virginia can be divided into periods of fifty years each. In the fifty years before Emancipation, tens of thousands of black Virginians found themselves making the trip from slavery in the Upper South to slavery in the Deep South. Then, in the half century after 1865, the river of humanity changed direction and flowed north to such cities as Baltimore, Philadelphia, and New York. Black Virginians also participated in the flood tide of migration, both black and white, from farm to city and from throughout the South into much of the North between 1915 and 1965, that is, during and long after World War I. But black Virginians were making the move in large numbers as early as the 1880s. Among the younger children of William and Josephine Campbell, former slaves in Montgomery County, Virginia, was Lucille, born in 1883. After attending Howard University, she moved in 1911 to New York City.

That same year, A. Philip Randolph moved from Florida to New York City. Also born in the 1880s, he was said to be descended from slaves belonging to John Randolph, the great Virginia planter-politician—slaves who had participated in the vast involuntary migration to the Deep South. Now, he joined the vanguard of migration to northern cities. Two years after both had arrived in New York, Lucille and Philip met each other. Some months later, they married.

These two people, both the progeny of Virginia slaves but born late enough to be born free, chose to leave the South. They arrived in ample time to enjoy, indeed contribute to, the Harlem Renaissance. And they did more. They found that black freedom in New York was not the same as white freedom, but they found that it was more, even far more, than black freedom in the South. Mr. Randolph had an unquestioned right to vote, even to run for political office, in New York. By the 1920s, both he and Mrs. Randolph had voted, and both had run for political office. The world of Jim Crow, with its segregation and disfranchisement, held black northerners with a grip less tight than it did black southerners. And, like those Virginians who left the slave South for the nonslave North before the Civil War, this new collection of ex-Virginians played a central role in bringing change to the region they had left behind.

The Randolphs' actions point toward some of the sources of change in the South. In the crucial early years of their married life together, Lucille made Philip's efforts as a political journalist and labor organizer financially possible, and eventually A. Philip Randolph became a household name in black households across America. As he later explained, without his wife's money he and partner Chandler Owen "couldn't have started the *Messenger*," and it was that labor periodical that brought Randolph to the attention of the workers who, in 1925, asked him to take the lead in organizing the Brotherhood of Sleeping Car Porters, forever after the basis of his power as a labor leader and black spokesman.

Demanding equal access to defense jobs and federal employment, as well as the desegregation of the armed services, Randolph organized the March on Washington movement—with a march on the nation's capital scheduled for July 1941, before the United States entered World War II but after the defense industries began building up to support Britain. And he gained the attention of U.S. presidents. In June 1941, in order to persuade Randolph to call off the march, President Franklin D. Roosevelt issued an executive order that jobs in defense industries be made available to workers regardless of their race. In 1948, after Randolph resumed his push for a desegregated military, with the nation about to resume a military draft to prepare for the Cold War, President Harry S. Truman ordered the racial desegregation of the U.S. armed forces. The greatest march that never was had tremendous consequences for the nation.

Quite aside from these actions, Philip and Lucille Randolph exercised the right to vote. They were only two among hundreds of thousands of black southerners who left behind the world of disfranchisement. As they entered the North, they picked up the right to vote, one entitlement that belonged to black as well as white citizens there.

John Mercer Langston, though his time in the U.S. House of Representatives proved very short, remained into the 1990s the only black congressman ever elected from Virginia, but he was by no means the only one from the South in the years after the Civil War. In 1901, however, George H. White, a black representative from North Carolina who had been reelected in 1898 but defeated in 1900, ended his term, and not until 1928 would another black candidate win election to Congress. That congressman, Oscar DePriest—like many of his constituents, a transplanted native of Alabama—came from a northern district, in Chicago. Other black congressmen subsequently gained election from northern districts in the 1930s and 1940s, including Adam Clayton Powell Jr., elected from New York City's Harlem, the Randolphs' district. Congressman Powell served as a representative of all of black America, and year after year he pushed for civil rights legislation.

By the late 1940s, presidential candidates had to court black voters, just as they had to seek the support of white voters. Few black adults voted in Virginia, and fewer still in the Deep South. But their former neighbors, once they moved to the North, voted in large numbers, and they engaged in other actions, too, calling for change. In doing so, they began to bring change to Virginia.

Chapter 17

Southern Progressivism

At the Virginia constitutional convention that met in Richmond in 1901, Carter Glass promised that his suffrage plan would "eliminate the darkey as a political factor in this State in less than five years, so that in no single county of the Commonwealth will there be the least concern felt for the complete supremacy of the white race in the affairs of government." Challenged by one fellow delegate as to whether he would accomplish this by fraud or by discrimination, he explained that fraud would be unnecessary, but "Discrimination! Why that is exactly what we propose; that, exactly, is what this Convention was elected for—to discriminate to the very extremity of permissible action under the limitations of the Federal Constitution, with the view to the elimination of every negro voter who can be gotten rid of, legally, without materially impairing the numerical strength of the white electorate."

William A. Anderson, who soon became the Virginia attorney general, sang along: "An effective suffrage article" would be a "constitutional road to absolute Caucasian supremacy." Allen Caperton Braxton, who came from Staunton, in the Shenandoah Valley, west of the Blue Ridge, agreed that it was important "to relieve the great incubus of negro domination in the East." Going beyond substantial black disfranchisement, Braxton held that "negroes should be excluded from the right to hold office in this State."

Reducing and reconfiguring the electorate was the convention's key objective. But most delegates had other important aims as well. Carter Glass, who hailed from Lynchburg, east of the Blue Ridge, focused on reducing the number of black voters to as near zero as manageable—although, despite his rhetoric, he and his fellow delegates did not much mind losing some white voters as well, and in fact some welcomed the effect. At the same time as it restricted the electorate, the Constitution of 1902 expanded the number of state offices filled by popular election rather than by the legislature, among them the state superintendent of public instruction. As for Braxton, he addressed his top priority when he said of the need for state regulation of railroad corporations that the convention had to decide whether "the people or the railroads would control the government of the commonwealth."

Delegates went on to debate such matters as tax valuation (should railroads pay far more in taxes?), rate regulation (should the corporations set freight and passenger rates without public oversight?), employers' liability (what responsibility should the companies bear for the crippling injuries suffered by railway workers or for the damage that resulted from trains colliding with livestock?), and eminent domain (what restrictions should be placed on corporations' use of condemnation proceedings to gain control of rights of way?). Braxton observed: "We recognize that these great powers of transportation are, like fire and water, most excellent servants, but the most destructive and unreasonable masters."

The convention came up with a variety of ways to cut into the black electorate, including the restoration of the poll tax as a condition of voting. Another major result was the establishment of the State Corporation Commission (SCC), a twentieth-century version of the old Board of Public Works. The SCC soon developed into a powerful agent of state government, initially concentrating on reining in the power of railroad corporations, and swiftly bringing about a doubling of tax revenues from them. So the convention made significant changes to the Underwood constitution. Dating from 1869, that constitution reminded a great many white Virginians of Reconstruction. But a symbolic burial of the old constitution had to carry with it substantive change as well, and the SCC embodied that.

These two core innovations by the convention revealed the two faces of southern progressivism. The Progressive movement of the early years of the twentieth century was a national phenomenon. Everywhere it had multiple strands, including social welfare and social control, as well as political democratization and its antithesis. In the South, because racial segregation and black disfranchisement were central to the enterprise, the two faces of progressivism were more different than elsewhere. Virginia's disfranchisement provisions, coupled with the SCC, captured the two faces of southern progressivism.

In one other key development, spurring increased spending on education—and on pensions for Confederate veterans—by the beginning of the twentieth century, during the Progressive years, Virginia was beginning to pull out of the economic hard times that had beset its private citizens and its public coffers ever since the Civil War. Agricultural commodity prices turned up. Rising valuations on citizens' real and personal property generated greater tax revenue. So did higher tax rates on railroads under the SCC.

Transportation: Progressivism and the Good Roads Movement

The 1890s featured a decision by the Virginia Supreme Court that the traditional means of constructing and maintaining public roads would no longer do. Virginia, like most American states, had historically depended on a tax such as the French corvée, where taxpayers paid no cash to maintain the roads but instead provided labor, and laborers received no cash for doing the work. William F. Proffitt, when called out in 1892 for the customary two days of work on the roads that the law said he owed his Louisa County community each year, had refused. As his daughter explained a century later, "Young men had to go out and work on the road," and "he just contested it." Proffitt said it was a tax unauthorized by the state constitution, and the state's highest court agreed with him. The General Assembly initiated an effort to amend the constitution, but in the end local governments in Virginia began hiring paid labor to do what men had traditionally done as a tax paid in labor.

In the first decade of the new century, the state legislature wrote another chapter to the new dispensation in Virginia travel. First, as Governor Philip W. McKinney had noted back in 1893 while Proffitt's case was still in the courts, the Virginia constitution had to be amended before the state could invest in roads. The framers of the 1869 constitution, mindful that the postwar problems with the public debt originated in prewar investments in transportation schemes, barred the state from investing in "any work of internal improvement." Their counterparts in the convention of 1901–1902 qualified the flat prohibition from the 1869 constitution with the phrase "except public roads." The legislature was free to act.

Though efforts began immediately, big changes in state policy did not come until 1906. Urged on by Governor Andrew Jackson Montague and then, in particular, by his successor, Governor Claude A. Swanson, the legislature enacted a new framework for the promotion of road improvements in Virginia. One law created a State Highway Commission to include one civil engineering professor from each of the Virginia Military Institute, the University of Virginia, and Virginia Polytechnic Institute. Another law provided for employing large numbers of penitentiary inmates on convict road gangs. Two years later, in 1908, the legislature appropriated $250,000 for allocation to the counties, on a matching-funds basis, for road improvements. The state had provided a basis for a system of highways.

Beneath the political maneuvering of turn-of-the-century Virginia was a bedrock reality—black workers could be pressed into service under a new regime that replaced conscripts, regardless of race, with convicts, most of them

Radford Farm, Virginia. This oil painting by
Ernest Lawson—better known for his work on
scenes in the New York City area—was done
sometime in the 1930s on one of Lawson's
annual drives along Route 11 on his way to or
from Florida. Route 11, which followed the old
Indian path and settler path south through Virginia west of the Blue Ridge, was a part of the
federal highway system that took shape beginning with the National Highway Act of 1916—
which, while requiring each state to establish
a state highway commission, offered matching
federal funds to finance highway construction.
Virginia Historical Society, Richmond, Virginia,
Lora Robins Collection of Virginia Art.

black. The Virginia chain gang, made up largely of black workers—receiving no more compensation than had their conscript predecessors—labored in the years ahead to build better roads and bring Virginia into the automobile age. Meanwhile, for long past 1906, roads in black areas of towns or counties were far less likely to be improved than were roads in white areas.

Public Education: Progressivism, the May Campaign, and the Schools

Education in Virginia in the first decade of the twentieth century was in a takeoff mode. Not since the Readjuster years of the 1880s had so much been attempted and accomplished. The energies behind the educational crusade had various sources. For one thing, enhanced revenues in the state coffers made more possible. Moreover, when the University of Virginia gained a new president, Edwin A. Alderman, in 1904, he identified himself immediately with an agenda that reached far beyond his campus. He hoped to reach out and connect his school, he said, "with all its traditions and its powerful influence on southern thought, with the movement for the democratization of education."

More strongly associated with the campaign for better public schools, however, were such white women as Lila Meade Valentine. Her multiple trips to England in the 1890s, aside from affording her opportunities to indulge her keen interests in music and painting, led to her acquaintance with reform movements under way there. She discovered women joining in those reform efforts, and she returned with a commitment to promote social reform in Virginia. What emerged was an emphasis on education in the public schools, for girls as well as boys, and black children as well as white.

In April 1900, she and several other Richmond women, among them Mary-Cooke Branch Munford, organized the Richmond Education Association. Valentine served as president of the group through 1904. During that time, it pushed for an additional normal school for white women teachers in Virginia and better pay and longer terms for teachers throughout the state. For Richmond, it sought playgrounds, a public library, and, above all, the introduction of kindergartens and vocational training into the city's public schools. The group achieved some early success, including a school to train teachers for a model kindergarten.

In 1902, Valentine linked the Richmond Education Association with the Southern Education Board, founded the previous year. Her efforts led the Board to schedule its 1903 annual meeting in Richmond with an agenda that emphasized the education of black and poor white southerners. Her success at defusing opposition to a "Yankee Crusade" was evident from an editorial in the

Richmond Times-Dispatch on the eve of the convention characterizing the effort as "a Southern affair, pure and simple, . . . under the direction of our own kith and kin." In the aftermath of that meeting, Valentine and her colleagues pressed on with their work, writing articles for newspapers and giving speeches to civic groups, and achieved a small triumph in 1903 when the city council approved $5,000 for kindergartens and vocational education.

Valentine, Munford, and other educational leaders called for a May Campaign for 1905. For a month they canvassed the state to broadcast their goal of a radically better system of education in the Old Dominion. Such educational improvements would take more state money. They wanted a nine-month school term for all children, high schools even in the rural areas, school libraries everywhere, consolidated schools and transportation to them, industrial education, and greater emphasis on teacher training. In response, the legislative session of 1906 brought a doubling of state appropriations for public schooling. Pushing far beyond a universal system of elementary schools, the Mann High School Act called for a state system of high schools. The Richmond Education Association had called for a $600,000 appropriation for a new high school to replace a decrepit and filthy one, and by 1910 the group was able to hold its annual meeting in the auditorium of the new John Marshall High School.

New Colleges to Produce More Teachers

The new high schools, in particular, soon generated an enormous additional demand for trained teachers. Many Virginians argued that while the vast majority of teachers were women, the state supported four institutions of higher education for white men—the University of Virginia, Virginia Polytechnic Institute, Virginia Military Institute, and William and Mary—and only one for white women, the Farmville Female College. Surely, they said, the state should foster increased opportunities for training white women to teach. The state soon established three new teachers' colleges.

Virginia displayed a happy combination of will, need, and resources. Yet divided minds could still thwart decisions. Many towns across the Commonwealth—particularly towns outside the Southside, where Farmville was—jockeyed to obtain a normal school, among them Newport News and Manassas. Three towns Fredericksburg, Harrisonburg, and Radford—appeared to lead the pack, but few people were optimistic that more than one school, let alone three, would be established anytime soon. Perhaps none at all would be, for some legislators opposed squandering the state's money on more normal schools, and any combination of candidates might prevent any other town from reaching its goal. The battle over the normal schools had much the ring to it of the "War of the Colleges," when the land-grant money had been so avidly sought by competing schools in the early 1870s.

A majority of legislators in 1908 favored establishment of a new school, but the House of Delegates approved a college for the east in or near Fredericksburg, while the Virginia Senate settled on one in the west in the vicinity of Harrisonburg. Resolution came, by the narrowest of margins, when both schools gained approval. The biennial budget contained start-up money for Harrisonburg the first year and for Fredericksburg the second year. Both schools initially carried the cumbersome, generic name Normal and Industrial School for Women. One eventually became known as James Madison University, the other as the University of Mary Washington. In addition to the older school at Farmville and the new schools at Fredericksburg and Harrisonburg, the 1910 legislature established in the southwest a fourth school, later known as Radford University. By World War I, each quadrant of the state had one such school.

A decision in the legislature left much unfinished business. In each town, rival sections and landowners jousted over the exact location of the new school. Each school's new board of visitors had to decide on a president. The Fredericksburg school began operations in September 1911 with 110 students. Tuition—thirty dollars per year for paying students—was free for students who committed themselves to teach in the Virginia public schools for at least four years, so the school could advertise an education "free to day students who expect to teach." Various members of the faculty at Fredericksburg had obtained their schooling at Virginia Military Institute, the University of Virginia, or Longwood.

The 1910 law concerning Radford carried stipulations similar to those the 1908 one had regarding Fredericksburg and Harrisonburg. The new schools offered training opportunities in every major section of the state. Yet so spotty was the availability of a thorough high school education that these schools could not assume that the students they admitted had the preparation to begin college work. Like the colleges and normal schools that preceded them, the schools at Harrisonburg, Fredericksburg, and Radford worked with students at whatever level of preparation they brought to the encounter. Later, the schools could impose higher entrance requirements. Later, too, they would gain accreditation.

The College of William and Mary in the Progressive Era

The state saved William and Mary in 1888, when the college won support for a normal school there to train white male teachers. Since then, the college had maintained its traditional classical curriculum and the teacher-training program. Half the school's students were "state students," their tuition covered under the state stipend on the pledge that they would become teachers. Yet doubts arose from time to time that the college could count on the continuance of this arrangement. At the constitutional convention of 1901–1902, a proposal called for terminating all state support for any institution not owned by the state, and of course that would apply to William and Mary. Supporters of William and Mary turned back the threat, but President Lyon G. Tyler and his board of visitors recognized the school's chronic fiscal vulnerability.

The William and Mary crowd understood that the resolution of 1888, vital as it had been, no longer sufficed. President Tyler mused that the school was "neither fish . . . nor fowl," neither public nor private, neither free of the whims of any session's legislators nor independent of the annual stipend from the state. One member of his faculty, John Lesslie Hall, who constituted the departments of English and history, wrote to Tyler: "We *must* before long *give ourselves to the state.*"

And so it was. The legislature increased the school's annual stipend in 1904, but what the state gave, the state could take away. In 1906, the state accepted William and Mary's offer to give up such independence as it had to become a state institution. The legislature approved the change, and Governor Swanson signed the measure into the law. William and Mary continued to be half teachers' school and half college, but no longer would it be half private and half not. Like VMI, VPI, and the University of Virginia, the College of William and Mary was now a public institution of higher education. The same legislature in 1906 increased its stipend from $25,000 to $35,000 and in 1908 increased it to $40,000.

Collegiate Coeducation for White Women

Mary-Cooke Branch Munford, who had worked closely with Valentine on various initiatives, especially on K–12 education, pursued a related quest regarding higher education for white women. She once explained her passion: "Education has been my deepest interest from my girlhood, beginning with almost passionate desire for the best education for myself, which was denied because it was not the custom for girls in my class to receive a college education at that time." She launched a sustained effort in 1910 to open the University of Virginia to female enrollment. A great many influential alumni of the university, unamused at the prospect of such an intrusion, campaigned against her crusade. The legislature considered a bill that would have gone so far as to create a coordinate college for women in Charlottesville—one with separate classes and residence halls but shared faculty and library, something like Radcliffe and Harvard, or Barnard and Columbia. Despite the efforts of Munford and her many supporters, however,

Lynchburg College. After the Civil War, as before, private colleges, often affiliated with a Protestant denomination, provided opportunities across Virginia for higher education. Lynchburg College (its name beginning in 1919) originated in 1903 as Virginia Christian College, a coeducational school affiliated with the Christian Church (Disciples of Christ). Its only building before 1909 was Westover Hall—the former Westover Hotel, a failed resort as shown here, a building that was demolished in 1970. Virginia Historical Society, Richmond, Virginia.

such a bill failed in 1916 in the House of Delegates by a vote of 46–48. A similar effort failed in 1918. Something less than half a loaf was obtained in 1920 with a decision to open the university's graduate and professional programs to women.

At other white institutions of higher education, some change also took place at about that time. The College of William and Mary faced a crisis again when its male students went off to fight World War I or to work in wartime industries; the college leased a dormitory to the DuPont Company to house workers in its nearby powder plant. Moreover, in 1917 Congress had passed the Smith-Hughes Act, offering institutions of higher education funds to train high school teachers of home economics. President Lyon G. Tyler, an avid supporter of white women's voting rights as well as white women's higher education, pressed for legislative approval of a change of policy, and state senator Aubrey E. Strode of Amherst County, who had been supporting such a change for the University of Virginia, signed on. Unlike the UVA bill, the one for William and Mary passed, and the college dropped all formal obstacles to female enrollment. In 1918, Mary could at last join William at William and Mary. The same graduation requirements for the collegiate and normal courses applied to both men and women. People connected with the University of Virginia managed to prevent undergraduate female enrollment at their school, deflecting it to William and Mary, and William and Mary happily adopted the change. At his retirement in 1919, President Tyler looked back and saw that the school's "struggle up to 1906 was for permission to live." After that, in his words, "the Institution, like the Phoenix of old, risen from the ashes, was arrayed in plumage more attractive than it ever before possessed."

Soon afterwards, Virginia Polytechnic Institute amended its policy of female exclusion as well. Taking the helm as president in 1919 was Julian A. Burruss, coming off a stint as the founding president of the normal school at Harrisonburg, so he brought considerable administrative experience with female undergraduates. In early 1921 he took a proposal to his board of visitors. He pointed to the admissions changes at William and Mary and the state university, and he mentioned women's having gained the right to vote the year before, as well as their contributions to the nation's efforts in World War I. More than that, he observed that unless the school offered places to women as well as men, it would jeopardize receipt of federal funds for the training of high school teachers in home economics as well as agriculture. The board approved the proposal, and that fall five women began their studies full-time, as did others on a part-time basis. By 1923, transfer student Mary Brumfield had earned her degree and begun graduate work, and in 1925, when she completed her master's degree, four female classmates obtained bachelor's degrees. Excluded from the cadets' printed yearbook, the *Bugle,* the female class of 1925 stitched together its own version, the *Tin Horn.*

Virginia Normal and Industrial Institute

During the new century's first decade, the University of Virginia obtained its first increase in annual support since the time of the Readjusters, the College of William and Mary became a state institution and saw its annual stipend rapidly rise, and the state launched entire new schools to train white women teachers. The largesse that the General Assembly displayed toward white institutions of higher education was not matched at the black college near Petersburg. Virginia Normal and Collegiate Institute (VNCI), an artifact of the Readjuster revolution of the early 1880s, survived through the 1890s before getting its wings severely clipped. Since the late 1880s, VNCI had had to get by with an annuity of only $15,000, rather than the $20,000 specified in the 1882 law that had launched it. Beginning in 1890, the school's board of visitors was entirely white, a stark contrast with the original bill's requirement that six of the seven members be African American.

The 1902 legislature restructured the school's operations. That year, the legislature stripped the collegiate program and renamed the school the Virginia Normal and Industrial Institute. Members of the last graduating class in the collegiate department obtained their degrees in 1902; by then fifty students, among them one woman, had earned bachelor's degrees. In 1908, however, the legislature restored the full $20,000 annuity. Thus the Virginia Normal and Industrial Institute regained the level of state financial support it had enjoyed as the Virginia Normal and Collegiate Institution for a time in the 1880s, though the white schools were by that time receiving far greater funding than two decades earlier. During the same decade that the legislature greatly increased its support of higher education in general, and created three new schools to train white women teachers in particular, it narrowed the curriculum at the black school.

The 1901–1902 constitutional convention was called in part to address the perceived need to take away the right to vote from as many as possible of the kinds of people, black and white, who had voted for the Readjusters. That same convention left the Petersburg school off a list of institutions from which the state Board of Education was to be drawn. The board of visitors from each of Virginia's major public schools would nominate a member of the faculty for consideration by the Senate, which would select among these "experienced educators" three people to fill four-year terms on the state board. Those schools were the University of Virginia, Virginia Polytechnic Institute, Virginia Military Institute, the College of William and Mary (so long as it continued to receive annual state funds), the Virginia School for the Deaf and Blind, and the Farmville Female College (the other three teachers' colleges did not yet exist). The Senate did not even have the discretion to consider appointing a black Virginian to the state Board of Education.

The Executive Budget System, the Land-Grant Funds, and Black Higher Education

Governor Westmoreland Davis inaugurated one of the key features of modern fiscal policy in Virginia, the executive budget system, an approach consistent with his ideas of applying scientific management principles to state government.

Under the executive budget system, the governor proposes a budget to the General Assembly, and the legislature has limited authority to modify it. Amounts can be increased or reduced. As a rule, however, no proposal can be entirely cut out, nor can entirely new items be introduced. The General Assembly in 1918 approved the new system, which went into effect in 1920.

Truncated as the black school was in the aftermath of legislation in 1902, it nonetheless took on two new identities in the 1920s. One reflected the new executive budget system directly; the other did so indirectly. Governor Davis observed, in his proposed budget message in 1920, that in 1872 Virginia had designated Hampton Institute, a private institution, as the state's black land-grant school. In the 1880s, however, the state had launched a public institution of black higher education, Virginia Normal and Collegiate Institute, and he proposed that the legislature lift the land-grant designation from Hampton and reassign it to Virginia Normal. The legislature did so, and from that time to this the school in Petersburg, rather than the one in Hampton, has been the recipient of a share of Virginia's federal money from the Morrill Acts of 1862 and 1890 and related legislation.

In another change, the legislature restored the Petersburg institution's authority to offer baccalaureate degrees. President John M. Gandy saw an opportunity that stemmed from the school's new land-grant status. In 1922, two decades after it had had its collegiate wing clipped in 1902, he urged what he called "the pressing necessity of reinstating College work at the Institute." As more black high schools began operation, the state needed more black teachers with baccalaureate degrees. Moreover, the Morrill Act funds, he asserted, were intended for use at collegiate institutions. Indeed, federal money received under the Smith-Hughes Act of 1917 brought these two considerations together, for that act of Congress provided money to states to support the establishment of high school programs in agricultural education, industrial education, and home economics—and to support programs to train the teachers of such subjects. President Gandy compared VNCI with the four normal schools for white women, arguing that they should have the same ability to offer four-year degrees. VNCI should simply be permitted to catch up with those schools: "We are asking for a teacher's college not a college of the arts and sciences."

The state superintendent for public instruction approved the change, effective for the 1923–1924 school year, and three women earned bachelor's degrees in 1925, in history, science, and mathematics. President Gandy then began pushing for a new identity consistent with the school's new mission, and in 1930 the General Assembly agreed to a new name, the Virginia State College for Negroes. Newly designated as Virginia's black land-grant school, it became a black teachers' college as well, so it could be compared with Virginia Polytechnic Institute and also the four white women's institutions. Subsequently the state Board of Education supervised the Petersburg school, just as it did the normal schools at Farmville, Fredericksburg, Harrisonburg, and Radford. People at the school clearly resisted the prepositional phrase in the new name, however; the state board found it had to insist in 1931 that the full legal name be used on all letterheads and diplomas.

Race, Region, State Funds, and Educational Opportunity

The fate of Virginia Normal and Collegiate Institute in 1902, when it was downgraded to Virginia Normal and Industrial, symbolized the racial disparity in public funding of education. Black elementary schools lagged far behind white schools in the state spending they obtained in 1900. At that time, per capita spending on white children was roughly double that on black children. During the next three decades, schools at every level secured increased funding—white schools far more than black. In black-majority Surry County in 1915, as historian Louis Harlan has shown, twice as many black students attended school as white students, but the white schools received five times as much money, so per-student expenditures for white children were ten times those for their black counterparts. As for high schools in particular, most counties had them for whites; few had them for blacks. It was reported in 1920 that, across rural Virginia, 297 black students attended high school, compared with 22,061 white students.

Discrimination that denied black children an equal educational opportunity also worked against large numbers of white children. State funds were distributed on a per capita basis—but then, to nobody's surprise, white school boards allocated the bulk of their funds to white schools. Not only did this mean that black schools in black-majority counties received far less money per capita than did white ones there—where far more dollars for black children could be diverted to white schools—but white schools in majority-black counties also received far more than did white schools in predominantly white areas. In that sense, white schools in predominantly black counties were subsidized both by black students in black counties and by white students in white counties. The larger the black proportion—and in the early twentieth century, many eastern counties, like Surry, still had black majorities—the larger the subsidy by other Virginians to white students there.

Racial segregation permitted an enormous funding disparity between black and white; the funding formula itself permitted a tremendous disparity between western whites and easterners. This discrimination—this double discrimination,

Julius Rosenwald (1862–1932) of Chicago, president of Sears, Roebuck and Co., standing outside the White House in late 1929. Beginning in 1914, partly as a result of his acquaintance with Virginia native and Tuskegee Institute president Booker T. Washington, Rosenwald contributed to the construction of 5,000 schools—more than 300 of them in eighty-one counties in Virginia—for black children in fifteen southern states. He demanded matching funds from school boards, thus leveraging his contributions and also enhancing public support for black schools, to supplement the substantial private amounts that black communities were already supplying on their own. Photographs of many of the Virginia schools are in the Jackson Davis Collection at the University of Virginia and the Archie Richardson Collection at Virginia State University. Library of Congress, Prints and Photographs Division, LC-USZ62, 111719.

one a function of the other—did not pass unnoticed by white Virginians in the western, whiter counties. At the constitutional convention in 1901, a western delegate, Thomas W. Harrison, challenged his eastern counterparts: "You will tax the people in Frederick county to educate the negro children in the Black Belt, and then you will not apply it to the education of the negro children in the Black Belt." And that is what they did.

This behavior had implications for all three groups in terms of their access to higher education and their chances for success at such institutions. Black students who enrolled at Virginia Normal and Industrial Institute or at Hampton Institute, like white students from western Virginia who enrolled at VPI, generally brought with them to the encounter far less schooling—measured in

266

tax dollars, at least—than did the students, typically from eastern Virginia, who went off to the University of Virginia or to William and Mary. Similarly, as seems likely, students enrolling at the teachers' colleges at Radford or Harrisonburg typically came less well academically prepared than did students at Fredericksburg or Farmville.

The Prohibition Experiment

One of the hallmarks of the Progressive movement in America was the call for the total prohibition of alcoholic beverages. Prohibition went far beyond earlier private initiatives to promote temperance, a limited use of such beverages; it called for legal enforcement of a total ban on such beverages. Prohibition as a political movement embodied various dimensions of progressivism—an organized attack on a social ill, a resort to legislation to address it, an effort to promote social welfare, and a reliance on social control. It was by no means a characteristically regional phenomenon. But it did draw more support in rural areas than in small towns, and among native Protestants than among immigrant Catholics. Virginia sported a lot of people who fit the description of native Protestants living in small towns and rural surroundings.

In the 1910s, Rev. James Cannon Jr. led a statewide drive for prohibition in Virginia. Converted at a revival while a student at Randolph-Macon College, Cannon had become a Southern Methodist minister, but prohibition was his obsession and the basis of his prominence in public affairs. By 1904, he had become the Anti-Saloon League's leading figure, and some years later that group successfully sought an enabling act that provided for a referendum on prohibition if its proponents could secure the signatures of 18,000 voters. Cannon's organization obtained 71,000 signatures, so Governor Henry C. Stuart ordered the referendum, set for September 22, 1914.

A statewide campaign ensued, the outcome of the referendum weighing in the balance. On one side, ministers preached the gospel of prohibition, and the Anti-Saloon League flooded the state with propaganda. The Woman's Christian Temperance Union (WCTU) published leaflets with titles like "The Saloon Evil" and "Prohibition Promotes Prosperity." Postcards carried the message "Save the Boys." Women could not vote, but they could lean on their men to vote—for prohibition. The "drys" organized parades and public meetings. Though receptive to moral and religious arguments, drys more often argued that alcohol ruined people's health, led to poverty, lowered workers' efficiency, and contributed to accidents, crime, and prostitution—and that prohibition was the best way to curtail these sorry results. Drunk fathers were more likely to get hurt on the job, drink away their wages, lose their jobs, beat the kids. Parents, concerned about the well-being of their own children and of youth in general, also often supported prohibition. Drys insisted that even moderate drinking was harmful, and the state should curtail it.

On the other side, rejecting any such imposition of a statewide law, was the Virginia Association for Local Self Government. The Virginia Association launched its own campaign of booklets, pamphlets, newspapers, and editorials. Henry Tucker, a distinguished lawyer and Democrat, organized the statewide distribution of the association's message. Prohibition would force the liquor problem underground, said "wets." It would be as flagrantly violated in Virginia as it was in other states, would lead to disrespect for the law, and would lead to higher general taxes to make up for the revenue lost from taxes on alcohol. The wets held that temperance, not prohibition, was the way to go. The moral and practical problems associated with the use of alcohol could best be solved through character development, not a legal ban.

Reverend Cannon warned his opponents that God would punish them for "the men and the women and the little children damned by your partnership with the saloon." The association responded in kind, calling the prohibition campaign's leaders "intolerant bigots" and "professional slanderers." The wets attempted to gain the support of tobacco farmers by arguing that prohibition of alcohol would be followed by a crusade against tobacco. As the referendum approached, and it became more and more evident that the drys would win, some citizens stocked up on four-gallon jugs of whiskey.

On referendum day, the turnout was large, as churches held prayer meetings and rang their bells to remind men to do their Christian duty. Drys won big. They defeated the wets not only in rural areas but even in cities. Prohibition took effect on November 1, 1916. After that, it was illegal in Virginia to manufacture alcoholic beverages, transport them, sell them, or even give them away. By then, Cannon was pressing his case for a federal amendment. Prohibition came to Virginia before federal law would have brought it in 1920 anyway.

Into the 1920s

The Progressive movement brought to Virginia a wide range of changes, some of them reinforcing trends that had preceded the twentieth century, some of them going off in new directions. From the perspective of the dominant political forces—white Virginians in general, rural whites as voters, business interests as a rule—progress had been achieved on many fronts. Segregation and disfranchisement, from this perspective, made for good race relations and a good electorate. More money and more statewide administration made for good schools and good roads. Prohibition and the SCC made for a sober society and a better economy. These patterns persisted into the 1920s—in particular, the state poured even larger amounts of money into schools and roads. Prohibition went national. Segregation got shored up from an already high level.

All of these initiatives reflected the use of state power, not so much "states' rights" in the sense of putting up a deflector shield against federal intervention—since that was not a key concern during this time—as using state power to reinforce favored constituencies at the local level or to thwart local initiatives that found disfavor elsewhere. The Virginia Association for Local Self Government, in its opposition to statewide imposition of prohibition, captured one facet of this phenomenon. Then again, one reason for taking the approach Virginia did regarding the distribution of state money for public schools had to do with region, race, and class. If the state acted directly to discriminate grossly in favor of whites and against blacks, someone might go to federal court. By sending state money to the local governments, in an absolutely nondiscriminatory fashion, on the basis of how many school-age residents lived in the locality, the state turned over responsibility to local authorities. In black counties, local officials put most of the proceeds into white schools. The best public schools in rural Virginia—certainly the best financed—were, as a consequence, the white schools in eastern Virginia in counties with the greatest proportions of black residents. In an era of progress—in the use of state power to make things better—such an outcome was entirely consistent with the progress that the rulers of Virginia sought.

Chapter 18

Alternative Pasts—Preserved, Retrieved, Celebrated

....

Especially between the 1890s and the 1940s, Virginians looked to history to find sustenance, secure a collective identity, and along the way promote cultural tourism. The two major frames of reference were colonial Jamestown and the Civil War. Each of the two frames of reference drew from the past to focus on a different creation myth, but both emphasized major themes in Virginia's past, and both distinguished Virginia's history from that of the North in general and New England in particular. Other themes emerged as well, some of them in one way or another consistent with the two leading ones, others jarring, even deliberately, with them, as various Virginians contested over the meaning of the past. These varied claimants to a place lived in different presents, aspired to different futures, looked to different pasts. Each contributed much to the world that Virginians inhabited, whether in physical space or in their heads.

Jamestown, Williamsburg, Monticello, and Richmond's Monument Avenue—all four of these venues were either created or rediscovered and rehabilitated in the late nineteenth and early twentieth centuries. Engaged in the politics and culture of heritage history were the twins—or uncle and niece, father and daughter—the United Confederate Veterans and the United Daughters of the Confederacy (UDC). Another key organization that emerged in those years and proved active in commemorating Virginia history was the Association for the Preservation of Virginia Antiquities (APVA). Together, their voices dominated the political and cultural landscape, but other voices rang out, too, with very different words. A survey of some of these varied voices can help us glimpse or grasp what ideals animated different groups of Virginians and how they tried to understand their past and influence the future.

Across the nineteenth century, such Virginia venues as Monticello and James-town were largely neglected. Between the 1890s and the 1930s, by contrast, they were largely rehabilitated—their reputations enhanced, their physical surround-ings restored. Much of the work was aimed at dissident Virginians, including the Readjuster movement. More was aimed at outsiders, especially New Englanders who presumed to trumpet—in textbooks read by schoolchildren, in histories sold to a general readership—the primacy of their region as the cradle of Amer-ica. Often it was outsiders, however, who made possible the transformations that occurred, whether the Levy family in preserving Monticello across the nine-teenth century or John D. Rockefeller Jr. in bankrolling Colonial Williamsburg as it emerged in the 1930s.

Jamestown well represents the early-twentieth-century efforts to rehabilitate iconic Virginia venues and to connect Virginians in particular—and Americans in general—with their past, or, more precisely, with the version of the past that the proponents of historical preservation chose to emphasize. The APVA got organized in 1889, and to no other site did it resonate as it did to Jamestown. The site had been a peninsula three centuries earlier, but erosion from the James River had cut it off from the mainland, and the APVA sought symbolically to link Jamestown back up with the mainstream of American historical under-standing.

By 1893 the APVA had acquired twenty-two acres of land at Jamestown, in-cluding the church and cemetery. In 1895 it inaugurated Virginia Day, May 13, to commemorate the 1607 landing. Some 700 elite Virginians made their way on a pilgrimage by boat—the *Pocahontas*—to Jamestown, where they joined several thousand other celebrants. They walked among the ruins of the ancient cem-etery and church, and they heard speeches glorifying Virginia's past, including one by Lyon G. Tyler, president of the College of William and Mary in nearby Williamsburg and son of a former president of the United States. Tyler observed that the nation's "rightful name" was Virginia.

Tyler sometimes referred supportively to the APVA style of historic preser-vation as "a struggle for self-preservation." The so-called Lost Cause—of seces-sion, war, and Confederate independence—had been lost, and the white South in general, and Virginia in particular, must revive its prestige, its confidence, its historical significance. In a 1921 book titled *Virginia First,* Tyler touted James-town as the "Cradle of the Union," as having had the first of everything of con-sequence, political (the first legislative assembly), religious (the first Protestant church), or economic (the first wharf, glassworks, or ironworks). Celebrated as

Ellen Glasgow (1873–1945). In novel after novel, Glasgow re-created the Virginia past, whether depicting people in Richmond or in the Shenandoah Valley, and whether before, during, or after the Civil War. Virginia Historical Society, Richmond, Virginia.

key figures in the early history of Virginia were John Smith, Pocahontas, and Nathaniel Bacon. Bacon's historical rehabilitation stands out in this pantheon. During his uprising in 1676, he burned the colonial capital—leaving the ruined church that the APVA acquired in the 1890s. An APVA leader, Mary Newton, with reference to a memorial to Bacon, mused about him in 1900 that he was "the first Virginian to enjoy the distinction of being dubbed with the title of 'rebel'—since made so dear to Southern hearts." In that view, Bacon's Rebellion, the American Revolution, and the War between the States were each a legitimate expression of opposition to illegitimate power.

Delighted to see white schoolchildren visit Jamestown, people from the APVA expressed their pleasure that "interest in this hallowed place is spreading forth into another generation." Jamestown was home to a growing collection of monuments, but selectively so. In 1916, when President John M. Gandy of the Virginia Normal and Industrial Institute—the black school in Petersburg, monument to the Readjusters—urged a monument to the black immigrants of 1619, the APVA turned him down: "Jamestown was the first permanent Colony of the English speaking people in this Country . . . and the incident of bringing negroes by the Dutch ship to Jamestown forms no such part in the life of the Colony as will justify our granting permission to erect a memorial to that event."

As the tercentennial year, 1907, approached, APVA people sought funding from Congress to support a major commemoration. Congressmen from Virginia discovered to their dismay that many of their colleagues from other states had never heard of Jamestown and had no idea of its historical significance—all the more reason to push ahead and highlight their version of the past.

Histories Just and True

The United Daughters of the Confederacy undertook to memorialize Confederate veterans and the Civil War by tending veterans' graves, and they also promoted the production of monuments to the Confederacy, whether of stone or in words. Conflating "southerners" with the plantation elite, they sought to rally broad-based support for the region's more privileged people. Equating "South" with "Confederacy," they did all they could to repel all challenges to their views of the Confederate and Reconstruction/Readjuster past. Northern writings that criticized the large planters and leading politicians of the slave South were banned in schools and libraries as anti-South. The horrors of black power during Reconstruction were paired with the glories of brave Confederate soldiers. The UDC organized Virginia chapters of the Children of the Confederacy, as historian Fred Arthur Bailey has observed, the first of them in Richmond in 1912 and soon others, from Fredericksburg and Charlottesville to Roanoke and Bristol. Required reading—and catechizing—for all children in these chapters was the *U.D.C. Catechism for Children,* with its litany of images that not only justified the Confederate cause but at the same time rendered slavery benign and slaves contented and loyal.

The UDC committed itself "to endeavor to have used in all Southern schools only such histories as are just and true." One such book, by Beverley B. Munford, *Virginia's Attitude toward Slavery and Secession*—published in 1909, near the end of his life, and dedicated to his wife, Mary-Cooke Branch Munford—satisfied the UDC as being "just and true" and was adopted for use in the public schools, whose growth the Munfords had fostered as Virginia progressives. Munford, who had been a child in Richmond during the Civil War, was a celebrated lawyer, a leading member of the Sons of Confederate Veterans, and often a state legislator—an anti-Readjuster member of the House of Delegates representing Danville at the time of the 1883 preelection incident there that steamrolled the state elections and ended the Readjuster experiment, and a member of the Virginia Senate representing Richmond in the late 1890s when he spearheaded a crusade against northern textbooks. Munford's book set out to dispute what he took to be the prevailing notions in the North that Virginia had ever acted out of either devotion to slavery or hostility toward the Union. For principle, George Washington took the stand against the British Empire that he did in 1775, and for principle, according to Munford, Robert E. Lee did much the same in 1861 and the "American War of Secession."

Munford's book remains an intriguing account of Virginia's travails through the years from one political revolution to another. Bemoaning the poor performance of statesmen who permitted tensions to rise to such an extreme in 1861, it steers a course that sometimes deprecates both New England and the Deep South in the debate and compromise in 1787 over the international slave trade, and both the Lower South and the Republican Party in the secession winter of 1860–1861. A century after its publication, its main value is as a primary source, capturing and reflecting the views of elite white Virginians in the early twentieth century and revealing the text from which so many young Virginians learned their catechism and formed their ideas and sensibilities about the past.

According to Munford, white Virginians never really wanted slavery. They had had the institution imposed upon them, and such tremendous "difficulties and dangers" attended its abolition that no effective action against it could ever be taken. Twice he quotes George Mason's strong language against the continuance of the international slave trade into the new nation—but nowhere does he quote Mason's companion concerns that the new national government might prove hostile toward slavery itself. Sadly he watches in retrospect as the General Assembly fails to embrace a golden opportunity and enact legislation to rid the state of slavery—and rid the state, too, of free black residents—in 1832. The book's main burden—and why it met with such strong endorsement—is its sustained effort to show that Virginia had been an unfortunate victim, with slavery and then war both thrust upon it. No doubt Munford's book did much to confirm elders' sense of their place in the past, not to mention shaping youngsters' durable knowledge of a past that never was.

UDC Woman versus Former Confederate Hero

Two white Virginians suggested the possibilities in gazing back at slavery and the war, always in the context of race relations—or, rather, white supremacy. Writing in 1913 for a public presentation, a Mrs. Lindsey, a member of the UDC, had fond memories of slavery. But, she acknowledged, it was gone. "In God's providence slavery came and went," she observed, "and while the race question of today is a vexing problem, we can always feel sure that white supremacy is God-given and will last."

John Singleton Mosby, once revered as a Confederate military hero for his Civil War exploits, relinquished that status by addressing the past in terms that belied the romantic portrayal of slavery and also the UDC view of the Civil War. Years ago slavery had been the norm in his world, he said, and he had taken it for granted, but he had no patience with the dogmatic insistence that slavery had had nothing to do with the war. "Why not talk about witchcraft if . . . slavery was not the cause of the war," he demanded. "I always understood that we went to war on account of the thing we quarreled with the North about." In another letter, reflecting at once his past and his present, he wrote: "Now while I think as badly of slavery as Horace Greeley did I am not ashamed that my family were slaveholders. It was our inheritance. Neither am I ashamed that my ancestors were pirates and cattle thieves."

Speaking about his own roles in the war, Mosby concluded: "The South went to war on account of Slavery. . . . a soldier fights for his country—right or wrong—he is not responsible for the political merits of the course he fights in. The South was my country." Was. His apostasy directed him to a different future, and he left the region. As for the kind of history promoted by the likes of Beverley Munford, Mosby had this to say about another Confederate veteran, George L. Christian, who was also active in Lost Cause work: "According to Christian the Virginia people were the abolitionists and the Northern people were *pro-slavery*."

Monument Avenue

In 1890, a quarter century after Appomattox, a tremendous crowd of white Virginians celebrated the unveiling of a huge statue in Richmond on what became known as Monument Avenue. Robert E. Lee once again rode his faithful horse Traveller, and this time he would forever be up there. In the years to come, a pair of Lee's old comrades in Confederate uniform rejoined him. J. E. B. Stuart's statue—with Stuart also on horseback—went up in 1907. Also unveiled that spring was a towering statue of Confederate president Jefferson Davis. Stonewall Jackson returned to Richmond in 1919, also taking up permanent residence on Monument Avenue, perpetually riding Little Sorrell.

There was another perspective on such celebration, such commemoration, such reverence, such worship. At the time of Lee's celebration in 1890, the editor of the city's black newspaper the *Richmond Planet* published a dissenting view. On the day the statue was unveiled, John Mitchell Jr. rebuked the city for both the statue and the joy with which it was being unveiled as commemorating a

The Confederate Veterans Memorial at Arlington National Cemetery. Arlington House—which George Washington Parke Custis, the grandson of President George Washington's wife, Martha, built just across the Potomac River from Washington, D.C.—passed in 1857 to Custis's daughter Mary, whose husband was Robert E. Lee. The Lee family reluctantly moved away from the area when Virginia seceded, and in 1864, while the Civil War raged, the federal government, having purchased the estate at a tax sale, began using a portion of the grounds as a military cemetery. Most of the men interred there were Union soldiers and sailors, but some Confederates, if they died in northern prison camps or hospitals, were buried in scattered plots in the cemetery as well. A proposal in the late 1890s to reinter the Confederate dead there all together in one part of the cemetery gained approval, and Congress appropriated funds in 1900 for that purpose in a bill supported by veterans from both armies. Unveiled at the site on June 4, 1914, was a Confederate Veterans Memorial, designed by Sir Moses Jacob Ezekiel, who had fought in 1864 at New Market as a VMI cadet and was subsequently a sculptor working mostly in Europe. The memorial bears the inscription "To Our Dead Heroes by the United Daughters of the Confederacy." This photograph depicts veterans in gray streaming away from the dedication, at which the speakers included President Woodrow Wilson, who had lived in his native Virginia as a child during the Civil War. Library of Congress, Prints and Photographs Division, LC-USZ62-91974.

"legacy of treason and blood." Not only editor of a newspaper but also a member of the Richmond City Council, he was concerned about how people in the future might view the city's black citizens if they were negated in its monuments: "What does this display of Confederate emblems mean? What does it serve to teach the rising generations of the South?" He took pride in an alternative demonstration later that year, when he served as grand marshal of an Emancipation Day parade that stretched two miles. Black Richmonders laid claim to the city's streets, too.

Douglas Southall Freeman (1886–1953) and Lee's Lieutenants

Douglas Southall Freeman was born in Lynchburg but moved as a child with his family in 1892 to Richmond, the former capital of the Confederacy and a center of Confederate memorials and gatherings. His father, a Confederate veteran, had been with General Lee at Appomattox. As a seventeen-year-old third-year student at Richmond College (now the University of Richmond), in November 1903 Douglas accompanied his father to Petersburg to witness a reunion of General Mahone's aging troops and a reenactment of the Battle of the Crater. Already inclined to the study of history, so moved was he by the experience that he concluded: "If someone doesn't write the story of these men, it will be lost forever," and in fact "I'm going to do it." He would write the history of Lee's Army of Northern Virginia.

Within a year, Freeman had earned his B.A. and begun graduate work in history at the Johns Hopkins University. In February 1907, during his third year at Hopkins, after some work at the Virginia State Library back in Richmond, he received an invitation from the reference librarian there, in her role as a member of the Confederate Memorial Literary Society. Might he be available, she asked, to organize the papers at the Confederate Museum and compile a book on those holdings? It would, she declared, "help the cause of the Confederacy." He jumped at the chance. In reply, he described such a project as essential "if the real history of the War Between the States is ever to be written": "They say it is a lost cause. Perhaps it was; but it still lives in the hearts of the Southern people. Its career of arms ended these forty years ago; we only live for its justification. And this is not to be done in any other way than through the careful collection and statement of calm historical fact."

That summer, working in the dining room of the Confederate White House, Freeman largely completed the project. Then he returned to his dissertation, "The Attitude of Political Parties in Virginia to Slavery and Secession (1846–1861)." Designed as an extended prologue to his life's historical work on the Civil

War era, the dissertation ended with the appointment of Robert E. Lee to the command of Virginia's army. By the time Freeman was awarded the Ph.D. in June 1908, at the age of twenty-two, he had also published his first book, *A Calendar of Confederate Papers*. A few months later, the dissertation was singed, but not destroyed, in a fire at Hopkins. Freeman never returned to that part of the project, but the dissertation and the *Calendar* jointly launched the historical work that engaged him for much of the next forty-five years.

Freeman almost always followed two vocations at the same time, newspaper work and historical research and writing. Even as an undergraduate, Freeman had begun a newspaper career as a college correspondent for the *Richmond News Leader*. By 1915 he had become the *News Leader* editor, a position he held until his retirement in 1949 to gain what he called "freedom to follow my first love," historical research and writing. Each day on his drive to and from work at the *News Leader,* he had saluted Lee's statue on Monument Avenue.

A Calendar of Confederate Papers led to Freeman's next book, an edited collection of original sources, *Lee's Dispatches* (1915). To produce the copious annotation—identifying every person named, providing context for every engagement recounted—required a huge down payment toward his later work. When he had finished, he observed how good he felt each time he passed the general's statue (and saluted): "Thank God, I've done a little to keep alive his fame!" Freeman's latest book led to an invitation to write a short book on Lee. He agreed, but it proved anything but short. Freeman approached his work by writing through the eyes of his subject. Taking a "fog of war" approach, he related what Lee knew at any time, not what an omniscient observer might have seen. The four-volume *R. E. Lee: A Biography* (1934–1935) won a Pulitzer Prize. Before he finished *Lee,* he witnessed yet another reunion, this the forty-second annual gathering in Richmond of the United Confederate Veterans, and he wrote a celebration as an editorial, but it also came out as a book, *The Last Parade* (1932). After *Lee,* he wrote a three-volume work, *Lee's Lieutenants: A Study in Command* (1942–1944). Then came the seven-volume *George Washington: A Biography* (1948–1957), although its final volume was completed after his death. Like *Lee,* it was awarded a Pulitzer Prize. Freeman's work on Robert E. Lee—Freeman's *Lee*—continues to dominate academic and popular views of the man and the general.

Carter G. Woodson (1875–1950) and Black History

Carter G. Woodson was a near contemporary of Douglas Southall Freeman. Also born in Virginia, but his father a former slave rather than a Confederate veteran, Carter Woodson worked on his parents' small farm in Virginia and then moved with his family to West Virginia, where his father worked in railroad construction and he in coal mining. Eventually, in 1903, the year before Kentucky banned all integrated schools, he graduated from the biracial Berea College. Returning to Huntington, West Virginia, he taught at Frederick Douglass High School, which he had attended. Then he spent four years teaching in the Philippines, before earning a master's degree in history at the University of Chicago and, in 1912, a Ph.D. at Harvard.

Dr. Woodson, like Dr. Freeman, published books on the history of the United States. But in Woodson's many books he wrote of other pasts than those to be found in Freeman's many books. In *The Education of the Negro Prior to 1861* (1915), for example, he wrote of education for black Americans in an era in which, though Charles Fenton Mercer's Literary Fund was in place, state law prohibited teaching black Virginians to read or write. His books also included *A Century of Negro Migration* (1918), *A History of the Negro Church* (1921), *The Negro in Our History* (1922), *The Negro Wage Earner* (1930), and *The Negro Professional Man and the Community* (1934). Significant as his books were, though, more important were his other major professional activities. In 1915, Woodson established the Association for the Study of Negro Life and History and began editing the *Journal of Negro History.*

For the rest of his life, through much of the period that Freeman was editing the *Richmond News Leader,* Woodson continued to edit that journal. During the very long time that black scholars found it virtually, or even entirely, impossible to get published in the major mainstream historical journals—and white scholars did, too, if they were writing on matters of race from a perspective at variance with the dominant pre-1950 understanding among whites—the *Journal of Negro History* provided a critically important outlet. Contributors included black historians Luther Porter Jackson and John Hope Franklin, white scholars Herbert Aptheker and Fabian Linden, and people whose professional training lay in other disciplines than history, among them folklorist Zora Neale Hurston and political scientist Ralph Bunche. Particularly important articles on the history of Virginia included one by Kenneth Stampp on Thomas R. Dew and the 1832 legislative debate over slavery, as well as two very long ones by A. A. Taylor titled "The Negro in the Reconstruction of Virginia." Woodson's lifework laid a foundation on which many scholars and citizens continue to construct renewed understandings of a past in which African Americans had a central presence and, indeed, were essential players. The people whose past Woodson wrote of, and celebrated, were the people over whom many of Freeman's people were contesting against northern armies, and a people who helped shape an outcome to the war that Lee's warriors battled to prevent.

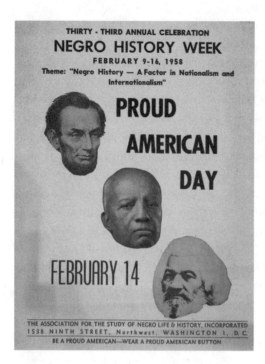

THIRTY - THIRD ANNUAL CELEBRATION

NEGRO HISTORY WEEK

FEBRUARY 9-16, 1958

Theme: "Negro History — A Factor in Nationalism and Internationalism"

PROUD

AMERICAN

DAY

FEBRUARY 14

THE ASSOCIATION FOR THE STUDY OF NEGRO LIFE & HISTORY, INCORPORATED
1538 NINTH STREET, Northwest, WASHINGTON 1, D.C.
BE A PROUD AMERICAN—WEAR A PROUD AMERICAN BUTTON

Dr. Carter G. Woodson (1875–1950). The cover of this 1958 program shows historian Carter G. Woodson, the originator of Negro History Week, flanked by President Abraham Lincoln and abolitionist Frederick Douglass, whose February birthdays inspired Woodson to pick that month for the celebration. Virginia Historical Society, Richmond, Virginia.

Freeman and Woodson each worked from primary sources, the raw materials of history, and each was scrupulous in his use of the materials. Critical differences between the two included Woodson's use of such previously unused sources as census information and slave testimony; his emphasis on the bottom of the social structure, not the great political and military leaders; and an approach to slavery that emphasized the institution and experience from the perspectives of black southerners. While Freeman was doing history in the interests of what he saw as an appropriate understanding of the Confederate experiment, Woodson was doing history to promote, among whites and blacks alike, a better understanding of the nation's racial past in general and of African American history in particular. In that spirit, Woodson developed the idea of Negro History Week, first celebrated in 1926 and marked during the second week of February to commemorate the birthdates of Abraham Lincoln and Frederick Douglass. Beginning in 1937, he also edited the *Negro History Bulletin,* like Negro History Week designed to circulate the ongoing research on black history to a wide audience that included teachers, students, and community people. Years after his death, Negro History Week became Black History Month, and the Association for the Study of Negro Life and History changed its name to Association for the Study of Afro-American Life and History.

Popular music also drew from the past and adapted it to the present. What have become known as the Bristol Recording Sessions of 1927 produced over a dozen new music acts of the "hillbilly" genre. Particularly prominent among the groups discovered at Bristol was the Carter Family trio from Pleasant Valley, Virginia—A.P. Carter, his wife, Sara, and his sister-in-law, Maybelle. Regarding A.P., musician Marty Stuart once said: "If you look at country music as if it were a musical bible, I'd say he would be in Genesis. Where God says, 'In the beginning, God created A.P. Carter.'"

The Carter Family was featured as a model American family, although the real story involved betrayal as well as love, and the struggles of simple beginnings in a hard time and place. Carters had lived in the shadow of Clinch Mountain since the Revolutionary War. Alvin Pleasant "A.P." Carter grew up in Poor Valley, where he learned to play the violin and sang in the church choir. Always described as an odd child, A.P. Carter was born with a tremor that caused him to shake and created a natural vibrato in his voice. Music gave A.P. a sanctuary and something he could excel in. But it could not put food on the table, so he worked on the railroad and sold fruit trees. While away at work one time, he met a young woman named Sara Dougherty, whose singing voice amazed him. In 1915 "they jumped the broomstick, got married," their son Joe Carter recounted much later, with an explanation like the one A.P. gave: "Music is what done it." In 1926, A.P.'s brother Ezra married Maybelle Addington, and the trio fell into place.

A.P. served as songwriter, Sara played autoharp and added her angelic singing voice, and Maybelle played guitar in her unique style. Maybelle later explained: "When I started playing the guitar I didn't have nobody to play with me, so that's how I developed the style of kicking in the rhythm too, you know, and they call it the Carter Scratch." A.P., the driving force behind the group, foresaw a great future for the trio, though to the average inhabitant of Poor Valley they were just another singing group. With A.P.'s mind always focused on music, he had a tough time seeing a crop through to harvest. Then he heard of Ralph Peer's newspaper advertisement for music acts, and he recognized his shot at making a living in music—even if the all-day, twenty-five-mile trek to Bristol held little appeal for Sara, let alone for eighteen-year-old Maybelle, then eight months pregnant.

After much convincing, the group headed to Bristol to audition for Peer, who later recounted: "As soon as I heard Sara's voice that was it." Peer knew America needed the trio's unique sound before America knew. The Carters also had something Peer needed—original material that could be copyrighted. Not only did the trio generate its own material, but as Carter Family historian Mark Zwonitzer has said, A.P.'s particular genius was "taking these old, old, songs . . . and remaking them." During those two days in August, the Carters recorded six songs. The group was paid $300 and sent back to Poor Valley. Months later, they learned of the release of their "Single Girl, Married Girl." Along with Jimmie Rodgers, the Carter Family was invited to a second recording session, this one in Camden, New Jersey. The Camden session produced hit after hit—"Wildwood Flower," "Forsaken Love," "Will You Miss Me When I'm Gone?"—each of which sold over 100,000 copies. The Carters were well on their way to becoming "the first family of country music," a status solidified when Maybelle's daughter June, at the age of ten, began performing with Sara and Maybelle.

The Carter Family repertoire kept growing, even while A.P.'s marriage fell apart. In the 1930s, during the Great Depression, he and his friend Lesley "Esley" Riddle ventured into the Deep South searching for local songs they could record—A.P. a tall, gangly, white man with the shakes and Esley a black man hobbling on one leg in the Jim Crow South. A.P. did not care much for family life, and Sara grew lonely back home in Poor Valley. A.P.'s absence and indifference toward her needs drove her into the arms of Coy Bays, one of A.P.'s many cousins in Poor Valley. A.P. and Sara divorced in 1936, but the trio managed to record dozens of additional songs together.

In 1938, the Carter Family began broadcasting on radio station XERA, just over the Rio Grande in Mexico, where it could broadcast at 500 kilowatts—ten times the U.S. limit for radio stations—and reach every American who had a radio. The weekly broadcasts on XERA provided the Carter Family with a steady flow of income as well as worldwide exposure. They received letters saying things like "I hope to meet you in heaven someday and I'm just a poor uneducated person and not good with words, but I want to tell you how much you mean to me." Many famous Virginia musicians followed the Carter Family into country stardom, but as *Richmond Times-Dispatch* writer Clarke Bustard has written: "A.P. Carter was unique. No modern Virginian echoed the commonwealth's musical heritage more authentically. None exerted a more profound influence on the future of American music."

A.P. Carter died in 1960, his legacy more than a hundred songs arranged and recorded. Maybelle "Mother" Carter passed away in 1978 leaving behind her singing daughters Anita, Helen, and June. June married a legend in his own right, Johnny Cash. The last surviving member of the original trio, Sara Carter Bays, died in 1979. Sara's children Janette and Joe Carter were instrumental in preserving the family heritage, creating the Carter Family Memorial Music Center in Poor Valley. Janette, the last surviving child of the original Carter Family, died at age eighty-two in January 2006. In 1998, meanwhile, Congress designated Bristol the "Birthplace of Country Music." The Carter Family had reached deep into the American past, multiple American pasts, to produce a music that, through the modern technologies of recordings and radio, reached across the nation. The merging of the Cash and Carter names perpetuated the Carter Family's legacy and introduced their music to new generations.

Retrieving a Political Past

Far from the southwestern reaches of the state, particularly in the east, elite Virginians did much to work their will in mythologizing the past. They embodied it on Monument Avenue, imposing a view of the past that privileged Virginians with white faces and Confederate antecedents. A statue of a Confederate soldier stood out in front of courthouses across the state. The constitutional convention of 1901–1902 sought to reach back before the Civil War, even before the Constitution of 1851, to construct a political system in which middling and prosperous white men ran public affairs. The political organization that emerged in Virginia in the aftermath of the Readjusters' defeat celebrated a past it wished to reconstitute and perpetuate. Under the leadership of Harry F. Byrd Sr., from the 1920s into the 1960s, elite rural white Virginians held sway in the state's electoral politics.

U.S. Senator Thomas F. Martin died in 1919, after four terms in the Senate. State senator Harry F. Byrd soon became Democratic Party chairman. He took the reins of the old Martin Organization, as it had been known—the party machine that dominated the Democratic Party, and with it the politics of Virginia, in the era after the Readjusters were thrust from power. What now became known as the Byrd Organization harked back to significant aspects of earlier periods in Virginia's political history, even the time of his ancestor William Byrd II.

By the 1920s, neither race nor gender was any longer an absolute bar to voting or running for office. Nonetheless, the Byrd Organization depended on a small electorate, even more limited than in either the colonial period or the first half of the nineteenth century. Moreover, county courthouses proved central to the operations of public affairs in both the eighteenth century and the early twentieth century. In colonial Virginia, officeholders were awarded additional responsibilities according to how they demonstrated their ability to run public affairs in the county courts. In the Byrd era, men worked their way up the organization ladder depending first of all on their political reliability at the county level, and

Harry Byrd held more power in determining office seekers' advancement, over a longer period, than any one Virginian ever had before, in the colonial period or the nineteenth century. Dependent as they were on their perceived loyalty to Byrd, the men around the courthouses could be counted on to support Byrd and his brand of Democratic Party politics. Such men constituted a large proportion of the total active electorate.

Chapter 19

Alternative Futures

....

Virginians often found their identities by drawing from the past, and they sought to steer a course to a preferred future by celebrating various aspects of Virginia's legacy, whether from the seventeenth century and the Jamestown beginnings, the eighteenth and the nation's Founders, or the nineteenth and the Civil War. Many sought some kind of emancipation from the past, sought to forge a very different future. Some changes emerged when new technology made mass entertainment possible, as when people could buy recordings, listen to a radio, or go to a movie. These varied developments took a wide range of shapes, as Virginia's men and women, blacks and whites, urbanites and rural folk, looked to a twentieth century that would serve their social, economic, cultural, or political interests. Members of each group worked with materials at hand to foster a future they desired. Among other ventures of the period, in the 1920s Richard E. Byrd emulated his ancestor William Byrd II's travels along the farther reaches of the North Carolina border by tackling the forbidding areas around the North and South poles.

Black Protest against Segregated Streetcars

Jim Crow came to Virginia in 1902—maybe. Virginia's public schools were segregated from their beginnings in 1870. But civil rights lawyer Samuel W. Tucker, who was born in Alexandria in 1913, told listeners that his father had often mused about the time "before they Jim Crowed us," and the elder Tucker might have been speaking either of voting rights and the 1902 constitution or of segregated transit, which came about the same time. The Tuckers, father and son, were acutely aware that they struggled for a future that contrasted sharply with the one they sought to slay.

Between 1900 and 1906, both before and after the constitutional convention that disfranchised black Virginians, the General Assembly passed a number of laws regarding the segregation of public transit. The legislature began with railway cars, then turned its attention to coastal steamboats and urban electric trolleys. A bill in 1902 proposed to cover the state but then was limited to Alexandria. A 1904 law authorized all transit companies in Virginia to segregate their trolley cars, although it did not require them to do so. When the Virginia Passenger and Power Company decided to segregate passengers in the Richmond area, black residents of the city mounted a boycott to persuade the company to reverse its decision. The protest had many leaders in the black community, among them John Mitchell Jr., the editor of the *Richmond Planet* and a former member of the Richmond City Council, and Maggie Lena Walker, head of the Independent Order of St. Luke, a black fraternal and cooperative insurance society, and president of the St. Luke Penny Savings Bank.

This form of protest was designed to turn back a decision that the company was legally free to make or unmake. Leaders of the boycott urged black citizens not to force the question by purchasing tickets and then sitting in white cars, but rather to stay off the trolley cars entirely. The company's decision rankled, just as enactment of the law did. Black residents were also concerned about the manner in which the new regulations might be enforced, rudely and capriciously.

And who would the new regulations be applied to? Mitchell joked that "white Negroes" would no doubt have to wear nametags when they boarded streetcars, so conductors would know where to direct them. Pursuing that theme, he chided proponents of segregation who had discovered the necessity of transit segregation so as to prevent "amalgamation," pointing out that the "white men who mixed the races and gave us our crop of white Negroes didn't do it on the street cars." Using his newspaper to promote the boycott, sustain the boycotters, and urge his readers on, Mitchell printed poems by a former teacher of his, including one that went:

All those who choose are free to go
And ride in the "Jim Crow" car,
But rain may fall and wind may blow,
I'll not take the "Jim Crow" car.

The boycott persisted for many months, though it had its up and downs as spring turned to summer and then to fall. When the legislature finally enacted a law making such segregation mandatory, there was no point of a boycott, at least if its aim was to convince a company to undo a decision it had not been bound to make in the first place. John Mitchell, for his part, stayed off the streetcars.

As late as 1913, when he returned to the city after a trip, loaded with luggage, he had a decision to make when his ride did not show. He walked the sixteen blocks home. "I make it a practice," he explained, "not to ride the streetcars in Richmond."

Mitchell had not been alone in his protest. The entire community had played a role. Nor had Richmond been the only city where black Virginians responded in such a manner to white Virginians' efforts to shape a new future. In cities across the state—in Norfolk, Portsmouth, Danville, Lynchburg, and Newport News—boycotts cropped up. Black residents sometimes tried to set up parallel enterprises, so blacks could ride on all-black, black-owned conveyances. But the costs were too great, and these efforts, too, trailed away.

By no means did black Virginians permanently mothball their protest efforts when the boycotts faded. In 1921, the Republican Party emphasized its "lily-white" nature in seeking white votes as an alternative to the Democratic Party. That year, which was also the first year women could vote in Virginia's state elections, a group of black Virginians organized what came to be called a "lily-black" ticket for state offices, including John Mitchell Jr. for governor, Maggie Lena Walker for state superintendent of public instruction, and lawyer J. Thomas Newsome for attorney general. The ticket was credited with few votes, but it registered the growing black dissatisfaction with the Republican Party and therefore pointed toward the subsequent transition of many black voters to the ranks of another locally unresponsive party, the Democrats.

Virginia's First Woman Lawyer?

In March 1894, Belva Lockwood packed her bag and boarded a train that would take her from Washington, D.C., where she carried on an extensive law practice, to Richmond, Virginia. There she hoped to become the first woman to be admitted to represent clients in the Virginia courts. She and numerous other women at the time sought to enhance their occupational options as individuals, and at the same time, they sought to change the legal status of all women.

Lockwood had a mission, to break the male monopoly on the legal profession in Virginia. It probably came as little surprise to her that she first met failure, though a Virginia statute detailed what "any person" must do to qualify to practice in Virginia. Rebuffed by a local judge, Lockwood appealed to the Virginia Supreme Court, which (with one of the five judges absent) upheld the lower-court judge on a vote of 2–2. She took her case to the U.S. Supreme Court, whose members knew her as an accomplished attorney in the nation's capital, but that court, too, turned her away. The justices told her that the Fourteenth Amendment had nothing to do with her case and that only Virginia could address her demands: the state legislature in enacting Virginia's laws, the state courts in interpreting and applying those laws—determining whether the meaning of the word "person" in such laws might be "confined to males."

Back in the Virginia Supreme Court, she gained a 3–2 victory—and was admitted to the bar of that court—in June 1894 when the absent judge, Robert A. Richardson, returned and sided with her. In October 1894 she obtained her license to practice law in Virginia. The *New York Times* published a front-page report of Lockwood's having "won a signal victory in Virginia today for women" and declared her later that year "the only woman ever licensed to practice law" there.

Thus she triumphed and became a "first"—or so she thought, until six months later, in April 1895, when she brought a case to the Virginia Supreme Court, the same court that had admitted her to practice the previous year. In 1895, however, the court had five new judges. All five of the men who had ruled on her application in 1894 had been elected by the Readjuster legislature in 1882, and their twelve-year terms ended on New Year's Day in 1895. The new court undid the innovation. It ruled unanimously that under the statute (despite its phrasing), Lockwood had to be a man to practice law in that court. It refused to permit her to represent her client and argue the case. As the city newspaper the next day reported: "She was much surprised and disappointed at the court's action. She said she had supposed that the decision of the old court was final, and she had no idea that this new court would reverse it." The General Assembly, at its next session, revised the statute on the admission of lawyers to read "any male citizen." Belva Lockwood's quest pointed toward a future that appeared to have arrived in 1894, only to vanish the next year.

Not until women's suffrage came in 1920, after Lockwood had died, did Virginia change the law so women could become lawyers there. The first woman to earn a law degree at the University of Virginia, once that school opened its doors to female students (the dean referred to "these new and strange beings"), was Elizabeth Tompkins, in 1923, who practiced her new profession for the rest of her long life.

Race, Gender, and the Professions

In the 1870s, several black lawyers, each of whom had trained at Howard University, practiced their craft in Virginia—Walthal G. Wynn, William C. Roane, and Robert Peel Brooks. Pointing as early as the 1860s toward new professional possibilities according to both race and gender was Rebecca Lee. The first African

American woman to earn an M.D. degree, Lee graduated from the New England Female Medical College in 1864, in her early thirties. She practiced medicine in Boston until she moved the next year to Richmond. In Virginia before the 1860s, at no time could she have legally attended any school, and even if she had been white she could not have gone to medical school. In postwar Richmond, though, she could hope to find an outlet for her medical training—what she called "a proper field for real missionary work, and one that would present ample opportunities to become acquainted with the diseases of women and children." She worked for a time with the Freedmen's Bureau and other groups. Later she returned to Boston and resumed the practice of medicine there. In 1883 Dr. Rebecca Lee Crumpler published a book drawn from her journals, *A Book of Medical Discourses*, the major source for information about her unusual life.

Archer Fleming Sr. was born in Virginia during slavery times, his wife shortly after. In a postslavery world, they raised three children in Newport News. In the 1920s their daughter Marian, the middle child, went with her two young children for a time to Washington, D.C., where she earned a law degree at Howard University in 1925. L. Marian Fleming Poe became Virginia's first black female lawyer. By the end of the decade, two other black women lawyers—Bertha L. Douglass in Norfolk and Inez C. Fields in Hampton—were also practicing in Virginia, and the three remained the only ones until after World War II.

Marian Poe's professional biography reveals the changes, and the limits of change, that came to Virginia in the two generations after the Civil War. By the time she was born, the barrier to black male entry into the legal profession had come down. Before the 1920s, however, her gender would have prevented her from attending law school or becoming a lawyer in Virginia. Then the gender barrier came down too, but the racial barrier to in-state schooling persisted. Not until the 1950s would it become possible for an African American to attend the University of Virginia. Poe's brothers, Archer Fleming Jr. and Daniel Fleming, also earned professional degrees at Howard. One became a doctor, the other a dentist.

The end of slavery and the beginning of black schooling opened tremendous new educational and occupational possibilities for black Virginians of Marian Poe's generation. She and her brothers found, however, that Virginia offered no such thing as "separate but equal" higher education. Rather, categorically excluded from in-state programs, they had to go out of state for their professional training. And when they returned to their homes in Virginia, they each developed a practice that depended on black clients in a thoroughly segregated Jim Crow world.

In medicine as in law, gender had long shaped professional opportunities, just as race had, but in both professions women were forging new paths and

When the racial boundary was legally moved (as it was in Virginia in 1910 and again in 1924), assigning new racial identities to some people, in almost all cases people formerly identified as white were categorized as black, and thus a marriage between two white people might become designated as interracial, as in the 1911 case *Moon v. Children's Home Society of Virginia*, 112 Va. 737. In a variation on that theme, here is a story published January 30, 1909, in a black newspaper, the *Richmond Planet*.

BOTH CONVICTED.
A Pitiable Case in Prince Edward County.—Race Prejudices and Its Insistences.

Richmond, Va., Jan. 20—Probably the most unique and pitiful case in the history of Virginia has developed in Farmville, where Marcus Lindsay and his wife, both believing themselves to be Negroes, have been sentenced to eighteen years each in the penitentiary, the court having adjudged the man to have sufficient white blood in his veins to be legally white.

Marcus Lindsay is the son of a white woman. He always accepted a story, however, that he had colored blood in his veins. Believing this, he had associated with Negroes from his infancy, lived with them, and attended their churches and schools. Some months ago Marcus was married to Sophy Jones, a Negress, and

pointing toward new futures. Dr. Emily Chenault Runyon, a white woman, came to Richmond in 1894 and practiced there for a dozen years. Born in Kentucky, the daughter of a doctor, she studied medicine at the University of Michigan and at Northwestern University Medical School for Women. She married and had two children, both still very young when her husband suddenly died, and then, with years of experience in Chicago, Wichita, and New York City, she accepted an invitation by a friend to make a fresh start in Virginia.

Women doctors in Virginia were rare in the 1890s, but the General Assembly, at almost the very time Dr. Runyon moved to Richmond, was considering a bill that would require female patients in the state's mental institutions to be attended by women physicians, so the idea that women might be doctors was gaining currency. Nonetheless, her attendance at a meeting of the Richmond Academy of Medicine caused a ruckus among some old-timers. Eventually she became the first female member of the Medical Society of Virginia as well as of the Richmond Academy of Medicine, although both organizations had to change their constitutions before she could gain full membership. She left Richmond in 1907 for a time, first briefly as a medical missionary to China, from which ill health forced an early return, and then for several years at the State College for Women in Mississippi. After that she returned to Richmond, where she lived out the rest of her very long life.

The Struggle for Votes for Women

In May 1870, Anna Whitehead Bodeker organized a meeting in Richmond that launched the first Virginia State Woman Suffrage Association. She even attempted to vote in a municipal election in 1871. Soon, however, her organization faded. In the 1890s, Lynchburg's Orra Gray Langhorne founded a successor organization, which met a similar fate. A third group, the Equal Suffrage League of Virginia, was formed in Richmond in 1909. Led by Lila Meade Valentine and including such influential fiction writers as Ellen Glasgow and Mary Johnston, it thrived.

Travel to England in the 1890s had energized Valentine in support of various reform possibilities, and further travel in England may have contributed to her discovery of women's suffrage, which proved to be the focus of her reform energies in the 1910s. She recognized that public authorities made decisions about funding such activities as public education and public health, and yet, leader though she was, she and the women she worked with had no say in the election of the city council or legislative members who made those decisions. "Questions concerning food, water, sanitation, education, light, heat, plumbing, treatment of diseases, child labor, hours of labor for women and children"—all these, she noted, related "peculiarly to women" as well as to "the expanding functions of government" and thus demanded "political handling."

At first, the Equal Suffrage League of Virginia sought a suffrage amendment to the state constitution. Toward that end, Valentine addressed the House of Delegates in January 1912, appealing to the legislators: "Suppose every law that you lived under was enacted by women, would you consider yourselves free?" Bringing her oratorical as well as her organizational skills to her task, she made more than 100 speeches throughout the state in 1913. By 1916, she had also spoken in other states, in both the South and the North.

The Equal Suffrage League of Virginia, seeking

the widow of a Negro and has since lived with her.

Indictments were brought against Lindsay on the grounds that he is a white man who has married a Negro woman and against his wife, Sophy, for having married a white man, being herself a Negress, the laws of Virginia prohibiting such intermarriage. The court, while dwelling at length upon the tragedy that has made this man and woman criminals without any intention on their part of committing a criminal act, declared the marriage null and void, and sentenced the prisoners to the penitentiary for having committed an interracial marriage.

The court added, however, that while under the law he was forced to pronounce sentence he would personally petition the Governor to pardon the prisoners without allowing them to be taken to the penitentiary, but upon condition that all marital relations between them should cease.

Although the story is probably true in most particulars, one statement is not to be believed—that the judge, whatever his feelings on the subject, gave them prison sentences far longer than the two-to-five years specified in the law. A local story in the *Farmville Herald* (January 22, 1909) leaves out the rich detail but is far more credible on that point: "Marcus Lindsay, charged with miscegenation, was given two years in the penitentiary. Sophia Jones was given like term on the same charge."

HE USED TO BE WHITE—
IS HE STILL?

A person's genealogical past had supreme importance. George Spencer—was he less than one-sixteenth black, and therefore a white person under the Virginia law of 1910? Should he win a case of libel against George Looney, the white man who, having once been a friend and fellow white man, came to insist in public that Spencer and his family were "nothing but God damned negroes"? Virtually everything in early-twentieth-century Virginia depended on one's racial identity, and when such questions came up, they had to be addressed. The case arose in Buchanan County. Judge Richard H. Cardwell spoke for the Virginia Supreme Court in 1914 in summarizing the facts of the case of *Spencer v. Looney*, 116 Va. 767:

It appears that plaintiff in error, who was about thirty years of age when this action was brought and who is a son of Jordan Spencer, Jr., and a grandson of Jordan Spencer, Sr., (now deceased) lived in Johnson county, State of Kentucky, until he was about fifteen years of age, and has since that time lived in Buchanan county, Va., where he some years ago married a daughter of Ray Justus, a citizen of Buchanan county, and they have several children, the oldest, about nine years of age, being Melvin above mentioned. The descendants of Jordan Spencer, Sr., have at all times for

to educate fellow citizens on the issue, argued that women wanted and deserved to vote and, moreover, that politics needed a woman's touch. In 1912, once the matter was presented to the General Assembly, opponents formed an organization to counter the league, holding that Virginia women had no interest in voting, and that involving them in the political sphere would sully them more than it contributed toward cleaning up politics. More than that, the opponents argued, granting women the right to vote would lead to voting by black women as well as white women.

Three times between 1912 and 1916, the issue of women's suffrage came before the General Assembly. No measure came close to passing, although support increased each time. Some Virginia women joined the more militant National Woman's Party, as all suffragists had to consider supporting a national amendment if a state measure could not pass, though the prospect of federal involvement in voting rights evoked white Virginians' concerns on the racial front. As for Valentine, her failure to convince southern legislatures to take positive action led her, after a 1916 defeat in the Virginia legislature, to embrace the Susan B. Anthony amendment to change the federal Constitution. A boost to the general idea of women voters came when Great Britain granted women the right to vote in 1918; and in 1919 Virginia native Nancy Astor became the first woman to serve in the British Parliament.

In June 1919, Congress approved the Nineteenth Amendment, granting women the right to vote, and it was up to the states whether to ratify the measure. Unmoved by the Equal Suffrage League's efforts, the Virginia General Assembly rejected the amendment. The legislature nonetheless passed a "machinery act" to provide for women to vote if the Nineteenth Amendment was ratified despite Virginia's rejection—which happened in August 1920. In a belated symbolic gesture, Virginia finally ratified it in 1952.

The suffrage amendment having gone into effect, white women converted the Equal Suffrage League into the Virginia League of Women Voters, to promote actual voting and to educate voters on the issues. Black women formed a parallel group, the Virginia Negro Women's League of Voters. In 1923, two white women were elected to the Virginia House of Delegates, Sarah Lee Fain from the city of Norfolk and Helen T. Henderson representing Russell and Buchanan counties.

In the former capital city of the Confederacy in summer 1920, Maggie Lena Walker urged black women to register, and she urged the employment of more registration officials, partly just to move the process along, partly because of what she understood as discrimination by white registrars, who often ignored black women waiting in line and then turned them away at the close of business. The first black woman to register and pay her poll tax in Richmond may have been Puralee Sampson, soon followed by teacher Rosa Y. De-Witt and 2,408 other black women.

In Hampton, too, white Virginians proved no more receptive to black women's voting than they were to voting by black men. Correspondence to the National Association for the Advancement of Colored People (NAACP) described how white registrars there blatantly discriminated against black women, made them feel humiliated, and threatened black teachers with loss of their jobs if they persisted in seeking to register. Two women whose husbands worked at Hampton Institute felt "murderous" at the ill treatment they received. One reported that at first the clerk of the court had been courteous to her, thinking her white. But then he saw her with a woman more unam-

fifty years or more been permitted to attend the white public schools of both the States of Kentucky and Virginia, and they and all of them have been treated and respected by their white neighbors and associates as white people, plaintiff in error and his father having in recent years worked for defendant in error and stayed at his home, where they were treated as white people, eating at his table and sleeping in his beds. About two years prior to the trouble out of which this suit arises Jack Spencer, a brother of plaintiff in error, was accused of killing one Henderson Looney, a brother of defendant in error, and after that time, as it appears, the latter began to raise objections to plaintiff in error's boy, Melvin, attending the white public free schools of Buchanan county, accusing plaintiff in error and his family of being negroes, and through strenuous efforts, involving costs and expenses, secured and published affidavits purporting to have been made by persons in Kentucky, by reason of which the boy, Melvin, was turned out and denied the privileges of the public schools of Buchanan county; and hence this action.

The outcome of the trial depended a great deal on what instructions the judge gave the jury. Spencer had wanted this instruction to be given, but the judge refused it:

The court tells the jury that if they believe that Jordon Spencer, Senior, the great-grandfather of Melvin, had less than one-half negro blood and more than one-half white or Indian blood and that if they believe that his wife was a white woman, with no negro blood in her, and that then Jordon Spencer, Junior, the grandfather of Melvin, would have less than one-fourth negro blood in him and then if they believe that the wife of Jordon Spencer, Jr., had no negro blood in her, that George Spencer, the father of Melvin, would have less than one-eighth negro blood in him, and that if they believe that the wife of George Spencer, and the mother of Melvin, was a white woman with no negro blood in her, that then Melvin Spencer has less than one-sixteenth of negro blood in him, and is a white person and is entitled under the laws of the State of Virginia to attend the public white free schools of Buchanan county, Virginia.

The jury found for Looney, the white man who had challenged the claim of another man, Spencer, to a white identity. Spencer appealed the ruling. Reversing the trial court and ordering a new trial, the Virginia Supreme Court ruled that the trial judge should have permitted the jury to consider additional evidence. The point here is not that the trial went one way or the appeal another (the Virginia Supreme Court often ruled that juries should be given more discretion, whatever they might decide), but rather the situation in controversy.

biguously African American, and his demeanor changed. He made it clear that "he did not intend to be bothered with a lot of colored women," but "intended to just let a few register." Developments in Virginia revealed stark limits to the truth of the general statement that "women gained the right to vote in 1920."

Daughters of a New South

Lila Meade Valentine, proponent of public schools, public health, and women's suffrage, was born in Richmond in 1865. So was Mary-Cooke Branch Munford, best known for championing higher education for women. Born as the Old South came to an end, they worked with dignity and earnestness to bring about a New South, certainly with regard to educational opportunities. So too was Janie Porter Barrett, also born in 1865 and like Valentine a social worker extraordinaire in Progressive-Era Virginia. As president of the Virginia State Federation of Colored Women's Clubs, Barrett worked to establish the Virginia Industrial School for Colored Girls, in Hanover County, just as earlier she had founded the Locust Street Settlement, also for work with young black females, in Hampton. Born the year the Civil War came to an end, these women—two white, one black—shared a zeal for fixing social problems, just as they reflected new social roles for women in Virginia during the Progressive Era.

Valentine's work regarding the public schools in Richmond in the early years of the twentieth century led her to recognize the poor health of many of the students. Her efforts, together with those of Sadie Heath Cabaniss, led in 1902 to the establishment of the Instructive Visiting Nurse Association (IVNA) of Richmond as well as to a city appropriation to pay the salary of one nurse. In

THE
WOMAN'S LAND ARMY
of AMERICA

TRAINING   SCHOOL
UNIVERSITY *of* VIRGINIA
JUNE 15 TO SEPTEMBER 15 - COURSES TWO WEEKS
TUITION FREE - BOARD $5.00 PER WEEK
Apply WOMAN'S LAND ARMY, U. S. EMPLOYMENT SERVICE, 910 E. Main Street, RICHMOND, VA.

Poster for the Woman's Land Army of America, by Herbert Andrew Paus. During World War I, regular students at the University of Virginia left for the military or joined the Reserve Officers Training Corps (ROTC), and some new students arrived in 1918 in the Students Army Training Corps (SATC) program. Women could not take regular classes at the University of Virginia, but World War I brought new obligations and opportunities, as this poster reflects. Two-week summer courses offered training at the university for white women filling the places of Virginia's farming men who had gone off to work in industry or to fight in Europe. The wording on posters varied, but the picture—of two women dressed for farm work carrying a basket of vegetables and one woman in uniform on horseback carrying an American flag—was used across the country. Modeled after Great Britain's wartime Women's Land Army, such a group—to meet the same need—recurred in World War II, in Great Britain, Australia, and the United States. The second iteration of the land army, like the first, served as a rural counterpart to Rosie the Riveter's industrial work. In Virginia during World War II, women in the "land army," or on the "farm front," proved particularly important as seasonal workers in peach and apple orchards. Library of Congress, Prints and Photographs Division, LC-USZ62-42546.

Harry F. Byrd Sr. (1887–1966), Virginia governor, 1926–1930, and U.S. senator, 1933–1965. This painting by Helen Schuyler Bailey was based on an original by Louis Lupas. Virginia Historical Society, Richmond, Virginia, gift of Senator Harry F. Byrd Jr.

1904, Valentine was chosen president of the IVNA, and she directed its new campaign against tuberculosis. Other Virginia communities soon sought to emulate the Richmond program, and the Richmond group made its nurses available to assist such efforts and thus promote the development of public health throughout the state.

By the time women's voting rights came to Virginia, so ill was Valentine that a registrar came to her room so she could register to vote. She died in 1921, and black and white, rich and poor, and followers of various faiths attended a memorial service at her church. The *Richmond Times-Dispatch* editorialized about this "aristocrat with her noblesse oblige" that "she blazed her own paths" and "captained her own soul." In 1936, a marble portrait of her was placed in the hall of the Virginia House of Delegates in the State Capitol.

Mary-Cooke Branch Munford long dreamed that women would be admitted as undergraduates at the University of Virginia. A defeat in 1916 in the House of Delegates was as close as the matter got during her lifetime, but she served on the university's board of visitors from 1926 until her death in 1938. In the Alderman Library—constructed with New Deal public works money and dedicated in June 1938, three weeks before Munford's death—a plaque was installed in 1941, commemorating her as having "carried the devotion of a great mind and a flaming spirit into unselfish service to public education throughout Virginia," and it concluded: "Her memorial is in numberless young lives set free." Meanwhile, white women had been enrolling in graduate and professional programs at the university since 1920, and when the school finally built a residence hall for them in 1951, it was named Mary Munford Hall. In 1944, the General Assembly designated the old normal school at Fredericksburg, Mary Washington College, as the women's coordinate undergraduate college of the University of Virginia.

Power and Politics in the 1920s

From the 1920s to the 1960s, Harry F. Byrd Sr. and the Byrd Organization dominated Virginia politics, their main base of power the white rural voters in the east—especially the Southside—and the Shenandoah Valley. An astute, experienced politician, with ties across the state, he spearheaded a Democratic sweep in the congressional elections of 1922, and the next year he successfully opposed a large bond issue to finance highway improvements, insisting on a pay-as-you-go approach financed with a new three-cent-a-gallon tax on gasoline. A high school dropout, Byrd never had much interest in public education. Knowing that his constituents had a keen interest in farm-to-market roads, he stressed state investment in such roads, financed by a user fee, not a state property tax. A lifelong publisher of a newspaper, he always had a megaphone with which he let his views be known. Long one of Virginia's biggest apple growers, he always had a businessman's eye on keeping labor costs low.

Byrd won election as governor in 1925. As governor (1926–1930), he successfully proposed a reorganization of state government, including a streamlined state bureaucracy. Moreover, a constitutional amendment in 1928 restored the gubernatorial appointment of four officials that had for the past quarter century been elected by the voters, shrinking the list of elected state officials back to three spots, the "short ballot." Ever since then, the only offices filled by the voters in statewide elections have been the governor, lieutenant governor, and attorney general. Constitutional changes in 1928 also modified the state supreme court. Until then, there had always been a president of the court, and the other members were called judges. Since then, there has been a chief justice and the other members have been called justices.

As for policy initiatives, aside from the gas tax—the foundation for his pay-as-you-go transportation policy—Governor Byrd pressed for tax reductions, and his low-tax approach to state government meant that, in the years ahead, Virginians paid relatively little as they went, so education and other social services suffered. Whether measured against population or wealth, Virginia's expenditures

1. Be it enacted by the general assembly of Virginia, That the State registrar of vital statistics may, as soon as practicable after the taking effect of this act, prepare a form whereon the racial composition of any individual, as Caucasian, Negro, Mongolian, American Indian, Asiatic Indian, Malay, or any mixture thereof, or any other non-Caucasic strains, and if there be any mixture, then, the racial composition of the parents and other ancestors, in so far as ascertainable, so as to show in what generation such mixture occurred, may be certified by such individual, which form shall be known as a registration certificate....

4. No marriage license shall be granted until the clerk or deputy clerk has reasonable assurance that the statements as to color of both man and woman are correct.

If there is reasonable cause to disbelieve that applicants are of pure white race, when that fact is stated, the clerk or deputy clerk shall withhold the granting of the license until satisfactory proof is produced that both applicants are "white persons" as provided for in this act.

The clerk or deputy clerk shall use the same care to assure himself that both applicants are colored, when that fact is declared.

5. It shall hereafter be unlawful for any white person in this State to marry any save a white person, or a person with no other admixture

on public education ranked low among American states. True it was that state education funds were allocated in ways that diminished the revenues available for black schools in the east and also white schools in the west, but true it also was that state funds were left at low enough levels that the schools were financially squeezed everywhere.

The General Assembly Session of 1924

The General Assembly of 1924 had a few things to say about the futures of Virginia and Virginians. In an act "to preserve racial integrity," it renovated the classification scheme that determined whether Virginians would be defined as white (see sidebars, pages 290, 292, and 298). Across the nineteenth century, Virginia law had classified as nonwhite anyone as much as one-fourth black, a racial definition that was changed in 1910 to one-sixteenth—leaping two generations, from one black grandparent to one black great-great-grandparent. The 1924 law introduced what is known as the one-drop definition of black racial identity, and once again some people previously classified as white could find themselves assigned to the other side of the great racial divide. Leaders of the effort to obtain passage of the new law were noted musician John Powell, whose Anglo-Saxon Clubs of America screamed about racial purity, and Walter Plecker, the hard-driving director of the Virginia Bureau of Vital Statistics. Armed with the new law, Plecker arranged for many people's identities to be officially changed from "white" or "Indian" to "colored"—a change that redefined them not only for purposes of selecting a marriage partner but also for attending the public schools.

In quest of its own vision of good government, in which there would be one dominant party and few voters, the General Assembly refined the means of controlling who would do the voting—beyond the poll tax and the challenges of registering—as a new law provided that only those classified as white could participate in the Democratic Party's primary elections. And seeking a eugenically improved future, the General Assembly authorized the surgical sterilization of what turned out to be a great many people of Virginia, especially women, whatever their racial identity.

The question of whether the legal apparatus of a state can legitimately determine who has children, and on what conditions, is as central as any a society faces. Many American states in the first half of the twentieth century enacted laws authorizing citizens' involuntary surgical sterilization. In 1920, Emma Buck was committed to the State Colony for Epileptics and Feeble-Minded in Lynchburg. In 1924, her daughter Carrie was committed as well, after her foster father came to regard her as a burden, once she gave birth to a daughter after having been raped by a member of her foster parents' family. Appraised as feebleminded—as was her seven-month-old daughter, Vivian (both appraisals were subsequently revealed to be inappropriate)—she was surgically sterilized under the 1924 law; so too was her sister Doris. In all, roughly 70,000 Americans were sterilized under authority of their states, 8,000 of them in Virginia between the 1920s and the 1970s—40 percent of them male, 60 percent female. As for Doris, told at the time of her procedure that she was having an appendectomy, she learned at last in 1979 what had happened to her. "I broke down and cried," she said then. "My husband and me wanted children desperate—we were crazy about them. I never knew what they'd done to me."

These three legislative schemes from 1924 had varying futures themselves. The white-only Dem-

of blood than white and American Indian. For the purpose of this act, the term "white person" shall apply only to the person who has no trace whatsoever of any blood other than Caucasian; but persons who have one-sixteenth or less of the blood of the American Indian and have no other non-Caucasic blood shall be deemed to be white persons. All laws heretofore passed and now in effect regarding the intermarriage of white and colored persons shall apply to marriages prohibited by this act.

The 1924 act did not make interracial marriage a crime, for it had long been so, nor did it change the penalty for conviction, two to five years in the penitentiary; but it did change the definition of interracial marriage by shifting the boundary, for the first time introducing the one-drop definition of black racial identity, and it also thrust people of Asian ancestry over to the non-white side.

ocratic primary had the shortest shelf life. The U.S. Supreme Court heard cases regarding white-only Democratic primaries from other states across the 1920s, 1930s, and 1940s but did not finally throw the practice out until 1944. Virginia's law, by contrast, fell in 1930 to a lower federal court ruling. As for the sterilization law, before Carrie Buck was sterilized, the State Colony's doctor and various supporters colluded to present her case in a contrived fashion so as to maximize their chances of judicial validation of the law, and they succeeded. In the case of *Buck v. Bell* (1927), the U.S. Supreme Court upheld the policy, which was applied well past World War II but gradually fell out of repute. And the matter of "racial integrity," with its connections to the legal ban on "interracial" marriage, lost its significance in 1967 when the U.S. Supreme Court, in the case *Loving v. Virginia,* threw out the ban.

For good or ill, these bills became law, and for good or ill, they shaped life in Virginia for some years. Regardless, just a few years after 1924, an economic and social disaster befell Virginia, along with the rest of the nation and the world. In response to the Great Depression, the New Deal comprised a tremendous number of new laws, at the federal level, that did much to reshape life in the Old Dominion, in ways that could not have been predicted in 1924.

Chapter 20

Great Depression and New Deal

....

Shortly after his 1932 election as president, Franklin D. Roosevelt nominated U.S. Senator Claude A. Swanson to be secretary of the navy. The move opened a vacancy soon filled by former governor Harry F. Byrd, who joined Carter Glass in the U.S. Senate. These moves made a big difference to Harry Byrd, and they made a big difference to Byrd's Organization, but they made less difference to Virginia over the next few years than did the election of the man who started the musical chairs by appointing Swanson in the first place. Carter Glass and Harry Byrd often opposed Roosevelt and the New Deal, but in the end the New Deal thrived, and the Byrd Organization persisted.

It is sometimes said that Virginia fared better than many other states as the nation's economy spiraled downward in the four years after the stock market crashed in 1929—its economy was more diversified, for example, and farm mortgages were fewer—but most Virginians had a very rough time of it, especially after the first year or two. In spring 1933, J. R. Forsyth wrote Governor John Garland Pollard from Staunton asking for a cow, since the "place I live on has plenty of pasture for a cow," and having one "would be quite a help to my family." In fall 1935, a letter to President Roosevelt from Beaverdam, in Hanover County, began with the thought, "first we are looking for work, but never can't find any to do," and ended, "seem so dishearten in life to live like this when it use to be plenty of work for every body." "With cold times coming on," and scant food or winter clothes, the writer observed, "just looks like we will have to freeze and starve." And finally: "No one know how it is until you experience it."

The New Deal, as Roosevelt soon named his very active response to the enormous hardships of the Great Depression, brought to Virginia a wide range of federal programs that made tremendous differences to large numbers of people, as historian Ronald Heinemann has detailed. These laws soon changed the rules that governed the marketplace in tobacco and other commercial crops, and they changed the rules that governed labor-management relations in industrial labor. Other laws created the Civilian Conservation Corps, the Federal Housing Administration, the Public Works Administration, the Social Security Administration, and a variety of other agencies and activities.

The New Deal is best understood as coming in three phases. The First New Deal, comprising legislation mostly enacted in 1933, emphasized immediate issues of relief for families distressed by unemployment, as well as employment to kick-start the economy and curtail the need for relief measures. The Second New Deal, enacted mostly in 1935, established new programs that went farther, including Social Security. The Third New Deal, enacted in 1937 and 1938, tacked on some important programs to address matters not already sufficiently looked after.

Relief and Employment

Deemed essential in 1933 was federal assistance to the millions of unemployed. Jobs were still disappearing, and state and local governments, as well as charities, had exhausted their ability to provide relief. So the New Deal began there, with relief on the one hand and jobs on the other. The Federal Emergency Relief Administration (FERA), established in 1933 by the Federal Emergency Relief Act, provided needy citizens with food, clothing, shelter, and employment. In Virginia, FERA spent $26 million and directly affected the lives of a half million people. In addition, the National Industrial Recovery Act of 1933 created the Public Works Administration (PWA), directed by Secretary of the Interior Harold L. Ickes. In Virginia the PWA worked greatly to improve facilities for secondary and higher education, and it also spent over $2 million in 1937 on public works ranging from harbor improvements in Newport News to a sewage system and treatment plant in Staunton.

The Civilian Conservation Corps (CCC) also had a noticeable impact on Virginians during the Great Depression. Designed to provide discipline, outdoor experience, and construction skills and to generate jobs and public works, the CCC sponsored camps where military and civilian supervisors offered training in a variety of vocational fields. By 1941 the CCC had contributed $109 million to Virginia, with much of the money paying the salaries of camp employees. The first CCC camp among nearly eighty established in Virginia was Camp Roosevelt, in George Washington National Forest near Luray. Among many projects and places in Virginia, CCC workers put a great deal of skilled effort into the Shenandoah National Park, which Congress had authorized in 1926. As for state parks, Virginia had none before the New Deal, but after much effort by CCC workers, in 1936 the first six parks in a new state system opened, among them Fairy Stone State Park, in Patrick County, and Seashore State Park, in what later became the city of Virginia Beach. Another CCC project, the Blue Ridge Parkway, not only highlights the natural beauty of the mountain range it passes through but also provides an enduring reminder of the New Deal in Virginia.

Industrial Labor—and the Right to Organize a Union

The New Deal did much to transform labor-management relations in America. It did so in stages that marked the progression of New Deal programs.

Workers tended to view labor unions as a vital means of collective bargaining over such core questions as wages and working conditions—how much they were paid, and how dangerous the conditions were under which they labored. Before the 1930s, however, Americans had no recognized right to form and join labor unions. That began to change in 1933, when Section 7 (a) of the National Industrial Recovery Act declared such a right. The Wagner Labor Relations Act of 1935 went farther, establishing the National Labor Relations Board (NLRB) to monitor labor-management relations. Soon, the Congress of Industrial Organizations, a rival to the traditional American Federation of Labor, was aggressively seeking to unionize workers in mass-production industries—for example, auto manufacture and steel production—that had previously gone unorganized. In 1938, the Fair Labor Standards Act set forth rules on wages and hours to govern labor-management relations where unions were not present. National policy would guarantee workers two main things: The regular workweek was gradually reduced to a ceiling of forty hours, and hourly pay moved up to a floor of forty cents.

In Virginia, workers engaged in a variety of job actions with a variety of outcomes. The Wagner Labor Relations Act came into play when workers in Richmond at the Friedman–Harry Marks Clothing Company tried to organize and were fired. They filed a grievance, and in 1936 the NLRB directed the company to give the workers back their jobs. After the U.S. Supreme Court upheld the Wagner Act in 1937, the Amalgamated Clothing Workers of America organized the company's workers, bringing union recognition and establishing a minimum wage of fourteen dollars per thirty-six-hour workweek. Also that year, hundreds of workers in Covington at the Industrial Rayon Corporation held a sit-down strike, but it led to disappointing gains. Against great odds, by contrast, black women at some tobacco plants in Richmond, after walking off their jobs and away from wages of as little as five cents an hour, managed to form a union and win a wage increase. Often in the new labor-policy environment, Virginia industrial management—in shipbuilding, at rayon plants, and in tobacco factories—successfully sought to forestall strike activity and organizing efforts by instituting modest wage increases.

Agriculture—and the Culture and Economics of Tobacco

By the 1930s, Virginia's economy depended less on agriculture than it traditionally had, but the farm sector still predominated in much of the state. Tobacco was in trouble early, and by 1932 the entire farm economy was in a shambles, with commodity prices half what they had been in 1929. The Agricultural Adjustment Administration (AAA) strode to the rescue.

The Agricultural Adjustment Act was passed too late in 1933 to have much effect before 1934, but by reducing commodity output, the new farm program drove up prices. The program called for voluntary reductions in output, but it was meant to work regardless. The Kerr-Smith Tobacco Act of 1934, for example, imposed a tax on farmers who chose not to sign up or who produced more than their allotment. With the AAA program fully in place in 1934, Virginia's tobacco crop doubled in price per pound, with a total value well over 50 percent above the previous year's figure. Cash payments for not producing as much were often diverted, however, staying with the landowner and not shared with his laborers, so the benefits were not evenly distributed.

By 1934, Senator Byrd had gone public with his opposition to the farm program in particular and the New Deal in general. Most Virginia farm owners, however, were having none of it. They saw a program in place that, though it imposed controls on them, did so for their benefit, and by an overwhelming margin they gave it their support. Ever suspicious of federal authority, Byrd might say of the agriculture secretary, Henry Wallace, "We do not want a Hitler of American agriculture," but John Flannagan, congressman from southwest Virginia, retorted: "I do not know of any farmers who think they are being Hitlerized."

The U.S. Supreme Court declared the AAA program unconstitutional in early 1936, but Virginia farmers hardly agreed with the Court, either. *Richmond Times-Dispatch* editor Virginius Dabney called the Court's ruling a "stunning blow," "as heedless of public welfare as the *Dred Scott* decision." Governor George C. Peery lobbied for new legislation that would satisfy the Court's objections, and he had reason to be pleased with the results enacted that year, the Soil Conservation and Domestic Allotment Act. As part of the Third New Deal, a new Agricultural Adjustment Act was passed in 1938, providing a longer-term basis for controlling agricultural production and evening out farm commodity prices so the farm sector could remain viable.

Miss Tobacco. Hallie Hubbard poses for publicity photos for the National Tobacco Festival in South Boston, Virginia, probably in 1937. A related photograph depicts Louise Patterson (later Louise Patterson Slayton), wearing a white dress, waving tobacco leaves, and riding a bicycle past a tobacco field. Seven decades later, still proud of her moment in the sun, Louise Slayton was volunteering at the museum that housed these images. Courtesy South Boston–Halifax County Museum of Fine Arts and History.

The Federal Housing Administration—and Jim Crow's New Deal

A monumental program of the New Deal was designed to restore the construction industry, and with it carpentry and other building trades as well as timber, transportation, and nail-making industries. This was the Federal Housing Administration (FHA), established by the National Housing Act in 1934 and designed to work miracles without costing federal dollars. It worked from multiple premises: The housing industry lay at the center of the American economy; if people could finance new homes, they would buy them; if mortgages had longer terms, say thirty years, monthly payments would be more manageable; and if banks were confident of their investment, they would loan the money to finance such purchases. So the FHA guaranteed mortgages for qualifying home buyers—provided those mortgages followed FHA guidelines—and then the entire cycle could kick into operation.

Dating from the origins of the FHA is the thirty-year mortgage, together with thousands of suburbs full of single-family detached dwellings. Millions of new homes went up in the suburbs, beginning in the 1930s and surging in the postwar 1940s and beyond. When the area surrounding Washington, D.C., was built up, the FHA was there to spur the process along. The same was true of suburban Richmond, Norfolk, and other cities. The dream of a home in the suburbs became a reality for millions of families. Toward the end of World War II, the Servicemen's Readjustment Act of 1944 (GI Bill) created a counterpart Veterans Administration (VA) program that adopted the FHA concept and criteria.

There were some limits and drawbacks, however. Experts in the business—bankers, realtors—set up the guidelines that governed the FHA's operations, and they brought all their collective wisdom at the time to the task. One absolute requirement was that mortgages could be guaranteed only if the properties carried restrictive covenants. The covenants had to specify that blacks would be forbidden to buy in areas open to white settlement. Just during the FHA's first three years of insuring mortgages for new homes, white Virginians borrowed $20 million to construct 5,000 homes.

In later years, particularly with regard to black-white ratios in public schools, people would routinely distinguish between two types of segregation, de jure and de facto, that is, those that were deliberately established by law and those that just happened. The race policies of the FHA and the VA give the lie to the notion that residential patterns are solely, perhaps even primarily, a function of individual preferences and market forces. As intended, the FHA accomplished many wonderful things. The downside, and it was huge too, was that, in Virginia and across America, the FHA can be called Jim Crow's New Deal.

Rural Life and Old Age—Electric Power and Social Security

Two major innovations in federal policy came in 1935 with the Social Security Act and the Rural Electrification Administration. One major provision of the Social Security Act established a retirement insurance program, funded jointly by employer and employee, with taxes to be withheld beginning in 1937 and pensions to be paid beginning in 1942. Workers would be encouraged to leave the work force at age sixty-five, opening up jobs for younger employees, and a great many Americans would be guaranteed a monthly stipend in their retirement years. Two large categories of Virginia workers would not, however, be covered: domestics and agricultural laborers, and disproportionate numbers of both groups were African American.

The Emergency Relief Appropriation Act of 1935 signaled the federal government's withdrawal from direct relief, relinquishing primary responsibility in that area back to state and local authorities. Replacing the kind of relief that FERA had provided would be a new emphasis on public works, with the Works Progress Administration (WPA) overseeing those projects.

Under the Emergency Relief Appropriation Act, an executive order in 1935 established the Rural Electrification Administration (REA), to create and administer a program of extending electrical power to rural areas not already covered. The REA spurred the development of electric power beyond the cities and towns that already had it, and it worked so effectively that by 1940 many farms throughout Virginia, and by 1950 most of them, had electric lights and water pumps.

The New Deal and Public Works

In a major emphasis of the New Deal response to the Great Depression, Congress supplied federal funds to create public works jobs. People could not buy if they had no money, and they had no money if they remained unemployed. Moreover, if they did not buy, then others could not sell, so still others could not produce. The way to break effectively through the downward cycle of employment in America, according to the New Deal approach, was to put people to work building things from which Americans would benefit for many years afterward. Outside Virginia, such projects took shape as the Key West Highway in Florida and LaGuardia Airport in New York.

In Virginia, major monuments to New Deal public works spending include the Blue Ridge Parkway and the University of Virginia's Alderman Library. Federal funds paid much of the cost of constructing a new building in Richmond

Mabry Mill, Floyd County, near the Blue Ridge Parkway. The mill was built by Edwin Boston Mabry (1867–1936) in the years after 1903 and was first a blacksmith and wheelwright shop, later a sawmill and then a gristmill. Jack Boucher photographed it in the 1930s for the Historic American Buildings Survey, a New Deal program whose photographs mostly depict prominent historic structures. Library of Congress, Prints and Photographs Division, HABS VA 32-1-1. A variant program, established by the Virginia Writers' Project, was the Virginia Historical Inventory, which emphasized such everyday structures as mills and churches built before 1860; and its photographs, available online, are at the Library of Virginia.

that, for many years, housed the Virginia State Library and the Virginia Supreme Court. Federal public works money made it possible for new construction to go up at various public institutions of higher education, among them Mary Washington College and the College of William and Mary. At Virginia State College, the state substantially upgraded the physical plant with the construction in 1937 of a cluster of new buildings—an administration building, Virginia Hall; a science building, Colson Hall; and a library, Johnston Hall (now the Lindsay-Montague Music Building)—as well as a men's residence hall, completed in 1940 and named for former president John Mercer Langston.

Similar monuments to the New Deal, all completed between 1936 and 1940, can be found on the campus of Virginia Tech. On one side of the drill field is the Teaching and Administration Building, later named after VPI president Julian A. Burruss. Across the drill field, Agricultural Hall went up (today's Hutcheson Hall), as did the Natural Science Building (Smyth), the Agricultural Engineering Hall (Seitz), and the Home Economics Building (Agnew). At another corner of the drill field is the Eggleston residence hall complex, and back of it Owens Dining Hall. New Deal buildings also include the Student Activities Building (today's Squires Student Center, twice since enlarged), as well as Hillcrest, a residence hall, originally just for women, that today also houses the university honors program. Never had there been such a spate of new construction at the school, and all this came as a result of the Great Depression. Across the state—and across the nation—New Deal programs created jobs for the jobless and, as one consequence, put permanent capital improvements in place.

Creating Jobs and Writing History—The WPA Interviews

Among the many monuments the New Deal left in Virginia, some were constructed with stone or brick; others were crafted of nouns and verbs. The Great Depression put people in a great many occupations out of work. The New Deal attempted to put them back to work, and among these reemployed workers were writers. Workers on public works were constructing parks or parkways, libraries or classroom buildings, edifices for which considerable social need was seen. So, too, writers were employed at tasks that were considered to have significant public interest and social benefit. The programs of the WPA included a Federal Writers' Project, Virginia's part in it the Virginia Writers' Project. Plans to publish much of the resulting material were shelved in the early 1940s, and these sources remained largely unknown and unused for many years thereafter. Then they began to come to light.

Most of the work of the Virginia Writers' Project took place in the context of interviews. Many of these had to do with collecting people's life stories, and a selection of these, together with a critical evaluation of them, appear in the book *Talk about Trouble* (1996). Under the leadership of Hampton Institute professor Roscoe E. Lewis, more particularly, numerous writers searched for former slaves to collect their stories. Material from the slave narratives, finally published as *Weevils in the Wheat* (1976), has appeared in various chapters of this book. Together, the two collections offer extraordinary glimpses of some combination of (1) the program and the writers employed in it, as well as the life and work of each person interviewed; (2) the economic and cultural patterns of Virginia during the decade of the Great Depression, the New Deal, and the eve of World War II; and (3) the history of Virginia across the preceding century. In short, what can be known about Virginia's history is greatly enhanced by the availability of so many materials from the Virginia Writers' Project.

Daughters of a Newer South

Lucy Randolph Mason was a contemporary of Carter G. Woodson and Douglas Southall Freeman. Descended from the First Families of Virginia, as she was fond of pointing out, Mason called on her pedigree to legitimate her lifelong efforts to make a very different Virginia from the one that Douglas Southall Freeman lived in or the one that Harry F. Byrd Sr. fought to defend. What political leaders like Byrd sought to perpetuate, she sought to renovate. She worked as industrial secretary for the Young Women's Christian Association in Richmond, and as its general secretary in the 1920s. While she worked for better working conditions for all workers, she also worked for the right of women to vote, first for the achievement of that right with the Equal Suffrage League, and then for the exercise of that right with the League of Women Voters. She presided over the Richmond branches of each group in turn.

Yet she is best known for her work during fifteen years with the Congress of Industrial Organizations (CIO), from 1937 to 1952, beginning as a public relations representative with the Textile Workers Organizing Committee. Her work often brought her home to Virginia—in 1938 she interceded successfully with Virginia governor James Price to free three workers in Covington, CIO members who had been jailed for illegal picketing—but it usually kept her busy in the Deep South. Seeking to transcend all the major barriers that divided southerners (or all Americans) in general and Virginians in particular, she worked to create unions that would include black workers as well as white, and women workers as well as men. Her public relations work focused on protecting the "civil rights" of workers to organize independent unions, to engage in collective bargaining, and to seek higher wages and safer working conditions. In a great many ways, she helped to create a South in which the civil rights movement of the 1950s and '60s might emerge. And she did much of it during the very years that Douglas Southall Freeman was writing his books on Lee's Lieutenants.

Outside agitator? Yankee rabble rouser? Why, she'd have you know that she was the great-great-great-granddaughter of George Mason, author of Virginia's Declaration of Rights. Moreover, John Marshall, the great chief justice of the U.S. Supreme Court, was her mother's great-great-uncle. Her father had fought in the Confederate army, and one of his cousins was Robert E. Lee. On the litany went. If she was not a true Virginian, no one could be. Yet she looked forward to creating an alternative Virginia future, even as she drew on the authorized version of the Virginia past to do so.

Alice Jackson grew up in Richmond, where she had been born in 1913. As historian Larissa Smith recounts the story, Alice Jackson's father, James Jackson Sr., a pharmacist who had trained at Howard University, took her and her younger brother James Jr., when they were children, to witness Confederate veterans marching down Monument Avenue past the statues of Robert E. Lee and Stonewall Jackson—not to celebrate the march or the marchers but, rather, to point to a phenomenon that black Virginians had reason to view as inimical to their interests. In the early 1930s, James Jr. attended Virginia Union University, where his activities included the National Student League, a biracial antisegregationist group with another affiliate at the University of Virginia. His sister Alice graduated from Virginia Union in 1934 and then did a year's graduate work at Smith College, in Massachusetts.

But the Great Depression made finances even tighter than usual in the Jackson household, and she wished to continue her studies within Virginia. Yet no graduate program there was available to African Americans. For black Virginians, the question was not one of segregated access to "separate but equal" programs but, rather, one of categorical black exclusion from a wide range of programs. The multiple Virginia Union connections led to a meeting between Alice Jackson and Charles Hamilton Houston, special counsel for the NAACP's program to attack racially discriminatory education, and she decided to apply to the University of Virginia.

Before 1920, she would have been rejected on the grounds that the university did not admit women, even into its graduate programs. That much had changed by 1935, but she was African American, so the university rejected her application on racial grounds. The matter went public, and the *Richmond Times-Dispatch* warned against integrated higher education: "There is sufficient danger of ultimate racial amalgamation now, without increasing that danger through the mingling of the races in schools, colleges, and universities." The NAACP, though eventually deciding not to pursue Alice Jackson's case, remained interested in the topic, and meanwhile, moving on a related front against Jim Crow education, encouraged efforts to demand that public schools' teachers' salaries be equalized across racial lines. The Jackson application led the state Board of Education to recommend establishment of selected graduate programs at Virginia State College, programs that soon took shape. Moreover, the General Assembly, at its next session, established an out-of-state scholarship program so that black Virginians like Alice Jackson might be deflected from attending in-state white schools. That was how, with modest financial aid from the state of Virginia, Alice Jackson began taking graduate classes in fall 1936 at Columbia University, where she earned a master's degree in 1939.

Susie Rosa Catherine Byrd, an Albemarle County native, graduated in 1913 from Virginia Normal and Industrial Institute, with a major in home economics and a state teacher's certificate. Still in her teens, she taught at the training school on campus, then at a rural one-room school in Dewitt (outside Petersburg), and then in Petersburg. As teachers often did, she studied one summer at Virginia Normal and another at Hampton Institute. Marriage followed for a time, then college-level work at Virginia State College, and then the Great Depression. In 1933, she began teaching at a Federal Emergency Relief Administration nursery school. By 1935 she was teaching night school on a WPA project. Her night school teaching, mostly with elderly members of Petersburg's black community, led to the forming of what her students named the Susie R. C. Byrd Literary Club, meeting at the homes of various members, where she would provide treats and her class members worked on their reading and writing.

These varied activities came together in 1937 when Susie Byrd began interviewing elderly African Americans, mostly in Petersburg, for the WPA's Federal Writers' Project. She already knew former slave Rev. John Brown, and he introduced her to others. Beginning with nine people, then thirteen, and subsequently forty people and more, the group gathered together. They first met at the home of Brown and his wife Liza, then at other people's places, including Susie Byrd's, to sing songs from slavery times, share stories "'bout dem back times," and help Byrd gather materials that became an important part of the larger collection of Virginia slave narratives. Rev. James Boatman observed, according to Byrd's rendition, that the group wanted to "help dem chillun to git all dat slave stuff jus' like twas, 'cause us ole folks will soon be dead." One night, when Virginia Writers' Project state director Eudora Ramsay Richardson, a white woman, came by, Rev. Israel Massie, with his impaired vision, kept on telling stories, some especially for her benefit, for it never occurred to him that the group wasn't all black. The next morning he told Susie Byrd: "Lawdy, Honey I ain't knowed I was talkin' to a white 'oman I jes' told dat thing jes' like hit was."

Pauli Murray never resided in Virginia, but she sometimes found herself in the state—and challenging the racial order there. A mixed-race child of the South, she grew up in Durham, North Carolina. In 1938 she applied to do graduate work at the University of North Carolina, where her white forebears had been prominent, but her black ancestry kept her out. In 1940, she and an ill girlfriend were on their way, by Greyhound bus, south from New York City, where she was working, to her family home in Durham when they were arrested in Petersburg for disobeying the driver's insistence that they remain in the very back row of seats, where the bumps hurt the most, or in a nearby broken seat. They were convicted of disorderly conduct and of violating the segregation law. Thwarted in her wish to carry her case to the U.S. Supreme Court, she was delighted six years later when in a similar case—*Morgan v. Virginia*, regarding a black woman traveling home by bus from Virginia to Baltimore—the Supreme Court banned state-enforced racial segregation in interstate bus travel.

The Workers Defense League wired the funds that paid the fines for Murray and her friend, finally ending the two young women's ordeal in Virginia, and through that connection, later in 1940, Murray became intensely involved in a capital murder case. Odell Waller, a black sharecropper from Pittsylvania County in Southside Virginia, was arrested in connection with the death of his white landlord, Oscar Davis, after a dispute in which Davis had seized the farm's entire crop and had evicted Waller's foster mother and his wife from their little shack. An all-white, poll-tax-paying jury convicted Waller of first-degree murder, and he was sentenced to the electric chair. For two years, Murray threw herself into a national effort to obtain another outcome, raising funds, generating publicity, and assisting with a tour by Waller's stepmother, Annie Waller. In New York City, for example, A. Philip Randolph, at a huge gathering at Madison Square Garden associated with the March on Washington movement, introduced Annie Waller to a noisily sympathetic crowd. But the Virginia Supreme Court, the U.S. Supreme Court, and the governor of Virginia all declined to intervene. Murray failed in her bid to save Waller's life, and the experience catalyzed her decision to go to law school. So she enrolled at Howard University, where her off-campus activities included sit-ins against segregated eating establishments in the nation's capital during World War II.

Legacies of the Great Depression and New Deal

The 1930s shaped Virginia and Virginians in countless ways. The Great Depression provided the backdrop against which Alice Jackson applied to the University of Virginia and Lucy Randolph Mason organized southern workers. A host of New Deal programs left a permanent imprint on Virginia, whether temporary measures that resulted in public buildings or long-term policies like Social Security. And the tremendous growth of the federal government supplied the basis for subsequent national initiatives, whether against racial segregation or voting restrictions, of the sort that southern political leaders like Senator Byrd had feared. Thus the New Deal's legacy included not only new construction on college campuses and price supports for agricultural commodities but also new terms on which Virginians would contest each other on matters of class and race. Meanwhile, Virginians both black and white, comfortable and poor, found themselves in a vast war that also did much to spur change and shape it.

Chapter 21

World War II

....

In Bedford, Virginia, on the morning of July 17, 1944, Elizabeth Teass began her shift at the town's small Western Union telegraph office, at Green's drugstore. She had been working the booth since graduating from Bedford High School in 1941, some months before the Japanese attack at Pearl Harbor. Turning on the teletype machine that morning, she connected to the Western Union office in Roanoke: "Good Morning. Go ahead. Bedford." By summer 1944, the United States had been in World War II for two and a half years, and Teass was accustomed to receiving one casualty message report in a typical week. There had already been one the day before, but this time, word came back to expect more: "Roanoke. We have casualties."

The report began inching out of the machine, brandishing the opening words "The Secretary of War desires me to express his deep regret." The rest of the message came into view, and as Teass clipped the strips and glued them to a telegram, she waited for the machine to go quiet. But it kept on that day, and more reports came in later, bringing to Bedford the awful news to local families of what had happened on the coast of northwestern France some six weeks before. Bedford Hoback had died, and his younger brother Raymond was missing in action. The machine would not stay quiet. Twenty-two Bedford County soldiers died in the D-day attack at Normandy.

All but one of those casualties came from the 29th Infantry Division's 116th Regiment, of which Company A included thirty-eight men from Bedford County. The 116th Infantry had originally been a regiment of the Virginia National Guard, and after being called into federal service in early 1941 and subsequently deployed across the Atlantic, a great many Virginians remained in its ranks. The army assigned Company A to the first wave of attack on Omaha Beach. On Tuesday June 6, 1944, at 4:00 a.m., the boys of Bedford and their fellow soldiers loaded into six boats and were lowered into the water from their warship, the *Empire Javelin*. As the boats came within 800 feet of the shore, the soldiers could hear artillery and mortar fire, and when the first ramps were dropped at 6:36 the men charged out into water over their heads and struggled to make it to shore. Most of the Bedford boys who lost their lives that day were dead within minutes. The entire 116th Infantry suffered 797 casualties, most of them Virginians.

Preparing for War

In 1939 and 1940, Virginians grew increasingly concerned that if the British and French were both defeated, there would be little to stop the Nazis from steaming across the ocean, and Virginia seemed a prime location for an attack. In May 1940, Governor James H. Price created the Virginia Defense Council (later replaced by the Virginia Office of Civilian Defense), headed by the editor of the *Richmond News Leader,* Douglas Southall Freeman. It was the first state defense council formed in the nation, and other state defense councils soon followed. The council's first meeting outlined its chief tasks. One was to replace the Virginia National Guard, soon to be called into federal service, so the Virginia Protective Force was created, as was the Committee on Civil Police Mobilization.

In 1940 and on into 1941, most Americans wanted to stay out of World War II, but they also wanted to help Great Britain stay in it, so a massive military buildup took place in the months before the attack on Pearl Harbor. By 1940, America began to ramp up its industrial and military strength, an effort that had a profound effect in Virginia through World War II and beyond. Located close to the nation's capital and also on the coast, the Commonwealth was a prime place for military sites. The state's many military posts and bases required thousands of civilian workers, and the state produced vast amounts of munitions. Virginia was second only to Texas among southern states in the value of war contracts, and its economy surged as a result of the increased demand for war-related products. Not only soldiers but also new government workers and munitions workers, together with their families, swarmed into the state, and Virginians themselves changed jobs. New jobs at high wages at a big arsenal on the New River near Radford, to take one example, drew labor away from area farms.

As early as spring 1940, the Army General Staff's War Plans Division began developing plans for possible huge military operations in both Europe and the Pacific. Over the next year, the army identified a site between the Chesapeake Bay and the nation's capital for heavy weapons and maneuver training facilities. In mid-1941, six months before the United States entered World War II, workers with the Civilian Conservation Corps, black and white, assisted in the evacuation of families living in a huge area of northern Caroline County that the federal government took over to establish Fort A. P. Hill, named for a prominent Confederate general from Virginia. The households that were removed ranged from well-off to dirt-poor, and many of the residents were relocated to new tracts, racially segregated, of prefabricated housing in the Milford area, south of Bowling Green. Long after World War II, the facility served the nation's military needs in other wars, from Korea to Vietnam and beyond.

The war caused tremendous change in northern Virginia near Washington, D.C. Even before the Japanese attack at Pearl Harbor, 24,000 people were employed by the War Department in Washington, and as defense efforts expanded, governmental administration jobs spread into Virginia. As the armed forces expanded, the number of employees increased and a need for centralized administration arose. On September 11, 1941, ground was broken for a massive new building, the Pentagon, designed to relieve the War Department's need for space and consolidate the department under one roof. To conserve steel, the edifice was constructed with reinforced concrete, a measure that saved enough steel to construct a battleship. A staggering 680,000 tons of sand and gravel were dredged from the Potomac River and made into 435,000 cubic yards of concrete. Despite its size, construction of the Pentagon took only sixteen months and was completed on January 15, 1943, at a cost of $83 million. The mammoth new structure replaced seventeen War Department buildings. Although its height was limited to three stories because of its location near Washington National Airport, the Pentagon remains the largest office building in the world, with three times the floor space of the Empire State Building.

The defense effort had a dramatic effect on eastern Virginia as well. In fact, Portsmouth, home of a federal naval yard, and the shipyard at Newport News saw the state's greatest population increases. The production of warships was perhaps Virginia's most memorable contribution to the war—and the industry that brought the greatest change to the state. The Virginia seacoast put the state at the forefront of naval construction and the battle for the Atlantic. Naval and military facilities were created or enlarged, and the numbers of sailors and shipyard workers in the Hampton Roads area rose sharply. In 1942 German subs mined the entrance to the Chesapeake Bay, and in March that year, U-boats sank American ships in the area at a rate of nearly one per day.

As early as 1939, defense industries in the Hampton Roads area—including the cities of Norfolk, Portsmouth, Newport News, and Hampton—expanded sharply, while military personnel and wartime workers flooded the region. From April 1, 1940, to November 1, 1943, the civilian population of Hampton Roads rose from 392,909 to 576,075, and the military population from 15,715 to 158,024.

Douglas Southall Freeman (1886–1953), journalist and historian. Freeman reported the news, editorialized on the news, and appeared in the news. The image shown here, created by artist Ernest Hamlin Baker, appeared on the cover of *Time* magazine on October 18, 1948 (TIME Magazine © 1948 Time Inc. Reprinted by permission). It shows Freeman together with his two major historical companions, George Washington and Robert E. Lee. Freeman's historical work emphasized the eighteenth and nineteenth centuries, but his work at the *Richmond News Leader* contributed to the public's understanding of developments in the twentieth. His daily editorials—on the political and military events of World War I and World War II, for example—gained him a wide hearing. Beginning in 1925 and continuing to the day of his death in 1953, he discussed the news in a regular fifteen-minute program on the radio, typically twice a day until his retirement from the *News Leader* in 1949 and once a day thereafter. Political and military leaders read his books as primers on leadership. He successfully urged in a May 1944 editorial that the forthcoming "invasion" of Europe be termed instead the "liberation" of Europe. An index he long kept to stories in the *Richmond Times-Dispatch* and in the *News Leader,* known as the "Freeman File," continues to provide researchers easy access to such materials for much of the twentieth century.

Most civilian newcomers came in shipbuilding and repair. Shipbuilders were in desperate need of workers, and from 1939 to 1943 the Newport News Shipbuilding and Dry Dock Company's employment soared from 13,000 to 70,000. During the war, the company built 33 warships and repaired 700, while the Norfolk Navy Yard constructed 42 vessels and repaired 7,283.

The surge in population in urban centers put an enormous strain on schools, hospitals, and housing. Families flooded the Norfolk area from many of the nation's poorer regions, often so desperate to start their jobs that they resorted to sleeping in shanties, trailer camps, and even cars, or they moved into houses that were not yet completed. Richmond, too, found itself swamped by the soldiers and sailors arriving in the city for short vacations away from their various camps, and many of these men found themselves sleeping on chairs or floors.

Not only was the Chesapeake area the nation's leading location for ship construction and repair, but the government also activated the Hampton Roads Port of Embarkation on June 15, 1942, and the massive numbers of personnel and amounts of materials going through the port generated many additional jobs. Hampton Roads drew a national reputation as a sinful place, as reports of prostitution and the mistreatment of servicemen spread across the country. Strangely, this seemed to draw more attention to the region and elicit more federal aid than did the problems of housing shortages, overcrowded schools and hospitals, inadequate transportation systems, and inadequate sewage and water systems. The shipbuilding jobs had very high rates of turnover, and poor living conditions may have contributed to the turnover.

Despite labor shortages, only limited efforts were made to permit African Americans to work to full potential. Work opportunities for black men were actually far more limited in southern shipyards during World War II than during World War I, in part because of unionized white workers' resistance to working alongside blacks. Moreover, training opportunities for white women often went unmatched for black women, and when they were permitted to go through training programs, black women found themselves barred from the jobs they had trained for. The Fair Employment Practices Committee, which had been set up in 1941 in response to black labor leader A. Philip Randolph's March on Washington movement, heard numerous complaints about racial discrimination in Norfolk, Newport News, and elsewhere. Meanwhile, in the Jim Crow world that included a segregated military, black servicemen hung out at black United Service Organization (USO) facilities, and whites at white ones.

Prisoner of War Camps in Virginia

Huge numbers of Virginians headed overseas, whether across the Atlantic or across the Pacific. A reverse migration brought substantial numbers of Italians and Germans to Virginia, where they lived in prisoner of war (POW) camps and worked on farms and elsewhere. In fact, the Italians and Germans tended to come westbound across the Atlantic on the same vessels that had carried GIs eastbound to war. Then they passed through the great Hampton Roads Port of Embarkation. Roughly 134,000 POWs disembarked there—more than seven-eighths of them Germans, but nearly 16,000 of them Italians. Most were then distributed to camps far from Virginia, but some remained in the state.

Twenty-seven camps in Virginia housed German POWs—two generations later, Virginians remembered camps south of Leesburg, north of Crozet, and at various other locations. Italian POWs, far fewer, soon found themselves in a different situation, once Italy withdrew from the Axis powers against which the United States and its allies were fighting—but POWs they were nonetheless. Germans were sometimes defiant, insisting that Hitler would prove victorious, but some took the approach that living in a POW camp in Virginia was a huge improvement over fighting in Russia. Italians often recognized that regular food and other supplies offered a substantial improvement over what they would be experiencing as soldiers or civilians back in wartime Italy.

Both groups were often welcomed by Virginians who needed their labor and wanted their own family members to be well treated if captured. The flip side of that approach came into view when Virginians remembered that these former soldiers had probably been shooting at GIs but were safe and well looked after while Virginians were off at the front. Yet some POWs married American women, and some returned after the war to become citizens.

War Bonds, Blood Donations, and Sugar Rationing

Besides sending brothers, sons, husbands, fathers, and friends off to fight, Virginians also made numerous adjustments and sacrifices at home. With the men off fighting, women and children had to take their places in the job market to keep things running. With men gone from their farms, and with many of the rural workers rushing into the cities to work in the booming factories, women could be found riding tractors, often declaring it "easier than cooking." Rosie not only pounded rivets but also drove tractors and made parachutes.

Calls for the purchase of war bonds could be found all over newspapers, in advertisements and public service announcements on almost every page. An ad for Hofheimer's shoe stores appeared in the *Richmond Times-Dispatch* on June 8, 1944, just after D-day:

> We hate to write this Advertisement. Yet . . . the only way to win this war is to realize that the finest armies and navies and air fleets in the world are only as good as the flow and abundance of their munitions and supplies. And people with families and futures to think of . . . should remember always that every dollar of their investment is guaranteed by the strongest, safest, richest country on earth. It is no crime in the Fifth War Loan to use your head and your heart at the same time. The only crime is to fail the Living[,] to neglect the Wounded[,] and to forget the Dead.

Federal and state officials set monthly quotas for the sale of bonds for states and small towns, and most newspapers kept a running tally to inform the readers how close they were. Parades, telethons, special promotions, and celebrity appearances were some of the ways Virginia organizations attempted to sell the bonds. By the end of the war, the American people had bought about $49 billion worth of war bonds, accounting for one-sixth of the revenue used to finance the war. Virginians did their share.

Virginians were encouraged daily to buy war bonds, but they were encouraged not to buy many other things. Rubber and sugar were the first consumer items to be rationed, but over 300 products soon followed, including bikes, waffle irons, beer cans, toothpaste tubes, and coat hangers, so Americans felt the impact of the war in little ways every day. *Time* magazine wrote: "The American male, his pants and socks dragging, his sports ruined, his wife bulging in the wrong places, his balloonless child teething on wood, his car tireless in the garage, riding off to work on a hard-benched bus or subway, unable to erase mistakes, or snap a rubber band around them, could now get down to really hating Japan and the Axis." The federal government tried to enforce the strict rations to allow the armed forces the resources they needed, prevent hoarding of what remained, and ensure fair distribution.

In May 1942, the federal government began requiring drivers in the eastern states to register to purchase gasoline. Most drivers fell under Category A, those whose driving was not essential to the war effort, and were allowed less than four gallons a week of gasoline. In November, the entire country required registration. At around the same time, the government imposed a nationwide thirty-five-mile-per-hour speed limit to save gas and rubber. In January 1943, the federal government imposed a restriction on "pleasure driving," defined as nonessential driving, in seventeen eastern states, including Virginia, but it was hard to enforce. Under the law, driving to funerals was permitted, but driving to weddings was not. If caught driving for pleasure, drivers could have their gas rations revoked and find themselves in court. The ban was lifted in September 1943, and Virginians were asked simply to do their patriotic duty and not use more gasoline than absolutely necessary. A Texaco ad on June 8, 1944, just after D-day, exclaimed, "Gasoline powers the attack"; it noted that "invasion needs may use up vital fuel even faster" and urged, "Don't waste a drop!"

Blood was needed, too. Embedded among the lists of "Virginia War Casualties"—Virginia's war dead—in the *Richmond Times-Dispatch* on July 6, 1944, was a call from the Red Cross: "Plasma prepared from the pints of blood you gave went in with our troops in Normandy and Saipan. But more is needed urgently. As you read the casualty lists . . . stop and think, could you have helped keep some of these names off this list? What you won't miss, men can't live without."

Children in World War II Virginia

With so many women working outside the home, questions of what to do with the children arose. Governor Colgate W. Darden appointed the nation's first State Child Care Committee to aid working mothers. Nonetheless, a sharp increase in juvenile delinquency concerned many Virginians. According to the *Staunton News-Leader* in April 1943, Staunton was not exempt from a national problem, "an epidemic of recalcitrant boys" who "stay out late at night and get into various kinds of mischief, including such serious things as burglary and arson." In Richmond, a group was formed to "make life so full and entertaining for boys that they would not have time to smash things."

Other children turned to work to help fill the spots the men had left behind. In 1939, the state of Virginia issued 1,322 work permits to children under the age of sixteen—a rate of 110 per month. Midway through the war, the rate was more than ten times as high. And as for purchasing war bonds or war stamps, even school-age Virginians found themselves caught up in the excitement. The *Northern Neck News* of April 15, 1943, printed a letter from a father in Warsaw:

> I have a son named Leslie, . . . and it has been his mother's practice to give him fifteen cents each day with which to purchase his lunch at school. We observed that he came home each day from school very hungry. After observing this for some time we asked him if he was using his money to purchase lunch or using it for candy, chewing gum and the like. He replied that he was spending five cents for his lunch each day and had used the remaining ten cents to purchase a War Stamp. . . . Leslie's stamp album revealed that $9 of his lunch money had been invested in War Stamps.

All Virginians experienced the war in their own ways on the home front, but many thousands experienced it directly overseas. Elizabeth Teass, when she pulled new bits of bad news off the teletype, connected the fates of overseas Virginians with their stateside loved ones. Far more troops lived than died, however, and lived to tell about the war.

In the aftermath of the landing at Normandy, for example, Virginians were among the vast numbers of GIs who made their way inland toward Germany. Among them, Darrell "Shifty" Powers, who hailed from the hills of Clinch County, had grown up with a weapon in his hands, and his instincts and precision served him and his comrades well in western Europe. One December 1944 day, in the Bastogne area, he reported to his sergeant that "there's a tree up there," nearly a mile away, that "wasn't there yesterday," so something must be up. Shifty had no binoculars, but even though the sergeant did, he could not see at first what Shifty was talking about. Then he detected evidence that, under camouflage, the Germans were installing antiaircraft weapons, and the Americans destroyed the position. Some days later, Allied troops were advancing but could not locate an enemy sniper who was picking off men, until Shifty called out, "I see 'im," and fired. The enemy gun went silent, and before long the troops came to the spot Shifty had fired at. The sniper had a bullet in his forehead. Said another soldier, Robert "Popeye" Winn, whose peacetime home was South Hill, "You know, it just doesn't pay to be shootin' at Shifty when he's got a rifle."

John F. "Jack" Poulton completed bachelor's (1935) and master's (1936) degrees in architectural engineering at VPI, married Jane Weaver, and worked for five years at his craft. Then war came. Jack Poulton spent the war with the navy's Seabees—CBs, or Construction Battalions—in the South Pacific, including at Guadalcanal. Jane Poulton, living in Richmond, worked and took classes at Richmond Professional Institute. Week after week, year after year, they wrote each other. Early on he mused on their having "planned something else—easier and more pleasant," and she reported, "war is hell for women," noting mostly that she missed him but also that "I am tired of women all the time in my social life." Their letters exchanged news and rumors about the war, spoke of earlier times in Front Royal and Blacksburg, and looked to their postwar future. Finally it arrived. He returned for keeps, and their son was born in 1946, in time to kick off the nation's postwar baby boom.

Black Virginians' civil rights struggle, like everything else, got caught up in the war. Civil rights lawyers Oliver W. Hill, Samuel W. Tucker, and Roland D. Ealey each went to war in either the Pacific or the European theater. When in-

General George C. Marshall (1880–1959), architect of war and peace. Descended from a Virginia family dating from the 1650s, Marshall, a 1901 graduate of Virginia Military Institute, served as the U.S. Army's chief of staff during World War II. *Time* magazine recognized him as Man of the Year for 1943. After the war, as secretary of state under President Harry S. Truman, he originated what came to be known as the Marshall Plan for the economic recovery of devastated Europe. This image first appeared in 1944 in the *New York Times*. Virginia Historical Society, Richmond, Virginia.

terviewed four decades later, Oliver Hill recalled the "segregated army" of World War II, including his unit, a "black regiment" with "practically all white officers." When he arrived in England, "white troops and black troops" were stationed near the same community, and "they had white night and black night," so "American troops who were fighting . . . a common enemy" were not permitted to go into "the same town of an ally on the same night. Because there'd be riots!" Asked by his interviewer whether his wartime experiences had reinforced his commitment to civil rights, Hill replied: "Well, I had the commitment before I went into the Army, and didn't anything while I was in the service tend to diminish it in any way."

The "V" in "Virginia" Is for "Victory"

Hard it would be to find two days in the history of Richmond so strikingly different than V-E (Victory in Europe) day, May 8, 1945, and V-J (Victory over Japan) day, August 15, 1945. A hushed somber mood filled the streets the day the Nazi army surrendered to Allied troops. In his national announcement, the new president, Harry S. Truman, requested a sober prayerful observance, and Richmond answered his plea. For the most part the streets were deserted, and while some private businesses chose to close for the day, governmental offices and many others stayed open, as people "remained at their daily tasks grimly determined that there shall be no letup until the war is ended in complete victory," the *Richmond Times-Dispatch* reported. Schoolchildren spent the day listening to Truman's broadcast from the night before, playing patriotic music, and reading prayers in assemblies. Virginians' hearts were stirred on hearing the news of Hitler's defeat, yet all knew that the war was far from over. Said an officer about the wounded service personnel at McGuire General Hospital, "You couldn't tell it was V-E Day," as the men showed little emotion but "talked in terms of their buddies overseas." A Miller and Rhoads department store advertisement (with the notice "store closed all day today") captured the mood:

> Today we rejoice, indeed—humbly, soberly, thankfully, and with the knowledge that our work is not yet done. Therefore, in the encouragement of this Victory let us go forward with greater determination. Let us remember those who have suffered to bring this day. Let us resolve to be worthy of their sacrifices, and the sacrifices of those who yet must die. Above all, let us resolve to be worthy in our peace-making of those who suffered to bring us peace. With God's help may we win that greatest Victory of all.

Before 7:00 p.m. on August 14, 1945, the streets looked very similar to the way they had a few months earlier on V-E day. Shops were closed for the evening, families sat inside enjoying dinner, and—if not for the popularity of radio— things might have remained quiet throughout the night. But then came news that Japan had surrendered. Truman made an impromptu speech to the nation from the steps of the White House, people began spilling out of houses, and the streets "became a streaming parade of automobiles, trucks, bicycles, and people—all moving aimlessly along making noise," the *Richmond Times-Dispatch* reported. American flags were passed out to everyone who could hold one, and fire engines rang their bells in jubilation.

As the *Times-Dispatch* described the continuous noise that rang through the streets, "Suddenly everyone was talking at once. One thought was expressed over and over, 'I'm going home.'" Shortly after 7:00 p.m., telephone traffic reached an all-time high. A sailor, just back from eighteen months in the southwest Pacific, said the sensation he felt when hearing the news was "better than falling in love." That may have been so, but servicemen were soon planting kisses on any women close enough to be grabbed. Governor Darden declared August 15 a holiday and said, "I urge our people to observe it in prayer and thanksgiving for our deliverance, and I ask them to rededicate themselves to those principles of humanity and justice without which a free society cannot exist." The next day, most Virginians headed to church, the only buildings open, in observance of peace. The bedlam calmed down, but streets remained covered in streamers.

After the War: A Boom in Babies, Schools, and Suburbs

World War II made the Great Depression fade in people's memories, at least to some degree, as shortages of labor replaced shortages of jobs, and wages rose. Workers left the farms of rural Virginia to serve in the military or to take defense-related production jobs in the cities, spurring a permanent downward trend in the relative numbers of rural Virginians. An absence of farmworkers fostered the mechanization of agriculture, and postwar technological advances caused even more people to leave rural Virginia. People moved off the farms and away from small towns into metropolitan centers. In addition, people moved into Virginia instead of away from the state. A pronounced shift in population—now much larger than before and increasingly concentrated in the areas around Hampton Roads and Washington, D.C.—moved the social, cultural, economic, and political center of gravity northward and eastward in the state, as well as to urban areas.

During the Cold War that soon followed, northern Virginia continued to be the center of the nation's defense administration, and many of the workers who had flooded the Hampton Roads area remained there. The nation's need for defense did not decline. The industrialization and urbanization in Virginia caused by World War II remained in place and in fact continued to grow. By 1950, for the first time, as many Virginians lived in urban areas as in rural.

These social and economic changes in general—and the population growth and redistribution in particular—were tremendous, and they epitomized the transformation under way in Virginia. At the turn of the twenty-first century and beyond, obituaries in newspapers recited, in one sketch after another, the stories of the young men from the 1940s who returned from overseas and married soon after the war. The baby boom that began in 1946 rippled through the rest of the century and beyond, requiring in turn grade schools and their teachers, high schools and their teachers, and then colleges and their professors, before supplying a new generation of highly trained workers and professionals.

More immediately, the GI Bill, enacted by Congress in 1944 in anticipation of postwar necessities and opportunities, sent countless men, and some women as well, to college, putting a generation through postsecondary education. The GI Bill also helped people start businesses. And like the FHA mortgage-guarantee program, the GI Bill enabled countless families to move to the suburbs. Each of these changes in itself was huge. In combination, they meant that just as the men and women of the "greatest generation" had reshaped the world overseas, their return reshaped the nation in general and Virginia in particular.

Part V

1945–2007

COLD WAR AND

GREAT SOCIETY

Virginia is one of the more defense-dependent states in the nation. It is home to the Pentagon and to Oceana Naval Air Station, Quantico, Fort A. P. Hill, and Fort Eustis. The defense economy has created a technology-based economy in northern Virginia and many naval jobs in the Hampton Roads area. World War II made Virginia increasingly urban and industrial, and this trend continued, as the Cold War followed.

The Cold War brought an occasional lengthy hot war, and large numbers of Virginians found themselves caught up in those wars as well. In July 1950, ten days after the Korean War broke out, the first three Virginians died fighting there, and according to official data an additional 846 died in the war in hostile action. As early as March 1961, Captain Oscar B. Weston Jr., of the U.S. Air Force, died in combat in Vietnam. Among the military personnel who fought in Korea was future Virginia governor L. Douglas Wilder. Among those who fought in Vietnam was Charles S. Robb, future governor of Virginia and Democratic senator.

Segregation was very much still in place in the military at the end of World War II, but that soon changed. The first Cold War president, Harry Truman, followed up in 1948 on his predecessor's 1941 executive order against discrimination in defense jobs by ordering the desegregation of the nation's armed forces.

The United States had one of its major institutions increasingly run with little regard to racial identity, a change that spilled over into conditions off military bases as well as on them. In addition, black civilians and returning veterans alike resumed or launched initiatives in the courts to bring about change on the racial front, and the U.S. Supreme Court proved notably receptive. Various changes contributed to, or comprised, an emerging civil rights movement as black Virginians became even more active than before, and certainly more successful, in their efforts to end discrimination.

Aside from matters military or racial, the Cold War shaped major developments that contributed to a transformation of the nation in general and Virginia in particular. In 1956, President Dwight D. Eisenhower signed the Interstate Highway Act, a measure whose constitutionality Eisenhower preferred to see in terms of the nation's defense. After the Soviet Union's launch in 1957 of a satellite, *Sputnik I*, Congress passed the National Defense Education Act of 1958, designed to produce far more scientists and engineers for American research and development. Directly and indirectly, these initiatives in education and transportation spurred the growth of the Virginia economy and its system of higher education.

Building on the programs of both the New Deal and the Cold War, Congress soon launched a wide range of new initiatives. Added in the mid-1960s to Social Security, for example, were Medicare and Medicaid. The National Defense Education Act was expanded in 1964 to promote advanced education in the humanities and social sciences, followed up by the Higher Education Act of 1965. Another huge initiative funneled massive financial support to elementary and secondary education, and Head Start added yet another dimension to education initiatives.

The Civil Rights Act of 1964 and the Voting Rights Act of 1965 propelled Virginia out of the era of segregation and disfranchisement. In combination, the Higher Education Act and the Civil Rights Act spurred private colleges as well as public institutions to abandon practices of black exclusion. By the time Congress passed its major civil rights legislation, all three branches of the federal government had signed on to a transformation in policy in racial matters. Jim Crow must go.

Within a quarter century of World War II, given these and other changes and sources of change, Virginia looked like a place very different from anything it had ever been before.

Chapter 22

The Road to *Brown v. Board of Education*

....

The Civil War's end in 1865 brought an end to the state law that prohibited schools for black Virginians. The Fourteenth Amendment, ratified in 1868, required "equal protection of the laws." In 1870, as directed by Virginia's new state constitution, the General Assembly established a system of public schools, open to all children, black and white—but the statute also mandated racial segregation in such schools. The 1901–1902 convention inserted the 1870 language requiring segregation into Virginia's new state constitution: "White and colored children shall not be taught in the same school but in separate schools." These developments supply the backdrop to any study of public education in mid-twentieth-century Virginia.

From time immemorial, the autocrat King Color had governed life in Virginia, and making any change—especially a lot of change—took heroic efforts against great opposition. We know that the U.S. Supreme Court banned segregation in public schools in 1954, and if we map back from that moment, we can track the long prologue in Virginia on the road to that ruling.

Throughout the 1940s, Virginians contested the meaning for public education of *Plessy v. Ferguson,* an 1896 U.S. Supreme Court decision that made famous the phrase "equal but separate," or "separate but equal." The Supreme Court's ruling in *Plessy* did not segregate a single Virginia school—Virginia's public schools had been born segregated in 1870, and they continued that way past 1896 without a ripple. *Plessy* did, however, eventually shape the debate in Virginia in two profound ways. For one thing, the 1896 decision seemed to make futile any constitutional challenge to segregation. For another, the phrase "separate but equal" provided a standard against which practice in a segregated system could be measured.

Schools could be segregated, so far as the U.S. Constitution was concerned, and in fact they had to be, as far as the Virginia constitution was concerned. Were those segregated schools "equal"? That issue is where the legal debate often took place, as the two sides to the controversy met in Virginia courtrooms.

Virginia's First Sit-in, 1939

The modern civil rights movement is often thought to have begun after *Brown v. Board of Education* (1954), especially with the Montgomery bus boycott that began the next year, or even with the sit-ins that began in Greensboro, North Carolina, in February 1960. An event in Alexandria, Virginia, in 1939 points up the fact that such activities could be found long before 1955 or 1960.

In August 1939, Samuel Tucker and his brother Otto engineered a pioneer sit-in. Two years earlier, Alexandria had opened a public library, available to whites only. The Tucker brothers agreed that the direct approach would be appropriate for addressing the segregated library that refused black citizens access. Some days later, a young black man, well dressed and well mannered, entered the library, took a book to the circulation desk, and asked to take it out. When politely refused, he solemnly took a seat at a table and began reading. Five minutes later, another young man repeated the ritual. Soon, five tables were taken. A policeman, when called, felt forced to arrest the five—William Evans, Edward Gaddis, Morris Murray, Clarence Strange, and Otto Tucker.

Meanwhile, Samuel Tucker, who had been running the show, had alerted the media, and the next day the *Washington Post* published a photograph along with a story about the encounter at the library. With reference to a labor tactic in big industrial plants in the late 1930s, it was called a "sit-down strike." Tucker and his colleagues did not manage to extract the privilege of using the public library. As a result of their efforts, however, some months later the city made good on the "equal" in "separate but equal," and a black library was opened. Today it is the home of the Alexandria Black History Resource Center, at which one can watch a short video, narrated by Julian Bond, about the incident.

Similarly, the struggle over the public schools was a vibrant enterprise as early as 1939.

The Legacy of "Separate but Equal"

An upsurge in state spending on public schools in Virginia during the quarter century after 1902 poured far more per capita money into white schools than into black ones. Much the greatest disparity could be found in counties with large proportions of black children, for there the state's contribution to public schools—which was allocated on the basis of the number of school-age children, regardless of race—was divided by white school boards and was largely diverted to the white schools. By every indicator—teachers' salaries, the length of the school year, the schools' physical facilities, curricular offerings beyond the elementary level, the availability of school buses to transport children to school—black schools, especially in predominantly black districts, compared poorly to their white counterparts.

Beginning in the late 1930s, and with mounting insistence after World War II, efforts emerged by black parents, black teachers, and other black Virginians to address these issues, beginning with the discrepancies in teachers' salaries. The greatest opposition to change could be expected from whites living in cities and counties with large black populations, that is, especially east of the Blue Ridge. They had the most to lose from any equalization of funds and opportunities, and later they perceived the most at stake when the issue changed to desegregation—as it did in the 1950s.

Luther Porter Jackson, among the key figures in Virginia pushing for change on the racial front across the 1940s, showed that the public schools were a principal venue, but never the only one, for achieving change. He joined the faculty of Virginia Normal and Industrial Institute in 1922, as President John M. Gandy was launching a campaign, successful the next year, to get its collegiate program restored. By 1937, the Virginia State College for Negroes, as the school had been renamed, began offering selected graduate programs, especially in education. That year, at the University of Chicago, Jackson completed his dissertation, which he went on to publish as *Free Negro Labor and Property Holding in Virginia, 1830–1860* (1942). Jackson also wrote *Negro Office Holders in Virginia, 1865–1895* (1946). Jackson was a whirlwind in Virginia, especially in the 1940s. Through the Virginia Teachers Association (VTA) and the Virginia Voters League as well as from his faculty position at Virginia State, he actively promoted public education for black children, better salaries as well as professional development for their teachers, and voting rights for their parents.

Struggling toward Equality within Segregation— Aline Black and Melvin Alston

Black teachers in Norfolk, as elsewhere across the South, suffered racial discrimination in their salaries. Regardless of credentials or experience, black teachers earned much lower salaries than did their white counterparts. In 1937 the Virginia Teachers Association, representing black teachers in the public schools

Dr. Luther Porter Jackson (1892–1950), historian and activist. This watercolor portrait, painted by T. King in 1955, hangs at the Luther Jackson Middle School in Falls Church, Virginia, which originally opened in 1954 as the Luther Porter Jackson High School for black students in Fairfax County. Before then, black high school students in Fairfax had to go to Washington, D.C., or to a training school in Manassas. In April 1949, the year before his sudden death from a heart attack, Jackson was the first black scholar to present a paper—"Virginia and the Civil Rights Program," on President Truman's initiatives—at an annual meeting of the Virginia Social Science Association. Courtesy of the family of Dr. Luther P. Jackson.

(together with its local branch, the Norfolk Teachers Association), joined forces with the NAACP to organize a joint committee to pursue salary equalization. By that, they meant all teachers were to be paid according to the white teachers' salary schedule rather than the lower, black teachers' schedule. The NAACP supplied legal assistance, and the VTA established a $1,000 fund that could indemnify against salary loss for any teacher who was fired in retribution for serving as plaintiff in a court case.

Aline Elizabeth Black Hicks has historical significance in the modern civil rights movement because of a court case she lost in 1939 regarding salary equalization of public school teachers. Melvin Ovenus Alston has significance because of a case he won the next year. Both were natives of Norfolk, graduates of Norfolk's Booker T. Washington High School, and teachers there. Aline Black graduated from Virginia Normal and Industrial Institute with a B.S. in 1926 and from the University of Pennsylvania with an M.S. in 1935 and was certified to teach

English, Spanish, science, and chemistry. She became a member of the NAACP as well as of the Norfolk Teachers Association. Alston attended the Virginia State College for Negroes, where he earned a B.S. in 1935, and then began teaching math at Booker T. Washington High. Beginning in 1937 he served as president of the Norfolk Teachers Association, and he also held local leadership positions in the Young Men's Christian Association and the First Calvary Baptist Church. That same year, the Virginia NAACP and the all-black VTA, together with its Norfolk affiliate, organized a joint committee to support efforts to obtain salary equalization for black teachers.

In late 1938, Black challenged her low pay, less than what she would have earned had she been white. She was an excellent candidate to play the role she took on. Not yet married and still living in her parents' home, she was not very vulnerable in economic terms. Her professional qualifications were clear, so she could certainly lay claim to the higher pay that her white counterparts were receiving. First, she petitioned the Norfolk School Board to have her salary pegged to the white salary schedule. Rebuffed, she brought a case in state court, where in 1939 she lost again. Before her case could be appealed to the Virginia Supreme Court, the school board declined to renew her contract—insisting that it would not hire her while she was a plaintiff against them—and when she lost her job, her lawyers concluded that she no longer had standing to sue about the terms of her contract.

Though her case ended, the effort to contest separate-and-unequal race-based salary schedules continued. With some reluctance, Black's colleague Alston took her place in the litigation. Alston's lawyers were the NAACP's big guns—Thurgood Marshall, Leon A. Ransom, and William H. Hastie—together with Virginia attorneys Oliver W. Hill and J. Thomas Hewin Jr., and they took the case to federal court rather than state court. As a teacher, Alston sought a permanent injunction against the school board's continuing to discriminate in its salary schedule on racial grounds, and as a taxpayer he also challenged the city's discriminatory allocation of the state school fund. He and his attorneys lost the case in February 1940 in federal district court, but in June that year they won on appeal in the U.S. Court of Appeals for the Fourth Circuit (*Alston v. Board of Education of the City of Norfolk*). Pending a determination of the case, the appeals court had directed the school board not to distribute contracts for the coming year until July, so Alston could not be denied his job and no teachers could be required to waive their rights for that year.

The appeals court determined that the Norfolk School Board had denied equal protection of the laws by paying black teachers lower salaries than white teachers solely on the basis of race. The court rejected the school board's contention that teachers, having signed contracts for the year, could not contest the terms to which they had agreed and that if they failed to sign, they would have no standing to sue. The court ruled that such waivers could not extend beyond the single year of the contract. Moreover, the appeals court overruled the district judge in the matter of whether the case concerned only Alston. Rather, it was a class action suit that affected all black teachers in the Norfolk system.

In October 1940 the U.S. Supreme Court let the decision stand. The outcome in the *Alston* case proved to be one of the NAACP's more important victories in its campaign in the courts for equalization of educational and occupational opportunities. It supplied a powerful precedent for other salary-equalization cases, both in Virginia and in various other southern states. And it shaped efforts to achieve progress on other fronts, too—equal busing, equal facilities, and equal curricula—in the public schools of the South.

In Richmond, as attorney for Antoinette E. Bowler and the Richmond Teachers Association, Oliver Hill challenged the school board to equalize teachers' salaries. The maximum salary for a black teacher, even a principal, there, at that time, was one dollar less—substance is important; symbols are, too—than the lowest salary of any white teacher. The black teachers' proposal called for equalization within five years. When the school board rejected that plan in favor of one that would take ten to fifteen years to secure parity, Hill filed suit in U.S. district court. Settling out of court in February 1942, the school board accepted a plan similar to the one it had previously rejected. Other such developments unfolded elsewhere in Virginia.

The Struggle in the Late 1940s

Hill and his colleagues never regarded salary equalization as the final goal. A lull in their struggle occurred in the mid-1940s, however, when such black Virginia lawyers as Oliver Hill and Samuel Tucker were away in Europe or the Pacific fighting World War II. Activity resumed after they returned, and by the late 1940s real results could be seen. Hill found what might seem an unlikely ally in a white Southside judge: C. Sterling Hutcheson, who was born in 1894 on a farm in Mecklenburg County and became a federal district judge in 1944. In the years that followed, Judge Hutcheson was often in the news as a consequence of his involvement in cases regarding "separate but equal" public schools. In the late 1940s, his decisions directing that segregated schools be equalized in terms of teachers' pay and curricula included *Kelly v. School Board of Surry County* and *Ashley v. School Board of Gloucester County*, both in 1948.

A concerted effort by Hill and his colleagues in 1948 and 1949 made considerable progress in squeezing greater equality out of the old "separate but equal" formula. The prevailing image of the formula that litigation followed in the 1940s—from salary equalization to bus transportation to physical facilities (or simply from salaries to facilities)—supplies a convenient shorthand way of getting at the shift in objectives. But it oversimplifies the story. For example, equality in physical facilities might be achieved, as Hill later mused, "brick for brick," but what about the schools' curricula? Such questions as this loomed large in the late 1940s. Hill had eventual desegregation in mind, but "right now," he said, "we want the brick for brick." He also wanted bus for bus, dollar for dollar, and, at the high school level, class for class.

The new wave of litigation struck pay dirt in federal district court. There, Judge Hutcheson ratcheted up the level of equality of segregated schooling that would be required in Virginia. In March 1948, Hutcheson determined that the school board in Surry County was discriminating in teachers' salaries, bus transportation, and physical facilities. Moreover, black children there were being denied an accredited high school and an equal curriculum. The judge demanded that Surry County school officials demonstrate progress in narrowing the substantial disparities between the opportunities of black and white children to obtain high school educations.

The *Surry* decision proved as important in the postwar surge as the *Alston* decision had been in the earlier effort. It supplied a precedent to build on and to take to other school boards, and it energized teachers and other black Virginians to take action to redress ancient inequities. The next month, Hill and his partners gained another victory in Judge Hutcheson's district court, in a decision governing cases from Chesterfield, King George, and Gloucester counties. At one point the judge found the Gloucester County authorities in contempt of court, leading the *Richmond Times-Dispatch* to editorialize that the jails might soon be clogged, "because it is well understood that nowhere in Virginia are colored school facilities quite up to the standards of the white schools, nor could the situation be swiftly remedied." Things did not always work out the way anyone wanted. When directed to equalize the local white high school and black "training school," King George County's school board at first complied by dropping chemistry, physics, biology, and geometry at the white school.

Harry Truman, Segregation, and Virginia

The year 1948 was a watershed in state and national politics. In sharp contrast with the era of Reconstruction, now the Democratic Party was clearly becoming the party of civil rights. Early in the year, President Truman, soon to be a candidate for reelection, made civil rights a centerpiece of his State of the Union message, followed shortly by a civil rights message. Then, in July, days after gaining his party's nomination to run again, Truman issued an executive order to desegregate the armed forces. Moreover, he directed the Justice Department to side with the plaintiffs in litigation before the Supreme Court on black exclusion from southern public institutions of higher education.

As in 1860, the Democratic Party divided over racial policy—in 1860 on slavery; in 1948, segregation—and, under the Dixiecrat banner, Strom Thurmond challenged the incumbent. Truman nonetheless gained reelection, and he won in Virginia, but with far fewer votes there than FDR had attracted four years earlier. Virginia voters who supported Thurmond instead of Truman moved four years later into the ranks of the Republican candidate, Dwight D. Eisenhower, who—with Virginia's support—won the presidency in 1952 and again in 1956.

Higher Education—Gregory Swanson and Irving Peddrew

While efforts were under way to achieve progress in elementary and high schools, higher education was another important venue in the contest over equal opportunity and segregated schools. Across the Deep South, the Upper South, and the Border South, seventeen states entered the twentieth century with dual systems of higher education. Through World War II, little if anything had weakened the barriers of racial segregation anywhere in the South. Virginia can stand as a case study in the erosion of those barriers.

Virginia entered the 1950s with one public institution of higher education for black residents and eight for white undergraduates. No white student could attend Virginia State, nor could any African American attend any of the white schools. None had, and none would—until federal policy changed across the land and intervened in Virginia. In 1950, federal policy did change and did intervene. The biggest switch came with a June 1950 U.S. Supreme Court decision, *Sweatt v. Painter*, invalidating an effort to exclude an otherwise-qualified black applicant from the law school at the University of Texas. That summer, Gregory Swanson, a black Virginian with a 1949 law degree from Howard University, applied to do graduate work at the University of Virginia law school. The university resisted, but, in view of *Sweatt v. Painter*, a federal district court directed that Swanson be admitted, and—125 years after the school opened its doors in 1825—a historically white public school in Virginia had its first black student. Events surrounding the admittance of Swanson jolted Sarah Patton Boyle, the wife of a faculty member, into becoming a rarity in 1950s Virginia, an activist white liberal on racial matters.

In view of the court decision in Swanson's case, the university also began admitting a few other black students in law, as well as an occasional black applicant to study medicine. In addition, given that Virginia State had developed master's programs but no doctoral programs in education, UVA admitted Walter Nathaniel Ridley into a doctoral program. Swanson did not complete his degree, but Ridley did. A member of the faculty at Virginia State who had earned a master's degree at Howard University under the out-of-state scholarship program, in 1953 Ridley completed a doctoral degree. So did another black doctoral candidate, Louise S. Hunter, the wife of Virginia State College dean J. M. Hunter.

Higher education in Virginia moved slowly toward desegregation after 1950. At the College of William and Mary, Edward Travis entered the law school in 1951 and graduated in 1954, William and Mary's first black alumnus. Throughout the 1950s, however, both the University of Virginia and the College of William and Mary continued to turn away black applicants to programs that were offered at Virginia State College. At the same time, additional black applicants from Virginia to professional or graduate programs unavailable at Virginia State—law school, for example, or engineering—sometimes gained admission at historically white schools in Virginia. That was true of the eight black undergraduates who entered Virginia Polytechnic Institute in the 1950s, beginning with Irving L. Peddrew in electrical engineering in 1953. As a high school senior at a black high school in Newport News, Peddrew had applied to white schools in Virginia as well as black ones. Virginia Military Institute urged him to go out of state to Howard University, but VPI admitted him to classes—although it required him to live off campus.

In 1954, three graduates of Booker T. Washington High School in Norfolk—Floyd Wilson, Matthew Winston, and Charlie Yates—also enrolled in engineering, and also roomed off campus, with Peddrew. Yates, who earned a bachelor's degree, with honors, in mechanical engineering in 1958, became the first black undergraduate to obtain a degree at any historically white public institution in Virginia, or for that matter at any historically white land-grant school across the former Confederacy, just as Peddrew had been the first to gain admission. Meanwhile, Essex Finney transferred in 1956 from one Virginia land-grant school to another, from the black one to the white one, so he could graduate in agricultural engineering, a program not offered at Virginia State College.

The University of Virginia accepted three black undergraduates in 1955. As at VPI, they had to be seeking degrees in engineering. One of them, Robert Bland, graduated in 1959—from an institution that, like VPI, had not yet moved beyond the point VPI had reached in 1953, still operating under "separate but equal" but willing on that basis to accept an occasional African American.

Black and Nonblack in the Age of Segregation

Jim Crow governed life in the segregated South in mysterious ways. Schools from the first half of the twentieth century have long been characterized as either "black" or "white," in fact often "all-white"—by people at the time and by scholars ever since. Could schools be anything else than all white during the age of Jim Crow, when black students were categorically excluded? Yes. Virginia Military Institute enrolled its first Chinese student in 1904—at the very time disfranchisement was pushing black voters away from ballot boxes and segregation was pushing black passengers out of "white" streetcars—and scores of Chinese cadets followed before the first black student enrolled at VMI in 1968. More than one Chinese cadet switched to nearby Washington and Lee University, which was private and civilian. Nor were colleges in VMI's hometown, Lexington, unusual in taking Chinese but not black students.

In the 1920s, students of Asian ancestry took degrees at the University of Virginia, Virginia Polytechnic Institute, and the College of William and Mary. At VPI, for example, Cato Lee, whose hometown was Hong Kong, graduated in mechanical engineering in 1927, having lived on campus and played on the varsity tennis and track teams. At William and Mary, Art Matsu—his mother Scottish and his father Japanese—quarterbacked the varsity football team from 1923 through 1926. Two sisters from China, Shiran and Rohran Tung, earned degrees at VPI at midcentury. Hung-Yu Loh, another native of China, not only earned a master's degree at VPI in 1943 but also, after completing his Ph.D. at Johns Hopkins in 1946, returned to VPI as a physics professor, and his children, one after another, graduated from VPI across the 1950s. For purposes of higher education in Virginia, Cato Lee and Art Matsu were evidently white, although during their time as students in Virginia, a new state law in 1924 declared them to be subject to imprisonment if they married a white classmate.

Two Glimpses of Desegregated Baseball in Virginia in 1951

In 1951, as Virginia's portion of the *Brown v. Board of Education* litigation got under way, in two places the baseball diamond seemed to point toward a possible end to segregation in the Old Dominion.

On June 4, in the inaugural game of the Norton Little League in the small southwest Virginia town of Norton, two African American boys, Johnny Blair and Robert Strong, played alongside white boys. Under Virginia law, they attended different schools, but on the diamond that summer they played together. As former Norton Little Leaguer Lann A. Malesky has recounted, the founder of Norton's Little League—a young optometrist named Charles Litton—made the decision, together with four fellow white military veterans, to integrate the league by placing one black player on each of the four teams, and local civic and political leaders as well as the players' parents permitted integrated baseball to continue in this fashion without a hitch throughout the summer.

The integrated approach created controversy elsewhere, however. Drawn from the town's four teams, Norton's all-star team featured Johnny Blair and another African American boy, Harold Mitchell. At the state tournament, the team was barred from playing on the segregated fields of Charlottesville. National Little League said the Norton team must play, but the four all-white teams balked. Resolution came when officials determined that the winner of the Charlottesville tournament would be named Eastern Virginia Regional Champion and would face off against the Norton team in Norton, with the winner of that game being named Virginia's state champion. The Charlottesville team won the tournament it hosted, so it went to Norton for the championship game on August 4 against the integrated Norton squad, which started Blair at first base. In front of a crowd of 1,500, the small-town boys pulled off a 12–3 victory, thus securing the Virginia Little League state championship. The picture on the front page of the next week's edition of Norton's local paper, the *Coalfield Progress*, showed pitcher Robert Lively, the star of the game, celebrating the win on the shoulders of his teammates, with a smiling Johnny Blair right out in front.

That same summer, on August 10, nineteen-year-old Percy Miller made his debut for the Danville Leafs, the first African American ever to play in the Carolina League. The team's decision to sign Miller was made not for the sake of equality but, rather, for economic reasons, as club owners hoped the move would boost the Leafs' sagging attendance. Initially it did, as Miller's debut featured a near-capacity crowd of 1,763 fans at Danville's League Park, one-third of them in the "colored grandstand." And when Miller slapped out a two-run single, he was enthusiastically cheered.

Within weeks of that fairy-tale start to his season, however, Miller faced jeers and taunts from Carolina League crowds. Whether because of the taunts he faced or his own lack of experience, Miller spent the rest of the season mired in a slump, and after the season the Leafs released him. Percy Miller's brief stint with the Leafs during summer 1951 paved the way for many other black players to play for the team in subsequent seasons, including future Major League stars Bill White and Willie McCovey. The significance of Miller's brief tenure with the Leafs was recognized in 1997, when he threw out the ceremonial first pitch in a Carolina League all-star game in Durham, North Carolina. Instead of taunts, that night Percy Miller heard enthusiastic applause.

. . . In each of the cases, minors of the Negro race, through their legal representatives, seek the aid of the courts in obtaining admission to the public schools of their community on a nonsegregated basis. . . .

. . . In the South [in the 1860s], the movement toward free common schools, supported by general taxation, had not yet taken hold. Education of white children was largely in the hands of private groups. Education of Negroes was almost nonexistent, and practically all of the race were illiterate. In fact, any education of Negroes was forbidden by law in some states. . . . As a consequence, it is not surprising that there should be so little in the history of the Fourteenth Amendment relating to its intended effect on public education.

In the first cases in this Court construing the Fourteenth Amendment, decided shortly after its adoption, the Court interpreted it as proscribing all state-imposed discriminations against the Negro race. The doctrine of "separate but equal" did not make its appearance in this Court until 1896 in the case of *Plessy v. Ferguson* . . . involving not education but transportation. . . .

In approaching this problem, we cannot turn the clock back to 1868 when the Amendment was adopted, or even to 1896 when *Plessy v. Ferguson* was written. We must

A Storm out of Prince Edward County— Barbara Johns and Oliver Hill

As the 1950s began, such civil rights lawyers as Oliver Hill and Samuel Tucker continued to pursue the kind of public school litigation that had taken so much of their energy in the late 1940s. Just weeks after the Supreme Court handed down its decision in *Sweatt v. Painter,* however, the national NAACP made a strategic decision to mount a direct attack against segregated public schooling, and in October 1950 the Virginia State Conference of the NAACP agreed to that policy. It had become time to gamble, to challenge the "separate" rather than to only insist on the "equal" in "separate but equal."

That was the situation in April 1951, when Barbara Johns, together with her classmates in the town of Farmville in Prince Edward County, went on strike against the poor physical facilities at Robert R. Moton High School. Located in Virginia's Southside, in the middle of Virginia's "black belt"—the region with historically high proportions, even majorities, of black residents— Prince Edward County had an unusually high rate of black landownership, so black residents were somewhat less vulnerable there than in most other black-belt counties to white economic retaliation for any expression of dissent against Jim Crow. Prince Edward featured a recent development in the world of "separate but equal," as black protest against being excluded from Virginia's state parks had led to the opening the year before of Prince Edward State Park for Negroes, offered as an equivalent to the nearby white park at Goodwin Lake. Among the black leaders in Prince Edward was Rev. L. Francis Griffin, a combat veteran of World War II, minister of Farmville's First Baptist Church, and leader of the local branch of the

NAACP. Moreover, one of Barbara Johns's uncles, Rev. Vernon Johns, was an outspoken leader who, having grown up in rural Prince Edward County, preceded Rev. Martin Luther King Jr. at Dexter Avenue Baptist Church in Montgomery, Alabama.

Johns and her striking classmates contacted attorneys Oliver Hill and Spottswood Robinson in Richmond to request their support. Hill and Robinson, who would soon have to pass through the town anyway on their way to looking after another school case farther west, promised to stop by at Farmville. There, however, they advised the black community that they would take the case only if, instead of merely seeking improved facilities of the sort that white schoolchildren in that county enjoyed, they contested the segregation itself. Agreement was reached.

The trial of *Davis v. County School Board of Prince Edward County* took place in federal district court in February 1952. The court found the physical facilities unequal at Moton High School and found the busing opportunities and curricular offerings unequal as well. But those could be fixed, and the fixes seemed to be under way. The court found no reason to overturn school segregation in Virginia. "Separate" remained constitutionally permissible, and "equal"—though not yet in place—was promised by local authorities in the near future. The Virginia case, together with cases from Delaware, South Carolina, and Kansas, went to the U.S. Supreme Court.

The U.S. Supreme Court Announces a Decision

On May 17, 1954, the Supreme Court handed down its decision, that public school segregation was unconstitutional. According to *Brown v. Board of Education,* the case from Kansas, segre-

consider public education in the light of its full development and its present place in American life throughout the Nation. Only in this way can it be determined if segregation in public schools deprives these plaintiffs of the equal protection of the laws.

Today, education is perhaps the most important function of state and local governments. Compulsory school attendance laws and the great expenditures for education both demonstrate our recognition of the importance of education to our democratic society. It is required in the performance of our most basic public responsibilities, even service in the armed forces. It is the very foundation of good citizenship. Today it is a principal instrument in awakening the child to cultural values, in preparing him for later professional training, and in helping him to adjust normally to his environment. In these days, it is doubtful that any child may reasonably be expected to succeed in life if he is denied the opportunity of an education. Such an opportunity, where the state has undertaken to provide it, is a right which must be made available to all on equal terms.

We come then to the question presented: Does segregation of children in public schools solely on the basis of race, even though the physical facilities and other "tangible" factors may be equal, deprive the children of the minority group of equal educational opportunities? We believe that it does.

. . . In *McLaurin v. Oklahoma State Regents*, the Court, in requiring that a Negro admitted to a white graduate school be treated like all other students, again resorted to intangible considerations: ". . . his ability to study, to engage in discussions and exchange views with other students, and, in general, to learn his profession." Such considerations apply with added force to children in grade and high schools. To separate them from others of similar age and qualifications solely because of their race generates a feeling of inferiority as to their status in the community that may affect their hearts and minds in a way unlikely ever to be undone. . . .

We conclude that in the field of public education the doctrine of "separate but equal" has no place. Separate educational facilities are inherently unequal. Therefore, we hold that the plaintiffs and others similarly situated . . . are, by reason of the segregation complained of, deprived of the equal protection of the laws guaranteed by the Fourteenth Amendment. . . .

gated public schools could not meet the standard that the Court's interpretation of the Fourteenth Amendment's equal protection clause had come to demand (see sidebar, page 342).

The decision in *Brown* was unanimous, as Chief Justice Earl Warren had worked hard to reach a consensus, for it seemed essential that the Court put up a united front in its call for the desegregation of the public schools. How would Prince Edward County respond? How, more generally, would the state of Virginia?

Aline Black and Melvin Alston after Their Pioneering Litigation

We began this chapter with Norfolk teachers Aline Black and Melvin Alston, and we end with them. Both of them entered their litigation over black teachers' salaries with an indemnity, a promise that they would receive a year's salary if either lost their job as a consequence of their bringing suit against the city. Moreover, a state fund—generated to avert desegregation of graduate programs, after Alice Jackson applied in 1935 to the University of Virginia—could help with expenses at an out-of-state school. When Black lost her job in 1939, the joint committee of the VTA and the NAACP paid her salary for the school year, and she went to New York City, taught school there, and took classes toward a doctorate at New York University.

In 1941, after two years away and no longer a litigant—by that time, Alston had won his case in the federal courts—Black returned to teaching in Norfolk. As she later explained: "I felt I owed something to the people who had fought [alongside] me and who felt that the victory would be complete if I came back." She married Frank A.

Hicks, though the marriage lasted only a few years, and she adopted a daughter, Nina, a niece.

Working mostly during the summers, in the 1940s Alston also pursued graduate study in New York City. At Columbia University, he earned an M.S. in mathematics education in 1942 and an Ed.D. in the same field in 1945. During 1945–1946 Alston was perhaps the only teacher in the Virginia public schools, black or white, with a doctoral degree. In 1946, with doctorate in hand but a salary still too low to support his growing family, Alston left the scene of his courtroom triumph and took a position at Florida Agricultural and Mechanical College, where Florida was trying to upgrade its black land-grant school to avert any desegregation at the University of Florida.

Meanwhile, through the years leading up to *Brown v. Board of Education* and well after the beginnings of desegregation in Norfolk, Aline B. Hicks continued teaching at Booker T. Washington High School, until in 1971 she became a reading specialist at Jacox Junior High School, where a former pupil of hers and Alston's, Charles Corprew, had become principal. In 1971 she also received the Backbone Award from the Education Association of Norfolk. After nearly half a century of teaching, she retired in 1973. She was honored as the teacher who pioneered the challenge to seize the "equal" in "separate but equal" public schools in the South—so much so that people in the African American community in Norfolk often credit her with the victory that actually came in the *Alston* case.

Chapter 23

Massive Resistance to School Desegregation

....

Senator Harry F. Byrd Sr. and his Byrd Organization, the leaders of Virginia politics, were taken by surprise when the Supreme Court announced its ruling in *Brown v. Board of Education* on May 17, 1954. No plans to oppose the Supreme Court were in place before the *Brown* decision came down. Nor did the fight to preserve segregation in the face of *Brown* begin immediately. Rather, the day was surprisingly quiet as, across the state, Virginians heard the news that the Supreme Court had declared segregated schools to be constitutionally dead.

Governor Thomas B. Stanley's initial pronouncements were guarded. In public, he called for "cool heads, calm study, and sound judgment." As he wrote Senator Byrd, he hoped a solution could be worked out that "would be acceptable to our people" without appearing either "surrendering" or "blustering." Other statements from white Virginians, especially from the Southside, were less measured. Letters to the governor from anxious constituents included one from a Southside woman who reported that her PTA—if it had to choose, and could choose—definitely preferred "the end of public education, rather than unsegregated schools."

Southside whites organized quickly. On June 19, in a Petersburg firehouse, Byrd Organization leaders—among them state legislators Garland Gray and Mills E. Godwin Jr.—organized around one core idea, what they called their "unalterable opposition to the principle of integration of the races in the schools." Days later, a delegation met with Governor Stanley, whose early apparent moderation had evaporated; he promised to "use every legal means at my command to continue segregated schools in Virginia." In August he appointed a commission, comprised solely of legislators, a disproportionate number of them from the Southside, whose task was to produce a "workable plan" to address what they saw as the threat of school desegregation. The group elected Garland Gray their chair, and the Gray Commission went about its work. Months passed. In May 1955 the Supreme Court issued a follow-up ruling, offering guidelines for implementing the 1954 decision. This ruling is often referred to as *Brown II* to distinguish it from the original ruling, *Brown I*, of the year before. In *Brown II*, the Court ordered that school desegregation be carried out with "all deliberate speed," and Byrd remarked: "The emphasis should be on 'deliberate' rather than on speed."

At last, on November 12, 1955, the Gray Commission issued its report. The Gray Plan sought to minimize, if it could not entirely prevent, school desegregation. Under a proposed new pupil-placement law, local authorities could assign students to schools in ways that would minimize change. The compulsory-education law should be amended so that parents could keep their children out of any desegregated school. If a school was either closed or integrated, state tuition grants might fund students' attendance at segregated private schools. This last measure would require an amendment to the state constitution, and Governor Stanley called a special legislative session to begin the process, which required approving a referendum on a constitutional convention to initiate such an amendment.

According to the so-called local option of the Gray Plan, localities would decide whether any desegregation would occur, and most, perhaps all, localities would no doubt have placed few if any black children in schools with whites. The approach had widespread support—probably a majority of white citizens were more or less comfortable with it. Many black Virginians, it is true, viewed it as a sham, designed to forestall meaningful change, if any change occurred at all. Some moderate spokesmen expressed concern that a move to private schools would damage the public schools. But even if the more adamant segregationists—in particular, Garland Gray and Mills Godwin—had signed off on the plan as commission members, they rejected its apparent concession that desegregation might occur at all anywhere. And in late November, soon after the report was issued, *Richmond News Leader* editor James J. Kilpatrick published a series of editorials offering a rationale for uncompromising resistance to the Supreme Court. Working from the premise that states have a right under the Tenth Amendment to intervene when their citizens are the victims of unconstitutional actions by the federal government, Kilpatrick set out to provide an intellectually respectable cover he called "interposition," a term dating back to the Virginia Resolution that Madison had authored in 1798 to defend the "rights" of "the states" against federal usurpation. Writing to Kilpatrick about the editorial

THE SOUTHERN MANIFESTO, MARCH 1956

We regard the decision of the Supreme Court in the school cases as clear abuse of judicial power. . . .

In the case of *Plessy v. Ferguson* in 1896 the Supreme Court expressly declared that under the Fourteenth Amendment no person was denied any of his rights if the states provided separate but equal public facilities. . . .

Though there has been no constitutional amendment or act of Congress changing this established legal principle almost a century old, the Supreme Court of the United States, with no legal basis for such action, undertook to exercise their naked power and substituted their personal political and social ideas for the established law of the land.

This unwarranted exercise of power by the court, contrary to the Constitution, is creating chaos and confusion in the states principally affected. It is destroying the amicable relations between the white and Negro races that have been created through ninety years of patient effort by the good people of both races. . . .

. . . If done, this is certain to destroy the system of public education in some of the states. . . .

We decry the Supreme Court's encroachments on rights reserved to the states. . . .

We commend the motives of those states which have declared the intention to resist forced integration by any lawful means. . . .

"Interposition Now," Senator Byrd said that it was "beautifully written" and added: "I wish we had gotten started on this sooner."

The legislature met in early December and called for a referendum the next month, on January 9, 1956. By a two-to-one margin, Virginia voters approved the convention. What followed can best be understood as a bait-and-switch tactic. Voters, whatever their own positions, had ample reason to understand the Gray Plan as leaving each locality in a position to decide on desegregation. The favorable vote on the single issue of tuition grants was generally taken, however, as approval of the entire Gray Plan; Byrd and his followers chose to see the willingness of so many Virginians to support the Gray Plan as a mandate to charge down a path that allowed for no local option, no compromise, and no desegregation whatever. In February, the General Assembly passed a resolution of nullification, or interposition, and Harry Byrd spoke of "passive resistance" and then, a few days later, of "massive resistance."

In the nation's capital, on March 12, 1956, under the leadership of U.S. Senators Strom Thurmond of South Carolina and Harry Byrd of Virginia, most members of Congress from the eleven states of the former Confederacy issued a "Southern Manifesto" in support of a movement that came to be called Massive Resistance (see sidebar). Like the Court's justices in *Brown*, the decision's opponents sought common ground with each other, so as to present a united front. The manifesto said, in part: "We commend the motives of those states which have declared the intention to resist forced integration by any lawful means." Those signing it included all ten of Virginia's congressmen as well as both its senators.

Soon, the Byrd Organization began to work up a program. Mills Godwin wrote Byrd in June 1956:

"I am convinced we should not pass any State law which would permit integration even in those localities where some may desire it." The next month, seven Southside members of the Gray Commission, the "Southside Seven," met with the senator—as well as with Congressmen Howard W. Smith, Bill Tuck, and Watkins Abbitt—in the conference room of Congressman Smith's House Rules Committee. In an exchange of letters soon afterward, Godwin said he "left the meeting believing we can find a way to prevent integration in Virginia," and Byrd responded: "I believe if the Southern States stand firm in massive resistance, we will win out." In August, the General Assembly met in special session to consider what was termed the "Stanley Plan"—a far cry from the Gray Plan. Tuition grants to private schools were one part of the new plan, as in the old one, but otherwise control of the process would shift to the state. No state funds would be available to any locality that permitted even one of its schools to desegregate, and in fact the governor would close any school a court ordered desegregated. Efforts to retain local option went down to defeat, 59–39 in the House of Delegates, 21–17 in the Senate. The Stanley Plan became law, and in 1958, at the next legislative session, the plan was further embellished. Massive Resistance was in place. Years had passed since *Brown I* or *Brown II,* and at no public elementary or high school in the state were black and white students attending together.

Leaders of the Byrd Organization frequently harked back to the era of Civil War and Reconstruction to situate what they saw as the crisis presented by the Supreme Court's rulings in *Brown v. Board of Education.* Byrd spoke of the "worst blow since Reconstruction," in fact "the greatest internal crisis since the War Between the States." Running for reelection to the Senate in 1958, Byrd

We pledge ourselves to use all lawful means to bring about a reversal of this decision which is contrary to the Constitution and to prevent the use of force in its implementation. . . .

David John Mays (1896–1971), prominent lawyer, law professor, and historian. Mays won the 1953 Pulitzer Prize for his 1952 two-volume biography of Revolutionary-era Virginia jurist Edmund Pendleton (1721–1803). Mays's interpretation of the U.S. Constitution emphasized the Tenth Amendment, not the Supreme Court's emerging understanding of the Fourteenth. During the years that followed *Brown v. Board of Education,* Mays put his legal talents to the defense of states' rights and racial segregation. He declined an invitation to serve on the Gray Commission, but he served as its counsel. As he wrote in his diary in May 1955 about the Massive Resisters, "the leaders know of no solution which will retain both the public school system and segregation." Mays shunned bluster, and he saw the ultimate futility of state legislation to forestall any and all school desegregation, yet he hoped other means of resistance would prove effective in curtailing change. When the General Assembly in March 1958 established the Virginia Commission on Constitutional Government (CCG) to function as a propaganda machine in support of segregation, Mays accepted the invitation to head it up. His diary makes frequent reference to "my CCG." The Virginia CCG, by the time it was disbanded in 1969, had distributed more than two million pamphlets and books, not only across the South but throughout the nation. One pamphlet—*Civil Rights and Federal Power,* which targeted what became the Civil Rights Act of 1964—had a cover depicting the Constitution being squeezed in a vise, and Senator Harry F. Byrd read the entire contents into the *Congressional Record* during his unsuccessful March 1964 filibuster against the bill. Virginia Historical Society, Richmond, Virginia.

wrote supporters that it was "undoubtedly the most important election we have had in Virginia since the days of Reconstruction." A Virginia legislator remembered Byrd's referring to "General Lee's long fight for his homeland in the face of clearly overwhelming odds." Supporters of Massive Resistance brandished Confederate battle flags. There were crucial differences, to be sure, between the 1860s and the 1950s—Byrd spoke of Virginians' "right to defy the Supreme Court" as long as they did so "without violence" and as long as they did not "try to overthrow the government."

As of May 1958—three years after *Brown II*, four years after *Brown I*—nothing had changed on the desegregation front. Perhaps nothing had been happening? But of course the resisters had been scrambling, month after month, to find a way to deflect any implementation of *Brown*. Resisting the resisters, meanwhile, were black parents and black lawyers. Civil rights lawyer Oliver Hill, for one, later reflected that he found himself in as many courts, after *Brown*, seeking to get schools desegregated as he had been in, before *Brown*, seeking to get schools in one way or another equalized. The task was doubly difficult in that, as a companion piece in the Massive Resistance laws, new legislation tried to make it impossible for the NAACP to go about its work.

But as with "General Lee's long fight," events proved that a successful struggle against any school desegregation at all could be maintained for only so long. Black parents in the city of Charlottesville, in the city of Norfolk, and elsewhere went into federal court to seek implementation of *Brown*. When a federal court directed that schools in each of those cities be desegregated, Governor Stanley closed them. Some months later, on January 19, 1959—the 152nd anniversary of Lee's birthday—those who had resisted the resisters won in both state court and federal court. Simultaneous rulings by Virginia's highest court and a federal district court threw out the legislative underpinnings of Massive Resistance. The federal court ruled that Massive Resistance violated the Fourteenth Amendment. The Virginia Supreme Court ruled that the school-closing plan violated Section 129 of the Virginia constitution, which committed the state to maintaining a system of public schools.

White Virginians: Better to Desegregate the Schools or to Close Them?

The resisters still had a way out, it seemed. Shut all the schools. Change the state constitution, drop the requirement about maintaining a system of public schools, and just abandon public education. Governor Lindsay Almond said as much when he called yet another special session of the legislature in early 1959.

The governor later remembered, however, how he had changed his mind, or at least his public stance, and what he had told a very unhappy Senator Byrd: "I said that the only way to prevent integration was to close down every public school in Virginia, and that I could not do." Facing the legislature, Almond announced that Massive Resistance was dead. With the legislature still in session, court-ordered school desegregation took place in Arlington and Norfolk, as black children began taking classes in white schools. For an ever-growing number of white Virginians, the main question had changed. Rather than "Should schools remain segregated?" the question became "Should schools remain open?"

The Perrow Commission, headed by a state senator, Mosby Perrow, had the task of coming up with a new set of proposals. Those proposals, no surprise, contrived new means to curtail desegregation, but they conceded some change. They looked, indeed, remarkably like the Gray Plan. In April 1959, the legislature considered the latest plan. By the narrowest of margins, legislators voted in favor of keeping public schools open, even if with some desegregation, rather than clos-ing them down to prevent any desegregation. The Virginia Senate approved the new approach, 20–19. The House of Delegates followed suit, by a vote of 53–45 rejecting a proposal to strip Section 129 from the constitution. The public school system had survived. Schools in places like Norfolk could reopen and stay open, on a formally desegregated basis, without jeopardizing the receipt of state funds. Some black students, in one locality or another, would attend classes with white students. Andrew Heidelberg, one of the "Norfolk 17," enrolled in February 1959 at that city's Norview High School, though he was terrified facing the enormous white throng awaiting him and a black friend, as they came up to the school the first day: "There was more white people there than I had ever seen in my life. In my life!" he recalled. "I didn't know if they were going to lynch us or what."

That summer, in primary elections to pick the Democratic nominees for the 1959 legislative elections, many districts featured Almond candidates versus Byrd candidates. Stripped to its core, the question remained, as it had been in April: "Schools or segregation?" With the results so very close in April, the entire issue seemed up for grabs as voters headed to the polls. The election results that summer left matters unchanged. The Almond faction would retain control of the legislature. Massive Resistance was as dead in the legislature as it was in the courts. Harry Byrd nonetheless professed himself a true believer: "I stand now as I stood when I first urged massive resistance." But the state was beginning to edge away from him. During the 1960s, as the electorate changed, and the scheme of legislative apportionment did, too, the state would move substantially away from where it had stood for a few years of crisis in the 1950s. Yet both before and after 1959, Massive Resistance shaped countless Virginians' lives.

Patsy Cline (1932–1963), country singer. Virginia Patterson Hensley was born in Winchester, Virginia, during the Great Depression. Like all Virginians of her generation, she attended segregated schools—whether in the Winchester area, elsewhere in western Virginia, or during World War II near Norfolk when her father worked in a shipyard there. When he deserted the family, she dropped out of Winchester's Hadley High School as a sophomore during the 1947–1948 school year to help support her mother and younger siblings; even a decade later Virginia's schools remained completely segregated. Meanwhile, originally "Ginny," she took the name "Patsy," and the name "Patsy Cline" reflected her first marriage, in 1953 to Gerald Cline. She burst on the national scene in 1957 when she sang "Walkin' after Midnight" on the television show *Arthur Godfrey's Talent Scouts*. Subsequent hits included "I Fall to Pieces" (a number-1 country hit in 1961), "Crazy" (number 2 that same year), and "She's Got You" (a number-1 country hit in 1962). Patsy Cline toured with Johnny Cash during the last year of her short life; she died in a plane crash in Tennessee in 1963. Her fame as a country music star lived on, and in 1993 a U.S. postage stamp, based on a painting by Richard Waldrep, commemorated her. Estate of Patsy Cline. Patsy Cline © 1993 United State Postal Service. All rights reserved. Used with permission.

In Warren County, in the Shenandoah Valley, Betty Ann Kilby was nine years old when the *Brown* decision was handed down. Her two older siblings were ten-year-old John and twelve-year-old James. All were in elementary school, and they continued to attend a black school near their home in western Virginia through the seventh grade. When each graduated from the elementary school, Warren County still had only one high school, and black students could not enroll there. Under Virginia's Massive Resistance legislation, any school that desegregated would be immediately shut down. In accordance with a companion law, Betty's father, James Wilson Kilby, signed a "pupil placement" form in 1956 as James was finishing the seventh grade, so young James could attend the all-black Manassas Regional High School (the only option made available on the form), located sixty miles away in Prince William County, a distance that meant that James had to board there and could return home only on weekends.

The following year, John also finished seventh grade, and Mr. Kilby insisted that the Johnson-Williams School in Berryville, thirty miles away, be made an option on the pupil placement form. The days would be long, but his children would return home each night. So the two boys began attending school in Berryville, and Betty figured she would begin attending that school with her brothers in 1958. That did not happen.

In spring 1958, thirteen-year-old Betty Kilby brought her pupil placement form home for her father to sign. He scratched out the only options listed, the schools at Manassas and Berryville, and wrote in "Warren County High School." Her teacher rejected the form filled out in that fashion, she rejected Mr. Kilby's second version with the same content, and someone from the school board phoned him at home after he did the same thing a third time. Years later, in her book *Wit, Will and Walls*, Betty recalled the exasperated words he spoke into the phone that evening in May 1958:

> This is Kilby, yes I did. Your form asked where I wanted to send Betty to high school. Well in 1956 I sent my son James to Manassas to the boarding school. Sixty miles away was too far even if it is only a weekly commute, and besides, James was too young to be away from home.... In 1957, I sent James and John to Berryville. Berryville was a 60 miles a day trip with the school bus picking my sons up at 6 AM and sometimes they didn't return until 7 or 7:30 PM. My boys had to walk half a mile to meet the "colored bus," while the bus carrying white kids drove past my boys walking.... I wasn't satisfied with that option

either. . . . I will not subject my kids to this kind of environment any more. You have the form. I wrote in my option of Warren County High School.

Later that evening, she heard him tell her mother, "Catherine, get ready for a fight because Betty ain't going to Manassas or Berryville, she is going to Warren County High School."

On behalf of his daughter Betty, so she could go to high school in her home county, Mr. Kilby went to court. Much of the summer was taken up with action in federal district court in nearby Harrisonburg. As white residents of the county began to ponder the possibilities, one woman mused: "I am in favor of separate schools but the main concern now is to keep the schools open." The high school senior class president observed of his schoolmates that, left to their own devices, "I believe that most of us would integrate rather than see the school closed." He continued: "We believe we could ignore" any black classmates "and go on as we always have."

On that score, neither the high school students nor the white woman had any more say than did the Kilby family. If the federal court ordered desegregation of Warren County High School, the governor would follow the legislature's mandate and close the school. Indeed, a desegregation order came down, and it led directly to the school's closing during fall 1958. White students rushed to make alternative arrangements, as did the black children. Court action continued.

In January 1959, as we have seen, the courts ruled against such closures; and U.S. district judge John Paul ordered on February 10 that Warren County High School be reopened in eight days, this time on a desegregated basis. The school was reopened, and its first black students enrolled. All through that winter and spring, the black students took classes there, but they were alone, as white students stayed with the arrangements they had made the previous fall. Terror outside the school began to contrast with serene times inside, and Betty later explained, "I felt safer in this building than I felt at home with the gunshots constantly being fired at the house, crosses burned in the yard, bloody sheet on the mailbox, the farm animals mutilated and the constant threatening phone calls."

But when classes resumed in fall 1959, Betty said about herself and the small number of her fellow black students: "It was time to put on our armor and become little soldiers." The white students had returned to the high school, and "I was the only Negro in most of my classes," Betty said. "We knew that it was not safe to walk the halls alone."

Judge Sterling Hutcheson and Prince Edward County

In the late 1940s, Judge C. Sterling Hutcheson often sided with Oliver W. Hill and other black NAACP lawyers when they insisted that segregated schools be equalized in terms of teachers' pay and high school curricula. But desegregation was another matter. In the school desegregation case that came out of Prince Edward County, Hutcheson was one of the three judges who ruled against the plaintiffs in 1952—a decision that the U.S. Supreme Court overturned in *Brown v. Board of Education*. As for implementing the *Brown* decision, in 1958 Judge Hutcheson ruled against efforts to open the white schools in Prince Edward to black students. When he declined to set a date when the schools must be desegregated, the Fourth Circuit Court of Appeals directed him to set a date. When he gave local authorities until 1965 to begin desegregating the schools, the Fourth Circuit Court of Appeals overruled him and directed that the schools be desegregated in September 1959.

Judge Hutcheson chose to retire when he could, at age sixty-five, in 1959. Time had passed him by. He had appeared in advance of white public opinion in the 1940s, but in the 1950s higher courts overruled him when he urged delay in school desegregation. Black lawyers like Oliver Hill remembered him as a judge who consistently supported segregation but just as insistently, within segregation, had mandated equalization. The judge had not changed. The nature of the questions before him had. He was prepared to accept what he saw as the full implications of *Plessy v. Ferguson* (1896). He regarded as impractical, and was unprepared to cooperate with, what he saw as precipitous efforts to implement that decision's reversal. As the *Richmond Times-Dispatch*, ever sympathetic to the positions Judge Hutcheson had taken in the 1950s, said in an editorial upon his announced retirement, "For an honorable, upright gentleman, such as he, resignation is preferable to following mandates from higher courts which are repugnant to his deeply-cherished beliefs."

The returns from 1959, in the courts and the legislature, revealed that Massive Resistance had been thrown out as a state policy. But a local version of it immediately emerged in Prince Edward County when, rather than desegregate as a federal court had finally ordered, the school board simply closed the public schools, and most white students moved into a new private academy, supported with public funds. A "lost generation" of black students, and a number of white students as well, had no schools to attend, or had to make other arrangements, bootlegging an education in a nearby county or boarding in a distant community.

Not until the U.S. Supreme Court's 1964 decision in *Griffin v. School Board of Prince Edward County* did the public schools there reopen. Now officially "desegregated," they did so with almost none but black students, although Richard Moss, son of Longwood College history professor C. G. Gordon Moss, also enrolled. The Prince Edward story continues to attract great attention, as it should, but in truth it reflected one county's actions, not an entire state's. Yet Massive Resistance at the state level affected far more people. White resistance, massive or otherwise, took a variety of forms.

"All Deliberate Speed"

That the implementation of *Brown v. Board of Education* might not come right away became clear, not only because the U.S. Supreme Court had used the phrase "all deliberate speed" in 1955, but also because so many white Virginians collectively put up such enormous resistance. Yet in 1959, simultaneous rulings by a federal court and the state supreme court had thrown out the policy of Massive Resistance, and some school desegregation had begun to occur, most notably in Norfolk and a few other cities.

Change continued, at what might appear to have been a glacial pace. New Kent County retained completely segregated schools all the way through the era of Massive Resistance, and then all the way through the time when Prince Edward County kept its public schools closed. Some limited change finally began when, using a "freedom of choice" approach, the county permitted students to petition to attend another school than the one to which they had been assigned on the basis of race. Small numbers of black students made it through the process and began attending a white school, though no white student attended a black school. When the county's student-assignment program was challenged, the U.S. District Court for the Eastern District of Virginia upheld it, and the Fourth Circuit Court of Appeals affirmed the district court ruling. The case—*Green v. County School Board of New Kent County*—then went to the U.S. Supreme Court. There, in 1968, the resisters lost. "The burden on a school board today," said the Court about the South in general and New Kent County in particular, "is to come forward with a plan that promises realistically to work, and promises realistically to work *now*."

Whether in 1959 or 1964 or 1969—or even later—more and more schools in Virginia made some degree of change from segregated schools, black or white, to integrated schools. A particularly notable instance came in fall 1970, when Governor Linwood Holton, in the first year of his term, escorted his thirteen-year-old daughter Tayloe to Richmond's John F. Kennedy High School for the new school year's first day of classes. His wife, Virginia ("Jinks"), meanwhile, took twelve-year-old Anne and eleven-year-old Woody to Mosby Middle School,

Governor Linwood Holton and his daughter Tayloe walking to the formerly all-black John F. Kennedy High School in Richmond on August 31, 1970, the new school year's first day of classes. In this gesture Holton, the first Republican to be elected governor of Virginia in 100 years, suggested how far Virginia politics had moved since Massive Resistance just a few years earlier. This photograph (courtesy the *New York Times*), by Lee Romero, also shows Major A. P. Tucker of the Capitol Police shadowing the governor and first daughter.

where each was the only white child in the classroom. The next year, the first year of widespread court-ordered busing to achieve desegregation in Richmond, sixth-grader Clara Silverstein took the school bus each day to Binford, a white girl in a black school. For the racial newcomers, black or white, the experience could be traumatic, though Anne Holton—in 2006 she returned to the governor's mansion as the wife of Tim Kaine—did not subsequently remember it that way. As for Governor Holton, years later he told historian Robert A. Pratt:

> Integration was morally right. No one could have had a better political opportunity than my family had that day to do something that was right, to show that it could be done without violence, and to show that people would support it because it was right. It was a thrill of a lifetime for me to have that opportunity.
>
> I wanted to make a plain demonstration that . . . this commonwealth was a law-abiding group and that we would comply with the orders of the courts. And I could see that picture of my daughter and me [entering Kennedy High

School] juxtaposed against the Ross Barnetts and the George Wallaces [of Mississippi and Alabama] saying, "you ain't a-comin." Makes me feel pretty good.

After "Desegregation"

The sustained crisis of the late 1950s had morphed into a chronic condition by the 1970s. The greatest political and judicial battles had been fought by 1964, when Prince Edward County was directed to reopen its public schools. Moreover, after Congress passed the Civil Rights Act in 1964, the promise of massive new Great Society federal aid to public education—especially under the Elementary and Secondary Education Act of 1965—carried a condition against racial segregation. State leaders moved on to other matters. All the while, beginning in 1959, change of one degree or another came to one community after another. The resisters of the 1950s found they could not prevent forever the desegregation of the Virginia public schools. Yet they managed to postpone the beginnings of change, and they succeeded in ensuring that change, when it came, would not only be gradual but also remain limited. The older strategy of containing race relations took a new shape, but in its new guise it persisted.

Children, black and white, experienced the pain as well as the new opportunities that came with desegregation. But youngsters like Betty Kilby were hardly the only pawns in the struggle over educational policy and practice in Virginia in the wake of *Brown v. Board of Education* and its subsequent implementation, which was generally carried out under the control of white residents and their leaders, with little or no input from black parents, black educators, or other local black citizens. Rarely was a black school desegregated, although Governor Holton's children illustrated such a pattern; rather, as in Warren County, black students began attending white schools. Black coaches and principals typically found themselves displaced, and black teachers frequently did, too. Black cheerleaders and football captains also often found themselves supplanted in their new high schools by their white counterparts. Yet black students often eventually found a measure of acceptance, at least after the first year. At Norfolk's Norview High School, Andrew Heidelberg was permitted in 1961, his senior year, to play varsity football, and he and his white teammates won the Eastern District championship.

Desegregation worked far more effectively in some places than in others. In Alexandria, black students and white students encountered each other in large numbers at the new consolidated T. C. Williams High School. In fall 1971, the football season began with what might just as well have been two varsity teams,

Christiansburg Institute after desegregation.
That desegregation, as implemented, could actually prove destructive to African Americans, whatever whites experienced, is seen in the closure of the Christiansburg Institute (CI) in Montgomery County. It had opened in 1866 as a Freedmen's Bureau school. Over the years it had schooled children in the elementary grades, had prepared black teachers to teach in black schools, had boarded students from near and far, and then had become a regional high school, with courses in academics and trades, to which black students were bused from as far away as Floyd and Pulaski counties. In 1966, after 100 years of service, when Montgomery County schools were desegregated, Christiansburg Institute was discarded. It was sold and most of it was demolished, as depicted in the 1980 photograph here of the wrecking ball and Baily Morris Hall. The building had been named after long-time CI supporters Elliston Morris and Joshua Baily, both of them leaders of the Philadelphia Friends' Freedmen's Association who had helped convince Booker T. Washington to assist the school. In the early twenty-first century, the main surviving structure, the Edward A. Long Building, was on the National Register of Historic Places, and loyal alumni were seeking to breathe new life into the old school, converting what remained of it into a museum and educational center. Photograph by Gene Dalton, *Roanoke Times* staff photographer; photograph courtesy of the *Roanoke Times*.

one white, one black. The senior football coach, Bill Yoast, was passed over, as a black coach, Herman Boone, was promoted to the head job, and Yoast agreed to be assistant coach. The coaches worked it out, and so did the team members. At the end of the season the Titans were the Virginia state high school champions, the students had come together, and to an extraordinary degree the community had as well. The 2000 movie *Remember the Titans* captures the developments at T. C. Williams High School that fall.

Meanwhile, *Brown* had other implications as well. In February 1960, twelve months after the first black students began attending white high schools in Virginia, a wave of sit-ins began in Greensboro, North Carolina, and spread to cities in Virginia as well as other states. In place after place, throughout his former dominion, King Color was losing control over how people, white and black, acted and how they interacted. Across the 1960s—as elementary and high schools were, or were not, becoming at least somewhat desegregated—events took place in voting booths, at lunch counters, and on college campuses that made the Virginia of the 1940s look increasingly like a distant time and place. Power flowed to new groups, whether from farm to city, white to black, or Southside to northern Virginia. By how they responded to new obligations and opportunities, Virginians determined to what degree there would have to be a loser for every winner, and to what degree there could be a great many winners.

Chapter 24

Power and Policy—
The Politics of the 1960s

In mid-1958, Harry F. Byrd Sr. had served in the U.S. Senate for thirty-five years, and he was running for yet another six-year term. His policy of Massive Resistance, Virginia's official response to *Brown v. Board of Education,* continued to govern the public elementary and high schools of Virginia, none of which had as yet become at all desegregated. The state's tradition of a small electorate, predictable in supporting the Byrd Organization and the state Democratic Party, remained largely intact. In both the U.S. Senate and the House of Representatives, Byrd and his colleagues from Virginia, as well as like-minded men from other southern states, from their powerful positions on leading committees—often as chairmen of those committees, given their tremendous seniority coming as they did from one-party states—continued to block liberal legislative proposals and to strengthen efforts to roll back liberal reforms, whether on race or labor or social welfare.

In that year's general election, though, Byrd faced a challenger, a newcomer to politics and to Virginia, Dr. Louise Wensel, who came to public notice in July 1958 when she wrote a letter to the editor of the *Richmond Times-Dispatch.* Upset about the policy of Massive Resistance, together with the Republican Party's failure to mount a challenge to Byrd, the white mother of five school-age children wrote: "How can we parents face our children if we sit back and accept the one-party rule of the Byrd machine with its plan for closing our public schools? Can we persuade our children that democracy is better than communism if we succumb to the dictatorship of an old man who proposes to destroy the very foundation of democracy—our public schools?" Approached by people who badly wanted someone to run against Byrd—in particular, by Harold Boyd, a leader of the AFL-CIO in Virginia—she agreed to run, though the deadline for announcing came only four days after her letter appeared. In the weeks ahead, Massive Resistance led to school closures in Warren County, Charlottesville, and Norfolk, so the emerging framework for understanding the central issue—whether to permit some desegregation or to close the schools—gained resonance. In some urban areas she picked up a great deal of support—39 percent of the vote in Norfolk—but Byrd nonetheless gained an easy victory.

Byrd's electoral victory notwithstanding, Massive Resistance soon came under attack in the courts. Before long, his political dominance faced challenges on many fronts. Within a decade, the world that had produced the Virginia Constitution of 1902, and then had been bolstered by it, came unraveled. The old social and political forces did not vanish, but during the 1960s they lost their easy control over state and society.

Virginia politics and policies in the 1950s, Virginia politics and policies in the 1970s—one scene had scant resemblance to the other. In part, social and economic patterns in Virginia were rapidly changing, as agriculture declined, urbanization continued, and more new people moved into the state. In part, mandates for change emerged from the nation's capital, whether because Congress enacted laws that brought change to Virginia, or because the U.S. Supreme Court ruled on key cases—often from Virginia—that changed the ways Virginians lived their lives. The broad social changes converged with the new federal policies to transform Virginia politics in a myriad of ways. By the end of the 1960s, Harry F. Byrd Sr. had died after five decades in public office, a Republican had been elected governor, and black Virginians were being elected to the legislature for the first time in the twentieth century.

What is sometimes termed a "Second Reconstruction" had emerged by the 1960s, in Virginia and elsewhere across the South, as the federal government once again intervened in the South to promote African Americans' civil and political rights. Long after ratification in 1868, the Fourteenth Amendment proved the basis for bringing an end to segregation laws in the 1950s and 1960s. The Voting Rights Act of 1965 was based on the Fifteenth Amendment, which had been ratified in 1870. Black voter registration in the 1960s returned black southerners to political participation, even political office, in Virginia and indeed in every southern state.

Institutions of higher education reflected the changes in race relations, gender relations, federal-state relations, and state policies of taxing and spending. A new Virginia emerged. By the end of the twentieth century, most Virginians—

black as well as white—would be hard pressed to comprehend how absolute the old rules had been during the reign of King Color, or how late it had been before any exceptions at all might be made to racial segregation.

The Case against Jim Crow

By the 1960s, federal courts had already been ruling for a number of years in ways that promised transformation on the racial front in Virginia. The biggest such decisions had come in *Brown v. Board of Education*, in 1954 and 1955. Soon decisions by the Supreme Court also overturned segregation laws and practices on other fronts, not all of them clearly in focus before 1960 as venues for overcoming Jim Crow. The kind of sit-ins at lunch counters that began in February 1960 in Greensboro, North Carolina, soon came to Richmond. Thirty-four black students from Virginia Union University were arrested for trespass when they took seats at the downtown Thalhimers department store, seeking to obtain service, and refused to leave when rebuffed. Convicted, they appealed the verdicts, first to the Virginia Supreme Court and then to the U.S. Supreme Court. In May 1963, in *Randolph v. Virginia,* the U.S. Supreme Court reversed the convictions, ruling that, the trespass statute having been deployed against people who were denied service because of their race, they had been denied due process of law.

The "Thalhimers Thirty-four" had included Ford T. Johnson Jr. as well as Raymond B. Randolph Jr., the Virginia Union student whose name appeared on the Supreme Court decision in *Randolph v. Virginia*. Another member was George W. Harris Jr., who had enrolled as an engineering student at the University of Virginia in 1955, found the place uncongenial, dropped out, and transferred to Virginia Union, where he was a senior in February 1960; he went on to law school and later served for twenty years as a state judge in Roanoke.

As for young Johnson, his name was on another Supreme Court case. Johnson was arrested in early 1962 for driving a car whose registration had expired, and when he showed up in the same courtroom he had been in two years earlier, he found that, in its incarnation as a traffic court, the place had segregated seating. When he failed to comply immediately with a directive from the judge to move from the white side to the black side of the courtroom, he was found in contempt of court. As in the sit-in case, he appealed the ruling. Just as the Supreme Court had ruled in the sit-in case that trespass laws could not be used to enforce racial segregation in public accommodations, in *Johnson v. Virginia* the Court ruled, in April 1963, that a person could not be found in contempt of court for failure to comply with the practice of segregated seating (see sidebar, page 364).

Ruth Tinsley (1901–1970). A prominent member of the black community in Richmond, Tinsley was fifty-eight in 1960 when this picture was taken. Long an adviser to the NAACP's Youth Group, she partnered in the civil rights struggle with her husband, Dr. J. M. Tinsley, who for many years, beginning in 1935, served as a leader of the NAACP in Virginia. On February 23, 1960, she was outside Thalhimers department store. Virginia Union University students had been arrested there the day before for sitting in at a lunch counter and a dining room. As she stood on the sidewalk, pickets were handing out leaflets, aimed at black shoppers, that read, "Don't buy where you cannot eat, and turn your charge plate in." She had one in her hand. Told repeatedly by police officers to move along, she stood her ground (she later said she had not been picketing but rather had been waiting for a friend to stop by and pick her up at that corner). When arrested, she neither resisted nor cooperated. The photo, taken by black Richmond photographer Scott Henderson, soon reached audiences worldwide, including readers of *Life* magazine's March 7 issue. Library of Congress, Prints and Photographs Division, LC-USZ62-119523.

JOHNSON V. VIRGINIA, 373 U.S. 61 (1963)

At the time Ford T. Johnson Jr. went to traffic court in April 1962, he was an undergraduate at Virginia Union University in Richmond; his father was a dentist in the city. The U.S. Supreme Court's opinion relates the facts of the case:

. . . The petitioner, Ford T. Johnson, Jr., was convicted of contempt of the Traffic Court of the City of Richmond, Virginia, and appealed his conviction to the Hustings Court, where he was tried without a jury and again convicted. The Supreme Court of Appeals of Virginia refused to grant a writ of error on the ground that the judgment appealed from was "plainly right." . . .

The evidence at petitioner's trial in the Hustings Court is summarized in an approved statement of facts. According to this statement, the witnesses for the State testified as follows: The petitioner, a Negro, was seated in the Traffic Court in a section reserved for whites, and when requested to move by the bailiff, refused to do so. The judge then summoned the petitioner to the bench and instructed him to be seated in the right-hand section of the courtroom, the section reserved for Negroes. The petitioner moved back in front of the counsel table and remained standing with his arms folded, stating that he preferred standing and indicating that he would not comply with the judge's order. Upon refusal to

Four years after these two cases from Richmond, the U.S. Supreme Court overruled another Virginia trial court's decision that had also been upheld by the Virginia Supreme Court. This case had to do with a law that made it a felony for two people to marry if one was white and the other not. Richard Loving was white. His bride, Mildred Jeter, was not. After going to Washington, D.C., in 1958 to get married, and then moving back to familiar surroundings in Caroline County, east of Fredericksburg, the couple that wanted to be Mr. and Mrs. Loving were arrested for their marriage, found guilty, and sentenced to a year in prison. The presiding judge, Leon M. Bazile, suspended the jail time on the condition that the couple accept banishment from Virginia for twenty-five years. They could remain married, but not in Virginia.

After four years of exile, living in Washington, D.C., they challenged the law under which they had been convicted. The original ruling was upheld in a return trip to the trial court, followed by an appeal to the Virginia Supreme Court. But in June 1967—just in time for their ninth wedding anniversary—the U.S. Supreme Court gave them the wedding present they had craved all those years. The Court ruled that states could, as they always had, regulate marriage in most respects. But the Fourteenth Amendment, in the Court's understanding by 1967, did not permit states to ban interracial marriage. Mr. and Mrs. Loving, their convictions overturned and the threat of further prosecution behind them, returned with their three young children to live permanently in Caroline County (see sidebar, page 366).

Thus, in one arena after another, Virginia customs and laws that governed people's behavior on the basis of their racial identities came under attack. Black Virginians contested the old rules.

State courts ruled against them. But in the 1960s the nation's highest court saw matters in a different light, and Virginia's ways had to change. Moreover, the U.S. Supreme Court was not acting alone in moving racial policies and practices out of the era of Jim Crow and on toward whatever might follow. Congress passed the Civil Rights Act of 1964 and the Voting Rights Act of 1965, and both were bound to help reshape black-white relations and black opportunities, whether at lunch counters or at polling venues.

Commemorating the Past—Jamestown 1957 and Civil War 1961–1965

During the years of Massive Resistance, Virginia commemorated the founding of Jamestown, and then, during several key years of direct action, litigation, and legislation on civil rights, Virginians marked the centennial of the Civil War. At the same time that key components of the state's racial history were being second-guessed and overruled, other key components of Virginia's history were being celebrated. Each attracted people whose identities resonated to certain chapters in the story of Virginia's past, and each engendered in countless people a lifelong fascination with chapters of the past.

Jamestown 1957—the Jamestown Festival 350th Celebration—included a dramatic production performed outdoors in an amphitheater, *The Founders,* authored by Paul Green (who had written a similar production, *The Lost Colony,* for the 350th anniversary of the 1587 settlement at Roanoke Island). Undeterred by the heat and humidity, visitors marveled at the church tower and grave sites; replicas of the triangular fort and the three ships from 1607; a visit by Queen Elizabeth II; and the production portraying John

obey the judge's further direction to be seated, the petitioner was arrested for contempt. At no time did he behave in a boisterous or abusive manner, and there was no disorder in the courtroom. The State, in its Brief in Opposition filed in this Court, concedes that in the section of the Richmond Traffic Court reserved for spectators, seating space "is assigned on the basis of racial designation, the seats on one side of the aisle being for use of Negro citizens and the seats on the other side being for the use of white citizens."

It is clear from the totality of circumstances, and particularly the fact that the petitioner was peaceably seated in the section reserved for whites before being summoned to the bench, that the arrest and conviction rested entirely on the refusal to comply with the segregated seating requirements imposed in this particular courtroom. Such a conviction cannot stand, for it is no longer open to question that a State may not constitutionally require segregation of public facilities. . . . State-compelled segregation in a court of justice is a manifest violation of the State's duty to deny no one the equal protection of its laws.

After hearing of his victory in this case, Johnson decided he would go to law school.

In June 1967, in a case that originated in Virginia, the U.S. Supreme Court declared that state
laws against interracial marriage
could no longer be enforced.
Demonstrating that by 1967 many
white Virginians could accept with
equanimity a decision that would
surely have ignited a firestorm in
earlier years, the *Roanoke Times*
had this to say on its June 14 editorial page:

Wedlock: A "Fundamental Freedom"

When the infamous Dred Scott
case was decided by the Supreme
Court in 1857, Chief Justice Taney
observed that the country's attitude toward Negroes was indicated
by its laws against interracial marriage. Those laws, he concluded,
put "a stigma of the deepest degradation upon the whole race." In
part, the court used that evidence
of public attitudes to justify its decision that Negroes could not be
American citizens.

Before the ink was barely dry on
the Dred Scott decision, the nation
was caught up in a tragic Civil War
that ultimately would reverse the
Supreme Court's non-citizenship
sentence for Negro Americans. But
for more than 100 years, there remained the "stigma of the deepest
degradation."

This week that stigma finally was
shattered. Appropriately enough, it
was the Supreme Court that again

Smith, Powhatan, Pocahontas, and John Rolfe. As
Jamestown 2007 approached, many people cherished memories of the 1957 celebration, including
attending as children in the company of grand-
parents who had experienced Jamestown 1907.

The year after the 1957 Jamestown celebration, the General Assembly established a Virginia
Civil War Commission, and Richmond reporter
James J. Geary accepted the position of executive
director. Early reactions to the commission were
mixed. Why, various people wanted to know, was
Virginia celebrating the Civil War, having lost so
catastrophically, or using such hallowed history to
attract tourists, or reopening ancient wounds at a
time when Richmond was embroiled in challenges
to segregation? In reply, Geary and his staff set out
to use the commemoration as an educational opportunity about the past, and in 1959 he published
the first of seventy-five monthly newsletters. On
the campus of the Medical College of Virginia
was constructed a Civil War Centennial Center,
which opened in 1961 on April 23 to coincide with
the anniversary of Robert E. Lee's acceptance of
the command of Virginia's military forces. A new
documentary film, *Manassas to Appomattox,* was
shown there. Two young historians got involved:
Lyon G. Tyler, the grandson of President John Tyler, served as assistant director and wrote *Virginia's Opportunity—the Civil War Centennial,* and
James I. Robertson Jr. wrote *Virginia, 1861–1865:
Iron Gate to the Confederacy.* Major public events
included a reenactment in July 1961 of the First
Battle of Manassas, reenactment of the May 1864
Battle of New Market, and an observance of the
centennial of General Lee's surrender to General
Grant, at which historian Bruce Catton spoke.

Geary went on to serve for many years as director of VMI's New Market Battlefield State Historical Park, established at the close of the Civil

War centennial. Tyler went on to a career as a historian first at VMI and then at the Citadel, and Robertson, after serving as executive director of the National Civil War Centennial Commission, went on to a career as a historian at Virginia Polytechnic Institute and State University.

New Playing Field, New Players

Virginia entered the 1960s with a political system that had undergone little change since even before Harry Byrd's term as governor in the 1920s. Virginia remained a one-party state, with Democrats so dominant in state politics that Republicans appeared to stand no chance of winning statewide office. The electorate remained small. Black voters remained especially few in number, yet race was hardly the only notable feature of the political landscape. The poll tax discouraged many impecunious whites, too, from voting. Moreover, in Virginia, as in many—or even most—American states, the system of legislative apportionment operated so as to enhance rural power and suppress urban residents' ability to pass laws that served their interests. City residents looked for help in undoing their competitive disadvantages, black citizens did too, and they looked primarily to Congress and the federal courts to undo their disabilities, bring down the barriers, and permit them to act more effectively—not only to vote, but to have their votes count for something.

Beginning in 1962, U.S. Supreme Court cases from other states—notably *Baker v. Carr*, from Tennessee—brought rulings often termed "one man, one vote," calling for redistricting in races for the U.S. House of Representatives and for reapportionment in races for seats in state legislatures. The core idea was that it should not take many more voters, or residents, in an urban dis-

was called upon to right a [grievous] wrong that still symbolized second-class citizenship for over 20 million Americans. Twelve years ago the court declined to take such action, desperately seeking to prevent a further outbreak of racial antagonism in Old Confederacy states still reeling from the previous year's historical school desegregation decision. . . .

To most Americans, marriage between whites and Negroes will continue to be viewed as wrong. If only because of social inhibitions, intermarriage will not occur except in a small percentage of cases. But the legal obstacle to such marriages has been erased . . . and so too the "stigma of the deepest degradation." The sensitive issue of race and sex will remain dominant in Negro-white relations for the foreseeable future, of course. But a state-administered caste system has been laid to final rest. . . .

"The law," Mrs. Loving once said, "should allow [people] to marry anyone [they want]." Because of *Loving v. Virginia*, the law so allows.

The couple seeking recognition as Mr. and Mrs. Loving, feeling free at last after their court victory in June 1967. Other well-known photographs of the couple, taken during the two years before the Supreme Court's ruling, suggest some combination of resignation and fury, instead of the quiet relief and satisfaction revealed here. Corbis.

trict to elect a representative than it did voters, or residents, in sparsely populated rural districts. In *Davis v. Mann* (1964), the U.S. Supreme Court ruled that Virginia must reapportion, granting such urban legislators as C. Harrison Mann Jr. and Kathryn H. Stone, who represented Arlington in the House of Delegates, the decision they had sought. Urban areas, such as northern Virginia, would, after that, have far more pull in Richmond than had been the situation before. In practice, the rapidly growing suburban areas most notably benefited from the new arrangements, but either way, the Virginia General Assembly often began to operate in new ways, especially in matters of taxing and spending.

Across the twentieth century, a poll tax had long kept many thousands of Virginians from voting. Virginians had brought court challenges to the tax several times in the 1940s, and there had been efforts in Congress, too, to eliminate it, but to no avail. Finally, the Twenty-fourth Amendment—which went into effect in time for the 1964 presidential election—prevented states from imposing a poll tax requirement for voters in federal elections. The Twenty-fourth Amendment left the poll tax intact in state elections, in Virginia and some other southern states, but in cases brought by two black women, Annie Harper in northern Virginia and Evelyn Butts in Norfolk, the U.S. Supreme Court ruled in 1966 that states could no longer require the payment of poll taxes for voters to participate in state elections either.

368

The 1964 presidential election signaled significant changes in Virginia politics, as historian James R. Sweeney has written. Chances are that the Virginia electorate would have picked Barry Goldwater over John F. Kennedy, but Kennedy's assassination in November 1963 meant that Lyndon B. Johnson would be the Democrats' standard bearer in 1964. Some tobacco and peanut farmers fretted that Goldwater might be hostile to the farm price supports they enjoyed. More important, the end of the poll tax restriction that year led to the registration of perhaps 80,000 additional black Virginians. Astute campaign leadership by political organizer Sidney Kellam led many white Democrats to support a straight-party ticket rather than join "Democrats for Byrd and Goldwater." In September, the Johnson campaign announced that the candidate's wife, Lady Bird Johnson, would travel by train through much of the South, including Virginia, in early October, and soon Governor Albertis S. Harrison Jr. and Lieutenant Governor Mills E. Godwin Jr. both announced they would join her on the Lady Bird Special for parts of the Virginia portion. His finger to the political winds, Godwin had become persuaded that such a gesture would help him shed his image as a Massive Resister, and he wanted to run for the governorship the next year. These various factors resulted in a Johnson victory in November.

As new rules came to govern the game of politics in Virginia, new players were chosen to represent Virginians, and the laws they wrote changed too. The voters chose another in a long string of Democrats as governor in 1965, but Mills Godwin sang different words to the ancient tune. Moreover, given the effect of reapportionment, the General Assembly looked very different after the 1965 elections. When the legislature convened in early 1966, Governor Godwin told lawmakers: "We can take no rest until all our public schools—not just some—will compare with any in the nation; until all our colleges and universities—not just some—can hold up their heads in any company"; and until "all our sons and daughters—not just some—have the same chance to train their minds and their skills to the utmost."

The 1966 session is known as the "sales tax" legislature. For the first time, under legislation enacted that session, the state, together with localities, would be collecting a tax on general sales. A tax of 2 percent would be collected by the state, with half the proceeds kept by the state and the other half distributed to localities on the basis of school-age population. In addition, a new 2 percent tax on the sale of automobiles was allocated to improvements in highways and roads. A new system of community colleges, together with vast increases in spending on existing four-year colleges and universities, revealed a far greater ability to spend, and willingness to pay, on education at every level than ever before. Moreover, the sales tax was slated to increase in 1968 from its initial level of 2 percent to a new permanent level of 3 percent. The three-pronged initiative in state policy—taxing more, and spending more on transportation and education—put the state in a posture of active support of public services, breathtaking in its sweep.

Change and Continuity in State and Federal Elections

The 1965 and 1966 elections reflected tremors under the political ground in ways that went beyond the outcome of the gubernatorial and legislative campaigns and the state legislation that quickly followed. In 1966, all of Virginia's congressmen were up for reelection, of course. So were both seats in the U.S. Senate, an unusual situation. In November 1965, an ailing Harry F. Byrd Sr. resigned his seat in the Senate, and Governor Albertis Harrison appointed state senator Harry F. Byrd Jr. as his successor on an interim basis. In 1966, Senator A. Willis Robertson would have been running for reelection anyway, but this development meant that voters would be filling the other U.S. Senate seat that year as well.

In the Democratic primary, Robertson, who had served in the Senate since 1946, faced William B. Spong Jr., a state senator from Portsmouth. Robertson should have won handily once again, but then again, he was seventy-nine years old, the poll tax was gone, black voters were participating in larger numbers than before, urban voters were far more numerous than six years earlier, and people inclined to oppose him had the sense that this time they might actually win, so it made sense to try. Spong edged the incumbent by 50.1 percent to 49.9 percent, or by about 600 votes. It could be said that any one of those many factors proved decisive, as Spong's victory depended on every one of them. Regardless, in a statewide election, a Byrd Organization stalwart had gone down to defeat.

How would Senator Byrd Jr. fare? Facing him was a longtime nemesis, northern Virginia's Armistead Boothe. In the 1950s, Byrd Jr., like his father, had been a leading proponent of Massive Resistance, and Boothe had opposed him. In 1966, Boothe merrily campaigned against Byrd with jibes that his opponent was "not a chip, or even a splinter, off the old block," in fact "hardly a feather off the old Byrd." Byrd held on to defeat Boothe, although by a scant margin, and he went on to win in the general election as well. Learning his political lesson, in subsequent campaigns—in 1970 and 1976—the younger Senator Byrd ran for reelection as an Independent, so as not to have to chance having to get past another liberal opponent like Boothe in the Democratic primary.

So the results in the June 1966 primary elections for the U.S. Senate showed a split decision, with Robertson losing but Byrd Jr. hanging on. The winners in Democratic primaries went on to victory in the general election that fall. Congressional races, contested in small portions of the state rather than before the entire Virginia electorate, took place in a similarly renovated political environment.

Congressman Howard W. Smith, running for reelection in the Eighth District, had never lost a race in all his fifty-eight years of public life. In the 1966 Democratic primary, he learned that he could not even secure his party's nomination. Congressional redistricting had brought into his district large numbers of Virginia natives who had not grown up knowing him as their congressman. On top of that, large numbers of people had been moving into the district, especially in Fairfax County, from out of state. And the poll tax no longer prevented anyone from voting. Congressman Smith went down to defeat to his challenger, George C. Rawlings Jr., a member of the House of Delegates from the Fredericksburg area. Prevented from returning to Congress, Smith could no longer chair the House Rules Committee, so—after years of blocking liberal legislation—he was no longer on hand to deflect congressional initiatives that the traditional rulers of Virginia found objectionable.

As for Governor Mills Godwin, his varied initiatives included a call for a convention to change the state constitution, which dated from 1902. In matters of governance, the Constitution of 1969 shortened the formal name of the state's highest court to the Virginia Supreme Court (dropping "of Appeals"), and it provided for annual, not biennial, sessions of the General Assembly. More important, measuring how far Virginia had come since the Massive Resistance era of just a few years earlier, the new fundamental law directed the General Assembly to "seek to ensure that an educational program of high quality is established and maintained." It also reflected the dismantling of racial and class barriers to voting since the 1902 constitution.

The next gubernatorial election cycle after the 1966 elections revealed how much had changed, how far the Byrd Organization had fallen. In the 1969 Democratic primary to pick a nominee for governor, the organization's first choice, Lieutenant Governor Fred G. Pollard, came in a distant third. In a run-off, William C. Battle defeated Henry E. Howell Jr., but in the general election A. Linwood Holton came out the victor, to become Virginia's first Republican governor in the twentieth century. Supporting the Republican Holton were such groups as the AFL-CIO, representing organized labor, and the Crusade for Voters, a black group, both of whom figured that a win by Holton, an attractive candidate anyway, would surely demonstrate that the old Byrd Organization had lost its dominance in state politics.

As governor, Holton brought a new day to Virginia politics. In his inaugural address, he spoke to the ghost of racial identity as the hallmark of southern politics. No Virginia citizen, he insisted, should any longer be "excluded from full participation in both the blessings and responsibilities of our society because of his race. . . . As Virginia has been a model for so much else in America in the past, let us now endeavor to make today's Virginia a model in race relations." On other fronts, Holton urged that the paltry state tax on cigarettes be doubled—a proposal that the House of Delegates quickly squelched—and he addressed environmental concerns, calling for action that might make Virginia's rivers "swimmable again." If he brought a new day, however, he did not bring a new epoch. The new Republican Party that Holton briefly headed did not stay the moderate course he had hoped it might, as it soon became the home of converted Byrd Democrats, and the new tenants took control of it.

Not only party but also race revealed notable change in Virginia elections in the 1960s and after. Black Virginians had won seats in the House of Delegates and the Virginia Senate through the 1870s and 1880s, but never again until the 1960s. In 1967, a black doctor in Richmond, W. Ferguson Reid, gained election to the House of Delegates. Reid won again in 1969 and 1971, and in 1969 William P. Robinson Sr. was elected from Norfolk. Also in 1969, L. Douglas Wilder won a seat in the Virginia Senate, in a special election in December after the Democratic incumbent, J. Sergeant Reynolds, was elected lieutenant governor. A former mayor of Richmond, running against Wilder as a Republican, came in second; Fred Pollard, having lost the gubernatorial race a few weeks earlier, again came in a distant third. Wilder gained reelection time and again (in 1973, 1977, and 1981), until he ran for the lieutenant governorship in 1985. He won that race and, four years later, became the nation's first African American to be elected state governor.

As the first black Virginia state senator in the twentieth century, Wilder aimed to make a difference. In February 1970, during Negro History Week, in his first Senate speech, he decried the state song "Carry Me Back to Old Virginny," with its line "there's where this ole darkey's heart am long'd to go." Beginning in 1975, he pushed for adoption of a day honoring Martin Luther King Jr.—although, when the proposal became law in 1984, King shared the day with Confederate heroes Stonewall Jackson and Robert E. Lee in a new Lee-Jackson-King Day. In 1997, legislative action gave the state song "emeritus" status, and in 2000, Lee-Jackson-King Day was divided, with Lee-Jackson Day a state holiday the Friday before Martin Luther King Day.

Race, Gender, and the University of Virginia

The new politics of public higher education also brought at least the beginnings of a transformation in the 1960s—in access by race, in access by gender, and in the sheer scope of the enterprise. Leroy Willis began his studies at Virginia State College's

L. Douglas Wilder (1931–). During his political career, Wilder often referred to himself as
a "grandson of slaves." His paternal grand-
parents, James W. Wilder and Agnes W. Johnson, were born into slavery in Virginia. They
had long since obtained their freedom and
become citizens when their thirteenth and
youngest child, Robert Judson Wilder, was
born in Richmond in 1886. He named the ninth
of his ten children, also born in Richmond,
after poet Paul Lawrence Dunbar and abolitionist Frederick Douglass. Lawrence Douglas

Wilder ran for a seat in the Virginia Senate in a
special election in 1969, and when he won, he
became the first black Virginia state senator in
the twentieth century. He served four terms in
the Senate before gaining election as lieutenant governor in 1985 and as governor in 1989,
the first African American elected to the governorship of any state in the nation. Virginia
Historical Society, Richmond, Virginia.

Norfolk division but transferred in 1959 to the University of Virginia as an engineering undergraduate. Two years later, in 1961, he broke through the barriers that had been preventing black students from switching out of engineering. Willis graduated in 1962 from the College of Arts and Sciences, with a degree in chemistry. He vowed never to return. But in 1993, he was back, watching his twin children, son Maceo and daughter Nia, graduate. Much had changed along the way.

The University of Virginia went through significant changes in student population in the years around 1970. The College of Arts and Sciences, the institution's core unit, enrolled more black students in fall 1968, twelve young black men, than had even applied the year before. One of the twelve was John Charles Thomas, whose leadership in the new Black Students for Freedom (renamed the Black Student Alliance in 1971) during his student days helped push the process of change at UVA along. Returning in 1994 to celebrate the Black Student Alliance's twenty-fifth anniversary, Thomas recalled how, when he arrived at the school as a freshman in 1968, it seemed like Confederate battle flags were everywhere; and the song "Dixie" could often be heard at Scott Stadium after the football team scored a touchdown. In between 1968 and 1994, Thomas had earned a law degree at UVA in 1975 and, in the 1980s, had served as the first black justice of the Virginia Supreme Court.

Proponents of change on the racial front at UVA in the late 1960s called for a vast array of changes in practices, symbolic and substantive—the recruitment of black faculty, establishment of a black studies program, appointment of a black member of the board of visitors, curtailment of the playing of "Dixie" and the display of the Confederate flag on campus, and many other initiatives, including the active recruitment of black students and a commitment to fostering an environment that would positively encourage black students to enroll and remain at the university. As a student, Thomas drove a state car all over Virginia, visiting high schools—some of them still segregated—and seeking to recruit additional black undergraduates.

An even bigger controversy at UVA, and a huge change, in the late 1960s and early 1970s had to do with gender—whether female students would be admitted on the same terms as men into the College of Arts and Sciences or would continue to be largely excluded. In 1967, the school's president, Edgar Shannon, acting partly in the expectation that litigation would force the question if the university failed to act on its own, appointed a committee to explore the matter. The next year, the university moved to implement a recommended policy of gradual change toward full coeducation. In the meantime, a suit in federal court resulted in a call for coeducation. The court permitted a two-year window—until fall

George Mason College, 1963, at the intersection of Route 7 and Columbia Pike, Bailey's Crossroads. In 1957, the University of Virginia leased this single building to house its northern Virginia branch, University College, a coeducational two-year institution that the General Assembly had authorized the year before. Renamed in 1960, George Mason College broke ground in August 1963 for a new campus, at 4400 University Drive, Fairfax, with four buildings. Authorized in 1966 to offer a four-year program of study, with access unrestricted by either race or gender, in 1972 it became a separate institution, George Mason University, twenty-four years after beginning operations as an extension of the University of Virginia. Its startling growth continued into the twenty-first century. GMU Archives Collection, Special Collections and Archives, George Mason University.

1972—within which to initiate full coeducation, and the school admitted about 500 women underclassmen each in fall 1970 and fall 1971. The new students that John Charles Thomas was recruiting, then, included some who were female as well as black. In the years to come, the female proportion in the College of Arts and Sciences approached 50 percent.

New Educational Institutions for Tidewater, Northern Virginia, and Elsewhere

The nine public colleges of the 1920s—eight white, one black—grew to a much larger number in the generation after World War II. To take one example, in response to efforts in the southwestern corner of Virginia, the University of Virginia established Clinch Valley College as a two-year branch in Wise. Always co-educational—as opposed to the all-male identity of the home campus in Charlottesville—by the 1970s it had become a four-year school, and in 1999 it became the University of Virginia's College at Wise.

In northern Virginia, meanwhile, George Mason University began in 1948 as an extension center of the University of Virginia. By 1956 it was a two-year branch campus of the university, with a coeducational clientele. In 1972 it became a separate institution, George Mason University. Two major driving forces in its continued development derived from its location in the D.C. metropolitan area. The large and rapidly growing population of the area not only generated large numbers of students but also translated into substantial support in the legislature for state funds. Long before the end of the century, it had a law school as well as doctoral programs in an array of academic disciplines.

In Richmond a new public university emerged during this period as well. The Medical College of Virginia dated from before the Civil War, and the Richmond Professional Institute originated in 1917 as the Richmond School of Social Work and Public Health, before becoming affiliated with the College of William and Mary. In 1968, the General Assembly combined the two units into Virginia Commonwealth University.

In Tidewater Virginia, several new campuses developed. What started out as a junior college in the 1930s as a branch of Virginia Union University, a private black institution in Richmond, was by 1944 the Norfolk division of Virginia State College. Gradually it developed its own identity as well as a more comprehensive curriculum, becoming Norfolk State College in 1969 and then Norfolk State University in 1979. Norfolk State gave Virginia two historically, and predominantly, black public universities. Also in Norfolk, a new white institution originated in 1930 as the Norfolk division of the College of William and Mary. By 1964, it offered undergraduate and master's programs as Old Dominion College, and in 1970 it became Old Dominion University. Across the river in Newport News, lagging behind the development of Old Dominion, in 1960 the College of William and Mary developed another branch campus, with a two-year program, closer to the home campus. Like Old Dominion, that branch developed into a four-year institution, separate from its parent—Christopher Newport College—and by 1992 it offered various graduate programs and had become Christopher Newport University.

The new politics of the 1960s, together with the post–World War II baby boomers' reaching college age, drove the rise of higher education in Virginia. Not only did the urban corridor develop various new public universities, but also a new system of public community colleges emerged, with dozens of campuses scattered across the state, rewarding legislators and giving citizens easier access to higher education. These two-year institutions were designed for two constituencies, students who wished to study technical programs beyond high school and students who wished to save money, live at home, and, whether on a full-time or part-time basis, complete the first year or two of college before transferring to a four-year institution.

Of all the initiatives in higher education that emerged in the 1960s, perhaps the community college system had greater importance to more Virginians. Some were new institutions entirely, while others, each a preexisting branch campus of a four-year institution, were folded into the new system. The largest were Northern Virginia Community College and Tidewater Community College, but smaller institutions could be found in Abingdon (Virginia Highlands Community College), Roanoke (Virginia Western Community College), Weyers Cave (Blue Ridge Community College), Martinsville (Patrick Henry Community College), Hampton (Thomas Nelson Community College), and a small host of other communities. The new system reflected the reapportioned General Assembly's willingness to enact a sales tax and other progressive legislation, and it also reflected the strong leadership of Governor Mills Godwin, as well as key support from such educators and politicians as the president of VPI, T. Marshall Hahn Jr., and the state senator from Chesterfield County, Lloyd C. Bird.

Higher education in Virginia by 1970 was a very different enterprise from what it had been just a decade earlier. Virginia Polytechnic Institute (VPI), whose enrollment had first reached 6,000 in 1962, became Virginia Polytechnic Institute and State University (Virginia Tech) in 1970 and had an enrollment that year of 12,000. The baby boom began to come on stream, from a college admissions perspective, in 1964. Desegregation was beginning to get under way by then, too. Exclusion by either race or gender was beginning to become a thing of the past. Traditionally parallel institutions, by race or gender, were soon significantly altered. At community colleges in particular, low cost and easy access would combine, the vision went, to bring higher education within reach of every family, every community. The decade brought new universities to every major population center of the state as well as new community colleges throughout the state. At the same time, a more rigorous level of academic exploration, a heightened emphasis on research at the major universities, brought new vibrancy to the classroom and laboratory and, moreover, as had long been the intent with regard to agricultural research, contributed social and economic benefits to citizens who never set foot on campus.

In the years to come, the vision would be contested and the role of the state in financing higher education diminished, but the transformation of the 1960s in higher education rippled on into the twenty-first century, as did the many other changes of that decade. A series of jolts along the way altered public attitudes toward higher education, imposing renewed limits on the willingness to use tax dollars. One was student rebellion on campuses, especially in the spring of 1970 at Virginia Tech and the University of Virginia, after President Richard Nixon widened the war in Southeast Asia to include Cambodia. Another was the sudden surge in gas prices, together with shortages at any price, in the mid-1970s and again at the end of the decade, resulting from production cutbacks by members of the Organization of Petroleum Exporting Countries and leading to economic downturns and revenue shortfalls.

Federal Policy and Private Colleges

At private colleges, as at public institutions, black and white students began attending classes together. The initial change at most private institutions took place in the wake of the Civil Rights Act of 1964, which demanded that institutions not engage in racial discrimination if they wished to benefit from federal programs. The Higher Education Act of 1965, by establishing new federal programs, with far more money attached, induced changes in institutional practice at one private school after another.

The combination of federal funds and federal conditions drove Danville's Averett College to end its policy of black exclusion in 1968. Before then, Roanoke College had admitted Virginia Maxine Fitzgerald in 1964, Lynchburg College had admitted its first black student in 1965, and Randolph-Macon College had enrolled its first in 1966. Sweet Briar College, learning in 1964 that federal loans or grants would no longer be available until the school permitted black students to enroll, went to court to free itself of a condition in the bequest that had launched the school in the first place, restricting admission to "white girls and young women." After lengthy legal jockeying, the school admitted its first African American student, Marshalyn Yeargin, in 1966. Washington and Lee University admitted two black students in 1966, freshman Dennis Haston and law student Leslie D. Smith Jr. Haston transferred after his first year, leaving no black undergraduates, but Smith stayed on to earn his law degree in 1969. In 1968, two black undergraduates enrolled, and the numbers grew from there.

At the University of Richmond (UR), news stories tracked the shift in racial policy and practice across the 1960s. The school's first black alumnus was a master's student who graduated in 1964. As for undergraduates, the school announced in June 1965 that it would end its segregation policy that September. It was reported in August 1968 that UR was under pressure from the federal government to hire black faculty. News came in February 1969 of the university's first black faculty member, Dr. James T. Guines, a part-time lecturer in psychology. And in May 1970 the school announced it was signing its first black scholarship athlete, Norman Williams.

Virginia Politics after the 1960s

Virginia helped Democrat Lyndon B. Johnson on his way to a landslide victory in the 1964 presidential campaign. Four years later, Virginia helped Richard M. Nixon, the Republican nominee, win a three-way race. Thus the 1964 election proved the exception, as Virginia quickly returned to the pattern of going Republican in presidential elections, a pattern that began in 1952 and 1956 with Dwight D. Eisenhower and continued, the 1964 aberration aside, all the way into the next century. Sometimes the race was fairly close, as in 1976 when southerner Jimmy Carter won the national election, or in 1992 and 1996, when Bill Clinton did. More often, the presidential contest was not very close in Virginia. But if Republicans could generally assume that Virginia would support their candidate every four years in presidential elections, nobody could assume the outcome in other statewide elections.

Linwood Holton's election as governor in 1969 proved no fluke, as Republicans won again in 1973 with former Democrat Mills Godwin and in 1977 with John N. Dalton. But then Charles S. Robb retrieved the state executive office for the Democrats in 1981. Gerald L. Baliles and L. Douglas Wilder held it for the Democrats in 1985 and 1989, but the Republican candidate, George F. Allen, won in 1993, as did Jim Gilmore in 1997. In turn, Mark Warner won for the Democrats in 2001, as did Tim Kaine in 2005 (see appendix 1).

Elections to the U.S. Senate revealed a similar back-and-forth pattern in the years after Harry Byrd Sr. left office. William Spong, a Democrat, lost a bid for reelection in the Nixon landslide of 1972 and was replaced by a Republican, William L. Scott, who also served a single term before another Republican, John W. Warner, gained election in 1978—and reelection in 1984, 1990, 1996, and 2002. As for Virginia's other seat in the Senate, when Harry Byrd Jr. declined to run again in 1982, a Republican, Paul S. Trible, took his place for a term. Then former governor Charles Robb, a Democrat, gained election in 1988 and served two terms before losing to another former governor, Republican George Allen, in 2000. During Robb's twelve years, Virginia had one Democratic senator and one Republican. During the six years before Robb's tenure, and again after it, two Republicans represented Virginia in the Senate (see appendix 2).

Gone were the days of the one-party state, where securing the Democratic nomination—whether for governor or for the U.S. Senate—virtually guaranteed victory in the general election. In that way, as in so many others, the 1960s proved a watershed decade, with Virginia's political as well as social history during the four decades after 1965 contrasting in many ways with the four decades before then. There was ample evidence of a shift from Democrat to Republican in the central tendency of Virginia politics, but it was not so pronounced that Democrats could not win statewide elections. In view of Tim Kaine's victory in 2005, a Democrat would be living in the governor's mansion when Virginia celebrated the 400th anniversary of the founding of Jamestown.

Chapter 25

Toward a New Dominion

Virginia since the 1970s

....

Virginia Military Institute enrolled five black cadets in 1968, the first African Americans ever to take classes at the school, and three graduated with their class in 1972. All five had an experience their entire first year that—though truly harsh and challenging, like that of many black pioneers at historically white but newly desegregated schools across the South—was, in contrast to that of black pioneers at other schools, not a matter of race. One of them, Richard Valentine, later recalled: "In the Rat Line, everyone was treated [harshly], and you don't think it's racially motivated because the white guy next to you is getting it too." All five lived on campus, and each had a white roommate. In 1997, at the class of 1972's twenty-fifth reunion, white alumnus Tom Hathaway told the story of the time, during their first year at VMI, when he suggested to his roommate, black cadet Harry Gore, that they sneak across the parade ground. Hathaway's point was that this was a privilege restricted to upperclassmen, so it would be danger-ous, but it was getting dark, so he told Gore, "They'll never be able to tell we're rats." "And Harry looks at me with this look on his face, and he says, 'Fool, there ain't no [blacks] in the upper classes.'"

VMI's first cohort of black students, coming as late as they did, were promptly integrated into the full run of campus activities, bypassing the kinds of restric-tions that the first black undergraduates at VPI and UVA had encountered. In the 1950s, VPI's first black students gained admittance under a new version of "separate but equal," having applied to study engineering, a curriculum unavail-able at Virginia State. Moreover, they never roomed on campus; they had to be in the VPI Corps of Cadets, but they had no place in the barracks. Even in the early 1960s, when black VPI students first obtained rooms on campus, none could play football for the school; the school's first black varsity athlete enrolled in 1967. By contrast, at VMI, electrical engineering major Richard Valentine Jr. played on the varsity football team and was sports editor of the VMI student yearbook, the *Bomb*. Harry W. Gore Jr., a dean's list student in math, served as managing editor of the campus newspaper, the *Cadet*. History major Philip L. Wilkerson Jr. was commander of F Company. Far from being ignored or forgotten, Larry H. Foster, who died in an accident after the first year, was memorialized in his class's 1972 yearbook.

By 1972, every public four-year college in Virginia counted black Virginians not only among its students but also among its graduates. The first cohort of African American cadets at VMI represented a transformation under way in public higher education in the South. When the three returned in 1997 for their reunion, they came to a campus that was once more going through the challenge of change.

In 1997, shops in Lexington were selling bumper stickers that said "Save the Males," as Beth Ann Hogan and other female cadets joined the VMI class of 2001. The Virginia Military Institute, after having enrolled none but male students ever since it began operations in 1839, embarked with considerable preparation but no obvious enthusiasm on a new venture, coeducation. When the school had enrolled its first black cadets twenty-nine years earlier, that extraordinary new departure caused nowhere near the strife, and had nowhere near the statewide—and in fact national—visibility that the events surrounding 1997 did. But that earlier change at VMI had been slow in coming, too. These changes, and the resistance to them, at VMI serve well as metaphors for the vast changes in society and politics as well as in higher education in Virginia during the final third of the twentieth century.

In Virginia in the 1970s, 1980s, and 1990s, some emerging social developments accelerated—migration into Virginia, especially from other lands, for example, and entry of women into the professions. Some changes in politics and government, though building on earlier patterns, constituted new departures, such as the nomination of black men and white women to state office and their appointment to state and federal judgeships. Some changes boosted economic well-being, as a new economy emerged in much of Virginia, particularly in the urban corridor of the east. And some changes came as economic and cultural shocks, bringing to an end patterns that had prevailed for generations, even centuries. Among these were a sharp decline in textile and wood-products manufacturing and, even more notably, an end to tobacco as a mainstay of the Southside economy. At the dawn of the new century, with race receding as a focal point of public and private life, a new issue emerged, as state legislation, to be reinforced with a proposed constitutional amendment, rolled back any advance in the rights of same-sex couples to control their own shared lives. Change as much as continuity, and conflict as much as consensus, continued to characterize the development of policy, culture, and economics in Virginia. Globalization had many dimensions; parochialism did too.

End to Sunday Closing Laws, Rise of the "Christian Right"

Legal barriers to doing business on Sunday came down in ways that resembled the decline of race-based barriers governing who could marry whom or where one could find a meal or lodging, or gender-based ones governing what professions one could or could not enter. Across much of the twentieth century, many businesses could not legally operate on Sundays. The ancient ban against regular commercial activity on the Sabbath went back to colonial times, or even to English law before the colonies were established.

Exceptions were permitted for "household or other work of necessity or charity." Judicial interpretations of these two terms of exception shaped commerce and entertainment in Virginia, beginning with decisions by the Virginia Supreme Court in the 1920s regarding Weyer's Cave in Augusta County; a swimming pool at an amusement park, Lakeside, in Salem; and a professional baseball game in Richmond. In case after case in the years that followed—about showing movies, for example, or selling groceries—Virginia courts sometimes expanded the definition of "necessity." At least as important, statute after statute permitted new exceptions. In a case in Roanoke in 1987, the trial judge changed his mind and ruled that Doug Carr could continue to operate his "best little warehouse in Virginia" on Sundays. Finally, in *Benderson Development Company v. Sciortino*, a 1988 case brought by big department stores in Virginia Beach, the state supreme court ruled that, with so many exceptions in place, the original rule could no longer be applied to any place of business. To all intents and purposes, the Sunday closing laws were no more.

The decline of Sunday closing laws resulted from the growth of commercial life and the development of constitutional law—it did not closely track the degree of commitment by large numbers of Virginians to organized religion. Indeed, Virginia in the late twentieth and early twenty-first centuries featured the powerful presence of two outspoken Southern Baptist figures, Jerry Falwell in Lynchburg and Pat Robertson in Virginia Beach. Each developed a tremendous television ministry, campaigned against abortion and gay rights, and developed a complex of facilities that included a university designed to promote his brand of Christianity. Founder of the Moral Majority movement in 1979,

Jerry Falwell began by founding the Thomas Road Baptist Church in 1956, as well as the all-white Lynchburg Christian Academy in 1967. His Liberty Baptist College, founded in 1971, in 1985 became Liberty University, which grew into one of Virginia's largest institutions of higher education. Pat Robertson, the son of longtime U.S. Senator A. Willis Robertson, founded the Christian Broadcasting Network, the Christian Coalition, and Regent University. He became widely known for hosting the Christian television program *The 700 Club*, running for the Republican Party nomination for the presidency in 1988, and commenting, in ways that often struck viewers as bizarre or unseemly, about international people and events.

Each of the two tugged the Virginia Republican Party—and thus sometimes the entire electorate—toward his social views, and each promoted the active participation by like-minded voters, so-called social conservatives of the Christian Right, in state and federal elections.

Northern Virginia, Hampton Roads, and the Defense Economy

Beginning with World War II, defense spending played an enormous role in the development of two large metropolitan areas in Virginia—the Hampton Roads region, where the James River flows into the Chesapeake Bay, and the Washington suburbs in northern Virginia. In the history of both regions, defense at some point caused a boom in employment opportunities and a surge in population growth, yet the influence of defense affected the regions in divergent ways. Northern Virginia developed a strong, vibrant, high-tech economy that, first spurred on by defense, then diversified into other sectors. Hampton Roads, by contrast, having remained heavily dependent on the manufacture of naval vessels, suffered whenever the military cut back on spending for ships.

Before the 1930s, federal employment was limited, and the D.C. economy small. But the New Deal greatly expanded the government bureaucracy, an expansion that continued into World War II as the number of people employed by the Department of War swelled. Such growth did not end when World War II did, for Cold War defense spending led to further growth in the area, and Great Society spending added more.

The emerging high-tech economy powered growth in the Washington suburbs. Not only was space hard to come by inside the city, but improved highway systems and enhanced incentives for home ownership after World War II made living in the D.C. suburbs more attractive, and edge cities developed at highway intersections. Proximity to the Pentagon, in Arlington, gave a competitive edge

Advance Auto Parts truck. Virginians led the development of any number of major new businesses, including retail chain stores, across the twentieth century. Among them is Advance Auto Parts, which had its beginnings when Arthur Taubman opened two Advance Stores in Roanoke and another in Lynchburg in 1932. Even during the Great Depression, and especially in the prosperous years after World War II, the auto industry played a central role in the new consumer economy, and such stores were crucial to that development. Another such business, reflecting the rise of consumer electronics, is Circuit City, which had its beginnings with a single Wards Company store in Richmond in 1949, opened by Sam Wurtzel and selling televisions and home appliances. By the early twenty-first century, both were Fortune 500 corporations. Photo courtesy of Advance Stores Company, Incorporated d/b/a Advance Auto Parts.

to defense contractors, and therefore much of the D.C. area's growth took place in northern Virginia.

Computer-based technologies had a tremendous effect on the Washington-area economy. High-tech products and services originally took hold in the region because the military created a demand, but companies in northern Virginia proved able to branch out and provide services to other government agencies and to private consumers. The development of weapons systems—the software systems required to control missiles, aircraft, and other military technologies—proved an important contributor to northern Virginia's economy. In the late 1980s and the 1990s, the federal government throttled back on defense spending, but in view of the need for technology services, contractors were largely successful in adapting to the changing economic landscape. As a result, northern Virginia's economy remained strong even when defense spending sputtered.

Defense spending also drove the growth of the Chesapeake region, but that region experienced less economic strength and diversity than did northern Virginia. The economy of the Hampton Roads region—the Norfolk–Newport News metropolitan area—has long depended on shipbuilding. By the end of World War II, patterns had developed in Hampton Roads that remained in place into the twenty-first century. The area's military-based economy expanded during the Cold War years, and the area kept close ties with Washington. The army, navy, air force, and National Aeronautics and Space Administration (NASA) established facilities in addition to the shipbuilding. With so much dependence on defense, the local economy went through cycles of growth and decline as Washington increased or reduced defense spending.

This cyclic economy caused many leaders in the area to seek a more diverse economy. Military facilities already occupied much of the developable land, however, making diversification difficult, and since military facilities do not directly generate tax revenue, many localities found themselves financially strapped. New institutions of higher education that emerged after World War II—Old Dominion University, Norfolk State University, and Christopher Newport University, as well as Tidewater Community College—brought some diversification to the area's economy. So did increased tourism at Virginia Beach. But the old economy remained the key to the region.

Hampton Roads remained dependent on the narrow employment base of military and shipbuilding jobs, so the community put great effort into retaining these activities and lobbying Washington for more spending. Relatively little sustained effort went into developing high-tech manufacturing. As a result, as the region celebrated the 400th anniversary of Jamestown, the economic makeup of Hampton Roads differed little from what it had been two decades earlier.

In the larger region surrounding it, as the twentieth century turned into the twenty-first, even the city of Suffolk—which merged in 1974 into what used to be Nansemond County—contained many farms, growing cattle, hogs, and poultry as well as wheat, corn, soybeans, cotton, and peanuts. The corn, wheat, cattle, and hogs had been around far longer than the cotton, peanuts, and soybeans, which were mostly twentieth-century developments. Suffolk had for many years billed itself as the "World's Largest Peanut Market," and it had a radio station, WLPM at 1450 AM, to advertise its case, though peanuts in the region, like tobacco farther west, came on increasingly hard times as Jamestown's 400th anniversary approached.

Migrants to the Old Dominion

Virginia was an importer of humanity in the seventeenth and eighteenth centuries, but after the American Revolution, it was a huge net exporter of people throughout the nineteenth century and into the twentieth. By World War II, large numbers of people were once again moving into the state, from other southern states and from outside the South. People who came to Washington, D.C., to work in the New Deal turned out to be many of the Old Dominion's new residents. World War II and the Cold War brought in more migrants, whether federal employees to the D.C. area, retired military to the Virginia Beach area, or recruits to the high-tech companies that sprouted along the urban corridor between those two areas. By the 1990s, half the state's residents had been born elsewhere. Less and less was northern Virginia, in particular, still clearly a part of the South.

More and more new Virginians were also coming from other countries. The Immigration Act of 1965 opened the nation's borders to greatly increased legal migration from both Asia and Latin America. Illegal immigration mounted as well. Many of those immigrants found their way to Virginia. By 2007, many of the newcomers had become citizens, and many of the students attending Virginia's public schools, and its institutions of higher education too, were first- or second-generation Americans from Asia and elsewhere.

In 1970, when growing numbers of Virginians were neither black nor white, Filipinos numbered 6,904, Japanese 3,457, and ethnic Chinese 2,303. In the year 2000, the census counted 5,120,110 Caucasians and 1,390,293 African Americans—and 264,971 Asians or Pacific Islanders, while 143,069 other residents claimed two or more racial identities. Quite aside from racial designations, in that year 329,540 of all Virginians were identified as Latino or Hispanic.

One could see the shift in the labor force, as Hispanic laborers worked tobacco and other crops and lived and worked in the Southside, in the Shenandoah Valley, or on the Eastern Shore. One could see it where Baptist and other churches in northern Virginia and, indeed throughout the state, had signs out front printed in hangul, indicating a welcome mat for people whose native language was Korean. The multiethnic communities that had for some time characterized the Hampton Roads area became commonplace throughout Virginia. More broadly, in the census year 2000, for the first time since long before the Civil War, Virginia's percentage of immigrants to the United States was nearing the national figure. Virginia's foreign-born population—which had long been negligible, but rose to 2 percent in 1970, 3 percent in 1980, and 5 percent in 1990—soared to 8 percent in 2000, compared with an official figure of 11 percent for the nation as a whole. The return of Pangaea—the coming together of multiple continents—reached much farther at the time of Virginia's quadricentennial than had ever before been the case, impressive as had been the post-Columbus coming together of Europe, Africa, and the Americas.

Among the notable changes coming into view at the turn of the century, people born outside Virginia, indeed outside the South, could be elected to public office, even to the governorship. George Allen, governor from 1994 to 1998, was born in California, and the first two Virginia governors elected in the twenty-first century were natives of northern states: Mark Warner, of Indiana, and Tim Kaine, of Minnesota. And a growing portion of the Virginia electorate was born not only in other states but even in other countries. While migration did much to reconfigure life in Virginia, so did enormous changes in the economics of small towns and rural areas, such as in the old tobacco belt.

Down in the Old Belt

In Danville, on a sunny November day in 1999, the auctioneer's call echoed across the sheets of tobacco arranged in long rows down the vast, dimly lit warehouse floor—and then stopped, as the 130th Danville tobacco-auction year ended. A small group of tobacco farmers, few of them under age sixty, sat along a bench near the office. Their mood was somber, a pall of uncertainty mixed with the roasted honey smell of cured tobacco leaves. Farmers routinely encountered a host of unknowns, and a philosophy of individualism, patience, and ingenuity helped them meet farming's hardships. Each year's harvest culminated at the warehouse. Here each farmer brought his crop, as generations had done before him. The payoff for the untold hours of labor to produce the "thirteen month-a-year crop" came down to the auction, and there the farmer confronted the core of his uncertainty—the global economy.

Having just sold this year's tobacco, the farmers in attendance turned their attention to the next season, which would bring a reduction in their quotas. One of them, Howard Kendrick, observed, "It looks like they want to do away with it." He went on: "And if they do away with it, I don't know how I am going to pay my taxes. It ain't nothing in wheat, nothing in corn. Back in the fifties, wheat was three dollar and a half a bushel, now it ain't but two dollars. And everything you put your hands on has gone up. So how are we going to stay in business?"

Interviewed in 1998, eighty-year-old Talbert Callands coaxed his aging tractor to life at the edge of his freshly turned and disked field, awaiting the spring planting of tobacco seedlings. He had farmed tobacco all his life, as had his father and his slave-born grandfather before him. Though technology had changed with time, much was the same. His rural farming community had followed the rhythms of the crop season for centuries. This, however, would be Callands's last crop of tobacco. He would retire, renting his small allotment to another farmer to work. "I worked out with the people who was farming," he said, recalling his farming life. "Sometimes they paid me fifty cents a day and sometimes we got a dollar. I worked out there some days and didn't get nothing, but still tobacco, I was working in tobacco, and I learned how to grow tobacco and when I got grown it was my business. I give tobacco credit for all of it. We bought our farm with tobacco money, the machinery that we have we bought it with tobacco money, everything."

Over the centuries, tobacco farming gave birth to a rich and complex culture in the many rural communities of Virginia's Old Belt—the region straddling the Virginia–North Carolina border, with Danville at its center, where Bright Leaf (flue-cured) tobacco was first developed and marketed. "Practically everyone who lived around here had some connection to the farming community back in those days," said Claude Whitehead Jr., whose prominent local tobacco-farming family goes back generations. "They may be running a store in one of the towns or something like that, but their parents still lived on the family farm or this type of thing. Everybody had a common thread, which was tobacco back in those days because that was the main crop, the main cash crop."

The tobacco culture of Virginia's Old Belt, centuries in the making, gained economic stability in the 1930s with the New Deal's Federal Tobacco Program. Under the tobacco program, farmers agreed to plant only their allotment, or share of the quota, which was established based on how much U.S. tobacco the companies wanted to buy. In exchange, the farmers received minimum-price guarantees for their crop. The tobacco program allowed smaller farmers, share-croppers and tenants, black and white, to break the cycle of peonage. "We raised eight children my wife and I, and tobacco did it. From day one until they left here," Talbert Callands said of his early years of farming. "That is the biggest thing I had to send my children to school from was tobacco, and all the children mostly through here were the same way."

As the new millennium dawned, tobacco farmers were concerned about losing the tobacco program. They wanted the program's minimum price supports, but the program limited farmers to growing their quota. And forcing cuts in their quotas was the fact that the price of U.S.-produced tobacco was double the price of tobacco on the world market, so tobacco companies bought less and less U.S. tobacco.

"It's a situation where as the profit margin gets closer and the quota is reduced more, I mean, it's a slow death," said John Ragsdale, who farms with his brother Allen. Another farmer, C. D. Bryant III, agreed: "We are now [this was 2004] growing the smallest crop of flue-cured tobacco that has ever been grown in this country," he said. "That puts more pressure on the farm. You don't know whether to try to hang on, do you exit, or a person like myself at my age you don't have a lot of options, and I don't want to leave the farm." Another farmer, Bernard Coles, wanted his legacy to be that he passed the family farm along intact to the next generation. But as a parent, he might have to break that tradition: "You want the best for your kids, and the way farming is going now you can't say farming is the best way for your kids now."

Farmers' quotas were all cut by the same proportion, and the smaller farmers were less able to adapt. "My daddy he raised tobacco, and I grew up on a farm so I helped him in tobacco. It was good going. All the family worked together. He passed away and left me the farm, and I started farming myself," said Douglas Cox, standing by his field, aware that the announced cuts for the 2004 season meant he could plant but half of what he used to. It was winter, and the bare brown tobacco stalks of last season's crop seemed a harbinger of what was to come. "I had about ten acres of tobacco and then they started cutting the quota," he said. "I don't see how I am going to make it. It's hard to live, there is no way you can make it off two acres of tobacco. I am trying to find me a job now, but it's hard for me to find a job at my age. So it's right bad because that is all I have ever known to do was to farm. It's hard for me to just go out and work, public, I would rather be living on my farm. I don't know what is going to happen."

On top of the pressure farmers felt from unprecedented quota cuts, tobacco companies began contracting directly with the farmer, bypassing the traditional marketing system and further weakening the tobacco quota program. Contracts went to the larger producers, leaving the smaller farmers to sell their tobacco in the dwindling number of auction warehouses still open. And as tobacco quotas declined and contracting took hold by 2002, another change, a more symbolic one, happened in the auctioning of tobacco. Handheld computers, with which tobacco buyers placed bids electronically, were replacing the tobacco auctioneer.

The chant of the auctioneer, this icon of tobacco culture, began in Danville in the 1860s. "It's a very sad situation," said Bob Cage, the 1984 World Champion Tobacco Auctioneer. "It is the best in the free market system way of selling. And it's been just an absolute tradition, it's been one of the nicest things that's ever happened to the South. The ambiance of the selling, people bringing in the tobacco, bringing their kids with them, bringing their wives, seeing people they don't generally see, is all gone. I miss it a lot. I wish it was still going. Whether it ever will again, I don't know. But I'm a dinosaur now, bones."

Planting a tobacco crop, early May 1999. In
northeast Pittsylvania County, near Mt. Airy on
a hill beside the Bannister River, Rev. Talbert
Callands is driving his 1950 John Deere tractor
on his place, as workers Sam Anderson and
Joyce Ann Irvin put in another thirteen-month
crop. Callands says he raised eight children
with that tractor. Courtesy James P. Crawford.

Howard Kendrick and his farmer friends on the warehouse bench back in
1999 knew change was coming, but they had no idea how much, how soon.
In the fall of 2004, Congress enacted the federal tobacco buyout, eliminating
the sixty-six-year-old federal tobacco program, signaling the end of the tobacco
culture of the Old Belt. "So, it's the ending of an era. I mean, it's the ending of
what we know as family production of tobacco in the Old Belt. It's the ending of
it," Bobby Conner said. "There are those individuals who, that's all they've ever
known and done is tobacco and they face difficult decisions." Douglas Cox, who
no longer farmed tobacco and was trying to find work off the farm, predicted:
"I don't think tobacco really will ever leave this area, but it might not be but one
or two people farming it."

In the years around 2000, economic and cultural changes were rapidly unfolding in this rural farming region. "I will be the last person that will be farming
all of this land right through here," said C. D. Bryant III, one of the larger-scale

Farming tobacco, early June 1999. Tommy
Martin on the tractor at Willie Thompson's
farm, and Jimmy Frost with a hoe, in Pittsylvania County. Also helping in the field was Willie
Thompson's daughter Frances Thompson (not
shown). Courtesy James P. Crawford.

tobacco farmers. "I don't foresee anyone else will come in behind me and farm this land." The impact of those changes on the region's environment is another unknown. "In this day and time when a farm is sold, it is so rare that a person like myself or another farmer can go in and buy that land. That land is broken up. It will never be farmed again, by anyone. That is gone," said Bryant. "So you change your landscape, the beauty that people talk about when they drive through Southside and the rolling hills and, 'Oh isn't that pretty?' Well you better look while you can, because I don't know how much longer it will be here."

The Decline of Mills and Mill Villages

The decline of tobacco around the turn of the twenty-first century revealed in particularly acute form the enormous changes taking place in the culture and economics of rural and small-town Virginia—and of America more widely. So many people had been involved in tobacco, in so much of Virginia's territory, and for so long—since the 1610s—that the sharp decline in tobacco stood above all similar changes in late-twentieth-century Virginia. Yet tobacco stood as a proxy for those other changes as well, with the social hurt, the loss of human capital, the end of the line in terms of transmitting to the next generation the know-how and the values that had worked well in the past. The combination of pride, regret, mourning, and hope that emanated from the Old Belt could be found in some fashion where other economic mainstays fell by the wayside. Farming more generally, not just tobacco, experienced comparable change.

Mills and mill towns captured such key phenomena as globalization of markets, changes in the technology of production and transportation, and vagaries of government policy. Imported textiles, imported furniture, all manner of goods came to market "made in China" or anywhere other than "made in the USA," and the shift had tremendous impact on people whose jobs went away. Though every mill and every mill town had its particular story, the mill town of Fries, in southwest Virginia, serves as a good example.

In the year 1900, Francis Henry Fries built a dam on the New River to power the machinery that a new company town, named after him, would soon be operating. Indoor plumbing and electric lights were just some amenities that the mill town introduced to the area. For many years, the main product was cotton flannel, used for producing work gloves. During the boom times of World War II, as many as 1,200 workers kept the machinery going, and the mill kept their families going. Then a long decline set in. By 1988, the town's population had shrunk to a mere 750, and that year the mill closed its doors.

Almost everyone in town was a former worker at the mill or the son or daughter of a former worker. But the tax base that had funded a fine school system went away, the jobs went away, the people went away, and the retirees among them found that their pensions had gone away as well. Looking back on what had been but would be no more, a local banker observed: "That mill has fed and clothed a lot of people over the years."

Many streams had fed into the economic river that tore through the town and brought it down. The machinery had once been state-of-the-art, but that day had long since passed. Talk by the Appalachian Power Company in the 1960s of a bigger dam downstream—one that would, if it came, flood the town—discouraged investment in new technology. The Occupational Safety and Health Administration demanded safeguards against brown lung, but the costs of retrofitting the old mill were seen as prohibitive. Freight costs went up. Imports did too.

Fries had been a special place for many people while it lasted. A highway marker proclaims a piece of its cultural and historical significance:

FRIES—CENTER OF EARLY RECORDED COUNTRY MUSIC. On Mar. 1, 1923, in New York City Henry Whitter of Fries, Va., recorded 2 songs, "The Wreck of the Old Southern 97" and "Lonesome Road Blues." These were among the first successful country recordings by a country artist. His records inspired many other local artists to record, including E. V. "Pop" Stoneman and Kelly Harrell. All three men were employees of the Fries Textile Plant.

Virginia's Heritage Music Trail—the Crooked Road

Virginia's Heritage Music Trail, dubbed "the Crooked Road," has multiple origins. Virginia west of the Southside and Blue Ridge always had its history and its culture, nurtured by the mountainous terrain and relative isolation. The area's constellation of backgrounds, beliefs, and livelihoods has fostered a musical expression that continues to define the region. Country music has long had a primary home in southwestern Virginia, even if folks elsewhere might think first of Nashville, Tennessee, or Branson, Missouri. The hit soundtrack to the 2000 movie *O Brother, Where Art Thou* demonstrated an extremely wide and strong interest in the area's music. Governor Mark Warner, who chaired the Appalachian Regional Commission during part of his 2002–2006 term, voiced a sustained commitment to the economic development of rural Virginia in general and the southwest in particular.

The General Assembly in 2004 created Virginia's Heritage Music Trail to highlight the extraordinary cultural richness of the region, especially its music. Funding the concept to get it launched were grants from such agencies as the Appalachian Regional Commission, the Virginia Department of Housing and Community Development, and the Virginia Coalfield Economic Development Authority; also used were funds from the Virginia Tobacco Indemnification and Community Revitalization Commission's 1998 tobacco settlement. So tobacco and coal might be replaced in part with music as an engine of economic well-being in the region. Some mainstays of the economy of the region might be replaced, and some mainstays of the culture might be reinforced, with a high-lighting of another cultural mainstay.

Much of the music of the area had its roots in the British Isles. Then again, the hybrid culture that emerged in the mountains fused the fiddle, with its European origins, and the banjo, of African origins. Musical monuments to the history of the area are legion, and the Crooked Road takes visitors, as well as local people, to any number of those. The city of Galax features its Old Fiddlers Convention each August. Floyd County has the Floyd County Store, with its Friday Night Jamboree. Ferrum College is home to the Blue Ridge Institute. Ralph Stanley has his own place, the Ralph Stanley Museum and Traditional Music Center, in Dickenson County. There's the Blue Ridge Music Center in Carroll County on the Blue Ridge Parkway. Bristol has the Birthplace of Country Music. In Scott County, the Carter Family Fold highlights the first family of country music, two of whose great stars of the second half of the twentieth century, Johnny Cash and June Carter Cash, were featured in the 2005 blockbuster movie *Walk the Line*.

Race, Sex, and Politics and the Professions

Beginning in the 1960s and 1970s, a range of changes in policy and culture opened doors to black Virginians, who strode through into medicine, law, politics, and other lines of work in far higher numbers than at any earlier time, and indeed in far larger numbers than could have been projected on the basis of trends visible as late as 1960. A similar cluster of changes led to a rapid rise in female enrollment in a wide range of professional schools, notably including law, human medicine, and veterinary medicine. In particular, Title IX of the federal Educational Amendments of 1972 banned discrimination in higher education on the basis of sex. By the end of the century, half of all law students were women, and a majority of vet students were. The combination of falling obstacles, by race and by gender, meant that growing numbers of black women appeared in law schools and medical schools in Virginia, as elsewhere, in the 1970s and 1980s.

Various changes in public life came into clear view in the 1980s in Virginia. Harry Byrd Sr.'s leading challenger to his reelection to the U.S. Senate in 1958 had been a woman doctor, Louise Wensel, who ran as an independent Republican. In 1961, Hazel K. Barger ran for lieutenant governor on the Republican ticket. In 1985, Mary Sue Terry ran for attorney general as a Democrat, and she won. Also in 1985, a black Democratic candidate, L. Douglas Wilder, ran for lieutenant governor, and he won, too. In 1989, in the general election to fill Virginia's three statewide offices, only three of the six candidates from the two major parties were white men. Wilder won the governorship, and Terry was reelected attorney general. For lieutenant governor, Donald Beyer came from behind to defeat his Republican opponent, Edwina P. Dalton, the widow of the popular former governor John Dalton, as the Democratic ticket swept that year.

The state judiciary revealed similar changes in race and gender in high office in Virginia. Before 1983, none but white men had ever served on the Virginia Supreme Court. That year, however, Democratic governor Charles S. Robb appointed John Charles Thomas to the court—an African American graduate of the University of Virginia—and in 1988, Democratic governor Gerald Baliles appointed Elizabeth B. Lacy. The General Assembly subsequently ratified both appointments by electing the two justices to full twelve-year terms. When Justice Thomas left the bench, his replacement was another African American, Leroy Rountree Hassell Sr. Justice Hassell stayed on, as did Justice Lacy, and other white women joined them, until white men held only three of the seven seats on the state's highest court. Beginning in 1997, three of the justices were white women—Elizabeth Lacy, Barbara M. Keenan, and Cynthia D. Kinser—and in 2003 Justice Hassell became the chief justice (see appendix 3).

Virginia's congressional delegation also revealed changes in race and gender and access to elective office. In 1992, voters in a northern Virginia district elected Leslie Byrne to Congress, the first woman ever to represent Virginians in the House of Representatives. That same year, a Tidewater district elected Robert C. Scott, only the second African American to win a congressional election in Virginia, a century after John Mercer Langston's short stay in Congress. When the 400th anniversary arrived, Bobby Scott was still representing his district.

Alice Jackson Returns to a Place She Had Never Been

In 1935, Richmond resident Alice Carlotta Jackson applied to do graduate work at the University of Virginia and was rejected because she was black. In 1990, the university's Office of Afro-American Affairs invited Alice Jackson Houston Stuart to come up to Charlottesville from Richmond and be the after-dinner speaker at an awards ceremony for black students at the university. Her prepared remarks concluded with these words:

> This invitation to address the children and grandchildren of my generation who are today the recipients of honors, citations and awards that they have earned and achieved in the name of this great university—the UNIVERSITY OF VIRGINIA—leaves me with a sense of great joy and long reminiscences. For you, it is a time of enjoyment, satisfaction and fulfillment. We share together.

Her notes for that talk offer more insight into the turmoil from long ago; the pain and joy associated with the invitation and her acceptance of it; her sense of closure, of reconciliation; and the tremendous change that had occurred since the 1930s. In one fragment she said: "I am left without words to convey to you what this moment means to me." In another she wrote: "More than a half century" ago, "I dreamed of perhaps someday, too, sitting where you now sit." Although that dream had gone unfulfilled, she observed: "Now more than three generations later, this institution where I had sought to continue my graduate education—the institution which I thought I might someday call Alma Mater—has invited me to be the Banquet Speaker for the 1990 Honors and Awards Day" for African American students at the University of Virginia. She mused: "This is my university, too, for I feel that in a very real sense—a little bit of me resides in every one of you who pass through these halls—I share your honors, I am proud of your achievements."

Alice Jackson Houston Stuart died in 2001, and in 2003 her son, Massachusetts judge Julian Towns Houston, donated her papers to the University of Virginia. Rebuffed in 1935, Alice Jackson never enrolled at the university. But her papers have a permanent home there in Special Collections.

A Same-Sex Family and a Virginia Law

Barbara Kenny and Tibby Middleton were high school classmates in the 1950s in Salt Lake City, Utah, but they were not close then. Years later, they met again, and this time they became lovers, although circumspect in public. Beginning in 1968 the two women shared a house, with Middleton, having separated from her husband, living upstairs with her two children and Kenny living in the basement. Middleton grew convinced that their living arrangement endangered her custody of the children, and if she lost custody, jeopardized her visiting rights.

So she made a wrenching decision—one might, with a nod to Virginia writer William Styron, term it "Tibby's choice."

Holly adored her father. Leaving her with him, Middleton fled Utah with her son James and with Kenny, and they moved east to Virginia. There, Middleton was repeatedly named "most popular female teacher" at her Fairfax County school, and Kenny ran a clinical social work practice. Eventually, in 1988, the couple settled together in Fredericksburg, where they made a home, in an accepting community and surroundings they loved, found a church, and began to let their relationship be just a bit more public. They took long walks through town, circled the track at Mary Washington College, and met loads of people who increasingly mattered to them. At last they were able not only to share their lives in private but also to create a shared life in their community.

One huge worry overtook them, though, when Kenny was diagnosed in 2001 with a brain aneurism. Next came Virginia's Affirmation of Marriage Act, in 2004, and they began to consider the prospect that, among the rights they could be denied, Middleton might be barred from making crucial decisions on Kenny's behalf in a medical emergency. Kenny in particular was terrified. Both of them remembered when Kenny had had surgery in Alexandria in 1984, and Middleton, barred from visiting her because she was not "family," had to wait for a change of shift, when she identified herself as Kenny's "sister" and was let in.

In another wrenching decision, they felt compelled to leave their home, exiled from Virginia because of the manifest legal threat to their shared lives that the new legislation seemed to pose. They moved to Frederick, Maryland, like Fredericksburg a college town, not too far from Germantown, Maryland, where Tibby's daughter Holly and granddaughter lived. Before leaving, they told their friends in Fredericksburg that the new law had "driven [us] to leave the state of Virginia." People had reason to move away from Virginia as well as to it: "We know we'll never be able to replace" in Maryland "the community . . . that we have here, and that is a great sadness." Knowing not a soul in their new town, at sixty-six, still together after some forty years, they started over. Another verse in the epic poem of dominant identity versus individual autonomy was unfolding, as was another verse in the long song of people moving to, or from, Virginia.

Epilogue

Into Virginia's Fifth Century—
Controversy and Commemoration

....

By Jamestown's 400th anniversary, the settlement itself was emerging into the historical light. Archaeologist William Kelso and his team began in 1994 to explore the ancient site. Among their greatest discoveries was the original fort, long thought to have been eroded away by the James River.

Virginians are very conscious of the potential their state offers in terms of cultural tourism, heritage tourism, or just local heritage and identity. With such a rich past to draw from, many different fragments of the past can be selected in one time or place or another for highlighting. Community colleges carry such names as Patrick Henry and John Tyler; universities are named after Christopher Newport, George Mason, and James Madison. In southwestern Virginia is Virginia's Heritage Music Trail, celebrating generations of recorded country music, music whose roots go back through colonial times and beyond. In the Shenandoah Valley is the Museum of Frontier American Culture. And of course the propinquitous Jamestown, Williamsburg, and Yorktown together capture iconic moments from permanent English settlement, through the eighteenth-century capital and the venerable College of William and Mary, to the final military victory in the American Revolution.

Virginia's centuries of history, often thought to exhibit harmony, consensus, and continuity, can just as readily—more readily—be seen as revealing tension, conflict, and change: between Native American and European, black and white, free and enslaved, eastern and western, and Union and Confederate, as well as between federal power and states' rights. Much has been at stake, and winners and losers in each encounter have radically different pasts. Yet black and white live together as free people in Virginia, and Virginia is in the Union, the national

Edgar Allan Poe (1809–1849). In the twenty-first century, many pasts—divergent in time, place, theme, and interpretation—get commemorated in one place or another in Virginia. Just as some emphasize Virginia's colonial beginnings, and others later developments, some have to do with political or military affairs, others with music or literature. Poe, author and editor, is best known for his poems and detective stories. He spent half of his short life outside the South but lived for most of his first twenty years in Richmond, where, having been orphaned at three, he was reared in the household of tobacco merchant John Allan. He briefly attended the new University of Virginia and toward the end of his tormented life returned for a time to Richmond. The city is home to the Edgar Allan Poe Museum. Library of Congress, Prints and Photographs Division, LC-USZ62-10610.

capital on its northern border—100 miles from the state capital, the former capital of the Confederacy.

Virginians take their history seriously. How then, could they not differ on who they are, what Virginia's history is, how it should be remembered, how it should be displayed and celebrated? Virginians have always seen disparate pasts and looked to alternate futures. At the 400th anniversary of Jamestown, it could not be otherwise than that there would be conflicting understandings, needs, wishes, and demands.

The state capital, Richmond, offers a series of recent examples of controversy associated with commemoration of the city's history. As the former capital of the Confederate States of America, Richmond has various museums and statues that highlight the Confederate past. The statues already in place have become more or less accepted, but new statues and murals have proved very controversial. Controversial, too, was an action by the Richmond City Council in 2000 taking Jeb Stuart's name off a bridge and replacing it with S. W. Tucker's, trading a Civil War general for a civil rights lawyer. Residents may want Richmond's history to be displayed, but they differ as to what part of that history ought to be commemorated, or how, or where. Within a few years of 2000, attacks against Robert E. Lee and Abraham Lincoln alike included references to treachery and comparisons to Hitler.

A Monument to Arthur Ashe

Arthur Ashe was born in Richmond during World War II, grew up there, and learned to play a mean game of tennis, but as a teenager he found himself, in what turned out to be the waning years of the Jim Crow era, barred from playing on public tennis courts, even as he starred on the tennis team at Maggie Walker High School. He went on to become the first African American man to win the U.S. Open or the Wimbledon tennis tournament. Tennis made Ashe famous, and then he decided what to do with his fame. Not only was he an exemplary athlete, but he also dedicated much of his life to speaking out against racism and apartheid and, in his later years, to promoting AIDS awareness after he contracted the disease in a 1983 blood transfusion gone awry. When he died in his hometown in 1993, still in his forties, he died a hero who transcended the world of sports.

Richmond launched plans in 1995 to honor Arthur Ashe. The city's planning commission supported erecting a statue to him, like other prominent Virginians, on Monument Avenue. Richmonders could, and many did, praise such a statute as a symbol of racial reconciliation. The proposed placement on Monument Avenue, however, sparked controversy, for those other prominent Virginians included the president of the Confederacy, Jefferson Davis, and famous generals who led the Confederate military, chief among them Robert E. Lee. The division might on first glance have looked like black against white, but it was far more complex than that. Many people who viewed the Confederacy with reverence thought Ashe a poor fit among those heroes from the 1860s, and many people who abhorred the Confederacy agreed. Thus, many members of both groups, regardless of how they saw Ashe and regardless of how they saw Lee, saw dissonance. Yet Monument Avenue is the place of choice for Richmond to place its more prominent memorials to famous Virginians.

Ashe's widow, Jeanne Moutoussamy-Ashe, publicly denounced the proposed location of her late husband's memorial as "the Avenue of Confederate Heroes." She proposed instead that the statue rest outside the proposed African-American Sports Hall of Fame in Richmond. In response, Viola Baskerville, a black member of the Richmond City Council, asserted that Ashe's humanitarian achievements far outweighed his athletic success, no matter how great that was. The Richmond City Council approved the Monument Avenue location, and in 1996 the statue went up. Effectively capturing Arthur Ashe's dual careers—and to him their relative importance—the granite statue depicts him holding a tennis racket in one hand and in the other, held higher than the racket, books. In time, a school in nearby Henrico County was named the Arthur Ashe Jr. Elementary School.

A decade later, people still held their variant yet intersecting views. Black Richmonders in particular still hailed the man who had made them so proud. They celebrated the mentoring program he had founded, Virginia Heroes Inc., to benefit children of all racial identities throughout his community. "There was a huge controversy about putting his statue here," observed Joyce Johnson, program coordinator for Virginia Heroes, standing at the statue. "Some people didn't want Arthur on the same road with all their Confederate war heroes." For his part, Brag Bowling, a state leader in the Sons of Confederate Veterans, said: "We have no problem with honoring him, but honor him in the appropriate place. Don't do it on . . . a street that is world-famous for honoring Confederate war heroes." Bowling pointed out that it might have been more appropriate—and not just to get the statue off Monument Avenue—to have placed it in Byrd Park, from which Ashe had been excluded as a child.

Whether on "the Avenue of Confederate Heroes" or in Byrd Park, whether compared with the time of the Civil War, or the time when the monuments to its heroes had gone up, or the era of Massive Resistance, the statue symbolized how much had changed—in Richmond, in Virginia, in America. Location completely aside, Henry Marsh III, the city's first black mayor, said of Ashe: "He was truly a Renaissance man. There are a great number of us here who get a very warm feeling when we think of Arthur, and regret tremendously that he left us so early."

A New Image of Lee

In 1999, the city revealed its new Canal Walk development project, with thirteen murals depicting various facets of the city's history. One was a large portrait of Robert E. Lee, wearing his Confederate uniform, and it quickly generated a huge controversy. Many white Richmond residents viewed Lee as a hero and welcomed the portrait. By contrast, to many black residents, the portrait was a reminder of the horrors of slavery, and they fought to have it removed. It was taken down after a black city councilman, Sa'ad El-Amin, met with the Richmond Historic Riverfront Foundation and threatened a boycott.

Instead, a different portrait of Robert E. Lee was installed, one that had been taken shortly after Appomattox. A few months later, though, someone destroyed it. The mural was then restored, but it too was vandalized, and, regardless, the controversy continued. Opponents of Lee's image, old or new, were not the only people distressed by the display. Brag Bowling, of the Sons of Confederate Veterans, expressed his distaste for the placement of Lee's image in a series that included Abraham Lincoln as well as a black Virginian, Powhatan Beaty, who had fought for the Union. New depictions of the past kept rousing passions in the present.

Lincoln in the Capital of the Confederacy

In early April 1865, shortly after Union troops occupied Richmond, President Abraham Lincoln made a brief visit to the devastated capital of the obliterated Confederacy. Accompanying him was his twelve-year-old son, Tad. On April 5, 2003, a striking event commemorated the visit. Lincoln would return to Richmond, this time permanently, but he would not raise hackles by claiming a position along Monument Avenue—organizers hoped to avoid replicating the controversy that had accompanied the installation of a statue to Arthur Ashe seven years before. At the city's Civil War Visitor Center, adjacent to the Tredegar Iron Works, a celebrating crowd of several hundred watched the unveiling of a bronze sculpture by David Frech. On a granite wall, behind the images of Tad Lincoln and his father, can be seen the president's pleading phrase, "To Bind Up the Nation's Wounds."

Days after Lincoln's 1865 visit to Richmond, General Lee's Army of Northern Virginia surrendered to General U. S. Grant at Appomattox Courthouse. Yet, as historian Bertram Wyatt-Brown has observed, the statue depicts a quiet moment of a father and his son, not the glory of a victory nearly completed. The sculpture shows a solemn president seated on a bench, his arm around Tad, the boy looking up earnestly at his father, Lincoln gazing down. Frech's representation of Lincoln contrasts with the statues along Richmond's famous Monument Avenue—Robert E. Lee, Stonewall Jackson, and J. E. B. Stuart. Mounted on horseback, forever ready to do battle with the Union, those figures suggest a starkly different stance.

At the Richmond ceremony in 2003, a small group of people attended not to commemorate but to deride the sense of a reunited country that Lincoln had sought to personify by his presence in the capital of the would-be separate nation. The protesters flourished Confederate banners and accused Lincoln of being a war criminal. Ron Wilson, the national commander of the Sons of Confederate Veterans, growled his opposition to this gesture of disrespect to the white South and the thwarted promise of the Confederate experiment. In the dissenters' view, the Confederacy that the Union had overcome was far superior to Lincoln's republic—representing not white supremacy, let alone enslavement, but a more democratic system that an imperious North could not, though it should have, let go its own way.

Supporters of the sculpture believed that commemoration of the visit to Richmond by the "Great Emancipator" was long overdue. Virginia should honor the man who played such a central role in ending slavery as well as in ending the war and reuniting the nation, and the 1865 trip to Richmond symbolized the dual hopes that accompanied the end of the dual horrors of slavery and war. These Lincoln supporters faced opposition, however, from Virginians who blamed Lincoln for the war in the first place. The latter perceived him instead as the perpetrator, through a brutal war, of an unconstitutional violation of states' rights. So, while many Virginians viewed the statue as a fitting memorial to the end of a long, destructive war, others rebuffed it as a symbolic renewed occupation. In this case, as in Arthur Ashe's, not all dissenting views opposed a statue, for Lincoln scholar Gabor Boritt mused that more appropriate might have been a statue depicting another moment during Lincoln's visit. In that scene, an old black man, newly freed, had bowed while lifting his hat, and Lincoln had replicated the gesture of deference by lifting his own hat, the famous stovepipe.

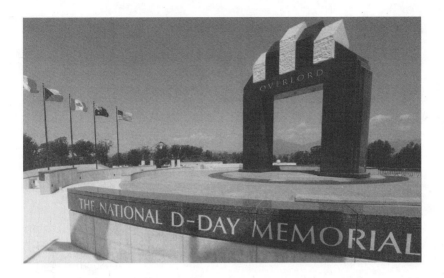

The National D-Day Memorial, Bedford, Virginia. Architect—Dickson Architects and Associates. Amid all the controversy over the meaning of past events, one exception commemorated the "greatest generation" and World War II. It is often said that on June 6, 1944, Bedford County lost more men than did any other community of its size in America. Years later, plans were launched to commemorate the events and the sacrifice—the sacrifice of those who never came home, and the sacrifice of those to whom they did not return. John Robert "Bob" Slaughter, a member of Company D at Omaha Beach, returned to his home in Roanoke after the war, married, raised a family, and worked his way up as a printer for the *Roanoke Times*. The specifics were his, but he embodied the postwar experience of the Omaha Beach veterans in particular and World War II GIs in general, and when he retired in 1987 he took on a new mission, as he established the D-Day Memorial Foundation. World War II's best-selling historian, Stephen Ambrose, signed on in support, as did *Peanuts* cartoonist Charles Schultz. The group broke ground in 1997 and dedicated the National D-Day Memorial on June 4, 2003, with President George W. Bush speaking. Meanwhile, in 1993, the state of Virginia designated U.S. Route 29, which runs north-south through Bedford, as "The 29th Infantry Division Memorial Highway."

Black as Well as White Jeffersons?

Facts are facts, at least sometimes. One is that Thomas Jefferson freed very few of his many slaves during his life or at his death. Another is that the children of Sally Hemings figured prominently among them—Sally Hemings was one slave mother in the early nineteenth century who saw her children gain their freedom. Yet another is that DNA evidence, as reported in *Nature* magazine in 1998, points to a male Jefferson as the father of at least the youngest Hemings child, Eston. The Thomas Jefferson Foundation, which runs Monticello, concluded that Thomas Jefferson was indeed the father of slaves he owned for years and finally freed.

The Monticello Association, which represents the third president's white descendants—the descendants of Martha Jefferson and her two daughters—resisted the foundation's conclusion, resisted the idea that Jefferson had descendants who were not white, resisted the quest by people who identified themselves as the white Jeffersons' mixed-race cousins to be included in the family tree, the yearly reunions, or the Monticello cemetery. Two centuries after Jefferson's presidency, the past still mattered, it seemed to have changed in light of new historical evidence, and it was being contested.

Jamestown at 400

Virginia may date back to the 1580s, but Jamestown does not. Commemoration of the first permanent English settlement in North America has led to periodic festive occasions, including those in 1907 and 1957. By the time the 400th anniversary approached, however, the present had been transformed, and thus the past as well. The 1907 celebration came barely a half-century after universal emancipation in Virginia, and just after the constitutional convention of 1901–1902 put what was meant to be a permanent end to post–Civil War black political power in the state. The 1957 date came in the midst of Massive Resistance against school desegregation, as many white Virginians took extreme measures to see that the work of both the Reconstruction legislature and the 1901–1902 convention be perpetuated in mandating absolute segregation in the schools. By 2007, disfranchisement and segregation were no longer the law of the state, the racial climate contrasted sharply with earlier eras, and the approach to commemoration had a very different tone.

Jamestown 400—the celebrations planned to mark Jamestown's 400th anniversary—inevitably encountered the complicating fact that different groups, with contrasting historical experiences though those 400 years, viewed the anniversary in different ways. Indians in Virginia were far fewer in number in the early twenty-first century than they had been in the early seventeenth. In the wake of Jamestown, their numbers were reduced, their sovereignty destroyed, their territory almost entirely taken, and even their identity denied. Virginia Indians often spoke of "paper genocide," referring especially to the 1924 "racial integrity" act, which divided all Virginians into "white" and "not white," and the strenuous efforts by Bureau of Vital Statistics registrar Walter Plecker to reclassify as "colored" all Virginians who identified themselves as Indians. Plecker to the contrary, as Jamestown 400 approached, more than 15,000 Virginians identified themselves as of Indian descent, and the General Assembly had extended "tribal recognition" to eight groups of Virginia Indians.

Some of the concerns raised with regard to Jamestown 400 had surfaced in the run-up to the 1992 marking of Columbus's first voyage west, but that 500th anniversary did not relate primarily to Virginia. Jamestown's 400th did. One important shift in rhetoric that took place early on was from "celebration" to "commemoration." People could mark the anniversary of the settlement of English Virginia without agreeing to see it as a matter for undiluted celebration.

During Jamestown 400, the colony's establishment in 1607 could scarcely be separated from subsequent developments, especially in 1619, when several of the founding features of Virginia—of early America—began to emerge. One of these was the House of Burgesses, later seen to herald the birth of democracy in English America. Another was the arrival of the first black Virginians, whose presence introduced new questions of race relations and equal rights and opportunities. In 1907 the Association for the Preservation of Virginia Antiquities rejected a proposal that the first black Virginians be recognized on the occasion of Jamestown 300. A hundred years later, as Virginians, whatever their racial identities, marked Jamestown 400, one-half of Virginia's dual history—as the birthplace of American democracy and the birthplace of American slavery—could not be so readily dismissed.

The history of Virginia, regardless of its heightened visibility at Jamestown 400, was important—but also contested. Had it not been so very important, there would have been no occasion for the contest over its meaning. Because of its importance, debate over its meaning was bound to be a vital part of the commemoration.

Four Centuries of Virginia History

Down through the generations after Jamestown's founding, from the first William Byrd or George Mason in the seventeenth century to Harry F. Byrd and

Lucy Randolph Mason in the twentieth, the First Families of Virginia shaped the colony, then the state, and the nation. So did less famous contemporaries, black and white, east and west. In the Revolution, George Washington and other Virginians fought from New England to the Carolinas, from the Atlantic Coast to the Mississippi River, and they won a war for national independence and secured a boundary far to the west of Jamestown. Thomas Jefferson's Louisiana Purchase doubled the new nation's size, and later Virginians brought to fruition a conception of territorial claims dating from Sir Francis Drake's stop at San Francisco.

Virginians wrote America's founding documents—George Mason the Declaration of Rights, Thomas Jefferson the Declaration of Independence. James Madison was the prime architect of the Constitution in Philadelphia in 1787, its ratification the next year in Richmond, and the Bill of Rights that soon followed. When native Virginians took up residence elsewhere, they influenced the shape of the nation. They did so when Sam Houston and Stephen Austin moved to Texas, when John Mercer Langston and William Henry Harrison found new homes in Ohio, and when Henry Clay moved to Kentucky, Cyrus McCormick to Illinois, Dred Scott to Missouri, or Lucille Campbell to New York.

As early as Opechancanough and his niece Pocahontas, the people of Virginia could differ, even profoundly, in their aspirations. Virginians variously authored the "Principles of 1798" and the leading decisions of John Marshall's Supreme Court. Virginians fought, generals and soldiers, on both sides in the Civil War in a massive struggle over the nation's destiny. In the time of the Readjusters, native Virginians challenged each other for control of the state and its policies. In exploring and recounting the past, historians Carter G. Woodson and Douglas Southall Freeman heard clashing muses. In the days of Massive Resistance, Oliver Hill and Samuel Tucker contested Harry Byrd and James J. Kilpatrick. Authentic Virginians all, they struggled for alternative futures.

Circumstances changed, alliances shifted. Patrick Henry, fervent Patriot in the Revolution, fervently opposed James Madison and the Constitution. George Mason, author of the Declaration of Rights for a newly independent state, was cool toward the Bill of Rights for a newly established nation. James Madison, Federalist in the 1780s, led the political opposition to the Federalists in the 1790s. Mills Godwin, proponent of Massive Resistance in the 1950s, revealed a new identity and mission as governor in the 1960s, when the state put far more money than ever before into public schools—desegregated schools. In 2007, a vibrant political culture saw Virginians continue to argue about, even as they cherished, a society that—revealing continuity and change, conflict and consensus—dated back 400 years.

Appendix 1

Governors of Virginia, 1776–2007

....

Beginning with the Constitution of 1776, governors were chosen by the General Assembly; beginning with the Constitution of 1851, they were chosen by popular election. Under the Constitution of 1776, governors were elected to one-year terms, for no more than three terms in succession. The Constitution of 1830 changed the term to three years, and the Constitution of 1851 changed it to four years, in each case with no eligibility for a second successive term.

Patrick Henry	1776–1779
Thomas Jefferson	1779–1781[a]
Thomas Nelson Jr.	1781[a]
Benjamin Harrison	1782–1784
Patrick Henry	1784–1786
Edmund Randolph	1786–1788
Beverley Randolph	1788–1791
Henry "Light Horse Harry" Lee	1791–1794 (Federalist)
Robert Brooke	1794–1796 (D-R)
James Wood	1796–1799[a] (Federalist)
James Monroe	1799–1802 (D-R)
John Page	1802–1805 (D-R)
William H. Cabell	1805–1808 (D-R)
John Tyler Sr.	1808–1811[a] (D-R)
James Monroe	1811[a] (D-R)
George William Smith	1811 (D-R)
James Barbour	1812–1814 (D-R)
Wilson Cary Nicholas	1814–1816 (D-R)
James Patton Preston	1816–1819 (D-R)
Thomas Mann Randolph	1819–1822 (D-R)

James Pleasants	1822–1825 (D-R)
John Tyler Jr.	1825–1827 (D-R)
William Branch Giles	1827–1830 (D)
John Floyd	1830–1834 (D)
Littleton Waller Tazewell	1834–1836[a]
David Campbell	1837–1840 (Whig)
Thomas Walker Gilmer	1840–1841[a] (Whig)
James McDowell	1843–1846[a] (D)
William Smith	1846–1849 (D)
John Buchanan Floyd	1849–1852 (D)
Joseph Johnson	1852–1856 (D)
Henry Alexander Wise	1856–1860 (D)
John Letcher	1860–1864 (D)
William Smith	1864–1865 (D)
Francis H. Pierpoint[b]	1861–1865 (governor of the Restored government, Unionist)
Francis H. Pierpont[b]	1865–1868 (provisional governor, R)
Henry Horatio Wells[b]	1868–1869 (provisional governor, R)
Gilbert C. Walker[b]	1869 (provisional governor, R)
Gilbert C. Walker	1870–1874 (R)
James Lawson Kemper	1874–1878 (Conservative)
Frederick William Mackey Holliday	1878–1882 (Conservative)
William E. Cameron	1882–1886 (Readjuster)
Fitzhugh Lee	1886–1890 (D)
Philip W. McKinney	1890–1894 (D)
Charles T. O'Ferrall	1894–1898 (D)
James Hoge Tyler	1898–1902 (D)
Andrew Jackson Montague	1902–1906 (D)
Claude A. Swanson	1906–1910 (D)
William Hodges Mann	1910–1914 (D)
Henry Carter Stuart	1914–1918 (D)
Westmoreland Davis	1918–1922 (D)
E. Lee Trinkle	1922–1926 (D)
Harry F. Byrd Sr.	1926–1930 (D)
John Garland Pollard	1930–1934 (D)
George C. Peery	1934–1938 (D)
James H. Price	1938–1942 (D)

Colgate W. Darden Jr.	1942–1946 (D)
William M. Tuck	1946–1950 (D)
John S. Battle	1950–1954 (D)
Thomas B. Stanley	1954–1958 (D)
J. Lindsay Almond Jr.	1958–1962 (D)
Albertis S. Harrison Jr.	1962–1966 (D)
Mills E. Godwin Jr.	1966–1970 (D)
A. Linwood Holton Jr.	1970–1974 (R)
Mills E. Godwin Jr.	1974–1978 (R)
John N. Dalton	1978–1982 (R)
Charles S. Robb	1982–1986 (D)
Gerald L. Baliles	1986–1990 (D)
L. Douglas Wilder	1990–1994 (D)
George Allen Jr.	1994–1998 (R)
James S. Gilmore III	1998–2002 (R)
Mark R. Warner	2002–2006 (D)
Timothy M. Kaine	2006–2010 (D)

Notes: D-R = Democratic-Republican; D = Democrat; R = Republican

[a] From the 1770s through the 1840s, if death or resignation caused a vacancy, a member (not named here) of the Council of State served as acting governor.

[b] During the Civil War, Francis H. Pierpoint served under Virginia's "Restored government," from 1861 to 1863 at Wheeling (before West Virginia became a state) and then from 1863 to 1865 at Alexandria. Between 1865 and 1870, the Union commanding general appointed a provisional governor.

Appendix 2

U.S. Senators from Virginia, 1789–2007

William Grayson	1789–1790 (D)	Richard Henry Lee	1789–1792 (D)
John Walker	1790 (Fed.)	John Taylor of Caroline	1792–1794 (D)
James Monroe	1790–1794 (D)	Henry Tazewell	1794–1799 (D)
Stevens T. Mason	1794–1803 (D)	Wilson C. Nicholas	1799–1804 (D)
John Taylor of Caroline	1803 (D)	Andrew Moore	1804 (D)
Abraham B. Venable	1803–1804 (D)	William Branch Giles	1804–1815 (D)
William Branch Giles	1804 (D)	Armistead T. Mason	1816–1817 (D)
Andrew Moore	1804–1809 (D)	John W. Eppes	1817–1819 (D)
Richard Brent	1809–1814 (D)	James Pleasants	1819–1822 (D)
James Barbour	1815–1825 (D)	John Taylor of Caroline	1822–1824 (D)
John Randolph	1825–1827 (D)	Littleton W. Tazewell	1824–1832 (D)
John Tyler	1827–1836 (D, W)	William C. Rives	1832–1834 (D)
William C. Rives	1836–1839 (D)	Benjamin W. Leigh	1834–1836 (W)
Vacant	1839–1841	Richard E. Parker	1836–1837 (D)
William C. Rives	1841–1845 (W)	William H. Roane	1837–1841 (D)
Isaac S. Pennybacker	1845–1847 (D)	William S. Archer	1841–1847 (W)
James M. Mason	1847–1861 (D)	Robert M. T. Hunter	1847–1861 (D)
Waitman T. Willey	1861–1863 (U)	John S. Carlile	1861–1865 (U)
Lemuel J. Bowden	1863–1864 (R)		

VACANT 1864–1870 (Reconstruction) VACANT 1865–1870 (Reconstruction)

John F. Lewis	1870–1875 (R)	John W. Johnston	1870–1883 (D)
Robert E. Withers	1875–1881 (D)	Harrison H. Riddleberger	1883–1889 (R)
William Mahone	1881–1887 (R)	John S. Barbour Jr.	1889–1892 (D)
John W. Daniel	1887–1910 (D)	Eppa Hunton	1892–1895 (D)

Claude A. Swanson	1910–1933 (D)	Thomas S. Martin	1895–1919 (D)
Harry F. Byrd Sr.	1933–1965 (D)	Carter Glass	1920–1946 (D)
Harry F. Byrd Jr.	1965–1983 (D, Ind.)	Thomas G. Burch	1946 (D)
Paul S. Trible Jr.	1983–1989 (R)	A. Willis Robertson	1946–1966 (D)
Charles S. Robb	19´89–2001 (D)	William B. Spong Jr.	1966–1973 (D)
George Allen	2001– (R)	William L. Scott	1973–1979 (R)
James Webb	2007– (D)	John W. Warner	1979– (R)

Notes: D = Democrat; Fed. = Federalist; R = Republican; U = Unionist; W = Whig

Appendix 3

Members of the Virginia Supreme Court, 1789–2007

....

The highest state court in Virginia, long called the Supreme Court of Appeals, became the Virginia Supreme Court under the Constitution of 1971. Since 1789, when the Supreme Court of Appeals began operations, judges have varied in number, from as few as three to as many as seven. Until 1928, members of the state supreme court were called judges and were headed by a president; since then they have been called justices, and have been headed by a chief justice. Except for when the Constitution of 1851 provided for popular election, judges of these various courts were always appointed by the General Assembly, though the governor has often filled vacancies pending the next session of the legislature.

Not only did the Civil War era bring a brief experiment with an elective state supreme court, but it also occasioned chronic institutional discontinuity. Judge George Hay Lee, who resided in what became West Virginia, never again sat on the court after Virginia seceded in April 1861. The others continued their service into 1865, even though elections would under normal conditions have been held in 1864. Under the restored state's Constitution of 1864, which ended the elective experiment, three judges were appointed in 1866, only one of whom, President Richard C. L. Moncure, was a holdover from the previous court. The judges whom the legislature had selected were unseated in 1869, when military authorities appointed three new men: Horace B. Burnham, Orlaff M. Dorman, and Westel Willoughby. In 1870, under yet another state constitution, a new court of five judges was appointed, with two members from 1866–1869 resuming their seats.

John Blair	1789
James Mercer	1789–1793
Henry Tazewell	1793–1794
Edmund Pendleton, president, 1789–1803	1789–1803
Paul Carrington	1789–1807
Peter Lyons, president, 1803–1809	1789–1809
William Fleming, president, 1809–1824	1789–1824
Spencer Roane	1795–1822
St. George Tucker	1804–1811
James Pleasants	1811
John Coalter	1811–1831
Francis T. Brooke, president, 1824–1831	1811–1851
William H. Cabell, president, 1842–1851	1811–1852
John W. Green	1822–1834
Dabney Carr	1824–1837
Henry St. George Tucker, president, 1831–1841	1831–1841
William Brockenbrough	1834–1838
Richard Elliott Parker	1837–1840
Robert Stanard	1838–1846
John J. Allen, president, 1851–1865	1840–1865
Briscoe G. Baldwin	1842–1852
William Daniel	1846–1865
Richard C. L. Moncure, president, 1866–1869, 1870–1882	1851–1866, 1866–1869, 1870–1882
Green B. Samuels	1852–1859
George Hay Lee	1852–1865
William J. Robertson	1859–1865
Alexander Rives	1866–1869
William T. Joynes	1866–1869, 1870–1872
Francis T. Anderson	1870–1882
Joseph Christian	1870–1882
Waller R. Staples	1870–1882
Wood Bouldin	1872–1876
Edward C. Burks	1876–1882
Lunsford L. Lewis, president, 1882–1894	1882–1894
Thomas T. Fauntleroy	1883–1894
Drury A. Hinton	1883–1894
Benjamin W. Lacy	1883–1894
Robert A. Richardson	1883–1894

John W. Riely	1895–1900
John A. Buchanan	1895–1915
James Keith, president, 1895–1916	1895–1916
Richard H. Cardwell, president, 1916	1895–1916
George M. Harrison, president, 1916–1917	1895–1917
Archer A. Phlegar	1900–1901
Stafford G. Whittle, president, 1917–1919	1901–1919
Joseph L. Kelly, president, 1920–1924, 1925	1915–1924, 1925
Frederick W. Sims, president, 1924–1925	1916–1925
Robert R. Prentis, president/chief justice, 1925–1931	1916–1931
Martin P. Burks	1917–1928
Edward W. Saunders	1920–1921
Jesse F. West	1922–1929
Preston W. Campbell, chief justice, 1931–1946	1924–1946
R. H. L. Chichester	1925–1930
Henry W. Holt, chief justice, 1946–1947	1928–1947
Louis S. Epes	1929–1935
George L. Browning	1930–1947
Herbert B. Gregory	1930–1951
Edward W. Hudgins, chief justice, 1947–1958	1930–1958
Joseph W. Chinn	1931–1936
John W. Eggleston, chief justice, 1958–1969	1935–1969
C. Vernon Spratley	1936–1967
Archibald Chapman Buchanan	1946–1969
Abram Penn Staples	1947–1951
Willis Dance Miller	1947–1960
Lemuel Franklin Smith	1951–1956
Kennon Caithness Whittle	1951–1965
Harold Fleming Snead, chief justice, 1969–1974	1957–1974
Lawrence W. I'Anson, chief justice, 1974–1981	1958–1981
Harry Lee Carrico, chief justice, 1981–2003	1961–2003
Thomas Christian Gordon Jr.	1965–1972
Albertis S. Harrison Jr.	1967–1981
Alex M. Harman Jr.	1969–1979
George M. Cochran	1969–1987
Richard Harding Poff	1972–1988
A. Christian Compton	1974–2000
W. Carrington Thompson	1980–1983
Roscoe B. Stephenson Jr.	1981–1997

Charles S. Russell	1982–1991
John Charles Thomas	1983–1989
Henry H. Whiting	1987–1995
Elizabeth B. Lacy	1988–
Leroy Rountree Hassell Sr., chief justice, 2003–	1989–
Barbara Milano Keenan	1991–
Lawrence L. Koontz Jr.	1995–
Cynthia D. Kinser	1997–
Donald W. Lemons	2000–
G. Steven Agee	2003–

For further reading: Thomas R. Morris, *The Virginia Supreme Court: An Institutional and Political Analysis* (1975); Margaret Virginia Nelson, *A Study of Judicial Review in Virginia, 1789–1928* (1947); Samuel N. Pincus, *The Virginia Supreme Court, Blacks, and the Law, 1870–1902* (1990); Peter Wallenstein, *Blue Laws and Black Codes: Conflict, Courts, and Change in Twentieth-Century Virginia* (2004).

Appendix 4

Virginia and Presidential Elections, 1789–2004

....

In the first nine presidential elections, Virginia cast its electoral college votes for a native son every time, and eight times the Virginia candidate won: George Washington twice (10 votes in 1789 and 21 in 1792, after the first federal census); Jefferson in 1796 and 1800 (21 votes each time) and again in 1804 (24 votes), the first election in which electoral votes were cast separately for president and vice president; Madison in 1808 (24 votes) and 1812 (25 votes); and James Monroe in 1816 and 1820 (25 each time).

In the elections that followed, the number of electors reflected shifts in the relative size of Virginia's population. The popular vote reflected not only party shifts and population growth (or decline in 1870, after the departure of West Virginia) but also changes in the electorate's size and its makeup by class, race, gender, and age.

Year	Presidential Candidates (Party) (* = national winner)	Absolute Vote	Percent	Electoral Vote
1824	William H. Crawford (D-R)	8,558	55.7	24
	* John Quincy Adams (D-R)	3,419	22.2	
	Andrew Jackson (D-R)	2,975	19.4	
	Henry Clay (D-R)	419	2.7	
1828	* Andrew Jackson (D-R)	26,854	69.0	24
	John Quincy Adams (National R)	12,070	31.0	

1832	* Andrew Jackson (D)	34,243	75.0	23
	Henry Clay (National R)	11,436	25.0	
	Other	3	0.0	
1836	* Martin Van Buren (D)	30,556	56.6	23
	Hugh L. White (Whig)	23,384	43.4	
	Other	5	0.0	
1840	Martin Van Buren (D)	43,757	50.6	23
	* William H. Harrison (Whig)	42,637	49.4	
1844	* James K. Polk (D)	50,679	53.0	17
	Henry Clay (Whig)	44,860	47.0	
1848	Lewis Cass (D)	46,739	50.8	17
	* Zachary Taylor (Whig)	45,265	49.2	
1852	* Franklin Pierce (D)	73,872	55.7	15
	Winfield Scott (Whig)	58,732	44.3	
1856	* James Buchanan (D)	90,083	60.0	15
	Millard Fillmore (Whig/American)	60,150	40.0	
1860	John Bell (Constitutional Union)	74,481	44.6	15
	John C. Breckinridge (Southern D)	74,325	44.5	
	Stephen A. Douglas (D)	16,198	9.7	
	* Abraham Lincoln (R)	1,887	1.1	
1864	Virginia did not participate			
1868	Virginia did not participate			
1872	* Ulysses S. Grant (R)	93,463	50.5	11
	Horace Greeley (D, Liberal R)	91,647	49.5	
	Other	85	0.1	
1876	Samuel J. Tilden (D)	140,770	59.6	11
	* Rutherford B. Hayes (R)	95,518	40.4	
1880	Winfield S. Hancock (D)	128,083	60.5	11
	* James A. Garfield (R)	83,533	39.5	

1884	*	Grover Cleveland (D)	145,491	51.1	12
		James G. Blaine (R)	139,356	48.9	
		Other	130	0.0	
1888		Grover Cleveland (D)	152,004	50.0	12
	*	Benjamin Harrison (R)	150,399	49.5	
		Other	1,684	0.6	
1892	*	Grover Cleveland (D)	164,136	56.2	12
		Benjamin Harrison (R)	113,098	38.7	
		James Weaver (People's)	12,275	4.2	
		Other	2,729	0.9	
1896		William Jennings Bryan (D)	154,708	52.5	12
	*	William McKinley (R)	135,379	45.9	
		Other	4,587	1.6	
1900		William Jennings Bryan (D)	146,079	55.3	12
	*	William McKinley (R)	115,769	43.8	
		Other	2,360	0.9	
1904		Alton Parker (D)	80,649	61.8	12
	*	Theodore Roosevelt (R)	48,180	37.0	
		Other	1,581	1.2	
1908		William Jennings Bryan (D)	82,946	60.5	12
	*	William Taft (R)	52,572	38.4	
		Other	1,547	1.1	
1912	*	Woodrow Wilson (D)	90,332	66.0	12
		William Taft (R)	23,288	17.0	
		Theodore Roosevelt (Progressive)	21,776	15.9	
		Other	1,559	1.2	
1916	*	Woodrow Wilson (D)	101,840	67.0	12
		Charles Evans Hughes (R)	48,384	31.8	
		Other	1,801	1.2	
1920		James Cox (D)	141,670	61.3	12
	*	Warren Harding (R)	87,456	37.9	
		Other	1,907	0.8	

1924		John W. Davis (D)	139,716	62.5	12
	*	Calvin Coolidge (R)	73,312	32.8	
		Robert LaFollette (Progressive)	10,377	4.6	
		Other	197	0.1	
1928	*	Herbert Hoover (R)	164,609	53.9	12
		Alfred Smith (D)	140,146	45.9	
		Other	603	0.2	
1932	*	Franklin D. Roosevelt (D)	203,979	68.5	11
		Herbert Hoover (R)	89,637	30.1	
		Other	4,326	1.5	
1936	*	Franklin D. Roosevelt (D)	234,980	70.2	11
		Alfred Landon (R)	98,336	29.4	
		Other	1,274	0.4	
1940	*	Franklin D. Roosevelt (D)	235,961	68.1	11
		Wendell Willkie (R)	109,363	31.6	
		Other	1,283	0.4	
1944	*	Franklin D. Roosevelt (D)	242,276	62.4	11
		Thomas Dewey (R)	145,243	37.4	
		Other	966	0.2	
1948	*	Harry S. Truman (D)	200,786	47.9	11
		Thomas Dewey (R)	172,070	41.0	
		J. Strom Thurmond (States' Rights)	43,393	10.4	
		Other	3,007	0.7	
1952	*	Dwight Eisenhower (R)	349,037	56.3	12
		Adlai Stevenson (D)	268,677	43.4	
		Other	1,975	0.3	
1956	*	Dwight Eisenhower (R)	386,459	55.4	12
		Adlai Stevenson (D)	267,760	38.4	
		T. Coleman Andrews (Constitution)	42,964	6.2	
		Other	795	0.1	
1960		Richard M. Nixon (R)	404,521	52.4	12
	*	John F. Kennedy (D)	362,327	47.0	
		Other	4,601	0.6	

1964	*	Lyndon B. Johnson (D)	558,038	53.5	12
		Barry Goldwater (R)	481,334	46.2	
		Other	2,895	0.3	
1968	*	Richard M. Nixon (R)	590,319	43.4	12
		Hubert Humphrey (D)	442,387	32.5	
		George Wallace (Am. Ind.)	321,833	23.6	
		Other	6,952	0.5	
1972	*	Richard M. Nixon (R)	988,493	67.8	11
		George McGovern (D)	438,887	30.1	
		John Hospers	0	0.0	1
		Other	11,839	2.0	
1976		Gerald R. Ford (R)	836,554	49.3	12
	*	James Earl Carter (D)	813,896	48.0	
		Other	46,644	2.7	
1980	*	Ronald Reagan (R)	989,609	53.0	12
		James Earl Carter (D)	752,174	40.3	
		John Anderson (Ind.)	95,418	5.1	
		Other	28,831	1.5	
1984	*	Ronald Reagan (R)	1,337,078	62.3	12
		Walter F. Mondale (D)	796,250	37.1	
		Other	13,307	0.6	
1988	*	George H. W. Bush (R)	1,309,162	59.7	12
		Michael Dukakis (D)	859,799	39.2	
		Other	22,648	1.0	
1992		George H. W. Bush (R)	1,150,517	45.0	13
	*	William J. Clinton (D)	1,038,650	40.6	
		Ross Perot (Independent)	348,639	13.6	
		Other	20,859	0.8	
1996		Robert Dole (R)	1,138,350	47.1	13
	*	William J. Clinton (D)	1,091,060	45.1	
		Ross Perot (Reform)	159,861	6.6	
		Other	27,371	1.1	

2000	*	George W. Bush (R)	1,437,490	52.5	13
		Albert Gore Jr. (D)	1,217,290	44.4	
		Ralph Nader (Green)	59,398	2.2	
		Other	25,269	0.9	
2004	*	George W. Bush (R)	1,716,959	53.7	13
		John Kerry (D)	1,454,742	45.5	
		Other	26,666	0.8	

Source: *Presidential Elections, 1789–2004* (2005).

Notes: Notes: D-R = Democratic-Republican; D = Democrat; R = Republican

Appendix 5

Virginia and the

Census Returns, 1790–2000

Population Figures for Post-1860s Virginia

Year	Total	White	Black	Other	State Rank
2000	7,078,515	5,120,110	1,390,253	568,152	12
1990	6,187,358	4,791,739	1,162,994	232,625	12
1980	5,346,818	4,229,798	1,008,668	108,352	14
1970	4,648,494	3,761,514	861,368	25,612	14
1960	3,966,949	3,142,443	816,258	8,248	14
1950	3,318,680	2,581,555	734,211	2,914	15
1940	2,677,773	2,015,583	661,449	741	19
1930	2,421,851	1,770,441	650,165	1,245	20
1920	2,309,187	1,617,909	690,017	1,261	20
1910	2,061,612	1,389,809	671,096	707	20
1900	1,854,184	1,192,855	660,722	607	17
1890	1,655,980	1,020,122	635,438	420	15
1880	1,512,565	880,858	631,616	91	14
1870	1,225,163	712,089	512,841	233	10

Population Figures for Pre-1860s Virginia (including what became West Virginia)

Year	Total	White	Slave	Free Person of Color	Rank
1860	1,596,318	1,047,299	490,865	58,154	5
1850	1,421,661	894,800	472,528	54,333	4
1840	1,249,764	740,968	450,361	58,435	4
1830	1,220,978	694,300	471,371	55,307	3
1820	1,075,069	603,335	427,005	44,729	2
1810	983,152	551,514	394,357	37,281	1
1800	886,149	514,280	345,796	24,901	1
1790	747,610	442,117	292,627	12,866	1

The Three Largest Cities in Virginia by Population, 1790–2000

Year	Richmond	Norfolk	Others in the Top Three	
2000	197,790 (4)	234,403 (2)	425,257 (1)	Virginia Beach
			199,184 (3)	Chesapeake
1990	203,056 (3)	261,229 (2)	393,069 (1)	Virginia Beach
1980	219,214 (2)	266,979 (1)	262,199 (3)	Virginia Beach
1970	249,621 (2)	307,951 (1)	172,106 (3)	Virginia Beach
1960	219,958 (2)	305,872 (1)	114,773 (3)	Portsmouth
1950	230,310 (1)	213,513 (2)	91,921 (3)	Roanoke
1940	193,042 (1)	144,332 (2)	69,287 (3)	Roanoke
1930	182,929 (1)	129,710 (2)	69,206 (3)	Roanoke
1920	171,667 (1)	115,777 (2)	54,387 (3)	Portsmouth
1910	127,628 (1)	67, 452 (2)	34,874 (3)	Roanoke
1900	85,050 (1)	46,624 (2)	21,810 (3)	Petersburg
1890	81,388 (1)	34,871 (2)	22,680 (3)	Petersburg
1880	63,600 (1)	21,966 (2)	21,656 (3)	Petersburg
1870	51,038 (1)	19,229 (2)	18,950 (3)	Petersburg
1860	37,910 (1)	14,620 (3)	18,266 (2)	Petersburg
1850	27,570 (1)	14,326 (2)	14,010 (3)	Petersburg
1840	20,153 (1)	10,920 (3)	11,136 (2)	Petersburg
1830	16,060 (1)	9,814 (2)	8,322 (3)	Petersburg
1820	12,067 (1)	8,478 (2)	6,690 (3)	Petersburg
1810	9,735 (1)	9,193 (2)	5,668 (3)	Petersburg
1800	5,737 (2)	6,926 (1)	3,521 (3)	Petersburg
1790	3,761 (1)	2,959 (2)	2,828 (3)	Petersburg

For Further Learning
about Virginia History

....

Reference Bibliography

Arnold, Scott David. *A Guidebook to Virginia's Historical Markers.* Charlottesville: University of Virginia Press, 2007.

Dinan, John J. *The Virginia State Constitution: A Reference Guide.* Westport, Conn.: Praeger, 2006.

Hening, William Waller, ed. *The Statutes at Large*, 1619–1792. 13 vols. 1809–1823. Reprint, Charlottesville: University Press of Virginia, 1969.

Howard, A. E. Dick. *Commentaries on the Constitution of Virginia.* 2 vols. Charlottesville: University Press of Virginia, 1974.

Kneebone, John T., et al., eds. *Dictionary of Virginia Biography.* 3 vols. to date. Richmond: Library of Virginia, 1998–.

Leonard, Cynthia Miller, comp. *The General Assembly of Virginia, July 30, 1619–January 11, 1978: A Bicentennial Register of Members.* Richmond: Virginia State Library, 1978.

Loth, Calder, ed. *The Virginia Landmarks Register.* Charlottesville: University Press of Virginia, 1999.

Minchinton, Walter, Celia King, and Peter Waite, eds. *Virginia Slave-Trade Statistics, 1698–1775.* Richmond: Virginia State Library, 1984.

Perdue, Charles L. Jr., Thomas E. Barden, and Robert K. Phillips, eds. *Weevils in the Wheat: Interviews with Virginia Ex-Slaves.* Charlottesville: University Press of Virginia, 1976.

Presidential Elections, 1789–2004. Washington, D.C.: CQ Press, 2005.

Rose, Willie Lee, ed. *A Documentary History of Slavery in North America.* New York: Oxford University Press, 1976.

Salmon, Emily J., et al., eds. *The Hornbook of Virginia History: A Ready-Reference Guide to the Old Dominion's People, Places, and Past.* 5th ed., rev. and enlarged. Richmond: Library of Virginia, 2007.

Stephenson, Richard W., and Marianne M. McKee, eds. *Virginia in Maps: Four Centuries of Settlement, Growth, and Development.* Richmond: Library of Virginia, 2000.

Younger, Edward, and James Tice Moore, eds. *The Governors of Virginia, 1860–1978.* Charlottesville: University Press of Virginia, 1982.

Websites on Early Virginia

The Geography of Slavery in Virginia: Virginia Runaways. http://www.vcdh.virginia .edu/gos/.

Valley of the Shadow. http://valley.vcdh.virgna.edu/.

Virtual Jamestown. http://www.virtualjamestown.org/.

Films on Twentieth-Century Virginia

The Carter Family: Will the Circle Be Unbroken? DVD. PBS, 2005. Transcript at http:// pbs.org/wgbh/amex/carterfamily/filmmore//pt.html.

Down in the Old Belt: Voices from the Tobacco South. Researched, written, produced, and directed by James P. Crawford. DVD video, 57 minutes. Swinging Gate Productions, 2005. Available from www.swinginggateproductions.com.

"It's Just Me …": The Integration of the Arlington Public Schools. Produced by Arlington Public Schools. VHS. Arlington Educational Television, 2001.

Massive Resistance. Produced by George H. Gilliam. Videocassette, 58 minutes. Community Idea Stations, 2000.

New Deal Virginia. Produced by George H. Gilliam; written by Tom McNeer. Production director Shawn M. Freude. Videocassette, 29 minutes. Central Virginia Educational Telecommunications Corporation, 1999.

The Road to Brown. Executive producer, William Elwood. Produced and directed by Mykola Kulish; written by William A. Elwood. Videocassette, 47 minutes. California Newsreel, 1990.

Virginia Fights World War II. Produced by George H. Gilliam. Videocassette, 60 minutes. Community Idea Stations, 2001.

Books for Further Reading

PART I. 1580S–1760S: BETWEEN TWO WORLDS

Helen C. Rountree, *Pocahontas, Powhatan, Opechancanough: Three Indian Lives Changed by Jamestown* (2005).

CHAPTER 1. ELIZABETHAN VIRGINIA

Stephen Adams, *The Best and Worst Country in the World: Perspectives on the Early Virginia Landscape* (2001); James Axtell, *After Columbus: Essays in the Ethnohistory of Colonial North America* (1988); Carl Bridenbaugh, *Early Americans* (1981); April

Lee Hatfield, *Atlantic Virginia: Intercolonial Relations in the Seventeenth Century* (2004); Paul E. Hoffman, *A New Andalucia and a Way to the Orient: The American Southeast during the Sixteenth Century* (1990); Paul Hulton, *America, 1585: The Complete Drawings of John White* (1984); Karen Ordahl Kupperman, *Roanoke: The Abandoned Colony* (1984); Clifford M. Lewis and Albert J. Loomie, *The Spanish Jesuit Mission in Virginia, 1570–1572* (1953); William H. MacLeish, *The Day before America* (1994); Peter C. Mancall, ed., *Envisioning America: English Plans for the Colonization of North America, 1580–1640* (1995); Lee Miller, *Roanoke: Solving the Mystery of England's Lost Colony* (2001); Giles Milton, *Big Chief Elizabeth: The Adventures and Fate of the First English Colonists in America* (2001); David G. Moore, *Catawba Valley Mississippian: Ceramics, Chronology, and Catawba Indians* (2002); Ivor Noël Hume, *The Virginia Adventure: Roanoke to James Towne, an Archaeological and Historical Odyssey* (1994); Helen C. Rountree and E. Randolph Turner III, *Before and after Jamestown: Virginia's Powhatans and Their Predecessors* (2002); Carl Ortwin Sauer, *Sixteenth Century North America: The Land and the People as Seen by the Europeans* (1971); Margaret Holmes Williamson, *Powhatan Lords of Life and Death: Command and Consent in Seventeenth-Century Virginia* (2003).

CHAPTER 2. JAMESTOWN

Ann Uhry Abrams, *The Pilgrims and Pocahontas: Rival Myths of American Origin* (1999); Diana Karter Appelbaum, *Thanksgiving: An American Holiday, An American History* (1984); Bernard Bailyn, *Atlantic History: Concepts and Contours* (2005); Warren M. Billings, *A Little Parliament: The Virginia General Assembly in the Seventeenth Century* (2004); Alfred W. Crosby, *The Columbian Exchange: Biological and Cultural Consequences of 1492* (1972); Alfred W. Crosby, *Ecological Imperialism: The Biological Expansion of Europe, 900–1900* (1986); Frederick W. Gleach, *Powhatan's World and Colonial Virginia: A Conflict of Cultures* (1997); James Horn, *A Land as God Made It: Jamestown and the Birth of America* (2005); William M. Kelso, *Jamestown: The Buried Truth* (2006); David A. Price, *Love and Hate in Jamestown: John Smith, Pocahontas, and the Heart of a New Nation* (2003); Helen C. Rountree, *Pocahontas, Powhatan, Opechancanough: Three Indian Lives Changed by Jamestown* (2005); Helen C. Rountree and E. Randolph Turner III, *Before and after Jamestown: Virginia's Powhatans and Their Predecessors* (2002); Susan Schmidt, *Landfall along the Chesapeake: In the Wake of Captain John Smith* (2006); Camilla Townsend, *Pocahontas and the Powhatan Dilemma: An American Portrait* (2004); Alden T. Vaughan, *American Genesis: Captain John Smith and the Founding of Virginia* (1975).

CHAPTER 3. LAND AND LABOR

Virginia DeJohn Anderson, *Creatures of Empire: How Domestic Animals Transformed Early America* (2004); Ira Berlin, *Many Thousands Gone: The First Two Centuries of Slavery in North America* (1998); Warren M. Billings, ed., *The Old Dominion in the Seventeenth Century: A Documentary History of Virginia, 1606–1689*

(1975); Warren M. Billings, *Sir William Berkeley and the Forging of Colonial Virginia* (2004); Edward L. Bond, *Damned Souls in a Tobacco Colony: Religion in Seventeenth-Century Virginia* (2000); T. H. Breen, *Tobacco Culture: The Mentality of the Great Tidewater Planters on the Eve of Revolution* (1985); T. H. Breen and Stephen Innes, *"Myne Owne Ground": Race and Freedom on Virginia's Eastern Shore, 1640–1676* (1980, 2005); Kathleen M. Brown, *Good Wives, Nasty Wenches, and Anxious Patriarchs: Gender, Race, and Power in Colonial Virginia* (1996); Lois Green Carr, Philip D. Morgan, and Jean B. Russo, eds., *Colonial Chesapeake Society* (1988); Douglas B. Chambers, *Murder at Montpelier: Igbo Africans in Virginia* (2005); Pamela C. Copeland and Richard K. MacMaster, *The Five George Masons: Patriots and Planters of Virginia and Maryland* (1975); Wesley Frank Craven, *White, Red, and Black: The Seventeenth Century Virginian* (1971); A. Roger Ekirch, *Bound for America: The Transportation of British Convicts to the Colonies, 1718–1775* (1987); Jack P. Greene, *Pursuits of Happiness: The Social Development of Early Modern British Colonies and the Formation of American Culture* (1988); Sally E. Hadden, *Slave Patrols: Law and Violence in Virginia and the Carolinas* (2001); April Lee Hatfield, *Atlantic Virginia: Intercolonial Relations in the Seventeenth Century* (2004); James Horn, *Adapting to a New World: English Society in the Seventeenth-Century Chesapeake* (1994); Rhys Isaac, *Landon Carter's Uneasy Kingdom: Revolution and Rebellion on a Virginia Plantation* (2004); Winthrop D. Jordan, *The White Man's Burden: Historical Origins of Racism in the United States* (1974); John Gilman Kolp, *Gentlemen and Freeholders: Electoral Politics in Colonial Virginia* (1998); Allen Kulikoff, *Tobacco and Slaves: The Development of Southern Cultures in the Chesapeake, 1680–1800* (1986); Kenneth A. Lockridge, *The Diary and Life of William Byrd II of Virginia, 1674–1744* (1987); T. O. Madden Jr., with Anne L. Miller, *We Were Always Free: The Maddens of Culpeper County, Virginia, a 200-Year Family History* (1992); William H. McNeil, *The Great Frontier: Freedom and Hierarchy in Modern Times* (1983); Edmund S. Morgan, *American Slavery, American Freedom: The Ordeal of Early Virginia* (1975); Philip D. Morgan, *Slave Counterpoint: Black Culture in the Eighteenth-Century Chesapeake and Lowcountry* (1998); Gerald W. Mullin, *Flight and Rebellion: Slave Resistance in Eighteenth-Century Virginia* (1972); John Ruston Pagan, *Anne Orthwood's Bastard: Sex and Law in Early Virginia* (2003); Anthony S. Parent Jr., *Foul Means: The Formation of a Slave Society in Virginia, 1660–1740* (2003); James R. Perry, *The Formation of a Society on Virginia's Eastern Shore, 1615–1655* (1990); Michal J. Rozbicki, *The Complete Colonial Gentleman: Cultural Legitimacy in Plantation America* (1998); Darrett B. Rutman and Anita H. Rutman, *A Place in Time: Middlesex County, Virginia, 1650–1750* (1984); Daniel Blake Smith, *Inside the Great House: Planter Family Life in Eighteenth-Century Chesapeake Society* (1980); Michel Sobel, *The World They Made Together: Black and White Values in Eighteenth-Century Virginia* (1987); Charles S. Sydnor, *Gentlemen Freeholders: Political Practices in Washington's Virginia* (1952; published subsequently as *American Revolutionaries in the Making* [1962]); Thad W. Tate and David L. Ammerman, eds., *The Chesapeake in the Seventeenth Century:*

Essays on Anglo-American Society and Politics (1979); Alden T. Vaughan, *Roots of American Racism: Essay on the Colonial Experience* (1995); Peter Wallenstein, *Tell the Court I Love My Wife: Race, Marriage, and Law—an American History* (2002); Lorena S. Walsh, *From Calabar to Carter's Grove: The History of a Virginia Slave Community* (1997); Stephen Saunders Webb, *1676: The End of American Independence* (1985).

CHAPTER 4. THE WEST

Fred Anderson, *The War That Made America: A Short History of the French and Indian War* (2005); James Axtell, *The European and the Indian: Essays in the Ethnohistory of Colonial North America* (1981); Colin G. Calloway, *The Scratch of a Pen: 1763 and the Transformation of America* (2006); John Egerton, *Generations: An American Family* (1983); Warren R. Hofstra, *The Planting of New Virginia: Settlement and Landscape in the Shenandoah Valley* (2004); Rhys Isaac, *The Transformation of Virginia, 1740–1790* (1982); Patricia Givens Johnson, *James Patton and the Appalachian Colonists* (1983); John Keegan, *Fields of Battle: The Wars for North America* (1995); Thomas A. Lewis, *West from Shenandoah: A Scotch-Irish Family Fights for America, 1729–1781* (2004); Stephen L. Longenecker, *Shenandoah Religion: Outsiders and the Mainstream, 1716–1865* (2002); Gerald W. McFarland, *A Scattered People: An American Family Moves West* (1985); Michael J. Puglisi, ed., *Diversity and Accommodation: Essays on the Cultural Composition of the Virginia Frontier* (1997); James Titus, *The Old Dominion at War: Society, Politics, and Warfare in Late Colonial Virginia* (1991); John Alexander Williams, *Appalachia: A History* (2002).

PART II. 1760S–1820S: POLITICAL INDEPENDENCE AND POLITICAL SLAVERY

Bernard Bailyn, *The Ideological Origins of the American Revolution* (1967); John van der Zee, *Bound Over: Indentured Servitude and American Conscience* (1985); Bertram Wyatt-Brown, *The Shaping of Southern Culture: Honor, Grace, and War, 1760s–1890s* (2001).

CHAPTER 5. CONSERVATIVE REVOLUTIONARIES: VIRGINIANS AND INDEPENDENCE

Lawrence E. Babits, *A Devil of a Whipping: The Battle of Cowpens* (1998); Jeff Broadwater, *George Mason, Forgotten Founder* (2006); R. B. Bernstein, *Thomas Jefferson* (2003); Robin L. Einhorn, *American Taxation, American Slavery* (2006); David Hackett Fischer, *Washington's Crossing* (2004); James Thomas Flexner, *Washington: The Indispensable Man* (1974); Lawrence Henry Gipson, *The Coming of the Revolution, 1763–1775* (1954); Jack P. Greene, *Peripheries and Center: Constitutional Development in the Extended Polities of the British Empire and the United States, 1607–1788* (1986); Sally E. Hadden, *Slave Patrols: Law and Violence in Virginia and the Carolinas* (2001); Lowell H. Harrison, *George Rogers Clark and the War in the West*

(1976); Don Higginbotham, *Daniel Morgan, Revolutionary Rifleman* (1961); Woody Holton, *Forced Founders: Indians, Debtors, Slaves, and the Making of the American Revolution in Virginia* (1999); Rhys Isaac, *Landon Carter's Uneasy Kingdom: Revolution and Rebellion on a Virginia Plantation* (2004); John Keegan, *Fields of Battle: The Wars for North America* (1995); Marc W. Kruman, *Between Authority and Liberty: State Constitution Making in Revolutionary America* (1997); Henry Mayer, *A Son of Thunder: Patrick Henry and the American Republic* (1991); Cassandra Pybus, *Epic Journeys of Freedom: Runaway Slaves of the American Revolution and Their Global Quest for Liberty* (2006); Bruce A. Ragsdale, *A Planters' Republic: The Search for Economic Independence in Revolutionary Virginia* (1996); Simon Schama, *Rough Crossings: Britain, the Slaves, and the American Revolution* (2006); John E. Selby, *The Revolution in Virginia, 1775–1983* (1988).

CHAPTER 6. PERFECTING INDEPENDENCE (I): POWER AND
POLICY IN POSTREVOLUTIONARY VIRGINIA

Ira Berlin, *Many Thousands Gone: The First Two Centuries of Slavery in North America* (1998); Thomas E. Buckley, *Church and State in Revolutionary Virginia, 1776–1877* (1977); Douglas R. Egerton, *Gabriel's Rebellion: The Virginia Slave Conspiracies of 1800 and 1802* (1993); Melvin Patrick Ely, *Israel on the Appomattox: A Southern Experiment in Black Freedom from the 1790s through the Civil War* (2004); Peter R. Henriques, *Realistic Visionary: A Portrait of George Washington* (2006); Rhys Isaac, *The Transformation of Virginia, 1740–1790* (1982); Allen Kulikoff, *Tobacco and Slaves: The Development of Southern Cultures in the Chesapeake, 1680–1800* (1986); Andrew Levy, *The First Emancipator: The Forgotten Story of Robert Carter, the Founding Father Who Freed His Slaves* (2005); Robert McColley, *Slavery and Jeffersonian Virginia* (1973); Merrill D. Peterson and Robert C. Vaughan, eds., *The Virginia Statute for Religious Freedom: Its Evolution and Consequences in American History* (1988); Joshua D. Rothman, *Notorious in the Neighborhood: Sex and Families across the Color Line in Virginia, 1787–1861* (2003); Philip J. Schwarz, *Slave Laws in Virginia* (1996); Garrett Ward Sheldon and Daniel L. Dreisbach, eds., *Religion and Political Culture in Jefferson's Virginia* (2000); James Sidbury, *Ploughshares into Swords: Race, Rebellion, and Identity in Gabriel's Virginia, 1730–1810* (1997); Peter Wallenstein, *Tell the Court I Love My Wife: Race, Marriage, and Law—an American History* (2002); Henry Wiencek, *An Imperfect God: George Washington, His Slaves, and the Creation of America* (2003).

CHAPTER 7. VIRGINIA AND A NEW UNION

Richard R. Beeman, *The Old Dominion and the New Nation, 1788–1801* (1972); Kenneth R. Bowling, *The Creation of Washington, D.C.: The Idea and Location of the American Capital* (1991); Don E. Fehrenbacher, completed and edited by Ward M. McAfee, *The Slaveholding Republic: An Account of the United States Government's*

Relations to Slavery (2001); Richard Hofstadter, *The Idea of a Party System: The Rise of Legitimate Opposition in the United States, 1780–1840* (1969); Richard Labunski, *James Madison and the Struggle for the Bill of Rights* (2006); John C. Miller, *The Federalist Era, 1789–1801* (1960); William Lee Miller, *The Business of May Next: James Madison and the Founding* (1992); Richard B. Morris, *The Forging of the Union, 1781–1789* (1987); Paul A. Rahe, *Republics Ancient and Modern*, vol. 3, *Inventions of Prudence: Constituting the American Regime* (1994); Norman K. Risjord, *Chesapeake Politics, 1781–1800* (1978).

CHAPTER 8. MOTHER OF PRESIDENTS, MOTHER OF STATES

Bruce Ackerman, *The Failure of the Founding Fathers: Jefferson, Marshall, and the Rise of Presidential Democracy* (2005); Harry Ammon, *James Monroe: The Quest for National Identity* (1971); James M. Banner Jr., *To the Hartford Convention: The Federalists and the Origins of Party Politics in Massachusetts, 1789–1815* (1970); Lance Banning, *Sacred Fire of Liberty: James Madison and the Founding of the Federal Republic* (1995); Joan E. Cashin, *A Family Venture: Men and Women on the Southern Frontier* (1991); John Ferling, *Adams vs. Jefferson: The Tumultuous Election of 1800* (2004); Paul Finkelman, *Slavery and the Founders: Race and Liberty in the Age of Jefferson* (1996, 2001); David Hackett Fischer and James C. Kelly, *Bound Away: Virginia and the Westward Movement* (2000); Nicholas Perkins Hardeman, *Wilderness Calling: The Hardeman Family in the American Westward Movement, 1750–1900* (1977); David Freeman Hawke, *Those Tremendous Mountains: The Story of the Lewis and Clark Expedition* (1980); Roger G. Kennedy, *Mr. Jefferson's Lost Cause: Land, Farmers, Slavery, and the Louisiana Purchase* (2003); Jon Kukla, *A Wilderness So Immense: The Louisiana Purchase and the Destiny of America* (2003); Drew R. McCoy, *The Last of the Fathers: James Madison and the Republican Legacy* (1989); Gerald W. McFarland, *A Scattered People: An American Family Moves West* (1985); Peter S. Onuf, ed., *Jeffersonian Legacies* (1993); Adam Rothman, *Slave Country: American Expansion and the Origins of the Deep South* (2005); James F. Simon, *What Kind of Nation: Thomas Jefferson, John Marshall, and the Epic Struggle to Create a United States* (2002); Thomas P. Slaughter, *Exploring Lewis and Clark: Reflections on Men and Wilderness* (2003); Daniel B. Thorp, *Lewis and Clark: An American Journey* (1998, 2004); Anthony F. C. Wallace, *Jefferson and the Indians: The Tragic Fate of the First Americans* (1999); Patrick G. Williams, S. Charles Bolton, and Jeannie M. Whayne, eds., *A Whole Country in Commotion: The Louisiana Purchase and the American Southwest* (2005); Garry Wills, *"Negro President": Jefferson and the Slave Power* (2003).

PART III. 1820S–1890S: AFTER JEFFERSON'S LOUISIANA PURCHASE

William W. Freehling, *The Road to Disunion: Secessionists at Bay, 1776–1854* (1990).

CHAPTER 9. PERFECTING INDEPENDENCE (II): POWER AND
POLICY IN EARLY NATIONAL VIRGINIA

Sean Patrick Adams, *Old Dominion, Industrial Commonwealth: Coal, Politics, and Economy in Antebellum America* (2004); Thomas E. Buckley, *The Great Catastrophe of My Life: Divorce in the Old Dominion* (2002); Eric Burin, *Slavery and the Peculiar Solution: A History of the American Colonization Society* (2005); Douglas R. Egerton, *Charles Fenton Mercer and the Trial of National Conservatism* (1989); Susan H. Goodson et al., *The College of William and Mary: A History* (1993); Robert F. Hunter and Edwin L. Dooley Jr., *Claudius Crozet: French Engineer in America, 1790–1864* (1989); Anya Jabour, *Marriage in the Early Republic: Elizabeth and William Wirt and the Companionate Ideal* (1998); Beth Barton Schweiger, *The Gospel Working Up: Progress and the Pulpit in Nineteenth-Century Virginia* (2000); William G. Shade, *Democratizing the Old Dominion: Virginia and the Second Party System, 1824–1861* (1996); C. W. Tazewell, ed., *Virginia's Ninth President, Joseph Jenkins Roberts* (1992); Elizabeth R. Varon, *We Mean to Be Counted: White Women and Politics in Antebellum Virginia* (1998); Garry Wills, *Mr. Jefferson's University* (2002).

CHAPTER 10. COLLISION OF THREE VIRGINIAS

Alison Goodyear Freehling, *Drift toward Dissolution: The Virginia Slavery Debate of 1831–1832* (1982); William W. Freehling, *The Road to Disunion: Secessionists at Bay, 1776–1854* (1990); Scot French, *The Rebellious Slave: Nat Turner in American Memory* (2004); Kenneth S. Greenberg, ed., *Nat Turner: A Slave Rebellion in History and Memory* (2003); Michael O'Brien, *Conjectures of Order: Intellectual Life and the American South, 1810–1860* (2004); Joseph Clarke Robert, *The Road from Monticello: A Study of the Virginia Slavery Debate of 1832* (1941); Walter C. Rucker, *The River Flows On: Black Resistance, Culture, and Identity Formation in Early America* (2006); William G. Shade, *Democratizing the Old Dominion: Virginia and the Second Party System, 1824–1861* (1996); Robert P. Sutton, *Revolution to Secession: Constitution Making in the Old Dominion* (1989).

CHAPTER 11. RACE AND SLAVERY, 1820S–1850S

Ira Berlin, *Generations of Captivity: A History of African-American Slaves* (2003); Ira Berlin, *Slaves without Masters: The Free Negro in the Antebellum South* (1974); Tommy Bogger, *Free Blacks in Norfolk, Virginia, 1790–1860: The Darker Side of Freedom* (1997); F. N. Boney, Richard L. Hume, and Rafia Zafar, eds., *God Made Man, Man Made the Slave: The Autobiography of George Teamoh* (1990); William Cheek and Aimee Lee Cheek, *John Mercer Langston and the Fight for Black Freedom, 1829–65* (1989); Daniel W. Crofts, *Old Southampton: Politics and Society in a Virginia County, 1834–1869* (1992); Charles B. Dew, *Bond of Iron: Master and Slave at Buffalo Forge* (1994); Steven Deyle, *Carry Me Back: The Domestic Slave Trade in American Life* (2005); Melvin Patrick Ely, *Israel on the Appomattox: A Southern Experiment in Black Freedom from the 1790s through the Civil War* (2004); Philip S. Foner and Josephine F. Pacheco, eds., *Three Who Dared: Prudence Crandall, Margaret Douglass, Myrtilla Miner—Champions of Antebellum Black Education* (1984); Eugene D. Genovese, *The World the Slaveholders Made: Two Essays in Interpretation* (1969); Robert H. Gudmestad, *A Troublesome Commerce: The Transformation of the Interstate Slave Trade* (2003); Gregg D. Kimball, *American City, Southern Place: A Cultural History of Antebellum Richmond* (2000); Suzanne Lebsock, *The Free Women of Petersburg: Status and Culture in a Southern Town, 1784–1860* (1984); Michael O'Brien, *Conjectures of Order: Intellectual Life and the American South, 1810–1860* (2004); Josephine F. Pacheco, *The Pearl: A Failed Slave Escape on the Potomac* (2005); Joshua D. Rothman, *Notorious in the Neighborhood: Sex and Families across the Color Line in Virginia, 1787–1861* (2003); Jeffrey Ruggles, *The Unboxing of Henry Brown* (2003); Philip J. Schwarz, *Migrants against Slavery: Virginians and the Nation* (2001); Philip J. Schwarz, *Slave Laws in Virginia* (1996); Mitchell Snay, *Gospel of Disunion: Religion and Separatism in the Antebellum South* (1993); Brenda E. Stevenson, *Life in Black and White: Family and Community in the Slave South* (1996); Henry Wiencek, *The Hairstons: An American Family in Black and White* (1999).

CHAPTER 12. THE COMPROMISES OF 1850–1851

Edward P. Crapol, *John Tyler, the Accidental President* (2006); Don E. Fehrenbacher, *The Dred Scott Case: Its Significance in American Law and Politics* (1978); Don E. Fehrenbacher, completed and edited by Ward M. McAfee, *The Slaveholding Republic: An Account of the United States Government's Relations to Slavery* (2001); Susan-Mary Grant, *North over South: Northern Nationalism and American Identity in the Antebellum Era* (2000); Michael F. Holt, *The Fate of the Country: Politicians, Slavery Extension, and the Coming of the Civil War* (2004); William A. Link, *Roots of Secession: Slavery and Politics in Antebellum Virginia* (2003); John McCardell, *The Idea of a Southern Nation: Southern Nationalists and Southern Nationalism, 1830–1860* (1979); Jane H. Pease and William H. Pease, *The Fugitive Slave Law and Anthony Burns: A Problem in Law Enforcement* (1975); David M. Potter, completed and edited by Don E. Fehrenbacher, *The Impending Crisis, 1848–1861* (1976); Leonard L. Richards, *The Slave Power: The Free North and Southern Domination, 1780–1860* (2000); Philip J. Schwarz, *Migrants against Slavery: Virginians and the Nation* (2001); Henry T. Shanks, *The Secession Movement in Virginia, 1847–1861* (1934); Joel H. Silbey, *Storm over Texas: The Annexation Controversy and the Road to Civil War* (2005); Craig M. Simpson, *A Good Southerner: The Life of Henry A. Wise of Virginia* (1985); Robert S. Tilton, *Pocahontas: The Evolution of an American Narrative* (1994); Albert J. Von Frank, *The Trials of Anthony Burns: Freedom and Slavery in Emerson's Boston* (1998).

CHAPTER 13. VIRGINIA'S ROAD TO SECESSION AND WAR

Daniel W. Crofts, *Reluctant Confederates: Upper South Unionists in the Secession Crisis* (1989); Charles B. Dew, *Apostles of Disunion: Southern Secession Commissioners and the Causes of the Civil War* (2001); Paul Finkelman, ed., *His Soul Goes Marching On: Responses to John Brown and the Harpers Ferry Raid* (1995); Robert William Fogel, *Without Consent or Contract: The Rise and Fall of American Slavery* (1989); William W. Freehling, *The Reintegration of American History: Slavery and the Civil War* (1994); Gregg D. Kimball, *American City, Southern Place: A Cultural History of Antebellum Richmond* (2000); William A. Link, *Roots of Secession: Slavery and Politics in Antebellum Virginia* (2003); Kenneth W. Noe, *Southwest Virginia's Railroad: Modernization and the Sectional Crisis* (1994); Stephen B. Oates, *To Purge This Land with Blood: A Biography of John Brown* (1970); David S. Reynolds, *John Brown, Abolitionist: The Man Who Killed Slavery, Sparked the Civil War, and Seeded Civil Rights* (2005); Peggy A. Russo and Paul Finkelman, eds., *Terrible Swift Sword: The Legacy of John Brown* (2005); Craig M. Simpson, *A Good Southerner: The Life of Henry A. Wise of Virginia* (1985); Peter Wallenstein and Bertram Wyatt-Brown, eds., *Virginia's Civil War* (2005); Eric H. Walther, *The Shattering of the Union: America in the 1850s* (2004).

CHAPTER 14. VIRGINIANS AT WAR

Edward L. Ayers, *In the Presence of Mine Enemies: War in the Heart of America, 1859–1863* (2003); Peter Carmichael, *The Last Generation: Young Virginians in Peace, War, and Reunion* (2005); William C. Davis, *The Battle of New Market* (1975); William C. Davis, *Look Away! A History of the Confederate States of America* (2002); Charles B. Dew, *Ironmaker to the Confederacy: Joseph R. Anderson and the Tredegar Iron Works* (1966); William W. Freehling, *The South vs. the South: How Anti-Confederate Southerners Shaped the Course of the Civil War* (2001); Gary W. Gallagher, *The Confederate War: How Popular Will, Nationalism, and Military Strategy Could Not Stave Off Defeat* (1997); Ervin L. Jordan Jr., *Black Confederates and Afro-Yankees in Civil War Virginia* (1995); William K. Klingaman, *Abraham Lincoln and the Road to Emancipation, 1861–1865* (2001); George G. Kundahl, *Alexandria Goes to War: Beyond Robert E. Lee* (2004); Nelson D. Lankford, *Richmond Burning: The Last Days of the Confederate Capital* (2002); Bruce Levine, *Confederate Emancipation: Southern Plans to Free and Arm Slaves during the Civil War* (2006); Cornelia Peake McDonald, *A Woman's Civil War: A Diary, with Reminiscences of the War, from March 1862* (1992); Brian D. McKnight, *Contested Borderland: The Civil War in Appalachian Kentucky and Virginia* (2006); Roger L. Ransom, *The Confederate States of America: What Might Have Been* (2005); Edwin S. Redkey, ed., *A Grand Army of Black Men: Letters from African-American Soldiers in the Union Army, 1861–1865* (1992); James I. Robertson Jr., *Civil War Virginia: Battleground for a Nation* (1991); James I. Robertson Jr., *Stonewall Jackson—the Man, the Soldier, the Legend* (1997); John

G. Selby, *Virginians at War: The Civil War Experiences of Seven Young Confederates* (2002); Daniel E. Sutherland, *Seasons of War: The Ordeal of a Confederate Community, 1861–1865* (1995); Emory M. Thomas, *The Confederate State of Richmond: A Biography of the Capital* (1971); Emory M. Thomas, *Robert E. Lee—a Biography* (1995); Steven Elliott Tripp, *Yankee Town, Southern City: Race and Class Relations in Civil War Lynchburg* (1997); Elizabeth R. Varon, *Southern Lady, Yankee Spy: The True Story of Elizabeth Van Lew, a Union Agent in the Heart of the Confederacy* (2003); Michael Vorenberg, *Final Freedom: The Civil War, the Abolition of Slavery, and the Thirteenth Amendment* (2001); Peter Wallenstein and Bertram Wyatt-Brown, eds., *Virginia's Civil War* (2005); Brian Steel Wills, *The War Hits Home: The Civil War in Southeastern Virginia* (2001).

CHAPTER 15. RECONSTRUCTING VIRGINIA—AFTER WAR AND EMANCIPATION

David F. Allmendinger Jr., *Ruffin: Family and Reform in the Old South* (1990); James E. Bond, *No Easy Walk to Freedom: Reconstruction and the Ratification of the Fourteenth Amendment* (1997); Robert Francis Engs, *Freedom's First Generation: Black Hampton, Virginia, 1861–1890* (1979); Eric Foner, *Reconstruction: America's Unfinished Revolution, 1863–1877* (1988); Louis R. Harlan, *Booker T. Washington: The Making of a Black Leader, 1856–1901* (1972); Joseph B. James, *The Framing of the Fourteenth Amendment* (1956); Richard Lowe, *Republicans and Reconstruction in Virginia, 1856–70* (1991); Jack P. Maddex Jr., *The Virginia Conservatives, 1867–1879: A Study in Reconstruction Politics* (1970); James L. Roark, *Masters without Slaves: Southern Planters in the Civil War and Reconstruction* (1977); Anne Sarah Rubin, *A Shattered Nation: The Rise and Fall of the Confederacy, 1861–1868* (2005); Diane Swann-Wright, *A Way out of No Way: Claiming Family and Freedom in the New South* (2002); Peter Wallenstein, *Tell the Court I Love My Wife: Race, Marriage, and Law—An American History* (2002); Heather Andrea Williams, *Self-Taught: African American Education in Slavery and Freedom* (2005).

CHAPTER 16. RAILROADS, SCHOOLS, AND READJUSTERS

Edward L. Ayers, *The Promise of the New South: Life after Reconstruction* (1992); W. Fitzhugh Brundage, *Lynching in the New South: Georgia and Virginia, 1880–1930* (1993); Jane Turner Censer, *The Reconstruction of White Southern Womanhood, 1865–1895* (2003); Jane Dailey, *Before Jim Crow: The Politics of Race in Postemancipation Virginia* (2000); Ronald D. Eller, *Millers, Millhands, and Mountaineers: Industrialization of the Appalachian South, 1880–1930* (1982); Steven Hahn, *A Nation under Our Feet: Black Political Struggles in the Rural South from Slavery to the Great Migration* (2003); Jeffrey R. Kerr-Ritchie, *Freedpeople in the Tobacco South: Virginia, 1860–1900* (1999); Suzanne Lebsock, *A Murder in Virginia: Southern Justice on Trial* (2003); William A. Link, *A Hard Country and a Lonely Place: Schooling, Society, and Reform in Rural Virginia, 1870–1920* (1986); Jack P. Maddex Jr., *The Virginia*

Conservatives, 1867–1879: A Study in Reconstruction Politics (1970); Nancy J. Martin-Perdue and Charles L. Perdue Jr., *Talk about Trouble: A New Deal Portrait of Virginians in the Great Depression* (1996); Allen W. Moger, *Virginia: Bourbonism to Byrd, 1870–1925* (1968); James Tice Moore, *Two Paths to the New South: The Virginia Debt Controversy, 1870–1883* (1974); Samuel N. Pincus, *The Virginia Supreme Court, Blacks, and the Law, 1870–1902* (1990); Howard N. Rabinowitz, *Race Relations in the Urban South, 1865–1890* (1978); Crandall A. Shifflett, *Coal Towns: Life, Work, and Culture in Company Towns of Southern Appalachia, 1880–1960* (1991); Edgar Toppin, *Loyal Sons and Daughters: Virginia State University, 1882 to 1992* (1992); John Alexander Williams, *Appalachia: A History* (2002).

PART IV. 1890S–1940S: THE POLITICS OF MIGRATION AND THE WINDS OF CHANGE

Jervis Anderson, *A. Philip Randolph: A Biographical Portrait* (1973); James N. Gregory, *The Southern Diaspora: How the Great Migrations of Black and White Southerners Transformed America* (2005).

CHAPTER 17. SOUTHERN PROGRESSIVISM

Edward Alvey Jr., *History of Mary Washington College, 1908–1972* (1974); Raymond C. Dingledine Jr., *Madison College: The First Fifty Years, 1908–1958* (1959); Susan H. Goodson et al., *The College of William and Mary: A History* (1993); Louis R. Harlan, *Separate and Unequal: Public School Campaigns and Racism in the Southern Seaboard States, 1901–1915* (1958); Wythe Holt, *Virginia's Constitutional Convention of 1901–1902* (1990); J. Morgan Kousser, *The Shaping of Southern Politics: Suffrage Restriction and the Establishment of the One-Party South, 1880–1910* (1974); William A. Link, *A Hard Country and a Lonely Place: Schooling, Society, and Reform in Rural Virginia, 1870–1920* (1986); Amy Thompson McCandless, *The Past in the Present: Women's Higher Education in the Twentieth-Century American South* (1999); Allen W. Moger, *Virginia: Bourbonism to Byrd, 1870–1925* (1968); Michael Perman, *Struggle for Mastery: Disfranchisement in the South, 1888–1908* (2001); Raymond H. Pulley, *Old Virginia Restored: An Interpretation of the Progressive Impulse, 1870–1930* (1968); William G. Thomas, *Lawyering for the Railroad: Business, Law, and Power in the New South* (1999); Edgar Toppin, *Loyal Sons and Daughters: Virginia State University, 1882 to 1992* (1992); Peter Wallenstein, *Blue Laws and Black Codes: Conflict, Courts, and Change in Twentieth-Century Virginia* (2004).

CHAPTER 18. ALTERNATIVE PASTS—PRESERVED, RETRIEVED, CELEBRATED

William A. Blair, *Cities of the Dead: Contesting the Memory of the Civil War in the South, 1865–1914* (2004); David W. Blight, *Race and Reunion: The Civil War in American Memory* (2001); Edward D. C. Campbell Jr. and Kym S. Rice, eds., *A Woman's War: Southern Women, Civil War, and the Confederate Legacy* (1996); Karen L. Cox,

Dixie's Daughters: The United Daughters of the Confederacy and the Preservation of Confederate Culture (2003); Sarah E. Gardner, *Blood and Irony: Southern White Women's Narratives of the Civil War, 1861–1937* (2004); Jacqueline Goggin, *Carter G. Woodson: A Life in Black History* (1993); Susan Goodman, *Ellen Glasgow: A Biography* (1998); David E. Johnson, *Douglas Southall Freeman* (2002); James M. Lindgren, *Preserving the Old Dominion: Historic Preservation and Virginia Traditionalism* (1993); August Meier and Elliott Rudwick, *Black History and the Historical Profession, 1915–1980* (1986); Cynthia Mills and Pamela H. Simpson, eds., *Monuments to the Lost Cause: Women, Art, and the Landscapes of Southern Memory* (2003); Charles C. Osborne, *Jubal: The Life and Times of General Jubal C. Early, CSA, Defender of the Lost Cause* (1992); Mark Zwonitzer and Charles Hirshberg, *Will You Miss Me When I'm Gone? The Carter Family and Their Legacy in American Music* (2002).

CHAPTER 19. ALTERNATIVE FUTURES

Ann Field Alexander, *Race Man: The Rise and Fall of the "Fighting Editor," John Mitchell Jr.* (2002); Walter Russell Bowie, *Sunrise in the South: The Life of Mary-Cooke Branch Munford* (1942); Elna C. Green, *Southern Strategies: Southern Women and the Woman Suffrage Question* (1997); Jim Haskins and N. R. Mitgang, *Mr. Bojangles: The Biography of Bill Robinson* (1988); Ronald L. Heinemann, *Harry Byrd of Virginia* (1996); "Mr. Justice Holmes and Three Generations of Imbeciles" (on Carrie Buck), in William E. Leuchtenburg, *The Supreme Court Reborn: The Constitutional Revolution in the Age of Roosevelt* (1995); Gertrude Woodruff Marlowe, *A Right Worthy Grand Mission: Maggie Lena Walker and the Quest for Black Economic Empowerment* (2003); J. Douglas Smith, *Managing White Supremacy: Race, Politics, and Citizenship in Jim Crow Virginia* (2002); Peter Wallenstein, *Blue Laws and Black Codes: Conflict, Courts, and Change in Twentieth-Century Virginia* (2004).

CHAPTER 20. GREAT DEPRESSION AND NEW DEAL

Pete Daniel, *Breaking the Land: The Transformation of Cotton, Tobacco, and Rice Cultures since 1880* (1985); Elna C. Green, *This Business of Relief: Confronting Poverty in a Southern City [Richmond], 1740–1940* (2003); Ronald L. Heinemann, *Depression and New Deal in Virginia: The Enduring Dominion* (1983); Kenneth T. Jackson, *Crabgrass Frontier: The Suburbanization of the United States* (1985); Brooks Johnson and Peter Stewart, comps., *Mountaineers to Main Streets: The Old Dominion as Seen through the Farm Security Administration Photographs* (1985); Harley E. Jolley, *The Blue Ridge Parkway* (1969); Nancy J. Martin-Perdue and Charles L. Perdue Jr., *Talk about Trouble: A New Deal Portrait of Virginians in the Great Depression* (1996); Pauli Murray, *Song in a Weary Throat: An American Pilgrimage* (1987; reprinted as *Pauli Murray* [1989]); Mary Poole, *The Segregated Origins of Social Security: African Americans and the Welfare State* (2006); John A. Salmond, *Miss Lucy of the CIO: The Life and Times of Lucy Randolph Mason, 1882–1959* (1988); Richard B. Sherman, *The Case of Odell Waller and Virginia Justice, 1940–1942* (1992); J. Douglas Smith,

Managing White Supremacy: Race, Politics, and Citizenship in Jim Crow Virginia (2002).

CHAPTER 21. WORLD WAR II

Stephen E. Ambrose, *Band of Brothers: E Company, 506th Regiment, 101st Airborne—from Normandy to Hitler's Eagle's Nest* (1992); Alex Kershaw, *The Bedford Boys: One American Town's Ultimate D-Day Sacrifice* (2003); Nancy J. Martin-Perdue and Charles L. Perdue Jr., *Talk about Trouble: A New Deal Portrait of Virginians in the Great Depression* (1996); Suzanne Mettler, *Soldiers to Citizens: The G.I. Bill and the Making of the Greatest Generation* (2005); James W. Morrison, *Bedford Goes to War: The Heroic Story of a Small Virginia Community in World War II* (2004); Thomas C. Parramore, with Peter C. Stewart and Tommy L. Bogger, *Norfolk: The First Four Centuries* (1994); Jane Weaver Poulton, ed., *A Better Legend: From the World War II Letters of Jack and Jane Poulton* (1993).

PART V. 1945–2007: COLD WAR AND GREAT SOCIETY

John J. Accordino, *Captives of the Cold War Economy: The Struggle for Defense Conversion in American Communities* (1991); Donald C. Harrison, *Distant Patrol: Virginia and the Korean War* (1989); Donald C. Harrison, *Distant Patrol: Virginia and the Vietnam War* (1989); Tom Lewis, *Divided Highways: Building the Interstate Highways, Transforming American Life* (1997); Robert Mann, *The Walls of Jericho: Lyndon Johnson, Hubert Humphrey, Richard Russell, and the Struggle for Civil Rights* (1996); Sherie Mershon and Steven Schlossman, *Foxholes and Color Lines: Desegregating the U.S. Armed Forces* (1998).

CHAPTER 22. THE ROAD TO
BROWN V. BOARD OF EDUCATION

Bruce Adelson, *Brushing Back Jim Crow: The Integration of Minor-League Baseball in the American South* (1999); Sarah Patton Boyle, *The Desegregated Heart* (1962); Taylor Branch, *Parting the Waters: America in the King Years, 1954–63* (1988); Michael Dennis, *Luther P. Jackson and a Life for Civil Rights* (2004); Michael R. Gardner, *Harry Truman and Civil Rights: Moral Courage and Political Risks* (2002); V. O. Key Jr., with the assistance of Alexander Heard, *Southern Politics in State and Nation* (1949); Michael J. Klarman, *From Jim Crow to Civil Rights: The Supreme Court and the Struggle for Racial Equality* (2004); Richard Kluger, *Simple Justice: The History of* Brown v. Board of Education *and Black America's Struggle for Equality* (1976); Eric W. Rise, *The Martinsville Seven: Race, Rape, and Capital Punishment* (1995); J. Douglas Smith, *Managing White Supremacy: Race, Politics, and Citizenship in Jim Crow Virginia* (2002); Mark V. Tushnet, *Making Civil Rights Law: Thurgood Marshall and the Supreme Court, 1936–1961* (1994); Peter Wallenstein, *Blue Laws and Black Codes: Conflict, Courts, and Change in Twentieth-Century Virginia* (2004); J. Harvie Wilkinson III, *Harry Byrd and the Changing Face of Virginia Politics, 1945–1966* (1968).

Mark Bego, *I Fall to Pieces: The Music and Life of Patsy Cline* (1995); James C. Cobb, *The Brown Decision, Jim Crow, and Southern Identity* (2005); John Egerton, *Shades of Gray: Dispatches from the Modern South* (1991); Betty Kilby Fisher, *Wit, Will and Walls* (2002); Ronald L. Heinemann, *Harry Byrd of Virginia* (1996); Matthew D. Lassiter, *The Silent Majority: Suburban Politics in the Sunbelt South* (2006); Matthew D. Lassiter and Andrew B. Lewis, eds., *The Moderates' Dilemma: Massive Resistance to School Desegregation in Virginia* (1998); Alexander S. Leidholdt, *Standing before the Shouting Mob: Lenoir Chambers and Virginia's Massive Resistance to Public-School Integration* (1997); George Lewis, *The White South and the Red Menace: Segregationists, Anticommunism, and Massive Resistance, 1945–1965* (2004); Robert A. Pratt, *The Color of Their Skin: Education and Race in Richmond, Virginia, 1954–89* (1992); Clara Silverstein, *White Girl: A Story of School Desegregation* (2004); Doug Smith, *Whirlwind: The Godfather of Black Tennis—the Life and Times of Dr. Robert Walter Johnson* (2004); Steve Sullivan, *Remember This Titan: The Bill Yoast Story, Lessons Learned from a Celebrated Coach's Journey* (2005); Mark V. Tushnet, *Making Civil Rights Law: Thurgood Marshall and the Supreme Court, 1936–1961* (1994); J. Harvie Wilkinson III, *Harry Byrd and the Changing Face of Virginia Politics, 1945–1966* (1968).

Frank B. Atkinson, *The Dynamic Dominion: Realignment and the Rise of Virginia's Republican Party since 1945* (1992); Donald P. Baker, *Wilder: Hold Fast to Dreams, a Biography of L. Douglas Wilder* (1989); Virginius Dabney, *Virginia Commonwealth University: A Sesquicentennial History* (1987); Bruce J. Dierenfield, *Keeper of the Rules: Congressman Howard W. Smith of Virginia* (1987); Ronald L. Heinemann, *Harry Byrd of Virginia* (1996); Matthew D. Lassiter, *The Silent Majority: Suburban Politics in the Sunbelt South* (2006); Phyl Newbeck, *Virginia Hasn't Always Been for Lovers: Interracial Bans and the Case of Richard and Mildred Loving* (2004); Warren H. Strother and Peter Wallenstein, *From VPI to State University: President T. Marshall Hahn Jr. and the Transformation of Virginia Tech, 1962–1974* (2004); George B. Vaughan, *Pursuing the American Dream: A History of the Virginia Community College System* (1987); Peter Wallenstein, *Blue Laws and Black Codes: Conflict, Courts, and Change in Twentieth-Century Virginia* (2004); J. Harvie Wilkinson III, *Harry Byrd and the Changing Face of Virginia Politics, 1945–1966* (1968); Brian Steel Wills, *No Ordinary College: A History of the University of Virginia's College at Wise* (2004).

CHAPTER 25. TOWARD A NEW DOMINION:

VIRGINIA SINCE THE 1970S

John J. Accordino, *Captives of the Cold War Economy: The Struggle for Defense Conversion in American Communities* (2000); Frank B. Atkinson, *Virginia in the Vanguard: Political Leadership in the 400-Year-Old Cradle of American Democracy, 1981–2006* (2006); Laura Fairchild Brodie, *Breaking Out: VMI and the Coming of Women* (2000); Frances FitzGerald, *Cities on a Hill: A Journey through Contemporary American Cultures* (1986); J. L. Jeffries, *Virginia's Native Son: The Election and Administration of Governor L. Douglas Wilder* (2000); Nancy Bondurant Jones, *Rooted on Blue Stone Hill: A History of James Madison University* (2004); Mark J. Rozelle and Clyde Wilcox, *Second Coming: The New Christian Right in Virginia Politics* (1996); Charles D. Thompson Jr., *The Old German Baptist Brethren: Faith, Farming, and Change in the Virginia Blue Ridge* (2006); Peter Wallenstein, *Blue Laws and Black Codes: Conflict, Courts, and Change in Twentieth-Century Virginia* (2004).

EPILOGUE. INTO VIRGINIA'S FIFTH CENTURY—

CONTROVERSY AND COMMEMORATION

Arthur Ashe and Arnold Rampersad, *Days of Grace: A Memoir* (1993); William M. Kelso with Beverly A. Straube, *Jamestown Rediscovery, 1994–2004* (2004).

Acknowledgments

....

I conceived this book in 1991, when I was teaching Virginia history every year at Virginia Tech, but I put it aside to develop related projects. This time around, many years and books later, it is more an accidental book, one that began with an e-mail message. University Honors office manager Patty Irwin inquired in March 2005 whether I might teach a colloquium for Honors in the fall. Definitely not, went my first thought, I already have a teaching schedule for fall. But then I reconsidered, deferred any decision, and stopped by the Honors office, where Patty and I and the program director, Jack Dudley, had a brief conversation. Maybe I would, after all, teach a colloquium—perhaps on marriage in U.S. history, I mused, more likely on higher education. Then came epiphany.

I have, for some years, pushed "undergraduate research at a research university" as a core value for the institution and as the hallmark of my own teaching. The 400th anniversary of the founding of Jamestown was nigh. In view of the timing—the start of 2007 was barely twenty months away—it was a preposterous thought, it would be a madman's dash, but why not? So I crafted a course description for fall 2005 for "Writing a History of Virginia for 2007." The opening sentence was a question: "Written a good book lately?" Then, as I grew into the idea, in May I approached the University Press of Kansas about it, and by the time the fall semester began, the project was under contract, with a delivery date for the completed manuscript set for January 2006.

Nine undergraduates in University Honors at Virginia Tech joined the adventure in August and stayed with the project through December. Sophomores, juniors, and seniors, the members of the colloquium came from various majors across the university, and they created a community of scholars, learning on the fly. I brought a detailed outline and various pieces of a possible book. All we had left to do was work hard, work fast, work well—and get to where we could give a timely affirmative answer to the question: "Written a good book lately?"

The nine's names are Letisha Beachy, Graham Burkholder, Anna DeSouza, Bridget Devlin, Kathryn "Katie" Hoffman, Jennifer Jessie, Michael Makara, Marc

Thomas, and Victoria "Torey" Wilson. During our first class meeting in August, Katie in particular dismissed my prosaic working title and urged a substitute, "Cradle of America," and she urged that we emphasize individual people, a notion with which I was already in full agreement. In the weeks to come she and her colleagues each broke into a chapter to get a feel for the project, and each subsequently moved into other areas as well.

Katie's contributions included "colonizing critters" for chapter 2 and material on the American Revolution and religious freedom. Letisha tried to get us all to write in English, and she herself worked on Virginia Indians and then headed west with Lewis and Clark. Torey's specialties included John Smith and Pocahontas. Mike worked on the New Deal and then moved to more recent developments. Jennifer wrote on Harry Byrd Sr. and Massive Resistance. Marc first set his sights on the political and military leaders of the American Revolution. Graham went first after the Readjusters and then moved into the Progressive Era, writing, for example, on prohibition and women's suffrage, and then later on Virginia's defense economy. Anna became acquainted with William Byrd II and then wrote on the Civil War—and she continued work in the spring on portions left unfinished. Bridget began with World War II and then, as "secretary of war," moved to the Civil War and worked on secession, followed by Reconstruction and the appendices on governors and senators. Though I prefer to think of undergraduate research as involving engagement with primary sources—the raw materials of history—the scholarship done for this book often had to work from published materials by historians, yet Bridget also plunged into the *New York Times* to get another perspective on secession and the *Richmond Times-Dispatch* to see for herself what was in the newspapers during World War II.

I massaged all such materials, but each student contributor helped develop the book, and each experienced a genuine opportunity to engage in real-world scholarship as an undergraduate. My voice is much the dominant one, but everyone's work appears in one place or another, every voice contributed to the overall effect.

Other people also helped move the book along. I knew that Jim Glanville, a retired professor of chemistry at Virginia Tech, had been doing some exciting work on the early Spanish presence west of the Blue Ridge, so I asked him to write about it, and the results appear in chapter 1. Knowing of my former graduate student Ellen Apperson Brown's work on her ancestor Mary Draper Ingles, I asked her to write something that appears in chapter 4. James P. Crawford had just finished up a wonderful film on tobacco culture in twentieth-century Virginia, so I asked him to write about it, and his work is vital to chapter 25.

A University Honors class in Virginia history, at Virginia Tech, fall 2005. Front row, left to right: Victoria Wilson, Bridget Devlin, and Michael Makara. Back row, left to right: Peter Wallenstein, Anna DeSouza, Jennifer Jessie, Marc Thomas, Kathryn Hoffman, Graham Burkholder, and Letisha Beachy.

Several students in my fall 2005 undergraduate Historical Methods class also appear in the book. Letisha had wanted something on her hometown, and Megan Peters obliged her by writing on Roanoke as a railroad town for chapter 16. Adam Proctor had written on the Carter Family, and I invited him to give me something for chapter 18. John Cassara summarized his work on race and baseball for chapter 22. Marcus Huffman's work brought me material on the desegregation of private colleges for chapter 24, and Chris Akers called my attention to the story of his hometown, Fries, for chapter 25.

Although I have drawn for many chapters on my own work over the years, I could never have produced this book without the fine publications of a great many other scholars. Particularly helpful in guiding my work, and that of my students, were two exemplary state historical journals. The *Virginia Cavalcade,* lamentably no longer being published, the victim of budget cuts imposed on the Library of Virginia, was a fine source of inspiration and material. So was the *Virginia Magazine of History and Biography,* published by the Virginia Historical Society; reviews of the literature on Virginia history, published in that journal in 1996, proved particularly helpful, especially a very long essay by Brent Tarter.

Conversations with, and the writings of, a number of additional people shaped the narrative at one point or another. These include Chuck Carey, William Freehling, Kevin Levin, and Daniel Sharfstein. William Dusinberre cheered the project along from England, and I wish I could have implemented more of his many thoughtful suggestions.

Before submitting the manuscript and obtaining feedback from the press's readers, I wanted to have chapters vetted by other scholars. Among my colleagues in history at Virginia Tech, Dan Thorp did what he could—and it was a lot—to save me from boneheaded statements in the first third of the book, Jack Davis did the same with the Civil War, and Marian Mollin did so with some twentieth-century chapters. Bill Harris, of the University of New Hampshire, gave close readings to the middle third of the book. Jim Glanville reviewed chapter 1, and Jim Crawford read a draft of chapter 25 and the epilogue. Each of these people has contributed significantly to the overall product, and I am grateful for their time, care, and counsel.

Many people and institutions made possible the inclusion of the various illustrations in this book, and I am deeply indebted to them all. At the Virginia Historical Society—"the Center for Virginia History"—Heather Dawn Beattie pulled together half of these images. Another quarter of them came from the Library of Congress, particularly the American Memory Web page. Jim Crawford supplied the twentieth-century images of tobacco production and culture, including some he had taken, and he helped with the captions and permissions. Geography graduate student Katie Pritchard produced the 2007 map of Virginia; and Science and Technology Studies graduate student Xiaolan Qiu provided technical assistance with several images. At Advance Auto Parts, Laurie Stacy supplied me one image. At the Virginia Military Institute, Diane B. Jacob helped with another, as did April Cheek at the National D-Day Memorial Foundation and Veronica L. Fletcher at George Mason University. For assistance in acquiring and using the image of Luther Porter Jackson, I thank biographer and historian Michael Dennis; University Press of Florida production manager David K. Graham; and Jackson's grandson, Edward F. Jackson, and his wife, DeLoris Jackson. For other images I am indebted to Marianne Martin, of the Colonial Williamsburg Foundation; Bill Burns, at Corbis; and Jason O. Watson. For funding that covered the bulk of the costs of obtaining these images and the right to use them—especially the more expensive ones, from Corbis, *Time* magazine, and the *New York Times*, as well as the great many from the VHS—I thank my department chair Dan Thorp as well as the department's Curtis Fund.

From the University Press of Kansas, I received all kinds of wonderful assistance. The proposal went to three outside readers, who were very helpful with their support and their suggestions. So indeed were the outside readers of the completed manuscript, who read it with great care and generously shared their expertise. Scholars who read the proposal, a completed draft of the book, or both include, as I have learned from them, David W. Coffey, James L. Roark, Larissa M. Smith, and Brian Steel Wills. In the closing stages, Susan McRory guided the

ACKNOWLEDGMENTS

book through the process of publication. To all these people, I am deeply grateful. Most of all, University Press of Kansas director Fred M. Woodward proved immediately receptive when I suggested this book, which meant postponing another book I had promised him for January 2006. Without a doubt, no Fred Woodward, no *Cradle of America*. He still wants that other book, too.

The dedication page supplies me an opportunity to salute several of my favorite people. Most are historians, some of whom I came to know as far back as my long-ago days as an undergraduate, when I first discovered historical research and writing. Another is a sociologist, Jack Dudley, who for many years has directed the University Honors Program at Virginia Tech—and who, with enthusiasm, conviction, and humor, urged this project along.

Index

Bird, Lloyd C., 377
birth certificates, 298
Birthplace of Country Music, 395, 283
Black, Aline, 332–333, 342–343
Black Codes, 218–219, 220
black Confederates, 204
Black History Month, 280
Blacksburg, 322
black Union soldiers, 202–205, 215
Blair, Johnny, 338–339
Blake, Robert, 203
Bland, Robert, 337
Blue Ridge Community College, 377
Blue Ridge Institute, 395
Blue Ridge Music Center, 395
Blue Ridge Parkway, 303, 307, 308, 395
Blue Ridge Railroad Company, 137–138
Board of Trade, 45, 56
Boatman, James, 312
Bodeker, Anna Whitehead, 290
Boleyn, Anne, 5
Bolling, Philip A., 146
Bonaparte, Napoleon, 110, 136
Bond, Horace Mann, 230
Bond, Julian, 330
Booker T. Washington High School (Norfolk), 332–333, 337, 343
Boone, Herman, 359
Boothe, Armistead, 370
Border Ruffians, 177, 181
Border South, 201
Boritt, Gabor, 404
Boston, Mass.: "era of good feelings" and, 117; fugitive Virginia slaves and, 162, 172–173; Revolution and, 70, 77; War of 1812 and, 113, 115. See also Massachusetts
Boston Port Act, 70, 115
Boston Tea Party, 70
Boteler, Alexander, 182
Botetourt, baron de, 69
Botetourt County, 54
Botts, John Minor, 186
Bowler, Antoinette E., 334
Bowling, Brag, 402, 403

boycotts, 69, 286–287, 403
Boyd, Harold, 361
Boyd, Isabella, 155
Boyle, Sarah Patton, 336
Braddock, Edward, 57
Brantley, Etheldred T., 143
Braxton, Allen Caperton, 253, 254
Bread Riot, 200
Breckinridge, John C., 181, 198
Bridenbaugh, Carl, 6–7
Bristol, 273, 282, 283, 395
Bristol Recording Sessions of 1927, 281
Broadnax, William H., 146
Brooke County, 142
Brooks, Robert Peel, 288
Brotherhood of Sleeping Car Porters, 250
Brown, Fannie, 155
Brown, Henry "Box," 161–162, 163, 164, 168
Brown, John: Harpers Ferry and, 177–180, 181, 184, 196, 233; Kansas Territory and, 177
Brown, John and Liza, 312
Brown, Kate, 217
Brown v. Board of Education (1954), 340–342, 344, 362
Brown v. Board of Education (1955), 345, 362
Bruce, Blanche K., 223
Brumfield, Mary, 262
Brunswick County, 147, 215
Bryant, C. D., III, 390, 391–393
Buchanan County, 244, 292–294
Buchanan, James, 173, 178
Buck, Carrie and Vivian, 299
Buck, Doris, 299
Buck, Emma, 299
Buckingham County, 146
Buckingham Female Collegiate Institute, 135
Buck v. Bell (1927), 300
Buffalo Forge, 151
Bull Run, first battle of, 193–194
Bunche, Ralph, 279

Friedman–Harry Marks Clothing Company, 303
Fries, 393–394
Fries, Francis Henry, 393
Fries Textile Plant, 394
Front Royal, 322
Fugitive Slave Act (1793), 168
Fugitive Slave Act (1850), 162, 169, 171–172
fugitive slave clause, 186
Funder Democrats, 233–234, 236, 238

Gabriel's Rebellion, 142
Gaddis, Edward, 330
Galax, 395
Gandy, John M., 264, 272, 331
Gardiner, James, 203
Garner, Cornelius, 205
Garrison, William Lloyd, 127, 148
gasoline: shortage of, during World War II, 320–321; tax on, for highways, 297
Gates, Horatio, 111
Gates, Sir Thomas, 17, 18, 19
Geary, James J., 366
George Mason University, 375, 376, 399
George Town, D.C., 104, 138
George Washington National Forest, 302
Georgia, 103; Indian removal, 111; secession and Civil War, 184–186, 196, 200, 202; slavery and slave trade, 98, 101, 164
Georgian style, 46
Germany, 152; immigration from, 49, 53, 58, 150, 151; World War II and, 315, 316, 319, 322
Gettysburg, battle of, 196
GI Bill, 306, 325
Gilbert, Sir Humphrey, 12, 13
Giles County, 51, 244
Gilmore, James S. "Jim," III, 379
Glasgow, Ellen, 272, 291
Glass, Carter, 253, 301
glebes, 84, 86–87
Gloucester County, 335
Godspeed (ship), 14
Godwin, Mills E., Jr.: governor, 369, 371,

377, 379; Massive Resistance and, 344, 345, 346–347, 369
gold, 8, 14; discovery of, in California, 168; search for, 8, 17, 18, 22
Goldwater, Barry, 369
Goode, William O., 145
Goodwin Lake, 340
Gore, Harry W., Jr., 381, 382
Gosport Navy Yard, 152, 232
Grandy, Charles, 214
Grant, Ulysses S., 196, 197, 209, 210, 224
Gray Commission, 344–345, 348
Gray, Garland, 344, 345
Gray Plan, 345–346, 350
Grayson, William, 102
Gray, Thomas R., 144
grayware, 7
Great Bridge, 71
Great Charter (1618), 20–21
Great Debate over slavery (1832), 144–147, 158
Great Depression, 325
Great Migration, 247, 249–251
Great Society, 328, 357, 384
Greeley, Horace, 275
Greene, Arthur, 154, 215
Greene, Nathanael, 78
Green, John W., 141
Green, Paul, 365
Greensboro, N.C., sit-ins in, 330, 359, 362
Green v. County School Board of New Kent Count (1968), 355
Gregory, James, 34
Grenville, Sir Richard, 10
Griffin, L. Francis, 340–341
Griffin v. School Board of Prince Edward County (1964), 354
Griffith, David, 86
Grimes, Leonard A., 172
Grimes, Loula, 213
Guadalcanal, 322
Guines, James T., 379
Gunston Hall, 41, 46
Gwyn, Hugh, 34

Hahn, T. Marshall, Jr., 377
Haiti, 231
Hakluyt, Richard, 12–13
Hall, John Lesslie, 260
Hallom, Robert, 51
Hamilton, Alexander, 99, 105
Hamilton, Henry, 74, 76
Hampden-Sydney College, 118, 135
Hampton, 289, 293–294, 316, 377
Hampton Institute, 231, 266, 293–294,
    309, 312
Hampton Normal and Agricultural In-
    stitute, 226–228; as land-grant school,
    226–228, 242; loses land-grant designa-
    tion, 264; teacher training at, 235
Hampton Roads, 316–319, 325, 384, 386
Hampton Roads Port of Embarkation,
    318, 319
Hanover County, 145, 294, 301
Harlan, Louis, 265
Harlem Renaissance, 250
Harper, Annie, 368
Harpers Ferry Raid, 177–180, 181, 184,
    196, 233
Harrell, Kelly, 394
Harris, Alfred William, 236
Harris, Anna, 155, 215
Harris, George W., Jr., 362
Harrison, Albertis S., Jr., 369, 370
Harrison, Benjamin, 71
Harrisonburg, 258–259, 353
Harrison, Thomas W., 266
Harrison, William Henry, 117, 119, 165
Hartford Convention, 113–115; resolutions
    of, 114–115
Harvard University, 279
Hassell, Leroy Rountree, Sr., 396
Hastie, William H., 333
Haston, Dennis, 378
Hatch Act (1887), 242–242
Hathaway, Tom, 381
Haymond, Thomas S., 169
headright system, 21, 23, 41

Head Start, 328
Heidelberg, Andrew, 350, 357
Heinemann, Ronald, 301
Helper, Hinton Rowan, 180
Hemings, Eston, 39, 90, 406
Hemings, John, 88
Hemings, Madison, 90
Hemings, Sally, 38–39, 406
Henderson, Helen T., 293
Hening, William Waller, 39
Henrico County, 402
Henry VIII, king of England, 5
Henry, Patrick, 146; governor, 73, 74, 85;
    multiple establishment and, 84–85, 86;
    opposes ratification of Bill of Rights,
    102–103; opposes ratification of
    Constitution, 99, 100; Revolution and,
    69, 70–71, 73, 74, 80; and Two-Penny
    Case, 67
Hewin, J. Thomas, Jr., 333
Hicks, Aline Elizabeth Black, 332–333,
    342–343
Hicks, Frank A., 342–343
higher education, 328; challenges to segre-
    gation in, 310–311, 336–338, 372–375, 381–
    382; late-nineteenth-century, 234–242;
    New Deal and, 308–309; in pre–Civil
    War era, 130, 134–137; in Progressive
    Era, 258–265; during Reconstruction,
    224–228; since World War II, 336–338,
    372–379, 381–382, 395–397. See also col-
    leges and universities, private
Higher Education Act (1965), 328, 378
high schools, 258, 264, 332–335, 340–341,
    352–359
highways and roads: federal funding for,
    116, 165, 256, 302, 307, 328; state and lo-
    cal funding for, 255–257, 297, 369–370
Hill, Oliver W., 243, 323, 341, 349; school
    equalization campaign, 333, 334–335,
    340, 354
Hispanics, 387
Historic American Buildings Survey, 308

Jamestown: APVA and, 271–273; black immigrants of 1619, 22, 23, 28, 272, 407; burned in Bacon's Rebellion, 34; expansion beyond, 19–26; first black women, 22; first settlement at, 13, 15–17; first white women, 17, 21–22, 24; fort at, 15, 19, 399; resettlement at, 17–19; ruins of, 118

Jamestown commemoration: 1907, 366, 406–408; 1957, 365–366, 406; 2007, 366, 406–408

Japan: immigrants from, 387; war against, 316, 323

Jay, John, 98

Jefferson, Martha, 406

Jefferson, Peter, 39

Jefferson, Thomas, 39, 80, 130, 137, 140, 145; church and state and, 83–85, 108; Declaration of Independence and, 63, 71, 73, 76–77, 108; first inauguration of, 109–110; governor, 73; Missouri Crisis and, 127; politics of 1790s and, 103, 105, 106; president, 107–113; race and slavery and, 38–39, 63, 71, 90, 406; University of Virginia and, 108, 130, 134, 137

Jerusalem (later Courtland), 144

Jeter, Jeremiah, 189

Jeter, Mildred, 364; Jim Crow schools and, 334, 344, 354–355

Jim Crow. See segregation

John F. Kennedy High School (Richmond), 355–357

John Marshall High School (Richmond), 258

Johns, Barbara, 340

Johns Hopkins University, 277, 278, 338

Johnson, Andrew, 211–212, 218, 221

Johnson, Anthony and Mary, 36

Johnson, Chapman, 141

Johnson, Ford T., Jr., 362–365

Johnson, Joyce, 402

Johnson, Lady Bird, 369

Johnson, Lyndon B., 369, 379

Johnson, Sarah Wooden, 157, 200

Johnson v. Virginia (1963), 362–365

Johnson, William A., 162

Johnson-Williams School (Berryville), 352–353, 357

Johnston, James Hugo, 240

Johnston, Mary, 291

Johns, Vernon, 341

John Tyler Community College, 399

Jonathan (ship), 22

Jones, Louise, 155

Jones, Sophia, 290–291

Journal of Negro History, 279

Kaine, Timothy M. "Tim," 356, 379, 380, 388

Kanawha County, 146

Kansas, 341–342

Kansas-Nebraska Act, 126, 173, 177

Kansas Territory, 126, 173, 177, 180, 181

Kaskaskia, 74

Keenan, Barbara M., 396

Kellam, Sidney, 369

Kelly v. School Board of Surry County (1948), 334

Kelso, William, 399

Kemper, James L., 179

Kendrick, Howard, 388, 391

Kennedy, John F., 369

Kenny, Barbara, 397–398

Kentucky, 73–74, 107, 122, 139, 182, 279, 293

Kerr-Smith Tobacco Act (1934), 304

Key West Highway, 307

Kilby, Betty Ann, 352–353, 357

Kilby, James and John, 352

Kilby, James Wilson, 352–353

Kilpatrick, James J., 345

King George County, 335

King, Martin Luther, Jr., 341, 372

King Philip's War, 33

King's Mountain (S.C.), battle of, 79

Kinser, Cynthia D., 396

Knights of the Golden Horseshoe, 52

Knox, Alexander G., 146

Korea: immigrants from, 387; war in, 316, 327

370–371, 406; emergence and application of, 346–356
Matsu, Art, 338
May Campaign (1905), 258
Mays, David John, 348
McCollum, Scott, 53
McCormick, Cyrus, 122
McCovey, Willie, 339
McCoy, George, 90
McDaniel, David, 172–173
McDonald, Cornelia Peake, 200–201
McDowell, James, 147
McGuire General Hospital, 324
McKim, James Miller, 162
McKinney, Philip W., 255
McLaurin v. Oklahoma State Regents (1950), 342
McLean, Wilmer, 209
Mecklenburg County, 145, 146, 334
Medal of Honor (congressional), 203
Medicaid, 328
Medical College of Virginia, 366
medical profession, race, gender, and, 288–290, 395–396
Medical Society of Virginia, 290
Medicare, 328
Meigs, Montgomery C., 138
Menendez, Luisa, 8
Mercer, Charles Fenton, 129–132, 279
Merchant of London (ship), 22
Messenger (publication), 250
Methodists, 84, 85, 135, 161, 176, 188, 226
Mexican War, 167, 196, 201–202
Mexico, 4, 6, 22, 282
Middleton, Tibby, 397–398
migration: from South to North, 247, 249–251; into twentieth-century Virginia, 315, 325, 387–388; out of Virginia, 120–123, 164, 246–247, 249; within Virginia, 315, 325. *See also* immigrants
Military District No. 1, 221–222
Milledge, John, 111
Miller and Rhoads department store, 324
Miller, Percy, 339

mill villages, 393–394
Minnegerode, Charles, 207–208
Minnegerode, Lucy, 207
Mississippi, 184, 218, 223, 290, 357
Mississippi River: Civil War and, 196; navigation of, 98, 110–111, 113; western U.S. boundary, 80
Missouri, 122, 125, 174, 223
Missouri Compromise, 126–127, 173, 182
Missouri Crisis, 117, 125–126
Mitchell, Harold, 339
Mitchell, John, Jr., 275–277, 286–287
Monroe, James, 116–117
Montague, Andrew Jackson, 255
Montgomery, Ala., 181, 193
Montgomery Bus Boycott, 330
Montgomery County, 54, 145, 153, 226, 249, 358
Monticello Association, 406
Montpelier, 105, 271, 406
Montreal (Quebec), 4
Monument Avenue (Richmond), 275–277, 283, 311, 401–403
Moon v. Children's Home Society of Virginia (1911), 290
Moore, David, 7
Moore, Henry, 243
Moore, Putnam, 143, 144
Moore, Thomas, 143
Moral Majority movement, 383
Morgan, Daniel, 78–79, 80
Morgan v. Virginia (1946), 312–313
Morrill Act of 1890, 242, 264
Morrill Land-Grant College Act of 1862, 128, 219, 224–228, 241–242, 264
Morris, Elliston, 358
Morris, Faith, 157
mortality, in early Virginia, 17, 18, 36
Mosby, John Singleton, 197, 275
Mosby Middle School (Richmond), 355–356
Moss, C. G. Gordon, 355
Moss, Richard, 355
Mount Rogers, 244
Mount Vernon, 42, 59, 76, 80, 89

Virginia Historical Society, 118

Virginia House of Burgesses, 29, 48, 69, 72, 108; enacts laws on race and slavery, 37–43; established, 21, 22–23

Virginia House of Delegates: established, 72; first black members of, 223, 224, 226, 227; first black members in twentieth century, 372; first women members, 293; Great Debate over slavery, 144–147; reapportionment of, 140–142, 170–171, 367–368, 369

Virginia Industrial School for Colored Girls, 294

Virginia League of Women Voters, 293

Virginia Military Institute (VMI), 179, 245, 255, 366–367; black male cadets at, 381–382; candidate for land-grant funds, 225, 226; Chinese cadets at, 338; Civil War and, 191, 196, 198, 276; female cadets at, 382; graduates of, 227, 231, 235, 259, 323; origins and early history, 134, 136, 137, 138

Virginia militia, 41, 45, 54, 57, 59, 68, 71, 144

Virginia National Guard, 314, 315

Virginia Negro Women's League of Voters, 293

Virginia Normal and Collegiate Institute, 238–240; becomes a land-grant school, 264; downgraded to "Normal and Industrial," 262–263, 265; established, 235–237

Virginia Normal and Industrial Institute, 263, 264–265, 266, 272, 311–312, 332; collegiate program of, restored, 331. *See also* Virginia State College for Negroes

Virginia Office of Civilian Defense, 315

Virginia Passenger and Power Company, 286

Virginia Plan, 96

Virginia Polytechnic Institute (VPI; 1896–1972), 227, 255, 266, 322; Chinese students and faculty at, 338; coeducation at, 262; New Deal construction at,

308–309; pioneer black students at, 337, 381–382

Virginia Polytechnic Institute and State University, 367, 377, 378

Virginia Protective Force, 315

Virginia School for the Deaf and Blind, 139, 263

Virginia secession convention, 133, 183–188, 192

Virginia secession ordinance, 104, 190–191

Virginia Senate, 72; first black members of, 223, 224, 226, 227; first black member in twentieth century, 372, 373

Virginia's Heritage Music Trail, 394–395, 399

Virginia Social Science Association, 332

Virginia State Board of Education, 234, 263, 265

Virginia State College, 308, 311, 336, 337

Virginia State College for Negroes, 264–265, 331, 333; graduate classes initiated at, 331

Virginia State College, Norfolk division, 373–374, 376

Virginia State Library, 277, 308

Virginia State School for Colored Deaf and Blind Children, 139

Virginia State Woman Suffrage Association, 290

Virginia Statute for Religious Freedom (1786), 85

Virginia Supreme Court, 87, 129, 308; black or female justices on, 374, 396; blue laws and, 383; courtroom segregation and, 362–365; "first" woman lawyer in Virginia and, 287–288; interracial marriage and, 364; Marshall Court and, 120; name of, shortened, 371; Massive Resistance and, 349; racial identity and jury discretion and, 292–294; racially discriminatory teacher salaries and, 333; sit-ins and trespass laws and, 362; titles for members of, 297; unpaid labor on public roads and, 255

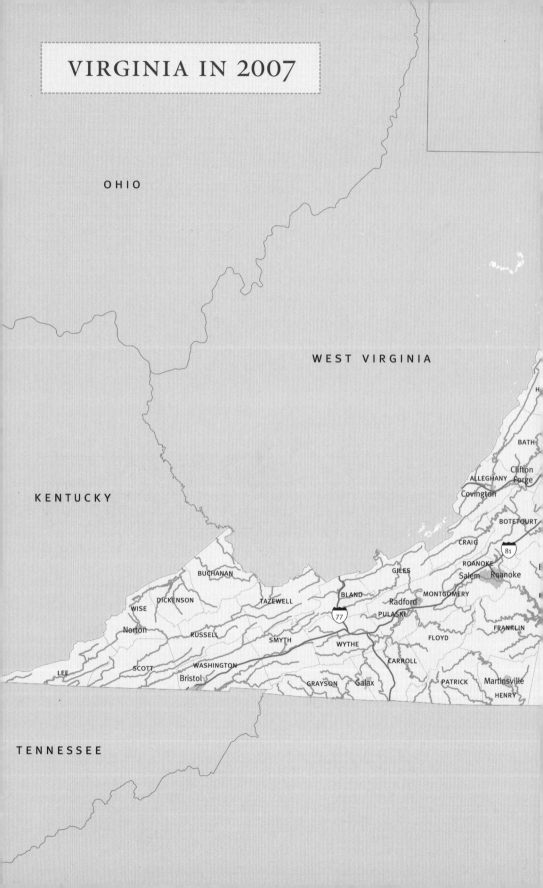

VIRGINIA IN 2007

OHIO

WEST VIRGINIA

KENTUCKY

TENNESSEE

BATH

Clifton Forge

ALLEGHANY

Covington

BOTETOURT

CRAIG

81

ROANOKE

GILES

Salem Roanoke

BUCHANAN

BLAND

Radford

MONTGOMERY

DICKENSON

TAZEWELL

WISE

77

PULASKI

Norton

RUSSELL

FLOYD

FRANKLIN

SMYTH

WYTHE

LEE

SCOTT

WASHINGTON

CARROLL

Bristol

GRAYSON Galax

PATRICK

Martinsville

HENRY